What **Resources** can I use when studying?

Pearson's *Integrated High School Mathematics* offers a range of resources that you can use out of class.

Student Worktext Your book is more than a textbook. Not only does it have important summaries of key math concepts and skills, it will also have your worked-out solutions to the *Got It?* and *Practice* exercises and your own notes for each lesson or problem. Use your book to:

- Refer back to your worked-out solutions and notes.
- Review the key concepts of each lesson by rereading the *Essential Understanding* and *Take Note* boxes.
- Access video tutorials of the concepts addressed in the lesson by scanning the QR codes.

Pearson SuccessNet You have full access to all of the resources on Pearson SuccessNet, including the **Interactive Digital Path** where you will find all of the *Solve Its!* and Problems presented in class. Revisit the animated, stepped-out problems presented in-class to clarify and solidify your math knowledge. Additional resources available to you include:

- Interactive Student Worktext
- Homework Video Tutors in English and Spanish
- Online Glossary with audio in English and Spanish
- MathXL for School Interactive Math Practice
- Math Tools and Online Manipulatives
- Multilingual Handbook
- Assessments with immediate feedback

Mobile eText You may wish to access your student book on the go, either online or offline via download. Pearson's *Integrated High School Mathematics* also offers you a complete mobile etext of the Student Worktext.

- Use the notes, highlight, and bookmark features to personalize your eText.
- Watch animated problem videos with step-by-step instruction for every lesson.

Pearson SuccessNet

Pearson SuccessNet is the gateway to all of the digital components of the program. You can use the online content to review the day's lesson, complete lessons independently, get help with your homework assignments, and prepare for and/or take an assessment. You will be given a username and password to log into www.pearsonsuccessnet.com.

The Homepage

The **To Do** tab contains a list of assignments that you need to complete. You can also access your gradebook and review past assignments.

The **Explore** tab provides you access to the Table of Contents and all of the digital content for the program.

You can also access the following student resources: Practice Worksheets, Homework Video Tutors, and a Multilingual Handbook

Your eText includes links to animated lesson videos, highlighting and note taking tools, and a visual glossary with audio.

Table of Contents

To access the Table of Contents, click on *Explore* from your Homepage.

Table of Contents
Chapter 7 > Lesson
▶ Chapter 7 My Math Video
⏻ Chapter 7 Virtual Nerd™ Video Tutorial
7-1: The Pythagorean Theorem and Its Converse
7-2: Special Right Triangles
7-3: Trigonometry
7-4: Angles of Elevation and Depression
7-5: Areas of Regular Polygons
Chapter 7 MathXL: End-of-Chapter Practice and Review

Student-developed videos bring real-life context to mathematics.

Step-by-step video tutorials offer additional support for every lesson.

Digital lessons include access to animated problems, math tools, homework exercises, and self-assessments.

MathXL for School exercises provide additional practice. Examples and tutorials support every problem, and instant feedback is provided as you complete each exercise.

Interactive Digital Path

To access the **Interactive Digital Path**, click on the appropriate lesson from the Table of Contents.

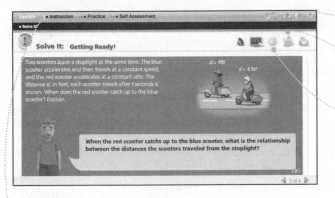

Math Tools help you explore and visualize concepts.

You'll find opportunities to review formulas, properties, and other key concepts.

Interactive Glossary is available in English and Spanish with audio.

Every lesson includes the following:

Launch: Interactive lesson opener connects the math to real-world applications.

Instruction: All lesson problems are stepped out with detailed instruction. You can complete the subsequent *Got It?* exercises in your Student Worktext.

Practice: Exercises from your Student Worktext are available for view.

Self-Assessment: You can take the self-check lesson quiz, and then check your answers on the second screen.

MathXL for School

To access *MathXL for School*, click on the Chapter Review and Practice link from the Table of Contents.

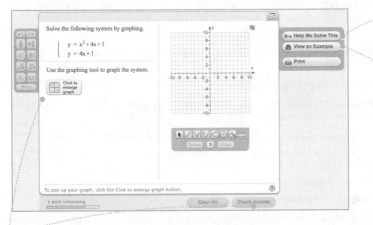

Select **Help Me Solve This** for an interactive step-by-step tutorial.

Select **View an Example** to see a similar worked out problem.

Input your answer and select **Check Answer** to get immediate feedback. After completing the exercise, a new exercise automatically regenerates, so you have unlimited practice opportunities.

Common Core *State Standards*

Mathematics II

Hi, I'm Max. Here is a list of the Common Core State Standards. You'll study algebra, functions, geometry, and statistics standards this year.

Number and Quantity

The Real Number System

Extend the properties of exponents to rational exponents.

N.RN.1 Explain how the definition of the meaning of rational exponents follows from extending the properties of integer exponents to those values, allowing for a notation for radicals in terms of rational exponents.

N.RN.2 Rewrite expressions involving radicals and rational exponents using the properties of exponents.

Use properties of rational and irrational numbers.

N.RN.3 Explain why the sum or product of rational numbers is rational; that the sum of a rational number and an irrational number is irrational; and that the product of a nonzero rational number and an irrational number is irrational.

Quantities

Reason quantitatively and use units to solve problems.

N.Q.2 Define appropriate quantities for the purpose of descriptive modeling. ★

The Complex Number System

Perform arithmetic operations with complex numbers.

N.CN.1 Know there is a complex number i such that $i^2 = -1$, and every complex number has the form $a + bi$ with a and b real.

N.CN.2 Use the relation $i^2 = -1$ and the commutative, associative, and distributive properties to add, subtract, and multiply complex numbers.

Use complex numbers in polynomial identities and equations.

N.CN.7 Solve quadratic equations with real coefficients that have complex solutions.

Algebra

Seeing Structure in Expressions

Interpret the structure of expressions

A.SSE.1 Interpret expressions that represent a quantity in terms of its context. ★

A.SSE.1b Interpret complicated expressions by viewing one or more of their parts as a single entity. *For example, interpret $P(1 + r)^n$ as the product of P and a factor not depending on P.* ★

A.SSE.2 Use the structure of an expression to identify ways to rewrite it. *For example, see $x^4 - y^4$ as $(x^2)^2 - (y^2)^2$, thus recognizing it as a difference of squares that can be factored as $(x^2 - y^2)(x^2 + y^2)$.*

Write expressions in equivalent forms to solve problems

A.SSE.3 Choose and produce an equivalent form of an expression to reveal and explain properties of the quantity represented by the expression. ★

A.SSE.3a Factor a quadratic expression to reveal the zeros of the function it defines. ★

A.SSE.3b Complete the square in a quadratic expression to reveal the maximum or minimum value of the function it defines. ★

Arithmetic with Polynomials and Rational Expressions

Perform arithmetic operations on polynomials

A.APR.1 Understand that polynomials form a system analogous to the integers, namely, they are closed under the operations of addition, subtraction, and multiplication; add, subtract, and multiply polynomials.

Creating Equations★

Create equations that describe numbers or relationships

A.CED.1   Create equations and inequalities in one variable and use them to solve problems. *Include equations arising from linear and quadratic functions, and simple rational and exponential functions.*★

A.CED.2   Create equations in two or more variables to represent relationships between quantities; graph equations on coordinate axes with labels and scales.★

A.CED.4   Rearrange formulas to highlight a quantity of interest, using the same reasoning as in solving equations. *For example, rearrange Ohm's law $V = IR$ to highlight resistance R.*★

Reasoning with Equations and Inequalities

Understand solving equations as a process of reasoning and explain the reasoning

A.REI.1   Explain each step in solving a simple equation as following from the equality of numbers asserted at the previous step, starting from the assumption that the original equation has a solution. Construct a viable argument to justify a solution method.

Solve equations and inequalities in one variable

A.REI.4   Solve quadratic equations in one variable.

A.REI.4a   Use the method of completing the square to transform any quadratic equation in x into an equation of the form $(x - p)^2 = q$ that has the same solutions. Derive the quadratic formula from this form.

A.REI.4b   Solve quadratic equations by inspection (e.g., for $x^2 = 49$), taking square roots, completing the square, the quadratic formula and factoring, as appropriate to the initial form of the equation. Recognize when the quadratic formula gives complex solutions and write them as $a \pm bi$ for real numbers a and b.

Solve systems of equations

A.REI.7   Solve a simple system consisting of a linear equation and a quadratic equation in two variables algebraically and graphically. *For example, find the points of intersection between the line $y = -3x$ and the circle $x^2 + y^2 = 3$.*

Functions

Interpreting Functions

Interpret functions that arise in applications in terms of the context

F.IF.4   For a function that models a relationship between two quantities, interpret key features of graphs and tables in terms of the quantities, and sketch graphs showing key features given a verbal description of the relationship. *Key features include: intercepts; intervals where the function is increasing, decreasing, positive, or negative; relative maximums and minimums; symmetries; end behavior; and periodicity.*★

F.IF.5   Relate the domain of a function to its graph and, where applicable, to the quantitative relationship it describes. *For example, if the function h(n) gives the number of person-hours it takes to assemble n engines in a factory, then the positive integers would be an appropriate domain for the function.*★

F.IF.6   Calculate and interpret the average rate of change of a function (presented symbolically or as a table) over a specified interval. Estimate the rate of change from a graph.★

Analyze functions using different representations

F.IF.7   Graph functions expressed symbolically and show key features of the graph, by hand in simple cases and using technology for more complicated cases.★

F.IF.7a   Graph linear and quadratic functions and show intercepts, maxima, and minima.★

Analyze functions using different representations

F.IF.7.b   Graph square root, cube root, and piecewise-defined functions, including step functions and absolute value functions.

F.IF.7.e   Graph exponential and logarithmic functions, showing intercepts and end behavior, and trigonometric functions, showing period, midline, and amplitude.

F.IF.8   Write a function defined by an expression in different but equivalent forms to reveal and explain different properties of the function.

F.IF.8a   Use the process of factoring and completing the square in a quadratic function to show zeros, extreme values, and symmetry of the graph, and interpret these in terms of a context.

F.IF.9   Compare properties of two functions each represented in a different way (algebraically, graphically, numerically in tables, or by verbal descriptions).

Building Functions

Build a function that models a relationship between two quantities

F.BF.1   Write a function that describes a relationship between two quantities. ★

F.BF.1a   Determine an explicit expression, a recursive process, or steps for calculation from a context.

F.BF.1b   Combine standard function types using arithmetic operations. *For example, build a function that models the temperature of a cooling body by adding a constant function to a decaying exponential, and relate these functions to the model.*

Build new functions from existing functions

F.BF.3   Identify the effect on the graph of replacing $f(x)$ by $f(x) + k$, $k\,f(x)$, $f(kx)$, and $f(x + k)$ for specific values of k (both positive and negative); find the value of k given the graphs. Experiment with cases and illustrate an explanation of the effects on the graph using technology. *Include recognizing even and odd functions from their graphs and algebraic expressions for them.*

> Look at the domains in bold and the clusters to get a good idea of the topics you'll study this year.

Geometry

Similarity, Right Triangles, and Trigonometry

Understand similarity in terms of similarity transformations

G.SRT.1   Verify experimentally the properties of dilations given by a center and a scale factor:

G.SRT.1a   A dilation takes a line not passing through the center of the dilation to a parallel line, and leaves a line passing through the center unchanged.

G.SRT.1b   The dilation of a line segment is longer or shorter in the ratio given by the scale factor.

G.SRT.2   Given two figures, use the definition of similarity in terms of similarity transformations to decide if they are similar; explain using similarity transformations the meaning of similarity for triangles as the equality of all corresponding pairs of angles and the proportionality of all corresponding pairs of sides.

G.SRT.3   Use the properties of similarity transformations to establish the AA criterion for two triangles to be similar.

Prove theorems involving similarity

G.SRT.4   Prove theorems about triangles. *Theorems include: a line parallel to one side of a triangle divides the other two proportionally, and conversely; the Pythagorean Theorem proved using triangle similarity.*

G.SRT.5   Use congruence and similarity criteria for triangles to solve problems and to prove relationships in geometric figures.

Define trigonometric ratios and solve problems involving right triangles

G.SRT.6   Understand that by similarity, side ratios in right triangles are properties of the angles in the triangle, leading to definitions of trigonometric ratios for acute angles.

G.SRT.7   Explain and use the relationship between the sine and cosine of complementary angles.

G.SRT.8   Use trigonometric ratios and the Pythagorean Theorem to solve right triangles in applied problems. ★

Geometric Measurement and Dimension

Explain volume formulas and use them to solve problems

G.GMD.1 Give an informal argument for the formulas for the circumference of a circle, area of a circle, volume of a cylinder, pyramid, and cone. *Use dissection arguments, Cavalieri's principle, and informal limit arguments*.

G.GMD.3 Use volume formulas for cylinders, pyramids, cones, and spheres to solve problems. ★

Statistics and Probability

Interpreting Categorical and Quantitative Data

Summarize, represent, and interpret data on two categorical and quantitative variables

S.ID.6 Represent data on two quantitative variables on a scatter plot, and describe how the variables are related.

S.ID.6a Fit a function to the data; use functions fitted to data to solve problems in the context of the data. *Use given functions or choose a function suggested by the context. Emphasize linear, quadratic, and exponential models*.

S.ID.6.b Informally assess the fit of a function by plotting and analyzing residuals.

Conditional Probability and the Rules of Probability

Understand independence and conditional probability and use them to interpret data

S.CP.1 Describe events as subsets of a sample space (the set of outcomes) using characteristics (or categories) of the outcomes, or as unions, intersections, or complements of other events ("or," "and," "not").

S.CP.2 Understand that two events A and B are independent if the probability of A and B occurring together is the product of their probabilities, and use this characterization to determine if they are independent.

S.CP.3 Understand the conditional probability of A given B as $P(A$ and $B)/P(B)$, and interpret independence of A and B as saying that the conditional probability of A given B is the same as the probability of A, and the conditional probability of B given A is the same as the probability of B.

S.CP.4 Construct and interpret two-way frequency tables of data when two categories are associated with each object being classified. Use the two-way table as a sample space to decide if events are independent and to approximate conditional probabilities.

S.CP.5 Recognize and explain the concepts of conditional probability and independence in everyday language and everyday situations.

Use the rules of probability to compute probabilities of compound events in a uniform probability model

S.CP.6 Find the conditional probability of A given B as the fraction of B's outcomes that also belong to A, and interpret the answer in terms of the model.

S.CP.7 Apply the Addition Rule, $P(A$ or $B) = P(A) + P(B) - P(A$ and $B)$, and interpret the answer in terms of the model.

Reasoning and Proof

Geometry

Congruence
Experiment with transformations in the plane
Prove geometric theorems
Make geometric constructions

Chapter 1

Proving Theorems About Lines and Angles

Geometry

Congruence
Experiment with transformations in the plane
Prove geometric theorems
Make geometric constructions

Chapter 2

3

Congruent Triangles

Chapter 3

Geometry

Congruence
Understand congruence in terms of rigid motions
Prove geometric theorems
Make geometric constructions

Geometry

Similarity, Right Triangles, and Trigonometry
Prove theorems involving similarity

4

Proving Theorems About Triangles

Chapter 4

Geometry

Congruence
Prove geometric theorems
Make geometric constructions

Geometry

Similarity, Right Triangles, and Trigonometry
Prove theorems involving similarity
Circles
Understand and apply theorems about circles

5

Proving Theorems About Quadrilaterals

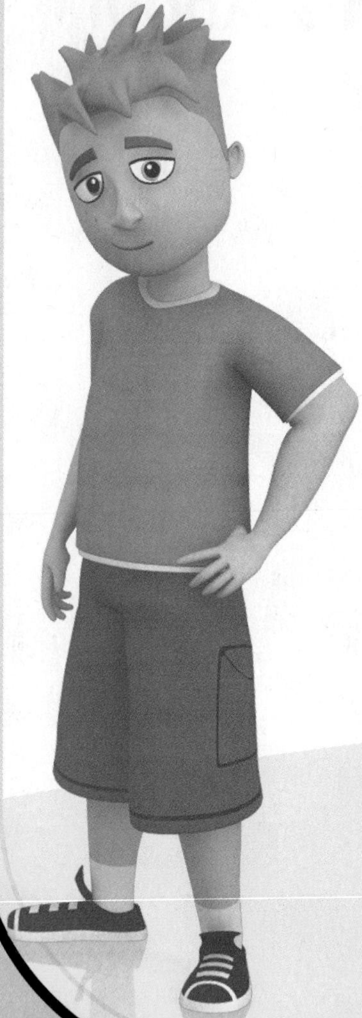

Chapter 5

Geometry

Congruence
Prove geometric theorems

Geometry

Similarity, Right Triangles, and Trigonometry
Prove theorems involving similarity

Similarity

Chapter 6

Geometry

Congruence
Make geometric constructions

Similarity, Right Triangles, and Trigonometry
Understand similarity in terms of similarity transformations
Prove theorems involving similarity

Geometry

Expressing Geometric Properties with Equations
Use coordinates to prove simple geometric theorems algebraically

Right Triangles and Trigonometry

Chapter 7

Geometry

Congruence
Make geometric constructions

Geometry

Similarity, Right Triangles, and Trigonometry
Prove theorems involving similarity
Define trigonometric ratios and solve problems involving right triangles

Circles

Geometry

Circles
   Understand and apply theorems about circles
   Find arc lengths and areas of sectors of circles

Chapter 8

This page intentionally left blank.

Get Ready!

Evaluating Expressions

Evaluate each expression for the given value of *x*.

1. $9x - 13$ for $x = 7$ **2.** $90 - 3x$ for $x = 31$ **3.** $\frac{1}{2}x + 14$ for $x = 23$

Solving Equations

Solve each equation.

4. $2x - 17 = 4$ **5.** $3x + 8 = 53$

6. $(10x + 5) + (6x - 1) = 180$ **7.** $14x = 2(5x + 14)$

8. $2(x + 4) = x + 13$ **9.** $7x + 5 = 5x + 17$

10. $(x + 21) + (2x + 9) = 90$ **11.** $2(3x - 4) + 10 = 5(x + 4)$

Segments and Angles

Use the figure at the right.

12. Name $\angle 1$ in two other ways.

13. If D is the midpoint of $\overline{AB}$, find the value of x.

14. If $\angle ACB$ is a right angle, $m\angle 1 = 4y$, and $m\angle 2 = 2y + 18$, find $m\angle 1$ and $m\angle 2$.

15. Name a pair of angles that form a linear pair.

16. Name a pair of adjacent angles that are not supplementary.

17. If $m\angle ADC + m\angle BDC = 180$, name the straight angle.

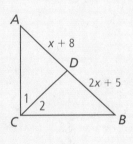

Looking Ahead Vocabulary

18. A scientist often makes an assumption, or *hypothesis*, about a scientific problem. Then the scientist uses experiments to test the *hypothesis* to see if it is true. How might a *hypothesis* in geometry be similar? How might it be different?

19. The *conclusion* of a novel answers questions raised by the story. How do you think the term *conclusion* applies in geometry?

20. A detective uses *deductive reasoning* to solve a case by gathering, combining, and analyzing clues. How might you use *deductive reasoning* in geometry?

CHAPTER 1

Reasoning and Proof

Big Ideas

Reasoning and Proof
Essential Question How can you make a conjecture and prove that it is true?

ⓒ Domains

- Congruence

Interactive Digital Path
Log in to **pearsonsuccessnet.com** and click on Interactive Digital Path to access the Solve Its and animated Problems.

Chapter Preview

Vocabulary

English/Spanish Vocabulary Audio Online:

English	Spanish
biconditional, *p. 26*	bicondicional
conclusion, *p. 19*	conclusión
conditional, *p. 19*	condicional
conjecture, *p. 12*	conjetura
contrapositive, *p. 22*	contrapositivo
converse, *p. 22*	recíproco
deductive reasoning, *p. 34*	razonamiento deductivo
hypothesis, *p. 19*	hipótesis
inductive reasoning, *p. 11*	razonamiento inductivo
inverse, *p. 22*	inverso
negation, *p. 22*	negación
perpendicular bisector, *p. 5*	mediatriz
theorem, *p. 48*	teorema

1-1 Basic Constructions

G.CO.12 Make formal geometric constructions with a variety of tools and methods (compass and straightedge . . .).

Objective To make basic constructions using a straightedge and a compass

Solve It! Write your solution to the Solve It in the space below.

In this lesson, you will learn another way to construct figures like the one in the Solve It.

Essential Understanding You can use special geometric tools to make a figure that is congruent to an original figure without measuring. This method is more accurate than sketching and drawing.

A **straightedge** is a ruler with no markings on it. A **compass** is a geometric tool used to draw circles and parts of circles called *arcs*. A **construction** is a geometric figure drawn using a straightedge and a compass.

Problem 1 Constructing Congruent Segments

Got It? Use a straightedge to draw $\overline{XY}$. Then construct $\overline{RS}$ so that $RS = 2XY$.

1. Construct $\overline{XY}$ congruent to $\overline{AB}$.

A   B

2. Construct $\overline{QJ}$ so that $QJ = TR - PS$.

T   R   P   S

Problem 2 **Constructing Congruent Angles**

Got It? **a.** Construct $\angle F$ so that $m\angle F = 2m\angle B$.

B

Think

Which postulate allows you to construct an angle with measure $2m\angle B$?

Ⓒ **b. Reasoning** How is constructing a congruent angle similar to constructing a congruent segment?

3. Construct $\angle D$ so that $\angle D \cong \angle C$.

4. Construct $\angle F$ so that $m\angle F = 2m\angle C$.

Perpendicular lines are two lines that intersect to form right angles. The symbol $\perp$ means "is perpendicular to." In the diagram at the right, $\overleftrightarrow{AB} \perp \overleftrightarrow{CD}$ and $\overleftrightarrow{CD} \perp \overleftrightarrow{AB}$.

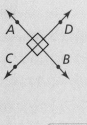

A **perpendicular bisector** of a segment is a line, segment, or ray that is perpendicular to the segment at its midpoint. In the diagram at the right, $\overleftrightarrow{EF}$ is the perpendicular bisector of $\overline{GH}$. The perpendicular bisector bisects the segment into two congruent segments. The construction in Problem 3 will show you how this works. You will justify the steps for this construction in Chapter 3, as well as for the other constructions in this lesson.

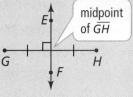

midpoint of $\overline{GH}$

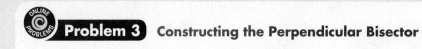

Problem 3   Constructing the Perpendicular Bisector

Got It?   Draw $\overline{ST}$. Construct its perpendicular bisector.

 Practice   **5.** Construct the perpendicular bisector of $\overline{AB}$.

A

B

6. Construct the perpendicular bisector of $\overline{TR}$.

Got It? Draw obtuse $\angle XYZ$. Then construct its bisector $\overrightarrow{YP}$.

Ⓐ Practice **7.** Draw acute $\angle PQR$. Then construct its bisector.

Lesson Check

Do you know HOW?

8. Construct a segment congruent to $\overline{PQ}$.

P •————————————• Q

P   Q

9. Construct the perpendicular bisector of $\overline{PQ}$.

P ●————————————● Q

10. Draw an obtuse ∠*JKL*. Construct its bisector.

Do you UNDERSTAND?

⊚ 11. Vocabulary What two tools do you use to make constructions?

© 12. Compare and Contrast Describe the difference in accuracy between sketching a figure, drawing a figure with a ruler and protractor, and constructing a figure. Explain.

© 13. Error Analysis Your friend constructs $\overleftrightarrow{XY}$ so that it is perpendicular to and contains the midpoint of $\overline{AB}$. He claims that $\overline{AB}$ is the perpendicular bisector of $\overleftrightarrow{XY}$. What is his error?

More Practice and Problem-Solving Exercises

Ⓑ Apply

Sketch the figure described. Explain how to construct it. Then do the construction.

14. $\overleftrightarrow{XY} \perp \overleftrightarrow{YZ}$ **15.** $\overrightarrow{ST}$ bisects right $\angle PSQ$.

© 16. Compare and Contrast How is constructing an angle bisector similar to constructing a perpendicular bisector?

© 17. Think About a Plan Draw an $\angle A$. Construct an angle whose measure is $\frac{1}{4}m\angle A$.
- How is the angle you need to construct related to the angle bisector of $\angle A$?
- How can you use previous constructions to help you?

18. Answer the questions about a segment in a plane. Explain each answer.
- **a.** How many midpoints does the segment have?
- **b.** How many bisectors does it have?
- **c.** How many lines in the plane are its perpendicular bisectors?
- **d.** How many lines in space are its perpendicular bisectors?

For Exercises 19–21, copy $\angle 1$ and $\angle 2$. Construct each angle described.

19. $\angle B$; $m\angle B = m\angle 1 + m\angle 2$

20. $\angle C$; $m\angle C = m\angle 1 - m\angle 2$

21. $\angle D$; $m\angle D = 2m\angle 2$

© 22. **Writing** Explain how to do each construction with a compass and straightedge.
   a. Draw a segment $\overline{PQ}$. Construct the midpoint of $\overline{PQ}$.
   b. Divide $\overline{PQ}$ into four congruent segments.

© 23. **a.** Draw a large triangle with three acute angles. Construct the bisectors of the three angles. What appears to be true about the three angle bisectors?
   b. Repeat the constructions with a triangle that has one obtuse angle.
   c. **Make a Conjecture** What appears to be true about the three angle bisectors of any triangle?

Use a ruler to draw segments of 2 cm, 4 cm, and 5 cm. Then construct each triangle with the given side measures, if possible. If it is not possible, explain why not.

24. 4 cm, 4 cm, and 5 cm   **25.** 2 cm, 5 cm, and 5 cm

26. 2 cm, 2 cm, and 5 cm   **27.** 2 cm, 2 cm, and 4 cm

© 28. **a.** Draw a segment, $\overline{XY}$. Construct a triangle with sides congruent to $\overline{XY}$.
   b. Measure the angles of the triangle.
   c. **Writing** Describe how to construct a 60° angle using what you know. Then describe how to construct a 30° angle.

29. Which steps best describe how to construct the pattern at the right?
   Ⓐ Use a straightedge to draw the segment and then a compass to draw five half circles.
   Ⓑ Use a straightedge to draw the segment and then a compass to draw six half circles.
   Ⓒ Use a compass to draw five half circles and then a straightedge to join their ends.
   Ⓓ Use a compass to draw six half circles and then a straightedge to join their ends.

Ⓒ **Challenge**

30. Study the figures. Complete the definition of a line perpendicular to a plane: A line is perpendicular to a plane if it is __?__ to every line in the plane that __?__.

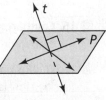

Line r ⊥ plane M.   Line t is not ⊥ plane P.

© 31. **a.** Use your compass to draw a circle. Locate three points A, B, and C on the circle.
   b. Draw $\overline{AB}$ and $\overline{BC}$. Then construct the perpendicular bisectors of $\overline{AB}$ and $\overline{BC}$.
   c. **Reasoning** Label the intersection of the two perpendicular bisectors as point O. What do you think is true about point O?

32. Two triangles are *congruent* if each side and each angle of one triangle is congruent to a side or angle of the other triangle. In Chapter 3, you will learn that if each side of one triangle is congruent to a side of the other triangle, then you can conclude that the triangles are congruent without finding the angles. Explain how you can use congruent triangles to justify the angle bisector construction.

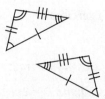

Patterns and Inductive Reasoning

Prepares for **G.CO.9** Prove theorems about lines and angles . . . Also prepares for **G.CO.10**, **G.CO.11**

Objective To use inductive reasoning to make conjectures

Solve It! Write your solution to the Solve It in the space below.

In the Solve It, you may have used inductive reasoning. **Inductive reasoning** is reasoning based on patterns you observe.

Essential Understanding You can observe patterns in some number sequences and some sequences of geometric figures to discover relationships.

Problem 1 Finding and Using a Pattern

Got It? What are the next two terms in each sequence?

    a. 45, 40, 35, 30, . . .

    b.

Practice Find a pattern for each sequence. Use the pattern to show the next two terms.

1. $1, \frac{1}{2}, \frac{1}{4}, \frac{1}{8}, \ldots$

2.

> You may want to find the tenth or the one-hundredth term in a sequence. In this case, rather than find every previous term, you can look for a pattern and make a conjecture. A **conjecture** is a conclusion you reach using inductive reasoning.

Problem 2 Using Inductive Reasoning

Got It? What conjecture can you make about the twenty-first term in R, W, B, R, W, B, . . .?

Plan

Do you need to extend the sequence to 21 terms?

Practice Use the sequence and inductive reasoning to make a conjecture.

3. What is the color of the thirtieth figure?

4. What is the shape of the fortieth figure?

> It is important to gather enough data before you make a conjecture. For example, you do not have enough information about the sequence 1, 3, . . . to make a reasonable conjecture. The next term could be $3 \cdot 3 = 9$ or $3 + 2 = 5$.

Got It? What conjecture can you make about the sum of the first 30 odd numbers?

Plan
What's the first step?

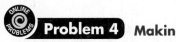 **Practice** Make a conjecture for each scenario. Show your work.

5. the sum of the first 100 positive even numbers

6. the product of two odd numbers

Got It? **a.** Use the graph of the sales information from Problem 4. What conjecture can you make about backpack sales in June?

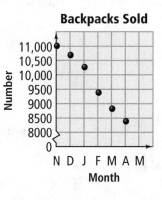

Backpacks Sold

© **b. Reasoning** Is it reasonable to use this graph to make a conjecture about sales in August? Explain.

STEM **7.** Lightning travels much faster than thunder, so you see lightning before you hear thunder. If you count 5 s between the lightning and thunder, how far away is the storm?

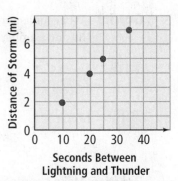

8. The speed at which a cricket chirps is affected by the temperature. If you hear 20 cricket chirps in 14 s, what is the temperature?

Number of Chirps per 14 Seconds	Temperature (°F)
5	45
10	55
15	65

Not all conjectures turn out to be true. You should test your conjecture multiple times. You can prove that a conjecture is false by finding *one* counterexample. A **counterexample** is an example that shows that a conjecture is incorrect.

 **Problem 5**   **Finding a Counterexample**

Got It?   What is a counterexample for each conjecture?

   a. If a flower is red, it is a rose.

   b. One and only one plane exists through any three points.

   c. When you multiply a number by 3, the product is divisible by 6.

A Practice Find one counterexample to show that each conjecture is false.

9. $\angle 1$ and $\angle 2$ are supplementary, so one of the angles is acute.

10. The sum of two numbers is greater than either number.

Lesson Check

Do you know HOW?

What are the next two terms in each sequence?

11. 7, 13, 19, 25, . . .

12.

13. What is a counterexample for the following conjecture?
All four-sided figures are squares.

Do you UNDERSTAND?

14. Vocabulary How does the word *counter* help you understand the term *counterexample*?

15. Compare and Contrast Clay thinks the next term in the sequence 2, 4, . . . is 6. Given the same pattern, Ott thinks the next term is 8, and Stacie thinks the next term is 7. What conjecture is each person making? Is there enough information to decide who is correct?

More Practice and Problem-Solving Exercises

B Apply

Find a pattern for each sequence. Use inductive reasoning to show the next two terms.

16. 1, 3, 7, 13, 21, . . .

17. 1, 2, 5, 6, 9, . . .

18. 0.1, 0.01, 0.001, . . .

19. 2, 6, 7, 21, 22, 66, 67, . . .

20. 1, 3, 7, 15, 31, . . .

21. $0, \frac{1}{2}, \frac{3}{4}, \frac{7}{8}, \frac{15}{16}, \ldots$

Predict the next term in each sequence. Use your calculator to verify your answer.

22. $12345679 \times 9 = 111111111$
$12345679 \times 18 = 222222222$
$12345679 \times 27 = 333333333$
$12345679 \times 36 = 444444444$
$12345679 \times 45 = \blacksquare$

23. $1 \times 1 = 1$
$11 \times 11 = 121$
$111 \times 111 = 12321$
$1111 \times 1111 = 1234321$
$11111 \times 11111 = \blacksquare$

24. Patterns Draw the next figure in the sequence. Make sure you think about color and shape.

Draw the next figure in each sequence.

25.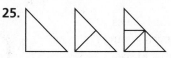

26.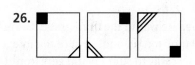

🅒 27. **Reasoning** Find the perimeter when 100 triangles are put together in the pattern shown. Assume that all triangle sides are 1 cm long.

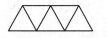

🅒 28. **Think About a Plan** Below are 15 points. Most of the points fit a pattern. Which does not? Explain.

$A(6, -2)$ $B(6, 5)$ $C(8, 0)$ $D(8, 7)$ $E(10, 2)$ $F(10, 6)$ $G(11, 4)$ $H(12, 3)$
$I(4, 0)$ $J(7, 6)$ $K(5, 6)$ $L(4, 7)$ $M(2, 2)$ $N(1, 4)$ $O(2, 6)$

- How can you draw a diagram to help you find a pattern?
- What pattern do the majority of the points fit?

🅒 29. **Language** Look for a pattern in the Chinese number system.
  a. What is the Chinese name for the numbers 43, 67, and 84?
  b. **Reasoning** Do you think that the Chinese number system is base 10? Explain.

🅒 30. **Open-Ended** Write two different number sequences that begin with the same two numbers.

🅒 31. **Error Analysis** For each of the past four years, Paulo has grown 2 in. every year. He is now 16 years old and is 5 ft 10 in. tall. He figures that when he is 22 years old he will be 6 ft 10 in. tall. What would you tell Paulo about his conjecture?

Chinese Number System

Number	Chinese Word	Number	Chinese Word
1	yī	9	jĭu
2	èr	10	shí
3	sān	11	shí-yī
4	sì	12	shí-èr
5	wŭ	⋮	⋮
6	lìu	20	èr-shí
7	qī	21	èr-shí-yī
8	bā	⋮	⋮
		30	sān-shí

32. **Bird Migration** During bird migration, volunteers get up early on Bird Day to record the number of bird species they observe in their community during a 24-h period. Results are posted online to help scientists and students track the migration.
  a. Make a graph of the data.
  b. Use the graph and inductive reasoning to make a conjecture about the number of bird species the volunteers in this community will observe in 2015.

🅒 33. **Writing** Describe a real-life situation in which you recently used inductive reasoning.

Bird Count

Year	Number of Species
2004	70
2005	83
2006	80
2007	85
2008	90

34. History When he was in the third grade, German mathematician Karl Gauss (1777–1855) took ten seconds to sum the integers from 1 to 100. Now it's your turn. Find a fast way to sum the integers from 1 to 100. Find a fast way to sum the integers from 1 to n. (*Hint:* Use patterns.)

35. Chess The small squares on a chessboard can be combined to form larger squares. For example, there are sixty-four 1×1 squares and one 8×8 square. Use inductive reasoning to determine how many 2×2 squares, 3×3 squares, and so on, are on a chessboard. What is the total number of squares on a chessboard?

36. a. Algebra Write the first six terms of the sequence that starts with 1, and for which the difference between consecutive terms is first 2, and then 3, 4, 5, and 6.

   b. Evaluate $\frac{n^2 + n}{2}$ for $n = 1, 2, 3, 4, 5,$ and 6. Compare the sequence you get with your answer for part (a).

   c. Examine the diagram at the right and explain how it illustrates a value of $\frac{n^2 + n}{2}$.

   d. Draw a similar diagram to represent $\frac{n^2 + n}{2}$ for $n = 5$.

$$
\begin{array}{c}
\quad\quad n+1 \\
n \left\{
\begin{array}{cccc}
\bullet & \bullet & \bullet & \bullet \\
\bullet & \bullet & \bullet & \bullet \\
\bullet & \bullet & \bullet & \bullet
\end{array}
\right.
\end{array}
$$

1-3 Conditional Statements

Prepares for **G.CO.10** Prove theorems about triangles . . . Also prepares for **G.CO.9, G.CO.11**

Objectives To recognize conditional statements and their parts
To write converses, inverses, and contrapositives of conditionals

Solve It! Write your solution to the Solve It in the space below.

The study of *if-then* statements and their truth values is a foundation of reasoning.

Essential Understanding You can describe some mathematical relationships using a variety of *if-then* statements.

take note

Key Concept Conditional Statements

Definition	Symbols	Diagram
A **conditional** is an *if-then* statement. The **hypothesis** is the part *p* following *if*. The **conclusion** is the part *q* following *then*.	$p \rightarrow q$ Read as "if *p* then *q*" or "*p* implies *q*."	

The Venn diagram above illustrates how the set of things that satisfy the hypothesis lies inside the set of things that satisfy the conclusion.

Problem 1 Identifying the Hypothesis and the Conclusion

Got It? What are the hypothesis and the conclusion of the conditional?
If an angle measures 130, then the angle is obtuse.

Think

What would a Venn diagram of the statement look like?

A Practice Identify the hypothesis and conclusion of each conditional.

1. If a figure is a rectangle, then it has four sides.

2. If you want to be healthy, then you should eat vegetables.

Problem 2 Writing a Conditional

Got It? How can you write "Dolphins are mammals" as a conditional?

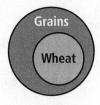

Think

Which part of the statement is the hypothesis, (*p*)?

A Practice **3. Algebra** Write the following sentence as a conditional.

$3x - 7 = 14$ implies that $3x = 21$.

4. Write a conditional statement that the Venn diagram illustrates.

Grains

Wheat

The **truth value** of a conditional is either *true* or *false*. To show that a conditional is true, show that every time the hypothesis is true, the conclusion is also true. To show that a conditional is false, find *only one* counterexample for which the hypothesis is true and the conclusion is false.

 Problem 3 Finding the Truth Value of a Conditional

Got It? Is the conditional *true* or *false*? If it is false, find a counterexample.

   a. If a month has 28 days, then it is February.

   b. If two angles form a linear pair, then they are supplementary.

Practice Determine if the conditional is *true* or *false*. If it is false, find a counterexample.

   5. If you live in a country that borders the United States, then you live in Canada.

   6. If an angle measures 80°, then it is acute.

The **negation** of a statement p is the opposite of the statement. The symbol is $\sim p$ and is read "not p." The negation of the statement "The sky is blue" is "The sky is *not* blue." You can use negations to write statements related to a conditional. Every conditional has three related conditional statements.

take note

Key Concept   Related Conditional Statements

Statement	How to Write It	Example	Symbols	How to Read it
Conditional	Use the given hypothesis and conclusion.	If $m\angle A = 15$, then $\angle A$ is acute.	$p \to q$	If p, then q.
Converse	Exchange the hypothesis and the conclusion.	If $\angle A$ is acute, then $m\angle A = 15$.	$q \to p$	If q, then p.
Inverse	Negate both the hypothesis and the conclusion of the conditional.	If $m\angle A \neq 15$, then $\angle A$ is not acute.	$\sim p \to \sim q$	If not p, then not q.
Contrapositive	Negate both the hypothesis and the conclusion of the converse.	If $\angle A$ is not acute, then $m\angle A \neq 15$.	$\sim q \to \sim p$	If not q, then not p.

Below are the truth values of the related statements above. **Equivalent statements** have the same truth value.

Statement	Example	Truth Value
Conditional	If $m\angle A = 15$, then $\angle A$ is acute.	True
Converse	If $\angle A$ is acute, then $m\angle A = 15$.	False
Inverse	If $m\angle A \neq 15$, then $\angle A$ is not acute.	False
Contrapositive	If $\angle A$ is not acute, then $m\angle A \neq 15$.	True

A conditional and its contrapositive are equivalent statements. They are either both true or both false. The converse and inverse of a statement are also equivalent statements.

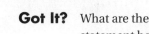

Problem 4 Writing and Finding Truth Values of Statements

Got It? What are the converse, inverse, and contrapositive of the conditional statement below? What are the truth values of each? If a statement is false, give a counterexample.

> If a vegetable is a carrot, then it contains beta carotene.

Practice If the given statement is not in *if-then* form, rewrite it. Write the converse, inverse, and contrapositive of the given conditional statement. Determine the truth value of all four statements. If a statement is false, give a counterexample.

7. Algebra If $4x + 8 = 28$, then $x = 5$.

8. Pianists are musicians.

Lesson Check

Do you know HOW?

9. What are the hypothesis and the conclusion of the following statement? Write it as a conditional.

> Residents of Key West live in Florida.

10. What are the converse, inverse, and contrapositive of the statement? Which statements are true?

> If a figure is a rectangle with sides 2 cm and 3 cm, then it has a perimeter of 10 cm.

Do you UNDERSTAND?

@ **11. Error Analysis** Your classmate rewrote the statement "You jog every Sunday" as the conditional below. What is your classmate's error? Correct it.

> If you jog, then it is Sunday.

@ **12. Reasoning** Suppose a conditional statement and its converse are both true. What are the truth values of the contrapositive and inverse? How do you know?

More Practice and Problem-Solving Exercises

B Apply

Write each statement as a conditional.

13. "We're half the people; we should be half the Congress." —Jeanette Rankin, former U.S. congresswoman, calling for more women in office

14. "Anyone who has never made a mistake has never tried anything new." —Albert Einstein

15. Probability An event with probability 1 is certain to occur.

@ **16. Think About a Plan** Your classmate claims that the conditional and contrapositive of the following statement are both true. Is he correct? Explain.

> If $x = 2$, then $x^2 = 4$.

- Can you find a counterexample of the conditional?
- Do you need to find a counterexample of the contrapositive to know its truth value?

17. Open-Ended Write a true conditional that has a true converse, and write a true conditional that has a false converse.

18. Multiple Representations Write three separate conditional statements that the Venn diagram illustrates.

19. Error Analysis A given conditional is true. Natalie claims its contrapositive is also true. Sean claims its contrapositive is false. Who is correct and how do you know?

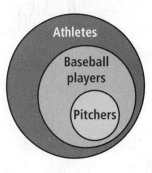

Draw a Venn diagram to illustrate each statement.

20. If an angle measures 100, then it is obtuse.

21. If you are the captain of your team, then you are a junior or senior.

22. Peace Corps volunteers want to help other people.

Algebra Write the converse of each statement. If the converse is true, write *true*. If it is not true, provide a counterexample.

23. If $x = -6$, then $|x| = 6$.

24. If y is negative, then $-y$ is positive.

25. If $x < 0$, then $x^3 < 0$.

26. If $x < 0$, then $x^2 > 0$.

27. Advertising Advertisements often suggest conditional statements. What conditional does the ad at the right imply?

Write each postulate as a conditional statement.

28. Two intersecting lines meet in exactly one point.

29. Two congruent figures have equal areas.

30. Through any two points there is exactly one line.

Challenge

Write a statement beginning with *all*, *some*, or *no* to match each Venn diagram.

31.

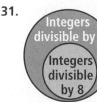

32.

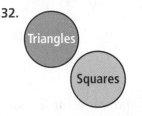

33.

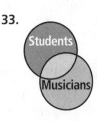

34. Let a represent an integer. Consider the five statements r, s, t, u, and v.

$r: a$ is even.　　$s: a$ is odd.　　$t: 2a$ is even.　　$u: 2a$ is odd.　　$v: 2a + 1$ is odd.

How many statements of the form $p \rightarrow q$ can you make from these statements? Decide which are true, and provide a counterexample if they are false.

1-4 Biconditionals and Definitions

Prepares for **G.CO.11** Prove theorems about parallelograms . . . Also prepares for **G.CO.9, G.CO.10**

Objective   To write biconditionals and recognize good definitions

 Solve It!   Write your solution to the Solve It in the space below.

In the Solve It, you used conditional statements. A **biconditional** is a single true statement that combines a true conditional and its true converse. You can write a biconditional by joining the two parts of each conditional with the phrase *if and only if*.

Essential Understanding   A definition is good if it can be written as a biconditional.

Problem 1   **Writing a Biconditional**

Got It?   What is the converse of the following true conditional? If the converse is also true, rewrite the statements as a biconditional.

If two angles have equal measure, then the angles are congruent.

Think

How do you form the converse of a conditional?

Practice Each conditional statement below is true. Write its converse. If the converse is also true, combine the statements as a biconditional.

    1. Algebra If $x = 3$, then $|x| = 3$.

    2. In the United States, if it is July 4, then it is Independence Day.

take note

Key Concept Biconditional Statements

A biconditional combines $p \rightarrow q$ and $q \rightarrow p$ as $p \leftrightarrow q$.

Example	**Symbols**	**How to Read It**
A point is a midpoint if and only if it divides a segment into two congruent segments.	$p \leftrightarrow q$	"p if and only if q"

You can write a biconditional as two conditionals that are converses.

Problem 2 Identifying the Conditionals in a Biconditional

Got It? What are the two conditionals that form this biconditional?

    Two numbers are reciprocals if and only if their product is 1.

Practice Write the two statements that form each biconditional.

    3. You live in Washington, D.C., if and only if you live in the capital of the United States.

    4. Algebra $x^2 = 144$ if and only if $x = 12$ or $x = -12$.

Undefined terms such as *point*, *line*, and *plane* are the building blocks of geometry. You understand the meanings of these terms intuitively. Then you use them to define other terms such as *segment*.

A good definition is a statement that can help you identify or classify an object. A good definition has several important components.

✓ A good definition uses clearly understood terms. These terms should be commonly understood or already defined.

✓ A good definition is precise. Good definitions avoid words such as *large, sort of*, and *almost*.

✓ A good definition is reversible. That means you can write a good definition as a true biconditional.

Problem 3 Writing a Definition as a Biconditional

Got It? Is this definition of *straight angle* reversible? If yes, write it as a true biconditional.

A straight angle is an angle that measures 180.

Think

How do you determine whether a definition is reversible?

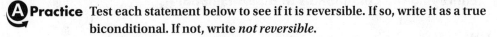**Practice** Test each statement below to see if it is reversible. If so, write it as a true biconditional. If not, write *not reversible*.

5. A perpendicular bisector of a segment is a line, segment, or ray that is perpendicular to a segment at its midpoint.

6. Two angles that form a linear pair are adjacent.

One way to show that a statement is *not* a good definition is to find a counterexample.

Problem 4 Identifying Good Definitions

Got It?   **a.** Is the following statement a good definition? Explain.

A square is a figure with four right angles.

ⓒ **b. Reasoning** How can you rewrite the statement "Obtuse angles have greater measures than acute angles" so that it is a good definition?

Ⓐ **Practice** Is each statement below a good definition? If not, explain.

7. A compass is a geometric tool.

8. Perpendicular lines are two lines that intersect to form right angles.

Lesson Check

Do you know HOW?

9. How can you write the following statement as two true conditionals?

   Collinear points are points that lie on the same line.

10. How can you combine the following statements as a biconditional?

    If this month is June, then next month is July.

    If next month is July, then this month is June.

11. Write the following definition as a biconditional.

    Vertical angles are two angles whose sides are opposite rays.

Do you UNDERSTAND?

○ 12. **Vocabulary** Explain how the term *biconditional* is fitting for a statement composed of *two* conditionals.

13. Error Analysis Why is the following statement a poor definition?

Elephants are gigantic animals.

14. Compare and Contrast Which of the following statements is a better definition of a linear pair? Explain.

A linear pair is a pair of supplementary angles.

A linear pair is a pair of adjacent angles with noncommon sides that are opposite rays.

More Practice and Problem-Solving Exercises

B Apply

15. Think About a Plan Is the following a good definition? Explain.
A ligament is a band of tough tissue connecting bones or holding organs in place.
- Can you write the statement as two true conditionals?
- Are the two true conditionals converses of each other?

16. Reasoning Is the following a good definition? Explain.
An obtuse angle is an angle with measure greater than 90.

17. Open-Ended Choose a definition from a dictionary or from a glossary. Explain what makes the statement a good definition.

18. Error Analysis Your friend defines a right angle as an angle that is greater than an acute angle. Use a biconditional to show that this is not a good definition.

19. Which conditional and its converse form a true biconditional?

    Ⓐ If $x > 0$, then $|x| > 0$.   Ⓒ If $x^3 = 5$, then $x = 125$.

    Ⓑ If $x = 3$, then $x^2 = 9$.   Ⓓ If $x = 19$, then $2x - 3 = 35$.

Write each statement as a biconditional.

20. Points in Quadrant III have two negative coordinates.

21. When the sum of the digits of an integer is divisible by 9, the integer is divisible by 9 and vice versa.

22. The whole numbers are the nonnegative integers.

23. A hexagon is a six-sided polygon.

Language For Exercises 24–27, use the chart below. Decide whether the description of each letter is a good definition. If not, provide a counterexample by giving another letter that could fit the definition.

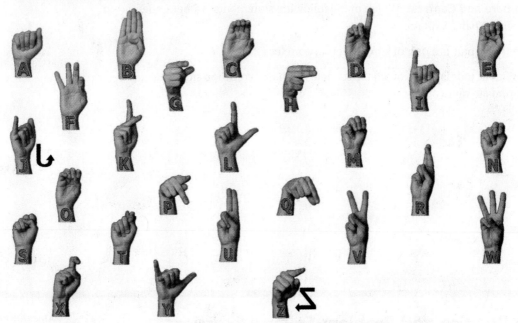

24. The letter *D* is formed by pointing straight up with the finger beside the thumb and folding the other fingers and the thumb so that they all touch.

25. The letter *K* is formed by making a *V* with the two fingers beside the thumb.

26. You have formed the letter *I* if and only if the smallest finger is sticking up and the other fingers are folded into the palm of your hand with your thumb folded over them and your hand is held still.

27. You form the letter *B* by holding all four fingers tightly together and pointing them straight up while your thumb is folded into the palm of your hand.

ⓒ Reading Math Let statements *p*, *q*, *r*, and *s* be as follows:

p: ∠*A* and ∠*B* are a linear pair.

q: ∠*A* and ∠*B* are supplementary angles.

r: ∠*A* and ∠*B* are adjacent angles.

s: ∠*A* and ∠*B* are adjacent and supplementary angles.

Substitute for *p*, *q*, *r*, and *s*, and write each statement the way you would read it.

28. $p \rightarrow q$ **29.** $p \rightarrow r$ **30.** $p \rightarrow s$ **31.** $p \leftrightarrow s$

ⓒ Challenge

32. Writing Use the figures to write a good definition of a *line* in spherical geometry.

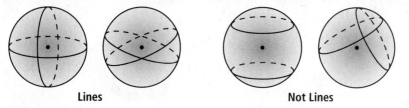

Lines   Not Lines

ⓒ 33. Multiple Representations You have illustrated true conditional statements with Venn diagrams. You can do the same thing with true biconditionals. Consider the following statement.

An integer is divisible by 10 if and only if its last digit is 0.

  a. Write the two conditional statements that make up this biconditional.
  b. Illustrate the first conditional from part (a) with a Venn diagram.
  c. Illustrate the second conditional from part (a) with a Venn diagram.
  d. Combine your two Venn diagrams from parts (b) and (c) to form a Venn diagram representing the biconditional statement.
  e. What must be true of the Venn diagram for any true biconditional statement?
  f. Reasoning How does your conclusion in part (e) help to explain why you can write a good definition as a biconditional?

1-5 Deductive Reasoning

Prepares for **G.CO.9** Prove theorems about lines and angles . . . Also prepares for **G.CO.10, G.CO.11**

Objective To use the Law of Detachment and the Law of Syllogism

 Solve It! Write your solution to the Solve It in the space below.

In the Solve It, you drew a conclusion based on several facts. You used deductive reasoning. **Deductive reasoning** (sometimes called logical reasoning) is the process of reasoning logically from given statements or facts to a conclusion.

Essential Understanding Given true statements, you can use deductive reasoning to make a valid or true conclusion.

take note

Property Law of Detachment

Law	Symbols
If the hypothesis of a true conditional is true, then the conclusion is true.	If $p \rightarrow q$ is true
	And p is true,
	Then q is true.

To use the Law of Detachment, identify the hypothesis of the given true conditional. If the second given statement matches the hypothesis of the conditional, then you can make a valid conclusion.

Problem 1 **Using the Law of Detachment**

Got It? What can you conclude from the given information?

Think
What conditions must be met for you to reach a valid conclusion?

a. If there is lightning, then it is not safe to be out in the open. Marla sees lightning from the soccer field.

b. If a figure is a square, then its sides have equal length. Figure *ABCD* has sides of equal length.

 Practice If possible, use the Law of Detachment to make a conclusion. If it is not possible to make a conclusion, tell why.

1. If a doctor suspects her patient has a broken bone, then she should take an X-ray. Dr. Ngemba suspects Lilly has a broken arm.

2. If three points are on the same line, then they are collinear. Points *X*, *Y*, and *Z* are on line *m*.

> Another law of deductive reasoning is the Law of Syllogism. The **Law of Syllogism** allows you to state a conclusion from two true conditional statements when the conclusion of one statement is the hypothesis of the other statement.

take note

Property Law of Syllogism

Symbols				Example
If	$p \rightarrow q$		is true	If it is July, then you are on summer vacation.
and		$q \rightarrow r$	is true,	If you are on summer vacation, then you work at a smoothie shop.
then	$p \rightarrow$	r	is true.	**You conclude:** If it is July, then you work at a smoothie shop.

Got It? What can you conclude from the given information? What is your reasoning?

    a. If a whole number ends in 0, then it is divisible by 10. If a whole number is divisible by 10, then it is divisible by 5.

Think

What conditions must be met for you to reach a valid conclusion?

    b. If $\overrightarrow{AB}$ and $\overrightarrow{AD}$ are opposite rays, then the two rays form a straight angle. If two rays are opposite rays, then the two rays form a straight angle.

Ⓐ Practice If possible, use the Law of Syllogism to make a conclusion. If it is not possible to make a conclusion, tell why.

STEM **3. Ecology** If an animal is a Florida panther, then its scientific name is *Puma concolor coryi*.

If an animal is a *Puma concolor coryi*, then it is endangered.

4. If a line intersects a segment at its midpoint, then the line bisects the segment.

If a line bisects a segment, then it divides the segment into two congruent segments.

You can use the Law of Syllogism and the Law of Detachment together to make conclusions.

Problem 3 Using the Laws of Syllogism and Detachment

Got It? **a.** What can you conclude from the given information? What is your reasoning?

If a river is more than 4000 mi long, then it is longer than the Amazon.

If a river is longer than the Amazon, then it is the longest river in the world. The Nile is 4132 mi long.

b. Reasoning In Problem 3, does it matter whether you use the Law of Syllogism or the Law of Detachment first? Explain.

 Practice Use the Law of Detachment and the Law of Syllogism to make conclusions from the following statements. If it is not possible to make a conclusion, tell why.

5. If a mountain is the highest in Alaska, then it is the highest in the United States.

If an Alaskan mountain is more than 20,300 ft high, then it is the highest in Alaska.

Alaska's Denali is 20,310 ft high.

6. If you live in the Bronx, then you live in New York.

Tracy lives in the Bronx.

If you live in New York, then you live in the eleventh state to enter the Union.

Lesson Check

Do you know HOW?

If possible, make a conclusion from the given true statements. What reasoning did you use?

7. If it is Tuesday, then you will go bowling. You go bowling.

8. If a figure is a three-sided polygon, then it is a triangle. Figure *ABC* is a three-sided polygon.

9. If it is Saturday, then you walk to work. If you walk to work, then you wear sneakers.

Do you UNDERSTAND?

Ⓒ 10. Error Analysis What is the error in the reasoning at the right?

Birds that weigh more than 50 pounds cannot fly. A kiwi cannot fly. So, a kiwi weighs more than 50 pounds.

Ⓒ 11. Compare and Contrast How is deductive reasoning different from inductive reasoning?

More Practice and Problem-Solving Exercises

B Apply

© **12. Think About a Plan** If it is the night of your weekly basketball game, your family eats at your favorite restaurant. When your family eats at your favorite restaurant, you always get chicken fingers. If it is Tuesday, then it is the night of your weekly basketball game. How much do you pay for chicken fingers after your game? Use the specials board at the right to decide. Explain your reasoning.

- How can you reorder and rewrite the sentences to help you?
- How can you use the Law of Syllogism to answer the question?

Beverages For Exercises 13–18, assume that the following statements are true.

A. If Maria is drinking juice, then it is breakfast time.

B. If it is lunchtime, then Kira is drinking milk and nothing else.

C. If it is mealtime, then Curtis is drinking water and nothing else.

D. If it is breakfast time, then Julio is drinking juice and nothing else.

E. Maria is drinking juice.

Use only the information given above. For each statement, write *must be true*, *may be true*, or *is not true*. Explain your reasoning.

13. Julio is drinking juice. | **14.** Curtis is drinking water.

15. Kira is drinking milk. | **16.** Curtis is drinking juice.

17. Maria is drinking water. | **18.** Julio is drinking milk.

STEM 19. Physics Quarks are subatomic particles identified by electric charge and rest energy. The table shows how to categorize quarks by their flavors. Show how the Law of Detachment and the table are used to identify the flavor of a quark with a charge of $-\frac{1}{3}$ e and rest energy 540 MeV.

Rest Energy and Charge of Quarks						
Rest Energy (MeV)	360	360	1500	540	173,000	5000
Electric Charge (e)	$+\frac{2}{3}$	$-\frac{1}{3}$	$+\frac{2}{3}$	$-\frac{1}{3}$	$+\frac{2}{3}$	$-\frac{1}{3}$
Flavor	Up	Down	Charmed	Strange	Top	Bottom

Write the first statement as a conditional. If possible, use the Law of Detachment to make a conclusion. If it is not possible to make a conclusion, tell why.

20. All national parks are interesting. Mammoth Cave is a national park.

21. All squares are rectangles. *ABCD* is a square.

22. The temperature is always above 32°F in Key West, Florida. The temperature is 62°F.

23. Every high school student likes art. Ling likes art.

Ⓖ 24. **Writing** Give an example of a rule used in your school that could be written as a conditional. Explain how the Law of Detachment is used in applying that rule.

Ⓒ **Challenge**

25. **Reasoning** Use the following algorithm: Choose an integer. Multiply the integer by 3. Add 6 to the product. Divide the sum by 3.
    a. Complete the algorithm for four different integers. Look for a pattern in the chosen integers and in the corresponding answers. Make a conjecture that relates the chosen integers to the answers.
    b. Let the variable x represent the chosen integer. Apply the algorithm to x. Simplify the resulting expression.
    c. How does your answer to part (b) confirm your conjecture in part (a)? Describe how inductive and deductive reasoning are exhibited in parts (a) and (b).

STEM 26. **Biology** Consider the following given statements and conclusion.
    Given: If an animal is a fish, then it has gills.
    A turtle does not have gills.

    You conclude: A turtle is not a fish.
    a. Make a Venn diagram to illustrate the given information.
    b. Use the Venn diagram to help explain why the argument uses good reasoning.

1-6 Reasoning in Algebra and Geometry

Prepares for **G.CO.10** Prove theorems about triangles . . . Also prepares for **G.CO.9, G.CO.11**

Objective   To connect reasoning in algebra and geometry

 Solve It!   Write your solution to the Solve It in the space below.

In the Solve It, you logically examined a series of steps. In this lesson, you will apply logical reasoning to algebraic and geometric situations.

Essential Understanding   Algebraic properties of equality are used in geometry. They will help you solve problems and justify each step you take.

In geometry you accept postulates and properties as true. Some of the properties that you accept as true are the properties of equality from algebra.

take note

Key Concept   Properties of Equality

Let a, b, and c be any real numbers.

Addition Property   If $a = b$, then $a + c = b + c$.

Subtraction Property   If $a = b$, then $a - c = b - c$.

Multiplication Property If $a = b$, then $a \cdot c = b \cdot c$.

Division Property   If $a = b$ and $c \neq 0$, then $\frac{a}{c} = \frac{b}{c}$.

Reflexive Property $a = a$

Symmetric Property If $a = b$, then $b = a$.

Transitive Property If $a = b$ and $b = c$, then $a = c$.

Substitution Property   If $a = b$, then b can replace a in any expression.

Key Concept The Distributive Property

Use multiplication to distribute a to each term of the sum or difference within the parentheses.

Sum:

$$a(b + c) = a(b + c) = ab + ac$$

Difference:

$$a(b - c) = a(b - c) = ab - ac$$

You use deductive reasoning when you solve an equation. You can justify each step with a postulate, a property, or a definition. For example, you can use the Distributive Property to justify combining like terms. If you think of the Distributive Property as $ab + ac = a(b + c)$ or $ab + ac = (b + c)a$, then $2x + x = (2 + 1)x = 3x$.

Problem 1 Justifying Steps When Solving an Equation

Got It? What is the value of x? Justify each step.

Given: $\overrightarrow{AB}$ bisects $\angle RAN$.

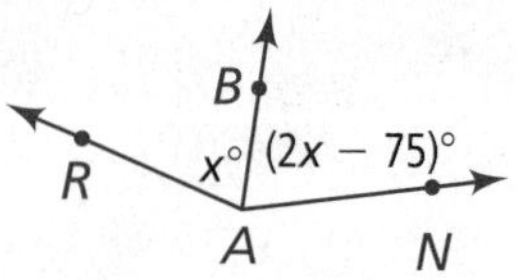

Plan

How can you use the given information?

Ⓐ Practice Algebra Fill in the reason that justifies each step.

1. $\frac{1}{2}x - 5 = 10$ Given

$2\left(\frac{1}{2}x - 5\right) = 20$ **a.** _____

$x - 10 = 20$ **b.** _____

$x = 30$ **c.** _____

2. $XY = 42$ Given

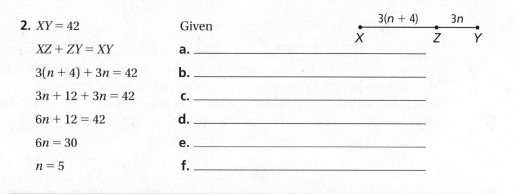

$XZ + ZY = XY$ **a.** _____

$3(n + 4) + 3n = 42$ **b.** _____

$3n + 12 + 3n = 42$ **c.** _____

$6n + 12 = 42$ **d.** _____

$6n = 30$ **e.** _____

$n = 5$ **f.** _____

Some properties of equality have corresponding properties of congruence.

Key Concept   Properties of Congruence

Reflexive Property $\overline{AB} \cong \overline{AB}$ $\angle A \cong \angle A$

Symmetric Property   If $\overline{AB} \cong \overline{CD}$, then $\overline{CD} \cong \overline{AB}$.
                   If $\angle A \cong \angle B$, then $\angle B \cong \angle A$.

Transitive Property   If $\overline{AB} \cong \overline{CD}$ and $\overline{CD} \cong \overline{EF}$, then $\overline{AB} \cong \overline{EF}$.
                   If $\angle A \cong \angle B$ and $\angle B \cong \angle C$, then $\angle A \cong \angle C$.
                   If $\angle B \cong \angle A$ and $\angle B \cong \angle C$, then $\angle A \cong \angle C$.

Problem 2   Using Properties of Equality and Congruence

Think

How do you know if each justification is a property of equality or congruence?

Got It?   For parts (a)–(c), what is the name of the property of equality or congruence that justifies going from the first statement to the second statement?

     a. $\overline{AR} \cong \overline{TY}$
        $\overline{TY} \cong \overline{AR}$

     b. $3(x + 5) = 9$
        $3x + 15 = 9$

     c. $\frac{1}{4}x = 7$
        $x = 28$

     ©**d. Reasoning** What property justifies the statement $m\angle R = m\angle R$?

Ⓐ Practice   Name the property of equality or congruence that justifies going from the first statement to the second statement.

     3. $\overline{ST} \cong \overline{QR}$
        $\overline{QR} \cong \overline{ST}$

     4. $AB - BC = 12$
        $AB = 12 + BC$

A **proof** is a convincing argument that uses deductive reasoning. A proof logically shows why a conjecture is true. A **two-column proof** lists each statement on the left. The justification, or the reason for each statement, is on the right. Each statement must follow logically from the steps before it. The diagram below shows the setup for a two-column proof. You will find the complete proof in Problem 3.

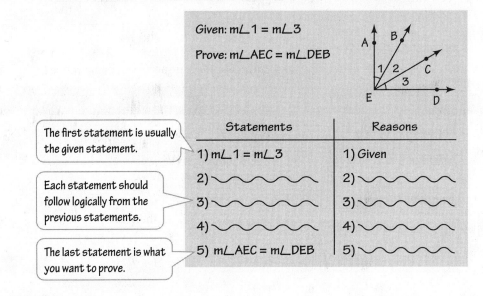

Given: m∠1 = m∠3

Prove: m∠AEC = m∠DEB

Statements	Reasons
1) m∠1 = m∠3	1) Given
2)	2)
3)	3)
4)	4)
5) m∠AEC = m∠DEB	5)

The first statement is usually the given statement.

Each statement should follow logically from the previous statements.

The last statement is what you want to prove.

Problem 3 Writing a Two-Column Proof

Got It?   **a.** Write a two-column proof.

Given: $\overline{AB} \cong \overline{CD}$

Prove: $\overline{AC} \cong \overline{BD}$

b. Reasoning In Problem 3, why is Statement 2 necessary in the proof?

⊕ 5. Developing Proof Fill in the missing statements or reasons for the following two-column proof.

Given: C is the midpoint of $\overline{AD}$.

Prove: $x = 6$

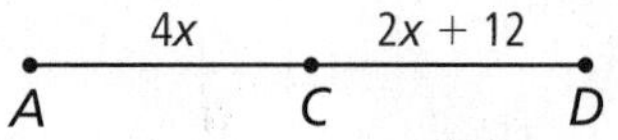

$$\overset{\displaystyle 4x \qquad\qquad 2x + 12}{\underset{\displaystyle A \qquad\qquad C \qquad\qquad D}{\bullet\!\!-\!\!-\!\!-\!\!-\!\!-\!\!-\!\!-\!\!\bullet\!\!-\!\!-\!\!-\!\!-\!\!-\!\!-\!\!-\!\!\bullet}}$$

Statements	Reasons
1) C is the midpoint of $\overline{AD}$.	**1)** a. _____
2) $\overline{AC} \cong \overline{CD}$	**2)** b. _____
3) $AC = CD$	**3)** $\cong$ segments have equal length.
4) $4x = 2x + 12$	**4)** c. _____
5) d. _____	**5)** Subtraction Property of Equality
6) $x = 6$	**6)** e. _____

✓ Lesson Check

Do you know HOW?

Name the property of equality or congruence that justifies going from the first statement to the second statement.

6. $m\angle A = m\angle S$ and $m\angle S = m\angle K$

  $m\angle A = m\angle K$

7. $3x + x + 7 = 23$

  $4x + 7 = 23$

8. $4x + 5 = 17$

  $4x = 12$

Do you UNDERSTAND?

9. Developing Proof Fill in the reasons for this algebraic proof.

Given: $5x + 1 = 21$

Prove: $x = 4$

Statements	Reasons
1) $5x + 1 = 21$	**1)** a. _____
2) $5x = 20$	**2)** b. _____
3) $x = 4$	**3)** c. _____

More Practice and Problem-Solving Exercises

B Apply

Use the given property to complete each statement.

10. Symmetric Property of Equality
If $AB = YU$, then _?_.

11. Symmetric Property of Congruence
If $\angle H \cong \angle K$, then _?_ $\cong \angle H$.

12. Reflexive Property of Congruence
$\angle POR \cong$ _?_

13. Distributive Property
$3(x - 1) = 3x -$ _?_

14. Substitution Property
If $LM = 7$ and $EF + LM = NP$,
then _?_ $= NP$.

15. Transitive Property of Congruence
If $\angle XYZ \cong \angle AOB$
and $\angle AOB \cong \angle WYT$, then _?_.

16. Think About a Plan A very important part in writing proofs is analyzing the diagram for key information. What true statements can you make based on the diagram at the right?
  • What theorems or definitions relate to the geometric figures in the diagram?
  • What types of markings show relationships between parts of geometric figures?

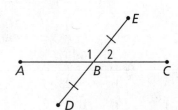

17. Writing Explain why the statements $\overline{LR} \cong \overline{RL}$ and $\angle CBA \cong \angle ABC$ are both true by the Reflexive Property of Congruence.

18. Reasoning Complete the following statement. Describe the reasoning that supports your answer.

The Transitive Property of Falling Dominoes: If Domino A causes Domino B to fall, and Domino B causes Domino C to fall, then Domino A causes Domino ? to fall.

Write a two-column proof.

Proof **19. Given:** $KM = 35$

      Prove: $KL = 15$

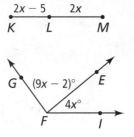

Proof **20. Given:** $m\angle GFI = 128$

      Prove: $m\angle EFI = 40$

Challenge

21. Error Analysis The steps below "show" that $1 = 2$. Describe the error.

$a = b$	Given
$ab = b^2$	Multiplication Property of Equality
$ab - a^2 = b^2 - a^2$	Subtraction Property of Equality
$a(b - a) = (b + a)(b - a)$	Distributive Property
$a = b + a$	Division Property of Equality
$a = a + a$	Substitution Property
$a = 2a$	Simplify.
$1 = 2$	Division Property of Equality

Relationships Consider the following relationships among people. Tell whether each relationship is *reflexive, symmetric, transitive,* or *none of these*. Explain.

Sample: The relationship "is younger than" is not reflexive because Sue is not younger than herself. It is not symmetric because if Sue is younger than Fred, then Fred is not younger than Sue. It is transitive because if Sue is younger than Fred and Fred is younger than Alana, then Sue is younger than Alana.

22. has the same birthday as

23. is taller than

24. lives in a different state than

1-7 Proving Angles Congruent

G.CO.9 Prove theorems about lines and angles . . . Theorems include: vertical angles are congruent . . .

Objective To prove and apply theorems about angles

 Solve It! Write your solution to the Solve It in the space below.

In the Solve It, you may have noticed a relationship between vertical angles. You can prove that this relationship is always true using deductive reasoning. A **theorem** is a conjecture or statement that you prove true.

Essential Understanding You can use given information, definitions, properties, postulates, and previously proven theorems as reasons in a proof.

take note

Theorem 1 Vertical Angles Theorem

Vertical angles are congruent.

$\angle 1 \cong \angle 3$ and $\angle 2 \cong \angle 4$

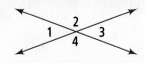

When you are writing a geometric proof, it may help to separate the theorem you want to prove into a hypothesis and conclusion. Another way to write the Vertical Angles Theorem is "If two angles are vertical, then they are congruent." The hypothesis becomes the given statement, and the conclusion becomes what you want to prove. A two-column proof of the Vertical Angles Theorem follows.

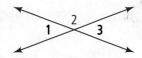

Proof Proof of Theorem 1: Vertical Angles Theorem

Given: ∠1 and ∠3 are vertical angles.

Prove: ∠1 ≅ ∠3

Statements	Reasons
1) ∠1 and ∠3 are vertical angles.	**1)** Given
2) ∠1 and ∠2 are supplementary. ∠2 and ∠3 are supplementary.	**2)** ⦞ that form a linear pair are supplementary.
3) $m\angle 1 + m\angle 2 = 180$ $m\angle 2 + m\angle 3 = 180$	**3)** The sum of the measures of supplementary ⦞ is 180.
4) $m\angle 1 + m\angle 2 = m\angle 2 + m\angle 3$	**4)** Transitive Property of Equality
5) $m\angle 1 = m\angle 3$	**5)** Subtraction Property of Equality
6) ∠1 ≅ ∠3	**6)** ⦞ with the same measure are ≅.

Problem 1 **Using the Vertical Angles Theorem**

Got It? What is the value of *x*?

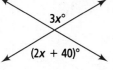

3x°

(2x + 40)°

> **Think**
> How can you check that your value of *x* is correct?

Ⓐ Practice **1.** Find the value of each variable.

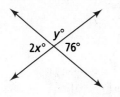

y°

2x° 76°

2. Find the measures of the labeled angles in Exercise 1.

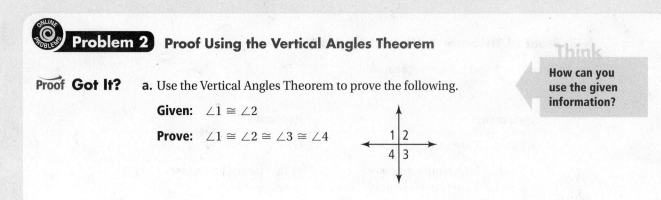

Problem 2 · Proof Using the Vertical Angles Theorem

Proof **Got It?**   **a.** Use the Vertical Angles Theorem to prove the following.

> **Given:** ∠1 ≅ ∠2
>
> **Prove:** ∠1 ≅ ∠2 ≅ ∠3 ≅ ∠4

Think

How can you use the given information?

ⓒ b. Reasoning How can you prove ∠1 ≅ ∠2 ≅ ∠3 ≅ ∠4 without using the Vertical Angles Theorem?

3. Developing Proof Complete the following proof by filling in the blanks.

Given: ∠1 ≅ ∠3

Prove: ∠6 ≅ ∠4

Statements	Reasons
1) ∠1 ≅ ∠3	**1)** Given
2) ∠3 ≅ ∠6	**2) a.** _____
3) b. _____	**3)** Transitive Property of Congruence
4) ∠1 ≅ ∠4	**4) c.** _____
5) ∠6 ≅ ∠4	**5) d.** _____

The proof in Problem 2 is two-column, but there are many ways to display a proof.

A **paragraph proof** is written as sentences in a paragraph. Below is the proof from Problem 2 in paragraph form. Each statement in the Problem 2 proof is red in the paragraph proof.

Proof **Given:** ∠1 ≅ ∠4

Prove: ∠2 ≅ ∠3

Proof: ∠1 ≅ ∠4 is given. ∠4 ≅ ∠2 because vertical angles are congruent. By the Transitive Property of Congruence, ∠1 ≅ ∠2. ∠1 ≅ ∠3 because vertical angles are congruent. By the Transitive Property of Congruence, ∠2 ≅ ∠3.

The Vertical Angles Theorem is a special case of the following theorem.

take note

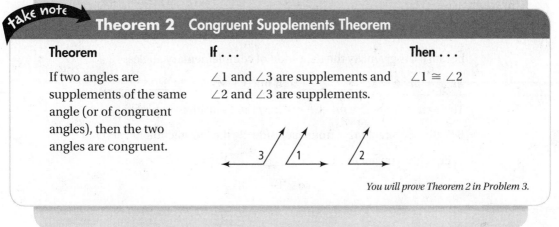

Theorem 2 Congruent Supplements Theorem

Theorem	If . . .	Then . . .
If two angles are supplements of the same angle (or of congruent angles), then the two angles are congruent.	∠1 and ∠3 are supplements and ∠2 and ∠3 are supplements.	∠1 ≅ ∠2

You will prove Theorem 2 in Problem 3.

Problem 3 Writing a Paragraph Proof

Proof **Got it?** Write a paragraph proof for the Vertical Angles Theorem.

Ⓐ Practice

Ⓒ **4. Developing Proof** Fill in the blanks to complete this proof of the
Congruent Complements Theorem (Theorem 3).

If two angles are complements of the same angle, then the two angles
are congruent.

Given: ∠1 and ∠2 are complementary.
∠3 and ∠2 are complementary.

Prove: ∠1 ≅ ∠3

Proof: ∠1 and ∠2 are complementary and ∠3 and ∠2 are complementary

because it is given. By the definition of complementary angles,

$m\angle1 + m\angle2 =$ **a.** _____ and $m\angle3 + m\angle2 =$ **b.** _____ .

Then $m\angle1 + m\angle2 = m\angle3 + m\angle2$ by the Transitive Property of

Equality. Subtract $m\angle2$ from each side. By the Subtraction Property

of Equality, you get $m\angle1 =$ **c.** _____ . Angles with the same

measure are **d.** _____ , so ∠1 ≅ ∠3.

The following theorems are similar to the Congruent Supplements Theorem.

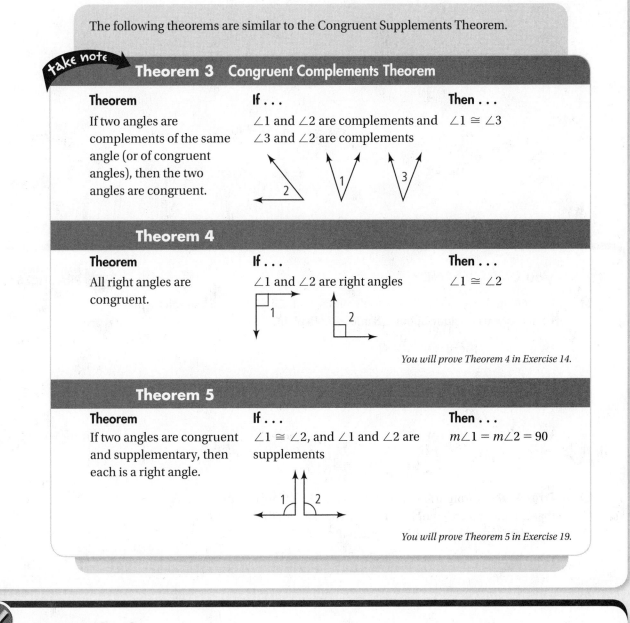

take note

Theorem 3   Congruent Complements Theorem

Theorem	If . . .	Then . . .
If two angles are complements of the same angle (or of congruent angles), then the two angles are congruent.	$\angle 1$ and $\angle 2$ are complements and $\angle 3$ and $\angle 2$ are complements	$\angle 1 \cong \angle 3$

Theorem 4

Theorem	If . . .	Then . . .
All right angles are congruent.	$\angle 1$ and $\angle 2$ are right angles	$\angle 1 \cong \angle 2$

You will prove Theorem 4 in Exercise 14.

Theorem 5

Theorem	If . . .	Then . . .
If two angles are congruent and supplementary, then each is a right angle.	$\angle 1 \cong \angle 2$, and $\angle 1$ and $\angle 2$ are supplements	$m\angle 1 = m\angle 2 = 90$

You will prove Theorem 5 in Exercise 19.

Lesson Check

Do you know HOW?

5. What are the measures of $\angle 1$, $\angle 2$, and $\angle 3$?

6. What is the value of x?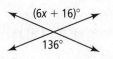

    Ⓐ 12   Ⓒ 120

    Ⓑ 20   Ⓓ 136

Do you UNDERSTAND?

MATHEMATICAL
PRACTICES

7. Reasoning If $\angle A$ and $\angle B$ are supplements, and $\angle A$ and $\angle C$ are supplements, what can you conclude about $\angle B$ and $\angle C$? Explain.

8. Error Analysis Your friend knows that $\angle 1$ and $\angle 2$ are complementary and that $\angle 1$ and $\angle 3$ are complementary. He concludes that $\angle 2$ and $\angle 3$ must be complementary. What is his error in reasoning?

9. Compare and Contrast How is a theorem different from a postulate?

More Practice and Problem-Solving Exercises

(C) MATHEMATICAL PRACTICES

(B) Apply

(C) 10. Think About a Plan What is the measure of the angle formed by Park St. and 116ᵗʰ St.?
- Can you make a connection between the angle you need to find and the labeled angle?
- How are angles that form a right angle related?

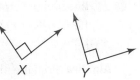

(C) 11. Open-Ended Give an example of vertical angles in your home or classroom.

Algebra Find the value of each variable and the measure of each labeled angle.

12.

$(x + 10)°$ $(4x - 35)°$

13.

$(3x + 8)°$ $(5x - 20)°$
$(5x + 4y)°$

(C) 14. Developing Proof Fill in the blanks to complete this proof of Theorem 4. All right angles are congruent.

Given: $\angle X$ and $\angle Y$ are right angles.

Prove: $\angle X \cong \angle Y$

Proof: $\angle X$ and **a.** ___?___ are right angles because it is given.
By the definition of **b.** ___?___, $m\angle X = 90$ and $m\angle Y = 90$.
By the Transitive Property of Equality, $m\angle X =$ **c.** ___?___.
Because angles of equal measure are congruent, **d.** ___?___.

X Y

15. Miniature Golf In the game of miniature golf, the ball bounces off the wall at the same angle it hit the wall. (This is the angle formed by the path of the ball and the line perpendicular to the wall at the point of contact.) In the diagram, the ball hits the wall at a 40° angle. Using Theorem 3, what are the values of x and y?

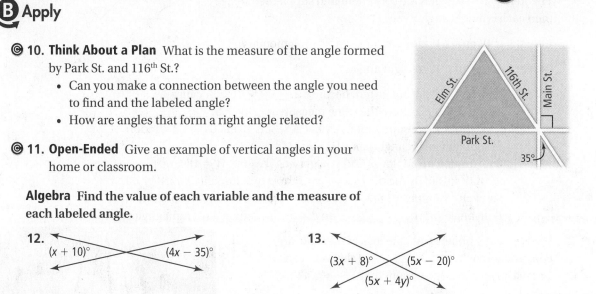

Name two pairs of congruent angles in each figure. Justify your answers.

16.

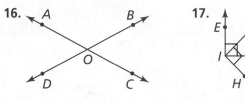

17.

18.

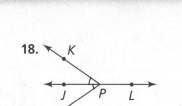

© 19. **Developing Proof** Fill in the blanks to complete this proof of Theorem 5. If two angles are congruent and supplementary, then each is a right angle.

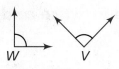

Given: ∠W and ∠V are congruent and supplementary.

Prove: ∠W and ∠V are right angles.

Proof: ∠W and ∠V are congruent because **a.** _____. Because congruent angles have the same measure, $m\angle W =$ **b.** _____. ∠W and ∠V are supplementary because it is given. By the definition of supplementary angles, $m\angle W + m\angle V =$ **c.** _____. Substituting $m\angle W$ for $m\angle V$, you get $m\angle W + m\angle W = 180$, or $2m\angle W = 180$. By the **d.** _____ Property of Equality, $m\angle W = 90$. Since $m\angle W = m\angle V$, $m\angle V = 90$ by the Transitive Property of Equality. Both angles are **e.** _____ angles by the definition of right angles.

20. **Design** In the photograph, the legs of the table are constructed so that $\angle 1 \cong \angle 2$. What theorem can you use to justify the statement that $\angle 3 \cong \angle 4$?

© 21. **Reasoning** Explain why this statement is true: If $m\angle ABC + m\angle XYZ = 180$ and $\angle ABC \cong \angle XYZ$, then $\angle ABC$ and $\angle XYZ$ are right angles.

Algebra Find the measure of each angle.

22. $\angle A$ is twice as large as its complement, $\angle B$.

23. $\angle A$ is half as large as its complement, $\angle B$.

24. $\angle A$ is twice as large as its supplement, $\angle B$.

25. $\angle A$ is half as large as twice its supplement, $\angle B$.

Proof 26. Write a proof for this form of Theorem 2. If two angles are supplements of congruent angles, then the two angles are congruent.

Given: ∠1 and ∠2 are supplementary.
∠3 and ∠4 are supplementary.
$\angle 2 \cong \angle 4$

Prove: $\angle 1 \cong \angle 3$

C Challenge

27. **Coordinate Geometry** ∠DOE contains points D(2, 3), O(0, 0), and E(5, 1). Find the coordinates of a point F so that $\overrightarrow{OF}$ is a side of an angle that is adjacent and supplementary to ∠DOE.

28. **Coordinate Geometry** ∠AOX contains points A(1, 3), O(0, 0), and X(4, 0).
    a. Find the coordinates of a point B so that ∠BOA and ∠AOX are adjacent complementary angles.
    b. Find the coordinates of a point C so that $\overrightarrow{OC}$ is a side of a different angle that is adjacent and complementary to ∠AOX.

Algebra Find the value of each variable and the measure of each angle.

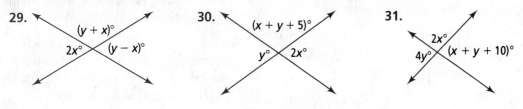

29. $(y + x)°$ $2x°$ $(y − x)°$

30. $(x + y + 5)°$ $y°$ $2x°$

31. $2x°$ $4y°$ $(x + y + 10)°$

① Chapter Review

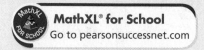

1-1 Basic Constructions

Quick Review

Construction is the process of making geometric figures using a **compass** and a **straightedge**. Four basic constructions involve congruent segments, congruent angles, and bisectors of segments and angles.

Example

Construct $\overline{AB}$ congruent to $\overline{EF}$. E————F

Step 1

Draw a ray with endpoint A. A——→

Step 2

Open the compass to the length of $\overline{EF}$. Keep that compass setting and put the compass point on point A. Draw an arc that intersects the ray. Label the point of intersection B.

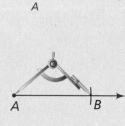

Exercises

1. Use a protractor to draw a 73° angle. Then construct an angle congruent to it.

2. Use a protractor to draw a 60° angle. Then construct the bisector of the angle.

3. Sketch $\overline{LM}$ on paper. Construct a line segment congruent to $\overline{LM}$. Then construct the perpendicular bisector of your line segment.

L————————M

4. a. Sketch $\angle B$ on paper. Construct an angle congruent to $\angle B$.
   b. Construct the bisector of your angle from part (a).

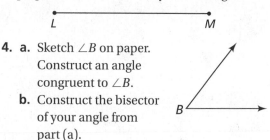

1-2 Patterns and Inductive Reasoning

Quick Review

You use **inductive reasoning** when you make conclusions based on patterns you observe. A **conjecture** is a conclusion you reach using inductive reasoning. A **counterexample** is an example that shows a conjecture is incorrect.

Example

Describe the pattern. What are the next two terms in the sequence?

$$1, -3, 9, -27, \ldots$$

Each term is -3 times the previous term. The next two terms are $-27 \times (-3) = 81$ and $81 \times (-3) = -243$.

Exercises

Find a pattern for each sequence. Describe the pattern and use it to show the next two terms.

5. 1000, 100, 10, . . .

6. 5, −5, 5, −5, . . .

7. 34, 27, 20, 13, . . .

8. 6, 24, 96, 384, . . .

Find a counterexample to show that each conjecture is false.

9. The product of any integer and 2 is greater than 2.

10. The city of Portland is in Oregon.

1-3 Conditional Statements

Quick Review

A **conditional** is an *if-then* statement. The symbolic form of a conditional is $p \rightarrow q$, where p is the **hypothesis** and q is the **conclusion**.

- To find the **converse**, switch the hypothesis and conclusion of the conditional ($q \rightarrow p$).
- To find the **inverse**, negate the hypothesis and the conclusion of the conditional ($\sim p \rightarrow \sim q$).
- To find the **contrapositive**, negate the hypothesis and the conclusion of the converse ($\sim q \rightarrow \sim p$).

Example

What is the converse of the conditional statement below? What is its truth value?

    If you are a teenager, then you are younger than 20.

Converse: If you are younger than 20, then you are a teenager.

A 7-year-old is not a teenager. The converse is false.

Exercises

Rewrite each sentence as a conditional statement.

11. All motorcyclists wear helmets.

12. Two nonparallel lines intersect in one point.

13. Angles that form a linear pair are supplementary.

14. School is closed on certain holidays.

Write the converse, inverse, and contrapositive of the given conditional. Then determine the truth value of each statement.

15. If an angle is obtuse, then its measure is greater than 90 and less than 180.

16. If a figure is a square, then it has four sides.

17. If you play the tuba, then you play an instrument.

18. If you baby-sit, then you are busy on Saturday night.

1-4 Biconditionals and Definitions

Quick Review

When a conditional and its converse are true, you can combine them as a true **biconditional** using the phrase *if and only if*. The symbolic form of a biconditional is $p \leftrightarrow q$. You can write a good **definition** as a true biconditional.

Example

Is the following definition reversible? If yes, write it as a true biconditional.

    A hexagon is a polygon with exactly six sides.

Yes. The conditional is true: If a figure is a hexagon, then it is a polygon with exactly six sides. Its converse is also true: If a figure is a polygon with exactly six sides, then it is a hexagon.

Biconditional: A figure is a hexagon *if and only if* it is a polygon with exactly six sides.

Exercises

Determine whether each statement is a good definition. If not, explain.

19. A newspaper has articles you read.

20. A linear pair is a pair of adjacent angles whose noncommon sides are opposite rays.

21. An angle is a geometric figure.

22. Write the following definition as a biconditional. An oxymoron is a phrase that contains contradictory terms.

23. Write the following biconditional as two statements, a conditional and its converse. Two angles are complementary if and only if the sum of their measures is 90.

1-5 Deductive Reasoning

Quick Review

Deductive reasoning is the process of reasoning logically from given statements to a conclusion.

Law of Detachment: If $p \rightarrow q$ is true and p is true, then q is true.

Law of Syllogism: If $p \rightarrow q$ and $q \rightarrow r$ are true, then $p \rightarrow r$ is true.

Example

What can you conclude from the given information?

Given: **If you play hockey, then you are on the team. If you are on the team, then you are a varsity athlete.**

The conclusion of the first statement matches the hypothesis of the second statement. Use the Law of Syllogism to conclude: If you play hockey, then you are a varsity athlete.

Exercises

Use the Law of Detachment to make a conclusion.

24. If you practice tennis every day, then you will become a better player. Colin practices tennis every day.

25. $\angle 1$ and $\angle 2$ are supplementary. If two angles are supplementary, then the sum of their measures is 180.

Use the Law of Syllogism to make a conclusion.

26. If two angles are vertical, then they are congruent. If two angles are congruent, then their measures are equal.

27. If your father buys new gardening gloves, then he will work in his garden. If he works in his garden, then he will plant tomatoes.

1-6 Reasoning in Algebra and Geometry

Quick Review

You use deductive reasoning and properties to solve equations and justify your reasoning. A **proof** is a convincing argument that uses deductive reasoning. A **two-column proof** lists each statement on the left and the justification for each statement on the right.

Example

What is the name of the property that justifies going from the first line to the second line?

$\angle A \cong \angle B$ and $\angle B \cong \angle C$
$\angle A \cong \angle C$

Transitive Property of Congruence

Exercises

28. Algebra Fill in the reason that justifies each step.

Given: $QS = 42$

Prove: $x = 13$

Statements	Reasons
1) $QS = 42$	1) a. _?_
2) $QR + RS = QS$	2) b. _?_
3) $(x + 3) + 2x = 42$	3) c. _?_
4) $3x + 3 = 42$	4) d. _?_
5) $3x = 39$	5) e. _?_
6) $x = 13$	6) f. _?_

Use the given property to complete the statement.

29. Division Property of Equality

If $2(AX) = 2(BY)$, then $AX = $ _?_ .

30. Distributive Property: $3p - 6q = 3(\underline{\ ?\ })$

1-7 Proving Angles Congruent

Quick Review

A statement that you prove true is a **theorem**. A proof written as a paragraph is a **paragraph proof**. In geometry, each statement in a proof is justified by given information, a property, postulate, definition, or theorem.

Example

Write a paragraph proof.

Given: $\angle 1 \cong \angle 4$

Prove: $\angle 2 \cong \angle 3$

$\angle 1 \cong \angle 4$ because it is given. $\angle 1 \cong \angle 2$ because vertical angles are congruent. $\angle 4 \cong \angle 2$ by the Transitive Property of Congruence. $\angle 4 \cong \angle 3$ because vertical angles are congruent. $\angle 2 \cong \angle 3$ by the Transitive Property of Congruence.

Exercises

Use the diagram for Exercises 31–34.

31. Find the value of y.

32. Find $m\angle AEC$.

33. Find $m\angle BED$.

34. Find $m\angle AEB$.

$(3y + 20)°$ $(5y - 16)°$

35. Given: $\angle 1$ and $\angle 2$ are complementary. $\angle 3$ and $\angle 4$ are complementary. $\angle 2 \cong \angle 4$

Prove: $\angle 1 \cong \angle 3$

 ASSESSMENT

Analyzing a Calendar Pattern

The figure shows a page from a calendar. Choose any four numbers from the calendar that lie inside a 2-by-2 square. One such set of numbers is shown below. Find the sum of the pair of numbers that lie on each diagonal of the square. What do you notice about the sums? Try this using other squares on the calendar and using calendar pages for different months.

MARCH						
SUN	MON	TUE	WED	THU	FRI	SAT
				1	2	3
4	5	6	7	8	9	10
11	12	13	14	15	16	17
18	19	20	21	22	23	24
25	26	27	28	29	30	31

Task Description

Use inductive reasoning to make a conjecture about the calendar pattern you observed. Then use deductive reasoning to prove your conjecture.

- How can you write your conjecture as a conditional statement?

- How can you use algebraic expressions to represent the four numbers that lie inside any 2-by-2 square on any calendar page?

Get Ready!

Identifying Angle Pairs

Identify all pairs of each type of angles in the diagram.

  1. linear pair

  2. complementary angles

  3. vertical angles

  4. supplementary angles

Justifying Statements

Name the property that justifies each statement.

  5. If $3x = 6$, then $x = 2$.

  6. If $\angle 1 \cong \angle 2$ and $\angle 2 \cong \angle 3$, then $\angle 1 \cong \angle 3$.

Solving Equations

Algebra Solve each equation.

  7. $3x + 11 = 7x - 5$ **8.** $(x - 4) + 52 = 109$ **9.** $(2x + 5) + (3x - 10) = 70$

 ## Looking Ahead Vocabulary

  10. The core of an apple is in the *interior* of the apple. The peel is on the *exterior*. How can the terms *interior* and *exterior* apply to geometric figures?

  11. A ship sailing from the United States to Europe makes a transatlantic voyage. What does the prefix *trans-* mean in this situation? A *transversal* is a special type of line in geometry. What might a *transversal* do? Explain.

  12. People in many jobs use *flow*charts to describe the logical steps of a particular process. How do you think you can use a *flow proof* in geometry?

Proving Theorems About Lines and Angles

Big Ideas

1 Reasoning and Proof
Essential Question How do you prove that two lines are parallel?

2 Measurement
Essential Question What is the sum of the measures of the angles of a triangle?

© Domains

- Congruence
- Modeling with Geometry

Chapter Preview

Interactive Digital Path

Log in to **pearsonsuccessnet.com** and click on Interactive Digital Path to access the Solve Its and animated Problems.

Vocabulary

English/Spanish Vocabulary Audio Online:

English	Spanish
alternate exterior angles, p. 67	ángulos alternos externos
alternate interior angles, p. 67	ángulos alternos internos
corresponding angles, p. 67	ángulos correspondientes
exterior angle of a polygon, p. 101	ángulo exterior de un polígono
parallel lines, p. 65	rectas paralelas
same-side interior angles, p. 67	ángulos internos del mismo lado
skew lines, p. 65	rectas cruzadas
transversal, p. 67	transversal

2-1 Lines and Angles

G.CO.1 Know precise definitions of . . . perpendicular line, parallel line . . . based on the undefined notions of point, line . . . Also prepares for **G.CO.9**

Objectives To identify relationships between figures in space
To identify angles formed by two lines and a transversal

Solve It! Write your solution to the Solve It in the space below.

In the Solve It, you used relationships among planes in space to write the instructions. In this lesson, you will explore relationships of nonintersecting lines and planes.

Essential Understanding Not all lines and not all planes intersect.

Key Concept Parallel and Skew

Definition	Symbols	Diagram
Parallel lines are coplanar lines that do not intersect. The symbol ∥ means "is parallel to."	$\overleftrightarrow{AE} \parallel \overleftrightarrow{BF}$ $\overleftrightarrow{AD} \parallel \overleftrightarrow{BC}$	
Skew lines are noncoplanar; they are not parallel and do not intersect.	$\overleftrightarrow{AB}$ and $\overleftrightarrow{CG}$ are skew.	
Parallel planes are planes that do not intersect.	plane $ABCD \parallel$ plane $EFGH$	

Use arrows to show
$\overleftrightarrow{AE} \parallel \overleftrightarrow{BF}$ and $\overleftrightarrow{AD} \parallel \overleftrightarrow{BC}$.

A line and a plane that do not intersect are parallel. Segments and rays can also be parallel or skew. They are parallel if they lie in parallel lines and skew if they lie in skew lines.

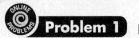
Got It? Use the figure in Problem 1, shown at the right.

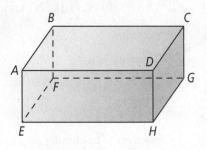

a. Which segments are parallel to $\overline{AD}$?

© **b. Reasoning** Explain why $\overline{FE}$ and $\overline{CD}$ are *not* skew.

c. What is another pair of parallel planes?

d. What are two segments parallel to plane $DCGH$?

 Practice Use the diagram to name each of the following. Assume that lines and planes that appear to be parallel are parallel.

1. two lines that are skew to $\overleftrightarrow{EJ}$

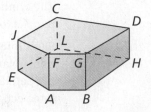

2. all lines that are parallel to plane $JFAE$

Essential Understanding When a line intersects two or more lines, the angles formed at the intersection points create special angle pairs.

A **transversal** is a line that intersects two or more coplanar lines at distinct points. The diagram below shows the eight angles formed by a transversal t and two lines ℓ and m.

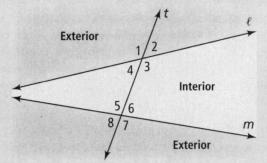

Notice that angles 3, 4, 5, and 6 lie between ℓ and m. They are *interior* angles. Angles 1, 2, 7, and 8 lie outside of ℓ and m. They are *exterior* angles.

Pairs of the eight angles have special names as suggested by their positions.

take note

Key Concept   Angle Pairs Formed by Transversals

Definition	Example	
Alternate interior angles are nonadjacent interior angles that lie on opposite sides of the transversal.	$\angle 4$ and $\angle 6$ $\angle 3$ and $\angle 5$	
Same-side interior angles are interior angles that lie on the same side of the transversal.	$\angle 4$ and $\angle 5$ $\angle 3$ and $\angle 6$	
Corresponding angles lie on the same side of the transversal t and in corresponding positions.	$\angle 1$ and $\angle 5$ $\angle 4$ and $\angle 8$ $\angle 2$ and $\angle 6$ $\angle 3$ and $\angle 7$	
Alternate exterior angles are nonadjacent exterior angles that lie on opposite sides of the transversal.	$\angle 1$ and $\angle 7$ $\angle 2$ and $\angle 8$	

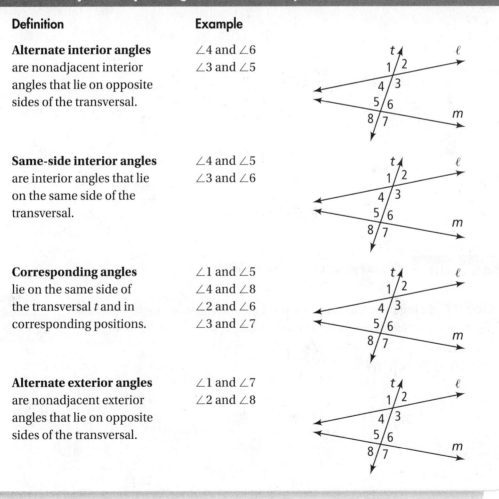

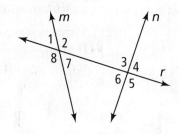

Problem 2　Identifying an Angle Pair

Got It?　Use the figure at the right. What are three pairs of
corresponding angles?

Ⓐ Practice　Identify all pairs of each type of angles in the diagram.
Name the two lines and the transversal that form each pair.

3. same-side interior angles

4. alternate exterior angles

Problem 3　Classifying an Angle Pair

Got It?　In Problem 3, are angles 1 and 3 *alternate interior angles, same-side
interior angles, corresponding angles,* or *alternate exterior angles*?

> **Think**
> How do the
> positions of ∠1
> and ∠3 compare?

5. Are the angles labeled in the same color *alternate interior angles, same-side interior angles, corresponding angles,* or *alternate exterior angles*?

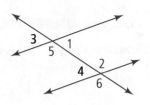

6. Aviation The photo shows an overhead view of airport runways. Are ∠1 and ∠2 *alternate interior angles, same-side interior angles, corresponding angles,* or *alternate exterior angles*?

Lesson Check

Do you know HOW?

Name one pair each of the segments, planes, or angles. Lines and planes that appear to be parallel are parallel.

7. parallel segments

8. skew segments

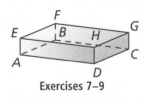

Exercises 7–9

9. parallel planes

10. alternate interior angles

11. same-side interior angles

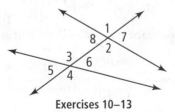

Exercises 10–13

12. corresponding angles

13. alternate exterior angles

Do you UNDERSTAND?

@ **14. Vocabulary** Why is the word *coplanar* included in the definition for parallel lines?

@ **15. Vocabulary** How does the phrase *alternate interior angles* describe the positions of the two angles?

@ **16. Error Analysis** In the figure at the right, lines and planes that appear to be parallel are parallel. Carly says $\overleftrightarrow{AB} \parallel \overleftrightarrow{HG}$. Juan says $\overleftrightarrow{AB}$ and $\overleftrightarrow{HG}$ are skew. Who is correct? Explain.

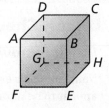

More Practice and Problem-Solving Exercises

B Apply

How many pairs of each type of angles do two lines and a transversal form?

17. alternate interior angles

18. corresponding angles

19. alternate exterior angles

20. vertical angles

21. Recreation You and a friend are driving go-karts on two different tracks. As you drive on a straight section heading east, your friend passes above you on a straight section heading south. Are these sections of the two tracks *parallel, skew,* or *neither*? Explain.

In Exercises 22–27, describe the statement as *true* or *false*. If false, explain. Assume that lines and planes that appear to be parallel are parallel.

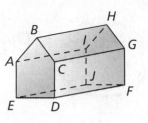

22. $\overleftrightarrow{CB} \parallel \overleftrightarrow{HG}$

23. $\overleftrightarrow{ED} \parallel \overleftrightarrow{HG}$

24. plane $AED \parallel$ plane FGH

25. plane $ABH \parallel$ plane CDF

26. $\overleftrightarrow{AB}$ and $\overleftrightarrow{HG}$ are skew lines.

27. $\overleftrightarrow{AE}$ and $\overleftrightarrow{BC}$ are skew lines.

28. Think About a Plan A rectangular rug covers the floor in a living room. One of the walls in the same living room is painted blue. Are the rug and the blue wall parallel? Explain.
- Can you visualize the rug and the wall as geometric figures?
- What must be true for these geometric figures to be parallel?

In Exercises 29–34, determine whether each statement is *always, sometimes,* or *never* true.

29. Two parallel lines are coplanar.

30. Two planes that do not intersect are parallel.

31. Two skew lines are coplanar.

32. Two lines that lie in parallel planes are parallel.

33. Two lines in intersecting planes are skew.

34. A line and a plane that do not intersect are skew.

35. a. Writing Describe the three ways in which two lines may be related.
   b. Give examples from the real world to illustrate each of the relationships you described in part (a).

36. Open-Ended The letter Z illustrates alternate interior angles. Find at least two other letters that illustrate pairs of angles presented in this lesson. Draw the letters. Then mark and describe the angles.

37. a. Reasoning Suppose two parallel planes A and B are each intersected by a third plane C. Make a conjecture about the intersection of planes A and C and the intersection of planes B and C.
   b. Find examples in your classroom to illustrate your conjecture in part (a).

Challenge

Use the figure at the right for Exercises 38 and 39.

38. Do planes A and B have other lines in common that are parallel to $\overleftrightarrow{CD}$? Explain.

39. Visualization Are there planes that intersect planes A and B in lines parallel to $\overleftrightarrow{CD}$? Draw a sketch to support your answer.

40. Draw a Diagram A transversal r intersects lines ℓ and m. If ℓ and r form $\angle 1$ and $\angle 2$ and m and r form $\angle 3$ and $\angle 4$, sketch a diagram that meets the following conditions.
- $\angle 1 \cong \angle 2$
- $\angle 3$ is an interior angle.
- $\angle 4$ is an exterior angle.
- $\angle 2$ and $\angle 4$ lie on opposite sides of r.
- $\angle 3$ and $\angle 4$ are supplementary.

Properties of Parallel Lines

G.CO.9 Prove theorems about lines and angles. Theorems include: . . . when a transversal crosses parallel lines, alternate interior angles are congruent . . .

Objectives To prove theorems about parallel lines
To use properties of parallel lines to find angle measures

Solve It! Write your solution to the Solve It in the space below.

In the Solve It, you identified several pairs of angles that appear congruent. You already know the relationship between vertical angles. In this lesson, you will explore the relationships between the angles you learned about in Lesson 2-1 when they are formed by *parallel* lines and a transversal.

Essential Understanding The special angle pairs formed by parallel lines and a transversal are congruent, supplementary, or both.

Postulate 11 Same-Side Interior Angles Postulate

Postulate	If . . .	Then . . .
If a transversal intersects two parallel lines, then same-side interior angles are supplementary.	$\ell \parallel m$	$m\angle 4 + m\angle 5 = 180$ $m\angle 3 + m\angle 6 = 180$

Problem 1 Identifying Supplementary Angles

© **Got It?** **Reasoning** If you know the measure of one of the angles, can you always find the measures of all 8 angles when two parallel lines are cut by a transversal? Explain.

Ⓐ **Practice** Identify all the numbered angles that are congruent to the given angle. Justify your answers.

1.

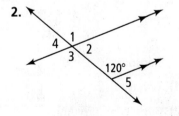

2.

You can use the Same-Side Interior Angles Postulate to prove other angle relationships.

take note

Theorem 6 Alternate Interior Angles Theorem

Theorem	If . . .	Then . . .
If a transversal intersects two parallel lines, then alternate interior angles are congruent.	$\ell \parallel m$	$\angle 4 \cong \angle 6$ $\angle 3 \cong \angle 5$

Theorem 7 Corresponding Angles Theorem

Theorem	If . . .	Then . . .
If a transversal intersects two parallel lines, then corresponding angles are congruent.	$\ell \parallel m$	$\angle 1 \cong \angle 5$ $\angle 2 \cong \angle 6$ $\angle 3 \cong \angle 7$ $\angle 4 \cong \angle 8$

You will prove Theorem 7 in Exercise 22.

Proof **Proof of Theorem 6: Alternate Interior Angles Theorem**

Given: $\ell \parallel m$

Prove: $\angle 4 \cong \angle 6$

Statement	Reasons
1) $\ell \parallel m$	1) Given
2) $m\angle 3 + m\angle 4 = 180$	2) Supplementary Angles
3) $m\angle 3 + m\angle 6 = 180$	3) Same-Side Interior Angles Postulate
4) $m\angle 3 + m\angle 4 = m\angle 3 + m\angle 6$	4) Transitive Property of Equality
5) $m\angle 4 = m\angle 6$	5) Subtraction Property of Equality
6) $\angle 4 \cong \angle 6$	6) Definition of Congruence

Proving an Angle Relationship

Got It? Let $a \parallel b$. Prove that $\angle 1 \cong \angle 7$.

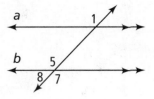

 Practice 3. **Developing Proof** Supply the missing reasons in the two-column proof.

Given: $a \parallel b, c \parallel d$

Prove: $\angle 1 \cong \angle 3$

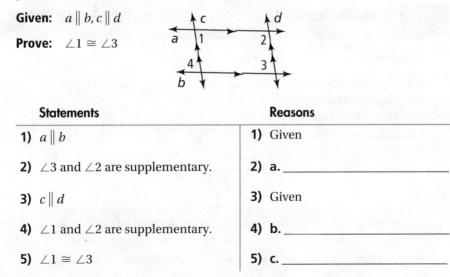

Statements	Reasons
1) $a \parallel b$	1) Given
2) $\angle 3$ and $\angle 2$ are supplementary.	2) a. _____
3) $c \parallel d$	3) Given
4) $\angle 1$ and $\angle 2$ are supplementary.	4) b. _____
5) $\angle 1 \cong \angle 3$	5) c. _____

Proof **4.** Write a two-column proof for Exercise 3 that does not use ∠2.

In the diagram for Problem 2, ∠1 and ∠7 are alternate exterior angles. In Got It 2, you proved the following theorem.

take note

Theorem 8   Alternate Exterior Angles Theorem

Theorem	If . . .	Then . . .
If a transversal intersects two parallel lines, then alternate exterior angles are congruent.	$\ell \parallel m$	$\angle 1 \cong \angle 7$ $\angle 2 \cong \angle 8$

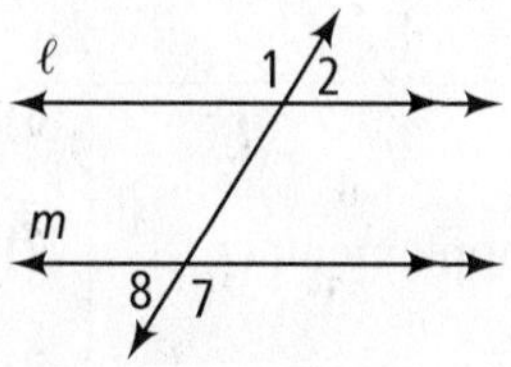

If you know the measure of one of the angles formed by two parallel lines and a transversal, you can use theorems and postulates to find the measures of the other angles.

Problem 3 **Finding Measures of Angles**

Got It? Use the diagram in Problem 3. What is the measure of each angle? Justify each answer.

> Think
>
> How does ∠4 relate to ∠1?

    a. ∠1   **b.** ∠2

    c. ∠5   **d.** ∠6

    e. ∠7   **f.** ∠8

Ⓐ **Practice** Find $m\angle 1$ and $m\angle 2$. Justify each answer.

5.

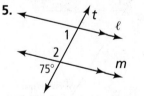

6.

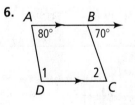

You can combine theorems and postulates with your knowledge of algebra to find angle measures.

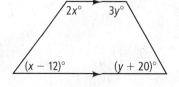 **Problem 4** **Finding an Angle Measure**

Got It? **a.** In the figure below, what are the values of *x* and *y*?

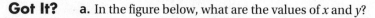

2*x*°   3*y*°

(*x* − 12)°   (*y* + 20)°

Think

What is the relationship between the two angles on the left side of the figure?

b. What are the measures of the four angles in the figure?

Ⓐ Practice **Algebra** Find the value of *x*. Then find the measure of each labeled angle.

7.

x°

(*x* − 50)°

8.

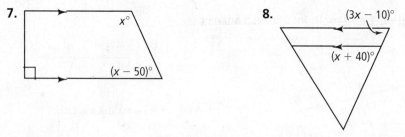

(3*x* − 10)°

(*x* + 40)°

Lesson Check

Do you know HOW?

Use the diagram for Exercises 9–12.

9. Identify four pairs of congruent angles. (Exclude vertical angle pairs.)

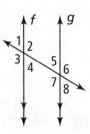

10. Identify two pairs of supplementary angles. (Exclude linear pairs.)

11. If $m\angle 1 = 70$, what is $m\angle 8$?

12. If $m\angle 4 = 70$ and $m\angle 7 = 2x$, what is the value of x?

© 13. **Compare and Contrast** How are the Alternate Interior Angles Theorem and the Alternate Exterior Angles Theorem alike? How are they different?

14. In Problem 2, you proved that ∠1 and ∠8, in the diagram at the right, are supplementary. What is a good name for this pair of angles? Explain.

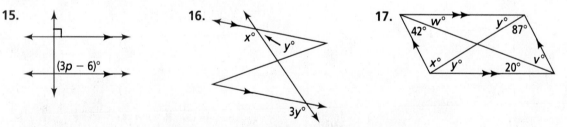

More Practice and Problem-Solving Exercises

 MATHEMATICAL PRACTICES

Ⓑ Apply

Algebra Find the values of the variables.

15.

16.

17.

© 18. **Think About a Plan** People in ancient Rome played a game called *terni lapilli*. The exact rules of this game are not known. Etchings on floors and walls in Rome suggest that the game required a grid of two intersecting pairs of parallel lines, similar to the modern game tick-tack-toe. The measure of one of the angles formed by the intersecting lines is 90°. Find the measure of each of the other 15 angles. Justify your answers.
- How can you use a diagram to help?
- You know the measure of one angle. How does the position of that angle relate to the position of each of the other angles?
- Which angles formed by two parallel lines and a transversal are congruent? Which angles are supplementary?

© 19. **Error Analysis** Which solution for the value of *x* in the figure at the right is incorrect? Explain.

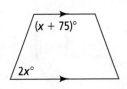

A.

$$2x = x + 75$$
$$x = 75$$

B.

$$2x + (x + 75) = 180$$
$$3x + 75 = 180$$
$$3x = 105$$
$$x = 35$$

20. **Outdoor Recreation** Campers often use a "bear bag" at night to avoid attracting animals to their food supply. In the bear bag system at the right, a camper pulls or releases one end of the rope to raise or lower the food bag.

a. Suppose a camper pulls the rope taut between the two parallel trees, as shown. What is $m\angle 1$?

b. Are $\angle 1$ and the given angle *alternate interior angles, same-side interior angles,* or *corresponding angles*?

© 21. **Writing** Are same-side interior angles ever congruent? Explain.

Proof 22. Write a two-column proof to prove the Corresponding Angles Theorem (Theorem 7).

Given: $\ell \parallel m$

Prove: $\angle 2$ and $\angle 6$ are congruent.

Proof 23. Write a two-column proof.

Given: $a \parallel b, \angle 1 \cong \angle 4$

Prove: $\angle 2 \cong \angle 3$

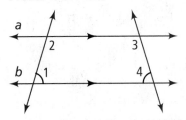

© **Challenge**

Use the diagram at the right for Exercises 24 and 25.

24. **Algebra** Suppose the measures of $\angle 1$ and $\angle 2$ are in a $4 : 11$ ratio. Find their measures. (Diagram is not to scale.)

© 25. **Error Analysis** The diagram at the right contains contradictory information. What is it? Why is it contradictory?

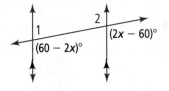

2-3 Proving Lines Parallel

G.CO.9 Prove theorems about lines and angles. Theorems include: . . . when a transversal crosses parallel lines, alternate interior angles are congruent and corresponding angles are congruent . . .

Objective To determine whether two lines are parallel

Solve It! Write your solution to the Solve It in the space below.

In the Solve It, you used parallel lines to find congruent and supplementary relationships of special angle pairs. In this lesson you will do the converse. You will use the congruent and supplementary relationships of the special angle pairs to prove lines parallel.

Essential Understanding You can use certain angle pairs to decide whether two lines are parallel.

Theorem 9 Converse of the Corresponding Angles Theorem

Theorem	If . . .	Then . . .
If two lines and a transversal form corresponding angles that are congruent, then the lines are parallel.	$\angle 2 \cong \angle 6$ 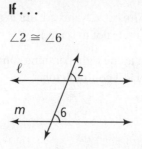	$\ell \parallel m$

You will prove Theorem 9 in Lesson 4-5.

Problem 1   Identifying Parallel Lines

Got It?   Which lines are parallel if $\angle 6 \cong \angle 7$? Justify your answer.

Think

Which line is the
transversal for
$\angle 6$ and $\angle 7$?

A Practice   Which lines or segments are parallel? Justify your answer.

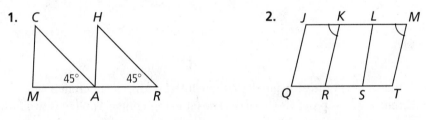

1.

2.

In the last lesson you proved theorems based on the Corresponding Angles
Theorem. You can use the Converse of the Corresponding Angles Theorem to prove
converses of the theorems and postulate you learned in the last lesson.

take note

Theorem 10   Converse of the Alternate Interior Angles Theorem

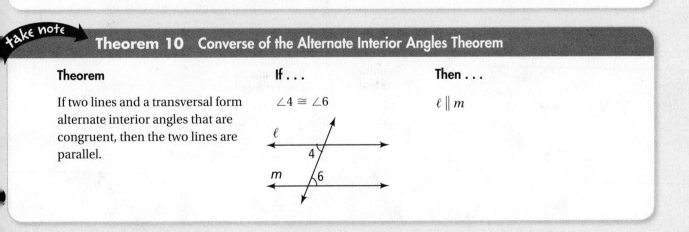

Theorem	If . . .	Then . . .
If two lines and a transversal form alternate interior angles that are congruent, then the two lines are parallel.	$\angle 4 \cong \angle 6$	$\ell \parallel m$

Theorem 11   Converse of the Same-Side Interior Angles Postulate

Theorem	If . . .	Then . . .
If two lines and a transversal form same-side interior angles that are supplementary, then the two lines are parallel.	$m\angle 3 + m\angle 6 = 180$	$\ell \parallel m$

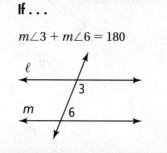

Theorem 12   Converse of the Alternate Exterior Angles Theorem

Theorem	If . . .	Then . . .
If two lines and a transversal form alternate exterior angles that are congruent, then the two lines are parallel.	$\angle 1 \cong \angle 7$	$\ell \parallel m$

The proof of the Converse of the Alternate Interior Angles Theorem below looks different than any proof you have seen so far in this course. You know two forms of proof—paragraph and two-column. In a third form, called **flow proof**, arrows show the logical connections between the statements. Reasons are written below the statements.

Proof Proof of Theorem 10: Converse of the Alternate Interior Angles Theorem

Given: $\angle 4 \cong \angle 6$

Prove: $\ell \parallel m$

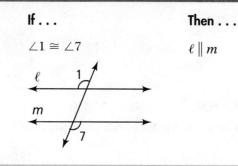

Got It? Use the same diagram used to prove Theorem 12 in Problem 2 to Prove Theorem 11.

Given: $m\angle 3 + m\angle 6 = 180$

Prove: $\ell \parallel m$

Ⓐ**Practice** **3. Developing Proof** Complete the flow proof below.

Given: $\angle 1$ and $\angle 3$ are supplementary.

Prove: $a \parallel b$

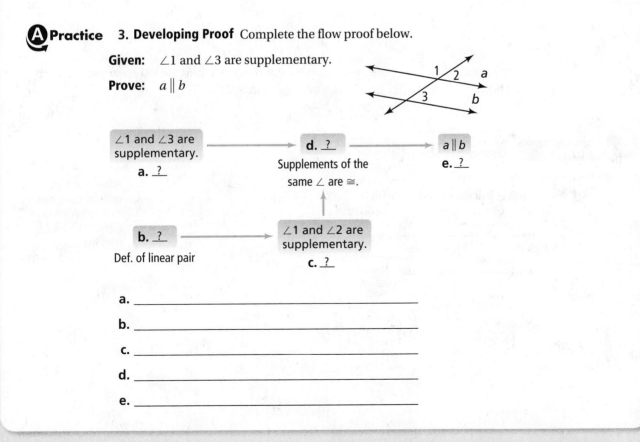

a. _____

b. _____

c. _____

d. _____

e. _____

The four theorems you have just learned provide you with four ways to determine if two lines are parallel.

ONLINE PROBLEMS **Problem 3** Determining Whether Lines are Parallel

Got It? In Problem 3, what is another way to explain why $r \parallel s$? Justify your answer.

Practice 4. **Parking** Two workers paint lines for angled parking spaces. One worker paints a line so that $m\angle 1 = 65$. The other worker paints a line so that $m\angle 2 = 65$. Are their lines parallel? Explain.

You can use algebra along with the postulates and theorems from the last lesson and this lesson to help you solve problems involving parallel lines.

ONLINE PROBLEMS **Problem 4** Using Algebra

Got It? What is the value of w for which $c \parallel d$?

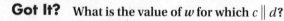
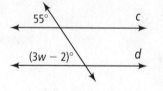

55° c

$(3w - 2)°$ d

Think

What must be true of the given angles for lines *c* and *d* to be parallel?

A Practice Algebra Find the value of x for which $\ell \parallel m$.

5.

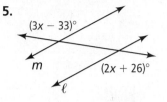

$(3x - 33)°$

m

$(2x + 26)°$

ℓ

6.

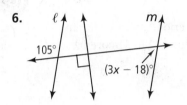

ℓ m

$105°$

$(3x - 18)°$

Lesson Check

Do you know HOW?

State the theorem or postulate that proves $a \parallel b$.

7.

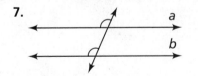

a

b

8.

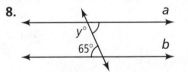

a

$y°$

$65°$

b

9. What is the value of y for which $a \parallel b$ in Exercise 8?

Do you UNDERSTAND?

10. Explain how you know when to use the Alternate Interior Angles Theorem and when to use the Converse of the Alternate Interior Angles Theorem.

11. Compare and Contrast How are flow proofs and two-column proofs alike? How are they different?

12. Error Analysis A classmate says that $\overleftrightarrow{AB} \parallel \overleftrightarrow{DC}$ based on the diagram at the right. Explain your classmate's error.

More Practice and Problem-Solving Exercises

Ⓒ **MATHEMATICAL PRACTICES**

Ⓑ **Apply**

Ⓒ **Developing Proof** Use the given information to determine which lines, if any, are parallel. Justify each conclusion with a theorem or postulate.

13. ∠2 is supplementary to ∠3.

14. ∠1 ≅ ∠3

15. ∠6 is supplementary to ∠7.

16. ∠9 ≅ ∠12

17. $m\angle 7 = 65$, $m\angle 9 = 115$

18. ∠2 ≅ ∠10

19. ∠1 ≅ ∠8

20. ∠8 ≅ ∠6

21. ∠11 ≅ ∠7

22. ∠5 ≅ ∠10

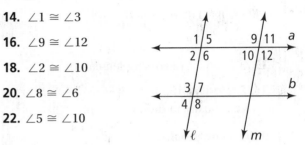

Algebra Find the value of x for which $\ell \parallel m$.

23.

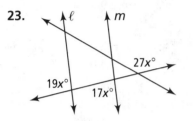

24.

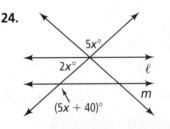

Ⓒ **25. Think About a Plan** If the rowing crew at the right strokes in unison, the oars sweep out angles of equal measure. Explain why the oars on each side of the shell stay parallel.

- What type of information do you need to prove lines parallel?
- How do the positions of the angles of equal measure relate?

Algebra Determine the value of x for which $r \parallel s$. Then find $m\angle 1$ and $m\angle 2$.

26. $m\angle 1 = 80 - x$, $m\angle 2 = 90 - 2x$

27. $m\angle 1 = 60 - 2x$, $m\angle 2 = 70 - 4x$

28. $m\angle 1 = 40 - 4x$, $m\angle 2 = 50 - 8x$

29. $m\angle 1 = 20 - 8x$, $m\angle 2 = 30 - 16x$

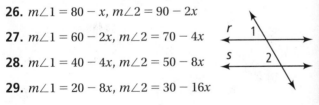

Use the diagram at the right below for Exercises 30–36.

Open-Ended Use the given information. State another fact about one of the given angles that will guarantee two lines are parallel. Tell which lines will be parallel and why.

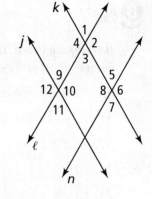

30. $\angle 1 \cong \angle 3$

31. $m\angle 8 = 110$, $m\angle 9 = 70$

32. $\angle 5 \cong \angle 11$

33. $\angle 11$ and $\angle 12$ are supplementary.

34. Reasoning If $\angle 1 \cong \angle 7$, what theorem or postulate can you use to show that $\ell \parallel n$?

Write a flow proof.

Proof 35. Given: $\ell \parallel n$, $\angle 12 \cong \angle 8$
 Prove: $j \parallel k$

Proof 36. Given: $j \parallel k$, $m\angle 8 + m\angle 9 = 180$
 Prove: $\ell \parallel n$

Challenge

Which sides of quadrilateral *PLAN* must be parallel? Explain.

37. $m\angle P = 72$, $m\angle L = 108$, $m\angle A = 72$, $m\angle N = 108$

38. $m\angle P = 59$, $m\angle L = 37$, $m\angle A = 143$, $m\angle N = 121$

39. $m\angle P = 67$, $m\angle L = 120$, $m\angle A = 73$, $m\angle N = 100$

40. $m\angle P = 56$, $m\angle L = 124$, $m\angle A = 124$, $m\angle N = 56$

Proof 41. Write a two-column proof to prove the following: If a transversal intersects two parallel lines, then the bisectors of two corresponding angles are parallel. (*Hint:* Start by drawing and marking a diagram.)

Parallel and Perpendicular Lines

G.CO.9 Prove theorems about lines and angles. Theorems include: . . . when a transversal crosses parallel lines . . .

Objective To relate parallel and perpendicular lines

Solve It! Write your solution to the Solve It in the space below.

In the Solve It, you likely made your conjecture about Oak Street and Court Road based on their relationships to Schoolhouse Road. In this lesson you will use similar reasoning to prove that lines are parallel or perpendicular.

Essential Understanding You can use the relationships of two lines to a third line to decide whether the two lines are parallel or perpendicular to each other.

take note

Theorem 13

Theorem	If . . .	Then . . .
If two lines are parallel to the same line, then they are parallel to each other.	$a \parallel b$ and $b \parallel c$ 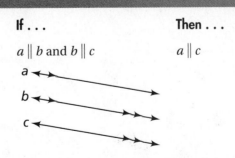	$a \parallel c$

You will prove Theorem 13 in Exercise 2.

take note

Theorem 14

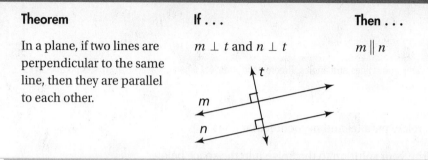

Theorem	If . . .	Then . . .
In a plane, if two lines are perpendicular to the same line, then they are parallel to each other.	$m \perp t$ and $n \perp t$	$m \parallel n$

Notice that Theorem 14 includes the phrase *in a plane*. In Exercise 17, you will consider why this phrase is necessary.

Proof **Proof of Theorem 14**

Given: In a plane, $r \perp t$ and $s \perp t$.

Prove: $r \parallel s$

Proof: $\angle 1$ and $\angle 2$ are right angles by the definition of perpendicular. So, $\angle 1 \cong \angle 2$. Since corresponding angles are congruent, $r \parallel s$.

ONLINE PROBLEMS

Problem 1 Solving a Problem With Parallel Lines

Got It? Can you assemble the pieces below to form a picture frame with opposite sides parallel? Explain.

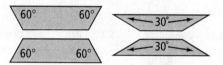

Think

How can a sketch help you visualize how to assemble the pieces?

Practice   **1.** A carpenter is building a trellis for vines to grow on. The completed trellis will have two sets of diagonal pieces of wood that overlap each other.

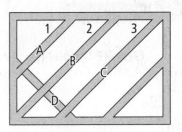

a. If pieces A, B, and C must be parallel, what must be true of ∠1, ∠2, and ∠3?

b. The carpenter attaches piece D so that it is perpendicular to piece A. If he wants to place more pieces parallel to piece D, how can he do so? Justify your answer using theorems from this lesson.

Theorems 13 and 14 give conditions that allow you to conclude that lines are parallel. The Perpendicular Transversal Theorem below provides a way for you to conclude that lines are perpendicular.

take note

Theorem 15   Perpendicular Transversal Theorem

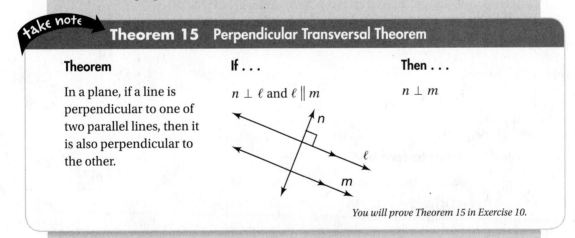

Theorem	**If . . .**	**Then . . .**
In a plane, if a line is perpendicular to one of two parallel lines, then it is also perpendicular to the other.	$n \perp \ell$ and $\ell \parallel m$	$n \perp m$

You will prove Theorem 15 in Exercise 10.

The Perpendicular Transversal Theorem states that the lines must be *in a plane*. The diagram at the right shows why. In the rectangular solid, $\overleftrightarrow{AC}$ and $\overleftrightarrow{BD}$ are parallel. $\overleftrightarrow{EC}$ is perpendicular to $\overleftrightarrow{AC}$, but it is not perpendicular to $\overleftrightarrow{BD}$. In fact, $\overleftrightarrow{EC}$ and $\overleftrightarrow{BD}$ are skew because they are not in the same plane.

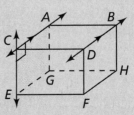

Got It?   In Problem 2, could you also conclude $a \parallel b$? Explain.

Think

How do lines *a* and *b* relate to line *d*?

 Practice

2. **Developing Proof** Copy and complete this paragraph proof of Theorem 13 for three coplanar lines.

Given: $\ell \parallel k$ and $m \parallel k$

Prove: $\ell \parallel m$

Proof: Since $\ell \parallel k$, $\angle 2 \cong \angle 1$ by the

a. __?__ Theorem. Since $m \parallel k$, **b.** __?__ $\cong$
c. __?__ for the same reason. By the Transitive Property of Congruence, $\angle 2 \cong \angle 3$. By the
d. __?__ Theorem, $\ell \parallel m$.

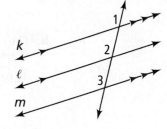

a. _____

b. _____

c. _____

d. _____

Proof 3. Write a paragraph proof.

Given: In a plane, $a \perp b$, $b \perp c$, and $c \parallel d$.

Prove: $a \parallel d$

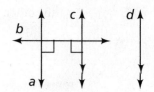

Lesson Check

Do you know HOW?

4. Main Street intersects Avenue A and Avenue B. Avenue A is parallel to Avenue B. Avenue A is also perpendicular to Main Street. How are Avenue B and Main Street related? Explain.

5. In the diagram at the right, lines *a*, *b*, and *c* are coplanar. What conclusion can you make about lines *a* and *b*? Explain.

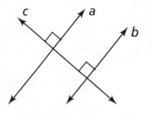

Do you UNDERSTAND?

6. Explain why the phrase *in a plane* is not necessary in Theorem 13.

7. Which theorem or postulate from earlier in the chapter supports the conclusion in Theorem 14? In the Perpendicular Transversal Theorem? Explain.

© **8. Error Analysis** Shiro sketched coplanar lines *m, n*, and *r* on his homework paper. He claims that it shows that lines *m* and *n* are parallel. What other information do you need about line *r* in order for Shiro's claim to be true? Explain.

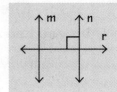

More Practice and Problem-Solving Exercises

(B) Apply

© **9. Think About a Plan** One traditional type of log cabin is a single rectangular room. Suppose you begin building a log cabin by placing four logs in the shape of a rectangle. What should you measure to guarantee that the logs on opposite walls are parallel? Explain.
- What type of information do you need to prove lines parallel?
- How can you use a diagram to help you?
- What do you know about the angles of the geometric shape?

Proof 10. Prove the Perpendicular Transversal Theorem (Theorem 15):
In a plane, if a line is perpendicular to one of two parallel lines, then it is also perpendicular to the other.

Given: In a plane, $a \perp b$ and $b \parallel c$.

Prove: $a \perp c$

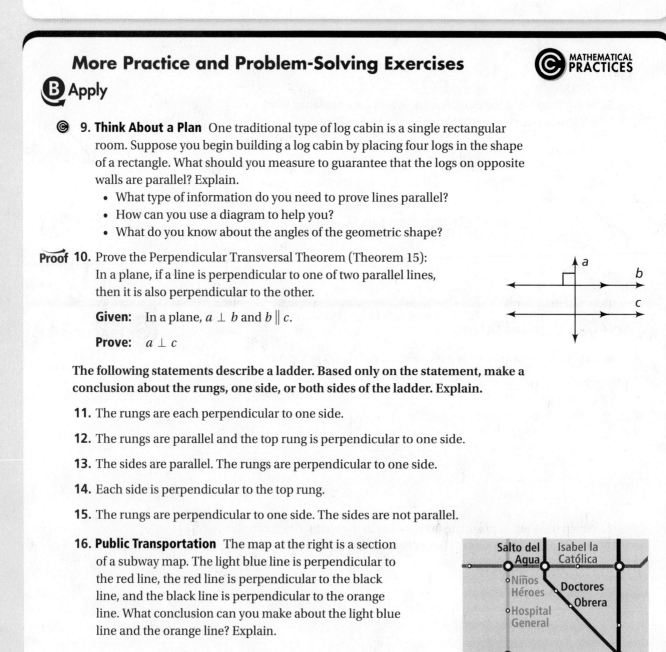

The following statements describe a ladder. Based only on the statement, make a conclusion about the rungs, one side, or both sides of the ladder. Explain.

11. The rungs are each perpendicular to one side.

12. The rungs are parallel and the top rung is perpendicular to one side.

13. The sides are parallel. The rungs are perpendicular to one side.

14. Each side is perpendicular to the top rung.

15. The rungs are perpendicular to one side. The sides are not parallel.

16. Public Transportation The map at the right is a section of a subway map. The light blue line is perpendicular to the red line, the red line is perpendicular to the black line, and the black line is perpendicular to the orange line. What conclusion can you make about the light blue line and the orange line? Explain.

17. Writing Theorem 14 states that in a plane, two lines perpendicular to the same line are parallel. Explain why the phrase *in a plane* is needed. (*Hint:* Refer to a rectangular solid to help you visualize the situation.)

18. Quilting You plan to sew two triangles of fabric together to make a square for a quilting project. The triangles are both right triangles and have the same side and angle measures. What must also be true about the triangles in order to guarantee that the opposite sides of the fabric square are parallel? Explain.

ⓒ Challenge

For Exercises 19–24, *a*, *b*, *c*, and *d* are distinct lines in the same plane. For each combination of relationships, tell how *a* and *d* relate. Justify your answer.

19. $a \parallel b, b \parallel c, c \parallel d$ **20.** $a \parallel b, b \parallel c, c \perp d$

21. $a \parallel b, b \perp c, c \parallel d$ **22.** $a \perp b, b \parallel c, c \parallel d$

23. $a \parallel b, b \perp c, c \perp d$ **24.** $a \perp b, b \parallel c, c \perp d$

25. Reasoning Review the reflexive, symmetric, and transitive properties for congruence in Lesson 1-6. Write reflexive, symmetric, and transitive statements for "is parallel to" ($\parallel$). Tell whether each statement is *true* or *false*. Justify your answer.

26. Reasoning Repeat Exercise 25 for "is perpendicular to" ($\perp$).

2-5 Parallel Lines and Triangles

G.CO.10 Prove theorems about triangles . . . measures of interior angles of a triangle sum to 180°. Also G.CO.9

Objectives To use parallel lines to prove a theorem about triangles
To find measures of angles of triangles

 Solve It! Write your solution to the Solve It in the space below.

In the Solve It, you may have discovered that you can rearrange the corners of the triangle to form a straight angle. You can do this for any triangle.

Essential Understanding The sum of the angle measures of a triangle is always the same.

The Solve It suggests an important theorem about triangles. To prove this theorem, you will need to use parallel lines.

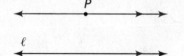

Postulate 12 Parallel Postulate

Through a point not on a line, there is one and only one line parallel to the given line.

P

ℓ

There is exactly one line through *P* parallel to ℓ.

Theorem 16 Triangle Angle-Sum Theorem

The sum of the measures of the angles of a triangle is 180.

$m\angle A + m\angle B + m\angle C = 180$

The proof of the Triangle Angle-Sum Theorem requires an *auxiliary line*. An **auxiliary line** is a line that you add to a diagram to help explain relationships in proofs. The red line in the diagram below is an auxiliary line.

Proof Proof of Theorem 16: Triangle Angle-Sum Theorem

Given: $\triangle ABC$

Prove: $m\angle A + m\angle 2 + m\angle C = 180$

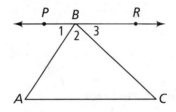

Statements	Reasons
1) Draw $\overleftrightarrow{PR}$ through B, parallel to $\overleftrightarrow{AC}$.	**1)** Parallel Postulate
2) $\angle PBC$ and $\angle 3$ are supplementary.	**2)** $\angle$s that form a linear pair are suppl.
3) $m\angle PBC + m\angle 3 = 180$	**3)** Definition of suppl. $\angle$s
4) $m\angle PBC = m\angle 1 + m\angle 2$	**4)** Angle Addition Postulate
5) $m\angle 1 + m\angle 2 + m\angle 3 = 180$	**5)** Substitution Property
6) $\angle 1 \cong \angle A$ and $\angle 3 \cong \angle C$	**6)** If lines are $\parallel$, then alternate interior $\angle$s are $\cong$.
7) $m\angle 1 = m\angle A$ and $m\angle 3 = m\angle C$	**7)** Congruent $\angle$s have equal measure.
8) $m\angle A + m\angle 2 + m\angle C = 180$	**8)** Substitution Property

When you know the measures of two angles of a triangle, you can use the Triangle Angle-Sum Theorem to find the measure of the third angle.

Problem 1   Using the Triangle Angle-Sum Theorem

Got It?   Use the diagram below. What is the value of z?

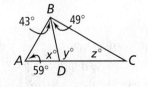

Plan

Which triangle will you use to find the value of z?

Practice   **1.** Find $m\angle 1$.

117°

1

33°

2. Algebra   Find the value of each variable.

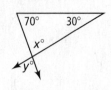

70°   30°

$x°$

$y°$

An **exterior angle of a polygon** is an angle formed by a side and an extension of an adjacent side. For each exterior angle of a triangle, the two nonadjacent interior angles are its **remote interior angles**. In each triangle below, ∠1 is an exterior angle and ∠2 and ∠3 are its remote interior angles.

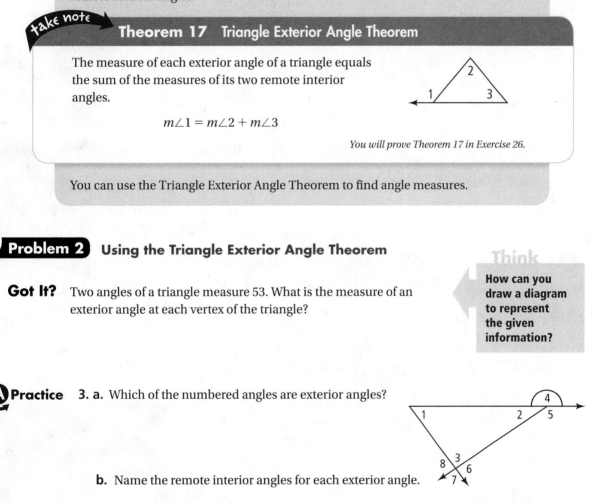

The theorem below states the relationship between an exterior angle and its two remote interior angles.

take note

Theorem 17   Triangle Exterior Angle Theorem

The measure of each exterior angle of a triangle equals the sum of the measures of its two remote interior angles.

$$m\angle 1 = m\angle 2 + m\angle 3$$

You will prove Theorem 17 in Exercise 26.

You can use the Triangle Exterior Angle Theorem to find angle measures.

Problem 2   Using the Triangle Exterior Angle Theorem

Got It?   Two angles of a triangle measure 53. What is the measure of an exterior angle at each vertex of the triangle?

Think

How can you draw a diagram to represent the given information?

Ⓐ Practice   **3. a.** Which of the numbered angles are exterior angles?

b. Name the remote interior angles for each exterior angle.

c. How are exterior angles 6 and 8 related?

4. Algebra Find the measure of ∠2.

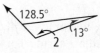

 Problem 3 **Applying the Triangle Theorems**

© **Got It?** **Reasoning** In Problem 3, can you find $m\angle A$ without using the Triangle Exterior Angle Theorem? Explain.

A Practice **5.** A ramp forms the angles shown at the right. What are the values of *a* and *b*?

6. A lounge chair has different settings that change the angles formed by its parts. Suppose $m\angle 2 = 71$ and $m\angle 3 = 43$. Find $m\angle 1$.

Lesson Check

Do you know HOW?

Find the measure of the third angle of a triangle given the measures of two angles.

7. 34 and 88

8. 45 and 90

9. 10 and 102

10. x and 50

In a triangle, $\angle 1$ is an exterior angle and $\angle 2$ and $\angle 3$ are its remote interior angles. Find the missing angle measure.

11. $m\angle 2 = 24$ and $m\angle 3 = 106$

12. $m\angle 1 = 70$ and $m\angle 2 = 32$

13. Explain how the Triangle Exterior Angle Theorem makes sense based on the Triangle Angle-Sum Theorem.

14. Error Analysis The measures of the interior angles of a triangle are 30, x, and $3x$. Which of the following methods for solving for x is incorrect? Explain.

A.
```
x + 3x = 30
   4x = 30
    x = 7.5
```

B.
```
x + 3x + 30 = 180
     4x + 30 = 180
          4x = 150
           x = 37.5
```

More Practice and Problem-Solving Exercises

B Apply

Algebra Use the given information to find the unknown angle measures in the triangle.

15. The ratio of the angle measures of the acute angles in a right triangle is $1 : 2$.

16. The measure of one angle of a triangle is 40. The measures of the other two angles are in a ratio of $3 : 4$.

17. The measure of one angle of a triangle is 108. The measures of the other two angles are in a ratio of $1 : 5$.

18. Think About a Plan The angle measures of $\triangle RST$ are represented by $2x$, $x + 14$, and $x - 38$. What are the angle measures of $\triangle RST$?
- How can you use the Triangle Angle-Sum Theorem to write an equation?
- How can you check your answer?

Proof **19.** Prove the following theorem: The acute angles of a right triangle are complementary.

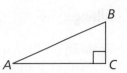

    Given: $\triangle ABC$ with right angle C

    Prove: $\angle A$ and $\angle B$ are complementary.

© 20. Reasoning What is the measure of each angle of an equiangular triangle? Explain.

© 21. Draw a Diagram Which diagram below correctly represents the following description? Explain your reasoning.

    Draw any triangle. Label it $\triangle ABC$. Extend two sides of the triangle to form two exterior angles at vertex A.

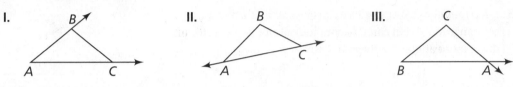

Find the values of the variables and the measures of the angles.

22.

23.

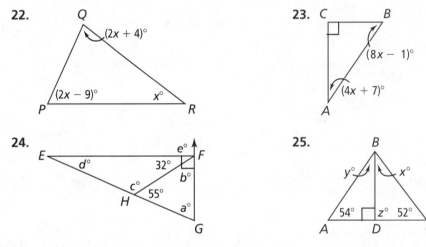

24.

25.

Proof **26.** Prove the Triangle Exterior Angle Theorem (Theorem 17). The measure of each exterior angle of a triangle equals the sum of the measures of its two remote interior angles.

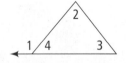

    Given: $\angle 1$ is an exterior angle of the triangle.

    Prove: $m\angle 1 = m\angle 2 + m\angle 3$

© 27. Reasoning Two angles of a triangle measure 64 and 48. What is the measure of the largest exterior angle of the triangle? Explain.

28. Algebra A right triangle has exterior angles at each of its acute angles with measures in the ratio 13 : 14. Find the measures of the two acute angles of the right triangle.

Probability In Exercises 29–33, you know only the given information about the measures of the angles of a triangle. Find the probability that the triangle is equiangular.

29. Each is a multiple of 30.　　　　　**30.** Each is a multiple of 20.

31. Each is a multiple of 60.　　　　　**32.** Each is a multiple of 12.

33. One angle is obtuse.

34. In the figure at the right, $\overline{CD} \perp \overline{AB}$ and $\overline{CD}$ bisects $\angle ACB$. Find $m\angle DBF$.

35. If the remote interior angles of an exterior angle of a triangle are congruent, what can you conclude about the bisector of the exterior angle? Justify your answer.

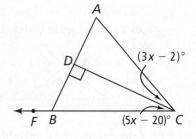

2-6 Constructing Parallel and Perpendicular Lines

G.CO.12 Make formal geometric constructions with a variety of tools and methods . . . constructing perpendicular lines . . . and constructing a line parallel to a given line through a point not on the line. Also **G.CO.13**

Objective To construct parallel and perpendicular lines

 Solve It! Write your solution to the Solve It in the space below.

In the Solve It, you used paper-folding to construct lines.

Essential Understanding You can also use a straightedge and a compass to construct parallel and perpendicular lines.

In Lesson 2-5, you learned that through a point not on a line, there is a unique line parallel to the given line. Problem 1 shows the construction of this line.

Problem 1 Constructing Parallel Lines

© **Got It?** **Reasoning** In Problem 1, why must lines ℓ and m be parallel?

Ⓐ **Practice** Construct the line through point J that is parallel to $\overleftrightarrow{AB}$.

1.

• J

$\overleftrightarrow{A \qquad\qquad B}$

2.

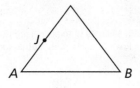

 **Problem 2** **Constructing a Special Quadrilateral**

Got It? **a.** Draw a segment. Label its length *m*. Construct quadrilateral *ABCD* with $\overleftrightarrow{AB} \parallel \overleftrightarrow{CD}$, so that $AB = m$ and $CD = 2m$.

b. Reasoning Suppose you and a friend both use the steps in Problem 2 to construct *ABYZ* independently. Will your quadrilaterals necessarily have the same angle measures and side lengths? Explain.

> **Think**
>
> **How can you test whether your answer to part (b) is correct?**

**Practice** Draw two segments. Label their lengths a and b. Construct a
quadrilateral with one pair of parallel sides as described.

3. The sides have length $2a$ and b.

4. The sides have length a and $\frac{1}{2}b$.

Problem 3 Perpendicular at a Point on a Line

Got It? Use a straightedge to draw $\overleftrightarrow{EF}$. Construct $\overleftrightarrow{FG}$ so that $\overleftrightarrow{FG} \perp \overleftrightarrow{EF}$ at point F.

Think

Can you use any
compass setting
when locating
point G?

Construct the line that is perpendicular to ℓ at point *P*.

5.

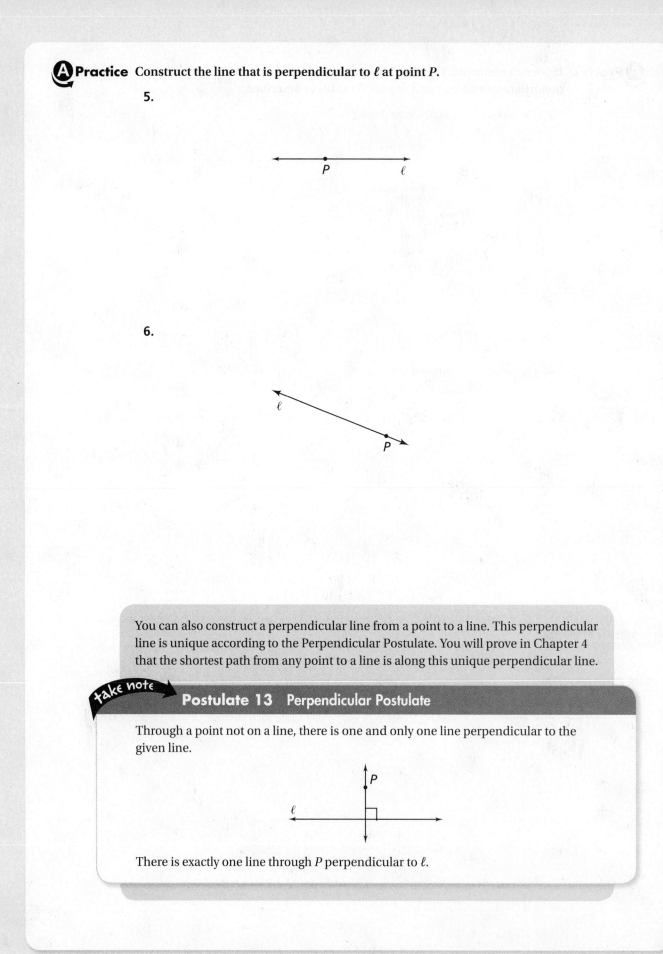

6.

You can also construct a perpendicular line from a point to a line. This perpendicular line is unique according to the Perpendicular Postulate. You will prove in Chapter 4 that the shortest path from any point to a line is along this unique perpendicular line.

take note

Postulate 13 Perpendicular Postulate

Through a point not on a line, there is one and only one line perpendicular to the given line.

There is exactly one line through *P* perpendicular to ℓ.

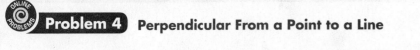

Got It? Draw $\overleftrightarrow{CX}$ and a point Z not on $\overleftrightarrow{CX}$. Construct $\overleftrightarrow{ZB}$ so that $\overleftrightarrow{ZB} \perp \overleftrightarrow{CX}$.

Ⓐ Practice Construct the line through point P that is perpendicular to $\overleftrightarrow{RS}$.

7.

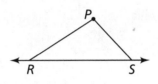

8.

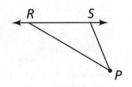

Lesson Check

Do you know HOW?

9. Draw a line ℓ and a point P not on the line. Construct the line through P parallel to line ℓ.

10. Draw $\overleftrightarrow{QR}$ and a point S on the line. Construct the line perpendicular to $\overleftrightarrow{QR}$ at point S.

11. Draw a line w and a point X not on the line. Construct the line perpendicular to line w at point X.

Do you UNDERSTAND?

12. In Problem 3, is $\overline{AC}$ congruent to $\overline{BC}$? Explain.

13. Suppose you use a wider compass setting in Step 1 of Problem 4. Will you construct a different perpendicular line? Explain.

ⓒ **14. Compare and Contrast** How are the constructions in Problems 3 and 4 similar? How are they different?

More Practice and Problem-Solving Exercises

ⓒ **MATHEMATICAL PRACTICES**

Ⓑ **Apply**

ⓒ **15. Think About a Plan** Draw an acute angle. Construct an angle congruent to your angle so that the two angles are alternate interior angles.
- What does a sketch of the angle look like?
- Which construction(s) should you use?

16. Constructions Construct a square with side length p.

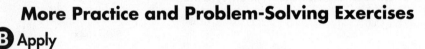
p

ⓒ **17. Writing** Explain how to use the Converse of the Alternate Interior Angles Theorem to construct a line parallel to the given line through a point not on the line. (*Hint:* See Exercise 15.)

For Exercises 18–24, use the segments at the right.

18. Draw a line *m*. Construct a segment of length *b* that is perpendicular to line *m*.

19. Construct a rectangle with base *b* and height *c*.

20. Construct a square with sides of length *a*.

21. Construct a rectangle with one side of length *a* and a diagonal of length *b*.

ⓒ **22. a.** Construct a quadrilateral with a pair of parallel sides of length *c*.
　　b. **Make a Conjecture** What appears to be true about the other pair of sides in the quadrilateral you constructed?
　　c. Use a protractor, a ruler, or both to check the conjecture you made in part (b).

23. Construct a right triangle with legs of lengths *a* and *b*.

ⓒ **24. a.** Construct a triangle with sides of lengths *a*, *b*, and *c*.
　　b. Construct the midpoint of each side of the triangle.
　　c. Form a new triangle by connecting the midpoints.
　　d. **Make a Conjecture** How do the sides of the smaller triangle and the sides of the larger triangle appear to be related?
　　e. Use a protractor, ruler, or both to check the conjecture you made in part (d).

25. Constructions The diagrams below show steps for a parallel line construction.

I.
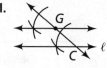

II. G
　　　　　　　　　　　　ℓ

III.
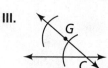

IV.
　　　　　　G
　　　　　　　　　ℓ
　　　C

　　a. List the construction steps in the correct order.
　　b. For the steps that use a compass, describe the location(s) of the compass point.

Ⓒ **Challenge**

Draw $\overline{DG}$. Construct a quadrilateral with diagonals that are congruent to $\overline{DG}$, bisect each other, and meet the given conditions. Describe the figure.

26. The diagonals are not perpendicular.　　　**27.** The diagonals are perpendicular.

Construct a rectangle with side lengths *a* and *b* that meets the given condition.

28. $b = 2a$　　　　**29.** $b = \frac{1}{2}a$　　　　**30.** $b = \frac{1}{3}a$　　　　**31.** $b = \frac{2}{3}a$

Construct a triangle with side lengths a, b, and c that meets the given conditions. If such a triangle is not possible, explain.

32. $a = b = c$　　　　**33.** $a = b = 2c$　　　　**34.** $a = 2b = 2c$　　　　**35.** $a = b + c$

2 Chapter Review

2-1 Lines and Angles

Quick Review

A **transversal** is a line that intersects two or more coplanar lines at distinct points.

∠1 and ∠3 are **corresponding angles.**

∠2 and ∠6 are **alternate interior angles.**

∠2 and ∠3 are **same-side interior angles.**

∠4 and ∠8 are **alternate exterior angles.**

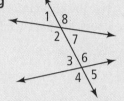

Example

Name two other pairs of corresponding angles in the diagram above.

∠5 and ∠7

∠2 and ∠4

Exercises

Identify all numbered angle pairs that form the given type of angle pair. Then name the two lines and transversal that form each pair.

1. alternate interior angles

2. same-side interior angles

3. corresponding angles

4. alternate exterior angles

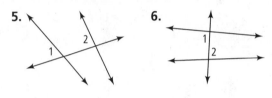

Classify the angle pair formed by ∠1 and ∠2.

5.

6.

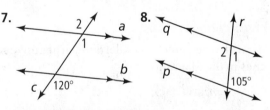

2-2 Properties of Parallel Lines

Quick Review

If two parallel lines are cut by a transversal, then

- corresponding angles, alternate interior angles, and alternate exterior angles are congruent
- same-side interior angles are supplementary

Example

Which other angles measure 110?

∠6 (corresponding angles)

∠3 (alternate interior angles)

∠8 (vertical angles)

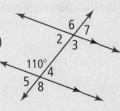

Exercises

Find $m\angle 1$ and $m\angle 2$. Justify your answers.

7.

8.

9. Find the values of x and y in the diagram below.

2-3 Proving Lines Parallel

Quick Review

If two lines and a transversal form

- congruent corresponding angles,
- congruent alternate interior angles,
- congruent alternate exterior angles, or
- supplementary same-side interior angles,

then the two lines are parallel.

Example

What is the value of *x* for which ℓ ‖ *m*?

The given angles are alternate interior angles. So, ℓ ‖ *m* if the given angles are congruent.

$2x = 106$ Congruent ⦞ have equal measures.

$x = 53$ Divide each side by 2.

Exercises

Find the value of *x* for which ℓ ‖ *m*.

10. 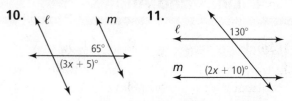 **11.**

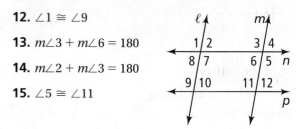

Use the given information to decide which lines, if any, are parallel. Justify your conclusion.

12. $\angle 1 \cong \angle 9$

13. $m\angle 3 + m\angle 6 = 180$

14. $m\angle 2 + m\angle 3 = 180$

15. $\angle 5 \cong \angle 11$

2-4 Parallel and Perpendicular Lines

Quick Review

- Two lines ‖ to the same line are ‖ to each other.
- In a plane, two lines ⊥ to the same line are ‖.
- In a plane, if one line is ⊥ to one of two ‖ lines, then it is ⊥ to both ‖ lines.

Example

What are the pairs of parallel and perpendicular lines in the diagram?

ℓ ‖ *n*, ℓ ‖ *m*, and *m* ‖ *n*.

$a \perp \ell$, $a \perp m$, and $a \perp n$.

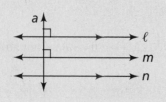

Exercises

Use the diagram at the right to complete each statement.

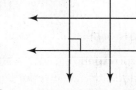

16. If $b \perp c$ and $b \perp d$, then c __?__ d.

17. If $c \parallel d$, then __?__ $\perp c$.

18. Maps Morris Avenue intersects both 1st Street and 3rd Street at right angles. 3rd Street is parallel to 5th Street. How are 1st Street and 5th Street related? Explain.

2-5 Parallel Lines and Triangles

Quick Review

The sum of the measures of the angles of a triangle is 180.

The measure of each **exterior angle** of a triangle equals the sum of the measures of its two **remote interior angles.**

Example

What are the values of x and y?

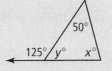

$$x + 50 = 125 \quad \text{Exterior Angle Theorem}$$
$$x = 75 \quad \text{Simplify.}$$
$$x + y + 50 = 180 \quad \text{Triangle Angle-Sum Theorem}$$
$$75 + y + 50 = 180 \quad \text{Substitute 75 for } x.$$
$$y = 55 \quad \text{Simplify.}$$

Exercises

Find the values of the variables.

19. **20.**

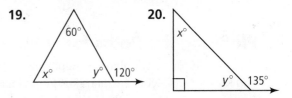

The measures of the three angles of a triangle are given. Find the value of x.

21. $x, 2x, 3x$

22. $x + 10, x - 20, x + 25$

23. $20x + 10, 30x - 2, 7x + 1$

2-6 Constructing Parallel and Perpendicular Lines

Quick Review

You can use a compass and a straightedge to construct

- a line parallel to a given line through a point not on the line
- a line perpendicular to a given line through a point on the line, or through a point not on the line

Example

Which step of the parallel lines construction guarantees the lines are parallel?

The parallel lines construction involves constructing a pair of congruent angles. Since the congruent angles are corresponding angles, the lines are parallel.

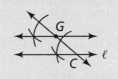

Exercises

24. Draw a line m and point Q not on m. Construct a line perpendicular to m through Q.

Use the segments below.

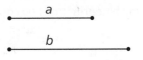

25. Construct a rectangle with side lengths a and b.

26. Construct a rectangle with side lengths a and $2b$.

27. Construct a quadrilateral with one pair of parallel opposite sides, each side of length $2a$.

Pull It **All Together**

Planning the Paths for a Park

Kiana works for a city's planning department. The city is developing a new park, and Kiana is reviewing the plans for the builders. The park is rectangular with two sets of parallel walkways that go through the park, as shown in the blueprint below.

Kiana notices that only a few angle measures are provided in the blueprint. She would like to add additional angle measures to make it easier for the builders to create the correct paths.

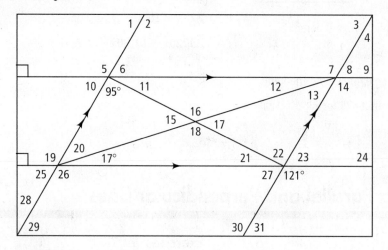

Task Description

Determine the measure of each numbered angle in the blueprint.

- Which postulates theorems can you use to help you find the angle measures?

- Which angles in the blueprint must be congruent to the 121° angle?

Get Ready!

The Distance Formula

Find the side lengths of △ABC.

1. $A(3, 1), B(-1, 1), C(-1, -2)$

2. $A(-3, 2), B(-3, -6), C(8, 6)$

3. $A(-1, -2), B(6, 1), C(2, 5)$

Proving Angles Congruent

Draw a conclusion based on the information given.

4. $\angle J$ is supplementary to $\angle K$;
$\angle L$ is supplementary to $\angle K$.

5. $\angle M$ is supplementary to $\angle N$;
$\angle M \cong \angle N$.

6. $\angle 1$ is complementary to $\angle 2$.

7. $\overrightarrow{FA} \perp \overrightarrow{FC}, \overrightarrow{FB} \perp \overrightarrow{FD}$

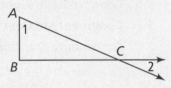

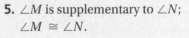

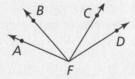

Parallel Lines and the Triangle Angle-Sum Theorem

What can you conclude about the angles in each diagram?

8. **9.** **10.**

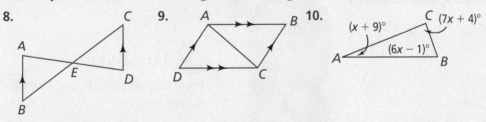

Looking Ahead Vocabulary

11. The foundation of a building is the *base* of the building. How would you describe the *base of an isosceles triangle* in geometry?

12. The *legs* of a table support the tabletop and are equal in length. How might they be similar to the *legs of an isosceles triangle*?

13. A postal worker delivers each piece of mail to the mailbox that *corresponds* to the address on the envelope. What might the term *corresponding parts* of geometric figures mean?

Congruent Triangles

Big Ideas

1 Visualization
Essential Question: How do you identify corresponding parts of congruent triangles?

2 Reasoning and Proof
Essential Question: How do you show that two triangles are congruent?

3 Reasoning and Proof
Essential Question: How can you tell whether a triangle is isosceles or equilateral?

© Domains

- Congruence
- Mathematical Practice: Construct viable arguments
- Modeling with Geometry

Chapter Preview

Interactive Digital Path

Log in to **pearsonsuccessnet.com** and click on Interactive Digital Path to access the Solve Its and animated Problems.

Vocabulary

English/Spanish Vocabulary Audio Online:

English	Spanish
base angles of an isosceles triangle, *p. 156*	ángulos de base de un triángulo isósceles
base of an isosceles triangle, *p. 156*	base de un triángulo isósceles
congruence transformation, *p. 186*	transformación de congruencia
congruent polygons, *p. 121*	polígonos congruentes
corollary, *p. 159*	corolario
hypotenuse, *p. 165*	hipotenusa
legs of an isosceles triangle, *p. 156*	catetos de un triángulo isósceles
legs of a right triangle, *p. 165*	catetos de un triángulo rectángulo
vertex angle of an isosceles triangle, *p. 156*	ángulo en vértice de un triángulo isósceles

Prepares for **G.CO.7** . . . Show that two triangles are congruent if and only if corresponding pairs of sides and corresponding pairs of angles are congruent. Also prepares for **G.SRT.5**

Objective   To recognize congruent figures and their corresponding parts

Solve It!   Write your solution to the Solve It in the space below.

Congruent figures have the same size and shape. When two figures are congruent, you can slide, flip, or turn one so that it fits exactly on the other one, as shown below. In this lesson, you will learn how to determine if geometric figures are congruent.

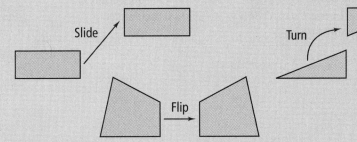

Slide   Turn   Flip

Essential Understanding You can determine whether two figures are congruent by comparing their corresponding parts.

take note

Key Concept   Congruent Figures

Definition

Congruent polygons have congruent corresponding parts—their matching sides and angles. When you name congruent polygons, you must list corresponding vertices in the same order.

Example

$ABCD \cong EFGH$

$\overline{AB} \cong \overline{EF}$ $\overline{BC} \cong \overline{FG}$
$\overline{CD} \cong \overline{GH}$ $\overline{DA} \cong \overline{HE}$

$\angle A \cong \angle E$ $\angle B \cong \angle F$
$\angle C \cong \angle G$ $\angle D \cong \angle H$

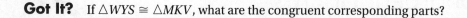

Problem 1   **Finding Congruent Parts**

Got It?   If △*WYS* ≅ △*MKV*, what are the congruent corresponding parts?

Practice   **1. Construction**   Builders use the king post truss for the top of a simple structure. In this truss, △*ABC* ≅ △*ABD*. List the congruent corresponding parts.

2. The attic frame truss provides open space in the center for storage. In this truss, △*EFG* ≅ △*HIJ*. List the congruent corresponding parts.

Problem 2   **Using Congruent Parts**

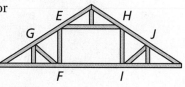

Plan

How do you know which sides and angles correspond?

Got It?   Suppose that △*WYS* ≅ △*MKV*. If $m\angle W = 62$ and $m\angle Y = 35$, what is $m\angle V$? Explain.

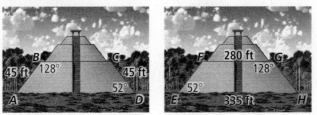

3. AD **4.** $m\angle DCB$

ONLINE PROBLEMS

Problem 3   **Finding Congruent Triangles**

Got It?   Is $\triangle ABD \cong \triangle CBD$? Justify your answer.

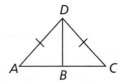

A Practice For Exercises 5 and 6, can you conclude that the triangles are congruent? Justify your answers.

5. $\triangle TRK$ and $\triangle TUK$

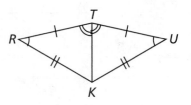

6. △*SPQ* and △*TUV*

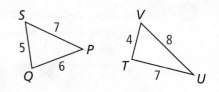

Recall the Triangle Angle-Sum Theorem: The sum of the measures of the angles in a triangle is 180. The next theorem follows from the Triangle Angle-Sum Theorem.

take note

Theorem 18   Third Angles Theorem

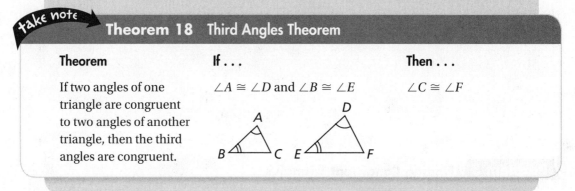

Theorem	If . . .	Then . . .
If two angles of one triangle are congruent to two angles of another triangle, then the third angles are congruent.	∠*A* ≅ ∠*D* and ∠*B* ≅ ∠*E*	∠*C* ≅ ∠*F*

Proof **Proof of Theorem 18: Third Angles Theorem**

Given: ∠*A* ≅ ∠*D*, ∠*B* ≅ ∠*E*
Prove: ∠*C* ≅ ∠*F*

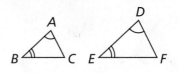

Statements	Reasons
1) ∠*A* ≅ ∠*D*, ∠*B* ≅ ∠*E*	**1)** Given
2) *m*∠*A* = *m*∠*D*, *m*∠*B* = *m*∠*E*	**2)** Def. of ≅ ⦦
3) *m*∠*A* + *m*∠*B* + *m*∠*C* = 180, *m*∠*D* + *m*∠*E* + *m*∠*F* = 180	**3)** △ Angle-Sum Thm.
4) *m*∠*A* + *m*∠*B* + *m*∠*C* = *m*∠*D* + *m*∠*E* + *m*∠*F*	**4)** Subst. Prop.
5) *m*∠*D* + *m*∠*E* + *m*∠*C* = *m*∠*D* + *m*∠*E* + *m*∠*F*	**5)** Subst. Prop.
6) *m*∠*C* = *m*∠*F*	**6)** Subtraction Prop. of =
7) ∠*C* ≅ ∠*F*	**7)** Def. of ≅ ⦦

Problem 4 Proving Triangles Congruent

Got It? **Given:** $\angle A \cong \angle D, \overline{AE} \cong \overline{DC},$ $\overline{EB} \cong \overline{CB}, \overline{BA} \cong \overline{BD}$

Prove: $\triangle AEB \cong \triangle DCB$

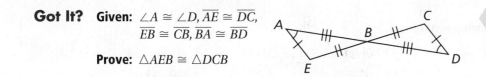

Plan

What else do you need to prove that the triangles are congruent?

Ⓐ **Practice** **7. Given:** $\overline{AB} \parallel \overline{DC}, \angle B \cong \angle D,$ Proof $\overline{AB} \cong \overline{DC}, \overline{BC} \cong \overline{AD}$

Prove: $\triangle ABC \cong \triangle CDA$

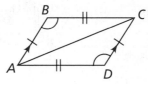

Lesson Check

Do you know HOW?

Complete the following statements.

8. Given: $\triangle QXR \cong \triangle NYC$

   a. $\overline{QX} \cong$ _____

   b. $\angle Y \cong$ _____

9. Given: $\triangle BAT \cong \triangle FOR$

   a. $\overline{TA} \cong$ _____

   b. $\angle R \cong$ _____

10. Given: $BAND \cong LUCK$

   a. $\angle U \cong$ _____

   b. $\overline{DB} \cong$ _____

   c. $NDBA \cong$ _____

11. In $\triangle MAP$ and $\triangle TIE$, $\angle A \cong \angle I$ and $\angle P \cong \angle E$.

   a. What is the relationship between $\angle M$ and $\angle T$?

   b. If $m\angle A = 52$ and $m\angle P = 36$, what is $m\angle T$?

Do you UNDERSTAND?

12. Open-Ended When do you think you might need to know that things are congruent in your everyday life?

13. If each angle in one triangle is congruent to its corresponding angle in another triangle, are the two triangles congruent? Explain.

© 14. Error Analysis Walter sketched the diagram at the right. He claims it shows that the two polygons are congruent. What information is missing to support his claim?

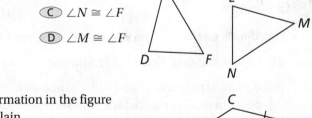

More Practice and Problem-Solving Exercises

© MATHEMATICAL PRACTICES

B Apply

15. If $\triangle DEF \cong \triangle LMN$, which of the following must be a correct congruence statement?

- Ⓐ $\overline{DE} \cong \overline{LN}$
- Ⓒ $\angle N \cong \angle F$
- Ⓑ $\overline{FE} \cong \overline{NL}$
- Ⓓ $\angle M \cong \angle F$

© 16. Reasoning Randall says he can use the information in the figure to prove $\triangle BCD \cong \triangle DAB$. Is he correct? Explain.

Algebra $\triangle ABC \cong \triangle DEF$. Find the measures of the given angles or the lengths of the given sides.

17. $m\angle A = x + 10, m\angle D = 2x$

18. $m\angle B = 3y, m\angle E = 6y - 12$

19. $BC = 3z + 2, EF = z + 6$

20. $AC = 7a + 5, DF = 5a + 9$

@ 21. Think About a Plan △ABC ≅ △DBE. Find the value of x.

- What does it mean for two triangles to be congruent?
- Which angle measures do you already know?
- How can you find the missing angle measure in a triangle?

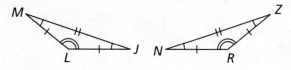

Algebra Find the values of the variables.

22.

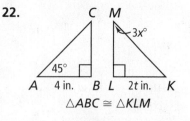

△ABC ≅ △KLM

23.

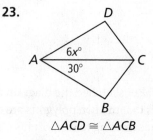

△ACD ≅ △ACB

24. Complete in two different ways: △JLM ≅ __?__ .

@ 25. Open-Ended Write a congruence statement for two triangles. List the congruent sides and angles.

Proof 26. Given: $\overline{AB} \perp \overline{AD}, \overline{BC} \perp \overline{CD}, \overline{AB} \cong \overline{CD}$
　　　　　$\overline{AD} \cong \overline{CB}, \overline{AB} \parallel \overline{CD}$
Prove: △ABD ≅ △CDB

Proof 27. Given: $\overline{PR} \parallel \overline{TQ}, \overline{PR} \cong \overline{TQ}, \overline{PS} \cong \overline{QS}, \overline{PQ}$ bisects $\overline{RT}$
Prove: △PRS ≅ △QTS

@ 28. Writing The 225 cards in Tracy's sports card collection are rectangles of three different sizes. How could Tracy quickly sort the cards?

C Challenge

Coordinate Geometry The vertices of △GHJ are $G(-2, -1), H(-2, 3),$ and $J(1, 3).$

29. △KLM ≅ △GHJ. Find $KL, LM,$ and KM.

30. If L and M have coordinates $L(3, -3)$ and $M(6, -3)$, how many pairs of coordinates are possible for K? Find one such pair.

31. a. A polygon is called *convex* if it has no diagonals with points outside the polygon. A polygon is called *concave* if it has at least one diagonal with points outside the polygon. How many quadrilaterals (convex and concave) with different shapes or sizes can you make on a three-by-three geoboard? Sketch them. One is shown at the right.
b. How many quadrilaterals of each type are there?

3-2

Triangle Congruence by SSS and SAS

G.SRT.5 Use congruence . . . criteria for triangles to solve problems and to prove relationships in geometric figures. Also prepares for **G.CO.8**

Objective   To prove two triangles congruent using the SSS and SAS Postulates

Solve It!   Write your solution to the Solve It in the space below.

In the Solve It, you looked for relationships between corresponding sides and angles. In Lesson 3-1, you learned that if two triangles have three pairs of congruent corresponding angles and three pairs of congruent corresponding sides, then the triangles are congruent.

If you know . . .

$\angle F \cong \angle J \quad \overline{FG} \cong \overline{JK}$
$\angle G \cong \angle K \quad \overline{GH} \cong \overline{KL}$
$\angle H \cong \angle L \quad \overline{FH} \cong \overline{JL}$

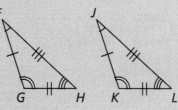

. . . then you know $\triangle FGH \cong \triangle JKL$.

However, this is more information about the corresponding parts than you need to prove triangles congruent.

Essential Understanding You can prove that two triangles are congruent without having to show that *all* corresponding parts are congruent. In this lesson, you will prove triangles congruent by using (1) three pairs of corresponding sides and (2) two pairs of corresponding sides and one pair of corresponding angles.

Postulate 14 Side-Side-Side (SSS) Postulate

Postulate	If . . .	Then . . .

If the three sides of one triangle are congruent to the three sides of another triangle, then the two triangles are congruent.

$\overline{AB} \cong \overline{DE}, \overline{BC} \cong \overline{EF}, \overline{AC} \cong \overline{DF}$

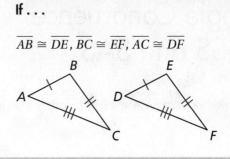

$\triangle ABC \cong \triangle DEF$

A postulate is an accepted statement of fact. The Side-Side-Side Postulate is perhaps the most logical fact about triangles. It agrees with the notion that triangles are rigid figures; their shape does not change until pressure on their sides forces them to break. This rigidity property is important to architects and engineers when they build things such as bicycle frames and steel bridges.

Problem 1   Using SSS

Got It?   **Given:** $\overline{BC} \cong \overline{BF}, \overline{CD} \cong \overline{FD}$

Prove: $\triangle BCD \cong \triangle BFD$

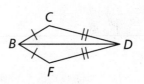

Plan

What else do you need to prove that the triangles are congruent?

**Practice**   **1. Developing Proof** Complete the flow proof.

Given: $\overline{JK} \cong \overline{LM}, \overline{JM} \cong \overline{LK}$

Prove: $\triangle JKM \cong \triangle LMK$

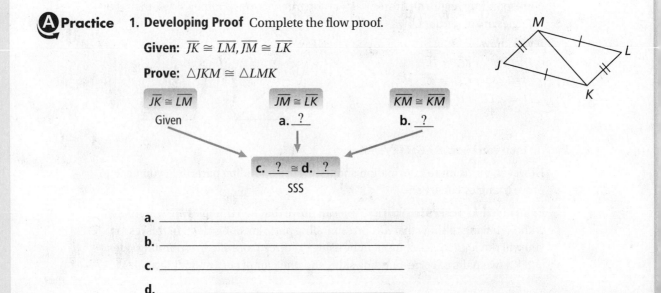

$\overline{JK} \cong \overline{LM}$	$\overline{JM} \cong \overline{LK}$	$\overline{KM} \cong \overline{KM}$
Given	**a.** ?	**b.** ?

c. ? $\cong$ **d.** ?

SSS

a. _____

b. _____

c. _____

d. _____

Proof 2. Given: $\overline{IE} \cong \overline{GH}$, $\overline{EF} \cong \overline{HF}$,
F is the midpoint of $\overline{GI}$

Prove: $\triangle EFI \cong \triangle HFG$

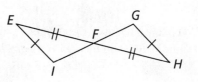

You can also show relationships between a pair of corresponding sides and an *included* angle.

The word *included* refers to the angles and the sides of a triangle, as shown at the right.

$\angle A$ is included between $\overline{BA}$ and $\overline{AC}$.

$\overline{BC}$ is included between $\angle B$ and $\angle C$.

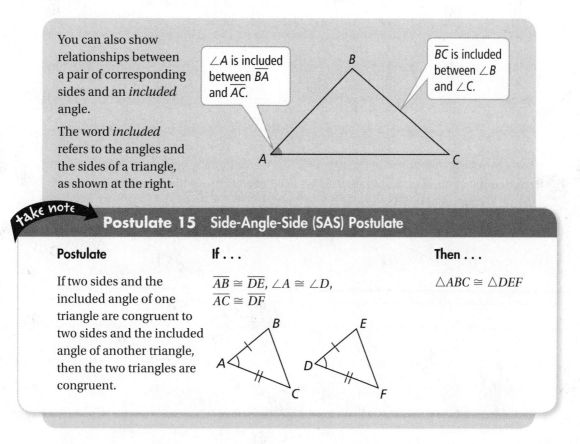

Postulate 15   Side-Angle-Side (SAS) Postulate

Postulate	If . . .	Then . . .
If two sides and the included angle of one triangle are congruent to two sides and the included angle of another triangle, then the two triangles are congruent.	$\overline{AB} \cong \overline{DE}$, $\angle A \cong \angle D$, $\overline{AC} \cong \overline{DF}$	$\triangle ABC \cong \triangle DEF$

You likely have used the properties of the Side-Angle-Side Postulate before. For example, SAS can help you determine whether a box will fit through a doorway.

Suppose you keep your arms at a fixed angle as you move from the box to the doorway. The triangle you form with the box is congruent to the triangle you form with the doorway. The two triangles are congruent because two sides and the included angle of one triangle are congruent to the two sides and the included angle of the other triangle.

Problem 2   Using SAS

Got It? What other information do you need to prove $\triangle LEB \cong \triangle BNL$ by SAS?

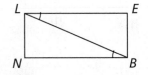

Practice What other information, if any, do you need to prove the two triangles congruent by SAS? Explain.

3.

4.

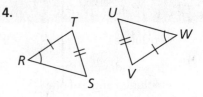

Recall that, in Lesson 1-1, you learned to construct segments using a compass open to a fixed angle. Now you can show that it works. Similar to the situation with the box and the doorway, the Side-Angle-Side Postulate tells you that the triangles outlined at the right are congruent. So, $\overline{AB} \cong \overline{CD}$.

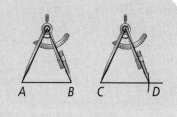

 Problem 3 Identifying Congruent Triangles

Got It? Would you use SSS or SAS to prove the triangles below congruent? Explain.

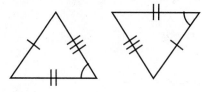

What should you look for first, congruent sides or congruent angles?

Ⓐ Practice Would you use SSS or SAS to prove the triangles congruent? If there is not enough information to prove the triangles congruent by SSS or SAS, write *not enough information*. Explain your answer.

5.

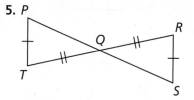

6.

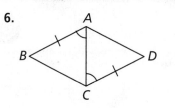

Lesson Check

Do you know HOW?

7. In $\triangle PEN$, name the angle that is included between the given sides.

    a. $\overline{PE}$ and $\overline{EN}$ **b.** $\overline{NP}$ and $\overline{PE}$

8. In $\triangle HAT$, between which sides is the given angle included?

    a. $\angle H$ **b.** $\angle T$

Name the postulate you would use to prove the triangles congruent.

9. 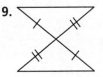   **10.**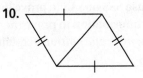

Do you UNDERSTAND?

11. Compare and Contrast How are the SSS Postulate and the SAS Postulate alike? How are they different?

12. Error Analysis Your friend thinks that the triangles shown at the right are congruent by SAS. Is your friend correct? Explain.

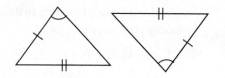

13. Reasoning A carpenter trims a triangular peak of a house with three 7-ft pieces of molding. The carpenter uses 21 ft of molding to trim a second triangular peak. Are the two triangles formed congruent? Explain.

More Practice and Problem-Solving Exercises

B Apply

MATHEMATICAL PRACTICES

14. Think About a Plan You and a friend are cutting triangles out of felt for an art project. You want all the triangles to be congruent. Your friend tells you that each triangle should have two 5-in. sides and a 40° angle. If you follow this rule, will all your felt triangles be congruent? Explain.
- How can you use diagrams to help you?
- Which postulate, SSS or SAS, are you likely to apply to the given situation?

Proof **15. Given:** $\overline{BC} \cong \overline{DA}$, $\angle CBD \cong \angle ADB$

Prove: $\triangle BCD \cong \triangle DAB$

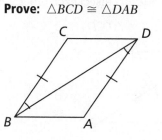

Proof **16. Given:** X is the midpoint of $\overline{AG}$ and $\overline{NR}$.

Prove: $\triangle ANX \cong \triangle GRX$

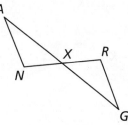

Use the Distance Formula to determine whether $\triangle ABC$ **and** $\triangle DEF$ **are congruent. Justify your answer.**

17. $A(1, 4)$, $B(5, 5)$, $C(2, 2)$;
$D(-5, 1)$, $E(-1, 0)$, $F(-4, 3)$

18. $A(3, 8)$, $B(8, 12)$, $C(10, 5)$;
$D(3, -1)$, $E(7, -7)$, $F(12, -2)$

19. $A(2, 9)$, $B(2, 4)$, $C(5, 4)$;
$D(1, -3)$, $E(1, 2)$, $F(-2, 2)$

20. Writing List three real-life uses of congruent triangles. For each real-life use, describe why you think congruence is necessary.

21. Sierpinski's Triangle Sierpinski's triangle is a famous geometric pattern. To draw Sierpinski's triangle, start with a single triangle and connect the midpoints of the sides to draw a smaller triangle. If you repeat this pattern over and over, you will form a figure like the one shown. This particular figure started with an isosceles triangle. Are the triangles outlined in red congruent? Explain.

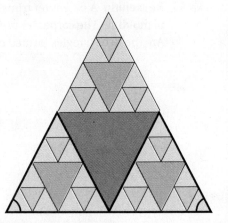

22. Constructions Use a straightedge to draw any triangle JKL. Then construct $\triangle MNP \cong \triangle JKL$ using the given postulate.
a. SSS
b. SAS

Can you prove the triangles congruent? If so, write the congruence statement and name the postulate you would use. If not, write *not enough information* **and tell what other information you would need.**

23.

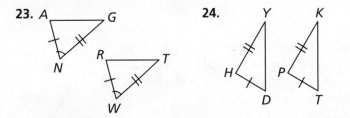

24.

25.

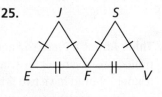

26. Reasoning Suppose $\overline{GH} \cong \overline{JK}$, $\overline{HI} \cong \overline{KL}$, and $\angle I \cong \angle L$. Is $\triangle GHI$ congruent to $\triangle JKL$? Explain.

Proof 27. Given: $\overrightarrow{GK}$ bisects $\angle JGM$, $\overline{GJ} \cong \overline{GM}$

Prove: $\triangle GJK \cong \triangle GMK$

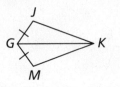

Proof 28. Given: $\overline{AE}$ and $\overline{BD}$ bisect each other.

Prove: $\triangle ACB \cong \triangle ECD$

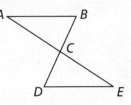

29. Given: $\overline{FG} \parallel \overline{KL}$, $\overline{FG} \cong \overline{KL}$

Proof **Prove:** $\triangle FGK \cong \triangle KLF$

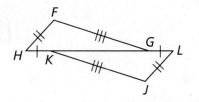

30. Given: $\overline{AB} \perp \overline{CM}$, $\overline{AB} \perp \overline{DB}$, $\overline{CM} \cong \overline{DB}$,
Proof M is the midpoint of $\overline{AB}$.

Prove: $\triangle AMC \cong \triangle MBD$

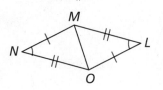

Challenge

31. Given: $\overline{HK} \cong \overline{LG}$, $\overline{HF} \cong \overline{LJ}$, $\overline{FG} \cong \overline{JK}$
Proof **Prove:** $\triangle FGH \cong \triangle JKL$

32. Given: $\angle N \cong \angle L$, $\overline{MN} \cong \overline{OL}$, $\overline{NO} \cong \overline{LM}$
Proof **Prove:** $\overline{MN} \parallel \overline{OL}$

© **33. Reasoning** Four sides of polygon *ABCD* are congruent, respectively, to the four sides of polygon *EFGH*. Are *ABCD* and *EFGH* congruent? Is a quadrilateral a rigid figure? If not, what could you add to make it a rigid figure? Explain.

3-3 | Triangle Congruence by ASA and AAS

G.SRT.5 Use congruence . . . criteria for triangles to solve problems and to prove relationships in geometric figures. Also prepares for **G.CO.8**

Objective To prove two triangles congruent using the ASA Postulate and the AAS Theorem

Solve It! Write your solution to the Solve It in the space below.

You already know that triangles are congruent if two pairs of sides and the included angles are congruent (SAS). You can also prove triangles congruent using other groupings of angles and sides.

Essential Understanding You can prove that two triangles are congruent without having to show that *all* corresponding parts are congruent. In this lesson, you will prove triangles congruent by using one pair of corresponding sides and two pairs of corresponding angles.

take note

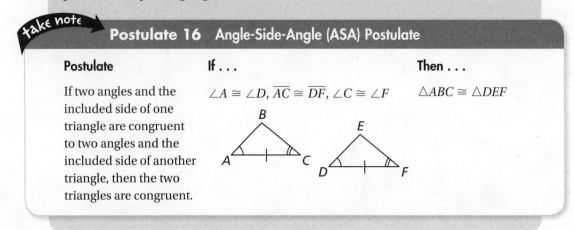

Postulate 16 Angle-Side-Angle (ASA) Postulate

Postulate

If two angles and the included side of one triangle are congruent to two angles and the included side of another triangle, then the two triangles are congruent.

If . . .

$\angle A \cong \angle D$, $\overline{AC} \cong \overline{DF}$, $\angle C \cong \angle F$

Then . . .

$\triangle ABC \cong \triangle DEF$

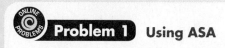

Problem 1 Using ASA

Got It? Which two triangles are congruent by ASA? Explain.

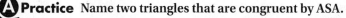

Think

When you use ASA, what must be true about the corresponding sides?

Practice Name two triangles that are congruent by ASA.

1.

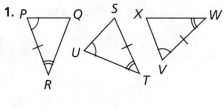

2.

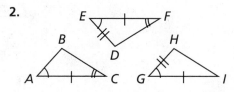

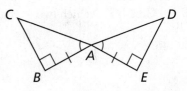

Problem 2 **Writing a Proof Using ASA**

Got It? **Given:** $\angle CAB \cong \angle DAE$, $\overline{BA} \cong \overline{EA}$, $\angle B$ and $\angle E$ are right angles

Prove: $\triangle ABC \cong \triangle AED$

 Practice 3. **Developing Proof** Complete the paragraph proof by filling in the blanks.

Given: $\angle LKM \cong \angle JKM$, $\angle LMK \cong \angle JMK$

Prove: $\triangle LKM \cong \triangle JKM$

Proof: $\angle LKM \cong \angle JKM$ and $\angle LMK \cong \angle JMK$ are given.

$\overline{KM} \cong \overline{KM}$ by the **a.** _____ Property of Congruence.

So, $\triangle LKM \cong \triangle JKM$ by **b.** _____.

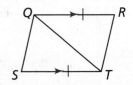

Proof 4. **Given:** $\overline{QR} \cong \overline{TS}$, $\overline{QR} \parallel \overline{TS}$

Prove: $\triangle QRT \cong \triangle TSQ$

You can also prove triangles congruent by using two angles and a nonincluded side, as stated in the theorem below.

Theorem 19   Angle-Angle-Side (AAS) Theorem

Theorem	**If . . .**	**Then . . .**
If two angles and a nonincluded side of one triangle are congruent to two angles and the corresponding nonincluded side of another triangle, then the triangles are congruent.	$\angle A \cong \angle D, \angle B \cong \angle E, \overline{AC} \cong \overline{DF}$ 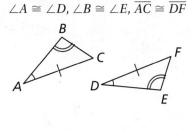	$\triangle ABC \cong \triangle DEF$

Proof **Proof of Theorem 19: Angle-Angle-Side Theorem**

Given: $\angle A \cong \angle D, \angle B \cong \angle E, \overline{AC} \cong \overline{DF}$

Prove: $\triangle ABC \cong \triangle DEF$

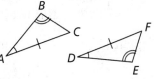

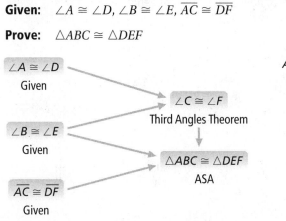

You have seen and used three methods of proof in this book—two-column, paragraph, and flow proof. Each method is equally as valid as the others. Unless told otherwise, you can choose any of the three methods to write a proof. Just be sure your proof always presents logical reasoning with justification.

Got It? **a. Given:** $\angle S \cong \angle Q$, $\overline{RP}$ bisects $\angle SRQ$

Prove: $\triangle SRP \cong \triangle QRP$

Think

How can you show on a diagram that $\overline{RP}$ bisects $\angle SRQ$?

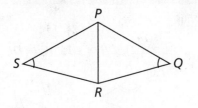

b. Reasoning In Problem 3, how could you prove that
$\triangle WMR \cong \triangle RKW$ by ASA? Explain.

Practice **5. Developing Proof** Complete the two-column proof
by filling in the blanks.

Given: $\angle N \cong \angle S$, line ℓ bisects $\overline{TR}$ at Q

Prove: $\triangle NQT \cong \triangle SQR$

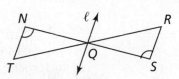

Statements	Reasons
1) $\angle N \cong \angle S$	**1)** Given
2) $\angle NQT \cong \angle SQR$	**2) a.** _____
3) Line ℓ bisects $\overline{TR}$ at Q.	**3) b.** _____
4) c. _____	**4)** Definition of bisect
5) $\triangle NQT \cong \triangle SQR$	**5) d.** _____

Proof 6. Given: $\overline{PQ} \perp \overline{QS}$, $\overline{RS} \perp \overline{SQ}$, T is the midpoint of $\overline{PR}$

   Prove: $\triangle PQT \cong \triangle RST$

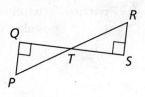

 **Problem 4** **Determining Whether Triangles Are Congruent**

Got It?   Are $\triangle PAR$ and $\triangle SIR$ congruent? Explain.

Practice Determine whether the triangles must be congruent. If so, name the postulate or theorem that justifies your answer. If not, explain.

7.

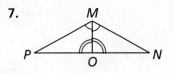

8.

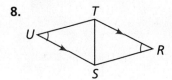

 Lesson Check

Do you know HOW?

9. In $\triangle RST$, which side is included between $\angle R$ and $\angle S$?

10. In $\triangle NOM$, $\overline{NO}$ is included between which angles?

Which postulate or theorem could you use to prove △ABC ≅ △DEF?

11.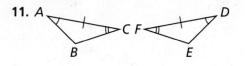

12.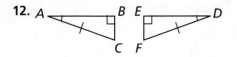

Do you UNDERSTAND?

13. Compare and Contrast How are the ASA Postulate and the SAS Postulate alike? How are they different?

14. Error Analysis Your friend asks you for help on a geometry exercise. To the right is your friend's paper. What error did your friend make? Explain.

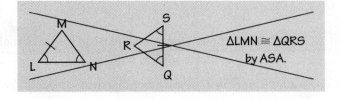

More Practice and Problem-Solving Exercises

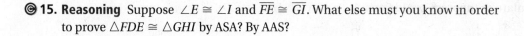
MATHEMATICAL
PRACTICES

B Apply

Proof **16. Given:** $\angle N \cong \angle P, \overline{MO} \cong \overline{QO}$

Prove: $\triangle MON \cong \triangle QOP$

Proof **17. Given:** $\angle FJG \cong \angle HGJ, \overline{FG} \parallel \overline{JH}$

Prove: $\triangle FGJ \cong \triangle HJG$

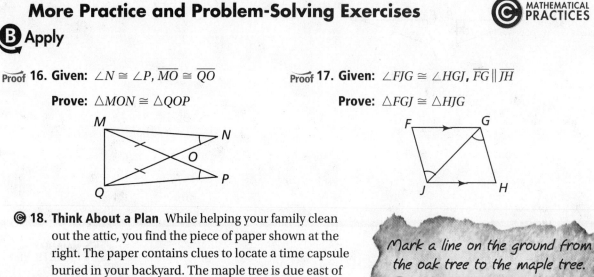

@ **18. Think About a Plan** While helping your family clean out the attic, you find the piece of paper shown at the right. The paper contains clues to locate a time capsule buried in your backyard. The maple tree is due east of the oak tree in your backyard. Will the clues always lead you to the correct spot? Explain.

- How can you use a diagram to help you?
- What type of geometric figure do the paths and the marked line form?
- How does the position of the marked line relate to the positions of the angles?

Mark a line on the ground from the oak tree to the maple tree. From the oak tree, walk along a path that forms a 70° angle with the marked line, keeping the maple tree to your right. From the maple tree, walk along a path that forms a 40° angle with the marked line. The time capsule is buried where the paths meet.

19. Constructions Use a straightedge to draw a triangle. Label it $\triangle JKL$. Construct $\triangle MNP$ so that $\triangle MNP \cong \triangle JKL$ by ASA.

@ **20. Reasoning** Can you prove that the triangles at the right are congruent? Justify your answer.

@ **21. Writing** Anita says that you can rewrite any proof that uses the AAS Theorem as a proof that uses the ASA Postulate. Do you agree with Anita? Explain.

Proof 22. Given: $\overline{AE} \parallel \overline{BD}$, $\overline{AE} \cong \overline{BD}$, $\angle E \cong \angle D$

Prove: $\triangle AEB \cong \triangle BDC$

Proof 23. Given: $\angle 1 \cong \angle 2$, and $\overline{DH}$ bisects $\angle BDF$.

Prove: $\triangle BDH \cong \triangle FDH$

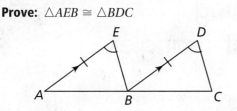

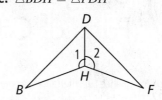

24. Draw a Diagram Draw two noncongruent triangles that have two pairs of congruent angles and one pair of congruent sides.

Proof 25. Given: $\overline{AB} \parallel \overline{DC}$, $\overline{DA} \parallel \overline{BC}$

Prove: $\triangle ABC \cong \triangle CDA$

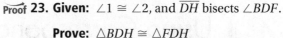

Challenge

26. Given $\overline{AD} \parallel \overline{BC}$ and $\overline{AB} \parallel \overline{DC}$, name as many pairs of congruent triangles as you can.

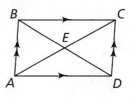

27. Constructions In $\triangle RST$ at the right, $RS = 5$, $RT = 9$, and $m\angle T = 30$. Show that there is no SSA congruence rule by constructing $\triangle UVW$ with $UV = RS$, $UW = RT$, and $m\angle W = m\angle T$, but with $\triangle UVW \ncong \triangle RST$.

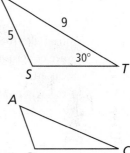

28. Probability Below are six statements about the triangles.

$\angle A \cong \angle X$ $\angle B \cong \angle Y$ $\angle C \cong \angle Z$

$\overline{AB} \cong \overline{XY}$ $\overline{AC} \cong \overline{XZ}$ $\overline{BC} \cong \overline{YZ}$

There are 20 ways to choose a group of three statements from these six. What is the probability that three statements chosen at random from the six will guarantee that the triangles are congruent?

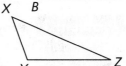

Using Corresponding Parts of Congruent Triangles

G.SRT.5 Use congruence . . . criteria for triangles to solve problems and to prove relationships in geometric figures. Also **G.CO.12**, prepares for **G.CO.7**

Objective To use triangle congruence and corresponding parts of congruent triangles to prove that parts of two triangles are congruent

Solve It! Write your solution to the Solve It in the space below.

With SSS, SAS, ASA, and AAS, you know how to use three congruent parts of two triangles to show that the triangles are congruent. Once you know that two triangles are congruent, you can make conclusions about their other corresponding parts because, by definition, corresponding parts of congruent triangles are congruent.

Essential Understanding If you know two triangles are congruent, then you know that every pair of their corresponding parts is also congruent.

 **Problem 1** **Proving Parts of Triangles Congruent**

Got It? **Given:** $\overline{BA} \cong \overline{DA}, \overline{CA} \cong \overline{EA}$

Prove: $\angle C \cong \angle E$

Think

In the diagram, which congruent pair is not marked?

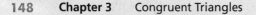

Practice

1. Developing Proof Tell why the two triangles are congruent. Give the congruence statement. Then list all the other corresponding parts of the triangles that are congruent.

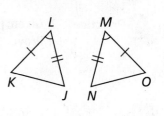

 **Problem 2** **Proving Triangle Parts Congruent to Measure Distance**

Plan

Which congruency rule can you use?

Got It? **a. Given:** $\overline{AB} \cong \overline{AC}$, M is the midpoint of $\overline{BC}$

Prove: $\angle AMB \cong \angle AMC$

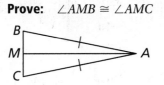

b. Reasoning If the landmark in Problem 2 were not at sea level, would the method in Problem 2 work? Explain.

2. Given: $\overline{OM} \cong \overline{ER}$, $\overline{ME} \cong \overline{RO}$
Proof **Prove:** $\angle M \cong \angle R$

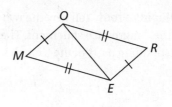

Ⓒ 3. Developing Proof A balalaika is a stringed instrument. Prove that the bases of the balalaikas are congruent.

Given: $\overline{RA} \cong \overline{NY}$, $\angle KRA \cong \angle JNY$,
$\angle KAR \cong \angle JYN$

Prove: $\overline{KA} \cong \overline{JY}$

Proof: It is given that two angles and the included side of one triangle are congruent to two angles and the included side of the other.

So, **a.** _____ $\cong \triangle JNY$ by **b.** _____.

$\overline{KA} \cong \overline{JY}$ because **c.** _____.

Lesson Check

Do you know HOW?

Name the postulate or theorem that you can use to show the triangles are congruent. Then explain why the statement is true.

4. $\overline{EA} \cong \overline{MA}$

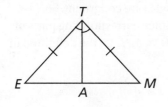

5. $\angle U \cong \angle E$

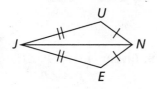

Do you UNDERSTAND?

6. Reasoning How does the fact that corresponding parts of congruent triangles are congruent relate to the definition of congruent triangles?

© 7. **Error Analysis** Find and correct the error(s) in the proof.

Given: $\overline{KH} \cong \overline{NH}$, $\angle L \cong \angle M$

Prove: H is the midpoint of $\overline{LM}$.

Proof: $\overline{KH} \cong \overline{NH}$ because it is given. $\angle L \cong \angle M$ because it is given. $\angle KHL \cong \angle NHM$ because vertical angles are congruent. So, $\triangle KHL \cong \triangle MHN$ by ASA Postulate. Since corresponding parts of congruent triangles are congruent, $\overline{LH} \cong \overline{MH}$. By the definition of midpoint, H is the midpoint of $\overline{LM}$.

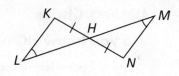

More Practice and Problem-Solving Exercises

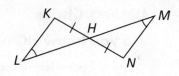
MATHEMATICAL
PRACTICES

B Apply

Proof **8. Given:** $\angle SPT \cong \angle OPT$, $\overline{SP} \cong \overline{OP}$

Prove: $\angle S \cong \angle O$

Proof **9. Given:** $\overline{YT} \cong \overline{YP}$, $\angle C \cong \angle R$, $\angle T \cong \angle P$

Prove: $\overline{CT} \cong \overline{RP}$

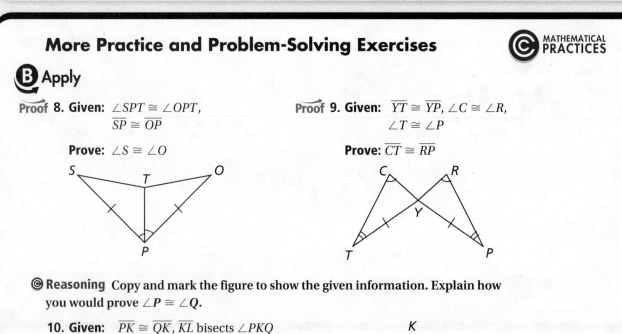

© **Reasoning** Copy and mark the figure to show the given information. Explain how you would prove $\angle P \cong \angle Q$.

10. Given: $\overline{PK} \cong \overline{QK}$, $\overline{KL}$ bisects $\angle PKQ$

11. Given: $\overline{KL}$ is the perpendicular bisector of $\overline{PQ}$.

12. Given: $\overline{KL} \perp \overline{PQ}$, $\overline{KL}$ bisects $\angle PKQ$

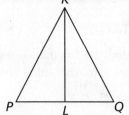

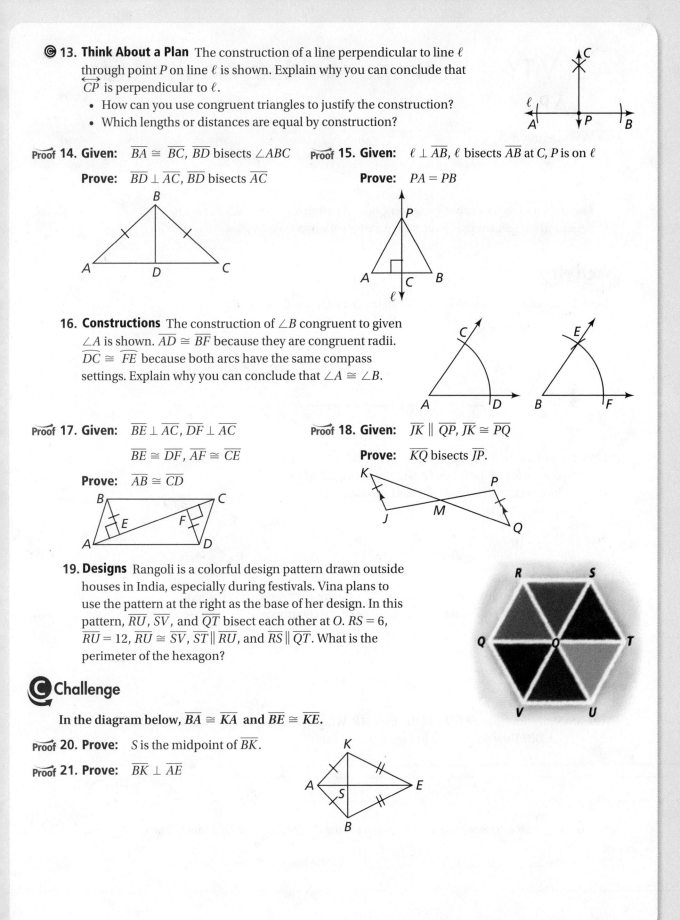

13. Think About a Plan The construction of a line perpendicular to line ℓ through point P on line ℓ is shown. Explain why you can conclude that $\overleftrightarrow{CP}$ is perpendicular to ℓ.
- How can you use congruent triangles to justify the construction?
- Which lengths or distances are equal by construction?

Proof 14. Given: $\overline{BA} \cong \overline{BC}$, $\overline{BD}$ bisects $\angle ABC$

Prove: $\overline{BD} \perp \overline{AC}$, $\overline{BD}$ bisects $\overline{AC}$

Proof 15. Given: $\ell \perp \overline{AB}$, ℓ bisects $\overline{AB}$ at C, P is on ℓ

Prove: $PA = PB$

16. Constructions The construction of $\angle B$ congruent to given $\angle A$ is shown. $\overline{AD} \cong \overline{BF}$ because they are congruent radii. $\overset{\frown}{DC} \cong \overset{\frown}{FE}$ because both arcs have the same compass settings. Explain why you can conclude that $\angle A \cong \angle B$.

Proof 17. Given: $\overline{BE} \perp \overline{AC}$, $\overline{DF} \perp \overline{AC}$

$\overline{BE} \cong \overline{DF}$, $\overline{AF} \cong \overline{CE}$

Prove: $\overline{AB} \cong \overline{CD}$

Proof 18. Given: $\overline{JK} \parallel \overline{QP}$, $\overline{JK} \cong \overline{PQ}$

Prove: $\overline{KQ}$ bisects $\overline{JP}$.

19. Designs Rangoli is a colorful design pattern drawn outside houses in India, especially during festivals. Vina plans to use the pattern at the right as the base of her design. In this pattern, $\overline{RU}$, $\overline{SV}$, and $\overline{QT}$ bisect each other at O. $RS = 6$, $\overline{RU} = 12$, $\overline{RU} \cong \overline{SV}$, $\overline{ST} \parallel \overline{RU}$, and $\overline{RS} \parallel \overline{QT}$. What is the perimeter of the hexagon?

C Challenge

In the diagram below, $\overline{BA} \cong \overline{KA}$ and $\overline{BE} \cong \overline{KE}$.

Proof 20. Prove: S is the midpoint of $\overline{BK}$.

Proof 21. Prove: $\overline{BK} \perp \overline{AE}$

Paper-Folding Conjectures

G.CO.12 Make formal geometric constructions with a variety of tools and methods (. . . paper folding . . .). Also prepares for **G.CO.10**

Isosceles triangles have two congruent sides. Folding one of the sides onto the other will suggest another important property of isosceles triangles.

Activity 1

Step 1 Construct an isosceles $\triangle ABC$ on tracing paper, with $\overline{AC} \cong \overline{BC}$.

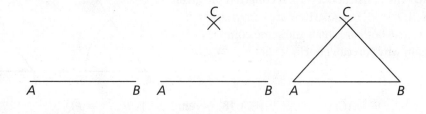

Step 2 Fold the paper so the two congruent sides fit exactly one on top of the other. Crease the paper. Label the intersection of the fold line and $\overline{AB}$ as point D.

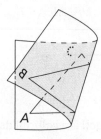

1. What do you notice about $\angle A$ and $\angle B$? Compare your results with others. Make a conjecture about the angles opposite the congruent sides in an isosceles triangle.

2. a. Study the fold line $\overline{CD}$ and the base $\overline{AB}$. What type of angles are $\angle CDA$ and $\angle CDB$? How do $\overline{AD}$ and $\overline{BD}$ seem to be related?

b. Use your answers to part (a) to complete the conjecture: The fold line $\overline{CD}$ is

the _____ of the base $\overline{AB}$ of isosceles $\triangle ABC$.

Activity 2

In Activity 1, you made a conjecture about angles opposite the congruent sides of a triangle. You can also fold paper to study whether the converse is true.

Step 1 On tracing paper, draw acute angle F and one side $\overline{FG}$. Construct $\angle G$ as shown, so that $\angle G \cong \angle F$.

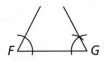

Step 2 Fold the paper so $\angle F$ and $\angle G$ fit exactly one on top of the other.

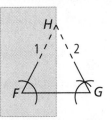

3. Why do sides 1 and 2 meet at point H on the fold line? Make a conjecture about sides $\overline{FH}$ and $\overline{GH}$ opposite congruent angles in a triangle.

4. Write your conjectures from Questions 1 and 3 as a biconditional.

3-5 Isosceles and Equilateral Triangles

G.CO.10 Prove theorems about triangles . . . base angles of isosceles triangles are congruent . . . Also **G.CO.13, G.SRT.5**

Objective To use and apply properties of isosceles and equilateral triangles

Solve It! Write your solution to the Solve It in the space below.

In the Solve It, you classified a triangle based on the lengths of its sides. You can also identify certain triangles based on information about their angles. In this lesson, you will learn how to use and apply properties of isosceles and equilateral triangles.

Essential Understanding The angles and sides of isosceles and equilateral triangles have special relationships.

Isosceles triangles are common in the real world. You can frequently see them in structures such as bridges and buildings, as well as in art and design. The congruent sides of an isosceles triangle are its **legs**. The third side is the **base**. The two congruent legs form the **vertex angle**. The other two angles are the **base angles**.

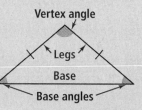

take note

Theorem 20 Isosceles Triangle Theorem

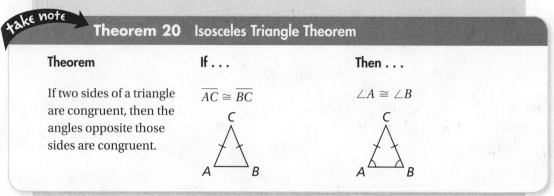

Theorem	If . . .	Then . . .
If two sides of a triangle are congruent, then the angles opposite those sides are congruent.	$\overline{AC} \cong \overline{BC}$	$\angle A \cong \angle B$

The proof of the Isosceles Triangle Theorem requires an auxiliary line.

Proof **Proof of Theorem 20: Isosceles Triangle Theorem**

Begin with isosceles $\triangle XYZ$ with $\overline{XY} \cong \overline{XZ}$. Draw $\overline{XB}$, the bisector of the vertex angle $\angle YXZ$.

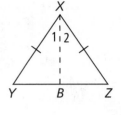

Given: $\overline{XY} \cong \overline{XZ}$, $\overline{XB}$ bisects $\angle YXZ$

Prove: $\angle Y \cong \angle Z$

Proof: $\overline{XY} \cong \overline{XZ}$ is given. By the definition of angle bisector, $\angle 1 \cong \angle 2$. By the Reflexive Property of Congruence, $\overline{XB} \cong \overline{XB}$. So by the SAS Postulate, $\triangle XYB \cong \triangle XZB$. $\angle Y \cong \angle Z$ since corresponding parts of congruent triangles are congruent.

Theorem 21   Converse of the Isosceles Triangle Theorem

Theorem	If . . .	Then . . .
If two angles of a triangle are congruent, then the sides opposite those angles are congruent.	$\angle A \cong \angle B$	$\overline{AC} \cong \overline{BC}$

You will prove Theorem 21 in Exercise 22.

Problem 1   **Using the Isosceles Triangle Theorems**

Got It?   **a.** Is $\angle WVS$ congruent to $\angle S$? Is $\overline{TR}$ congruent to $\overline{TS}$? Explain.

Think

What are you looking for in the diagram?

b. Reasoning Can you conclude that $\triangle RUV$ is isosceles? Explain.

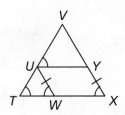

1. $\overline{VT} \cong$ _____

2. $\overline{UT} \cong$ _____ $\cong \overline{YX}$

3. $\overline{VU} \cong$ _____

4. $\angle VYU \cong$ _____

An isosceles triangle has a certain type of symmetry about a line through its vertex angle.

take note

Theorem 22

Theorem	**If . . .**	**Then . . .**
If a line bisects the vertex angle of an isosceles triangle, then the line is also the perpendicular bisector of the base.	$\overline{AC} \cong \overline{BC}$ and $\angle ACD \cong \angle BCD$	$\overline{CD} \perp \overline{AB}$ and $\overline{AD} \cong \overline{BD}$

You will prove Theorem 22 in Exercise 25.

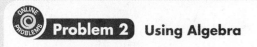

Problem 2 **Using Algebra**

Got It? Suppose $m\angle A = 27$. What is the value of x?

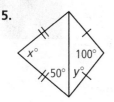

Think

How can you determine the measure of $\angle C$?

A Practice **Algebra** Find the values of x and y.

5.

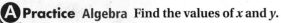

6.

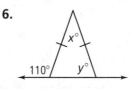

A **corollary** is a theorem that can be proved easily using another theorem. Since a corollary is a theorem, you can use it as a reason in a proof.

---

take note

Corollary to Theorem 20

Corollary

If a triangle is equilateral, then the triangle is equiangular.

If . . .

$\overline{XY} \cong \overline{YZ} \cong \overline{ZX}$

Then . . .

$\angle X \cong \angle Y \cong \angle Z$

Corollary to Theorem 21

Corollary

If a triangle is equiangular, then the triangle is equilateral.

If . . .

$\angle X \cong \angle Y \cong \angle Z$

Then . . .

$\overline{XY} \cong \overline{YZ} \cong \overline{ZX}$

Got It? Suppose the triangles in Problem 3 are isosceles triangles, where ∠ADE, ∠DEC, and ∠ECB are vertex angles. If the vertex angles each have a measure of 58, what are m∠A and m∠BCD?

 Practice **7.** The equilateral triangle and the isosceles triangle shown here share a common side. What is the measure of ∠ABC?

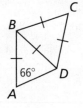

Lesson Check

Do you know HOW?

8. What is m∠A?

a.

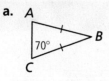

b.

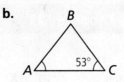

9. What is the value of *x*?

a.

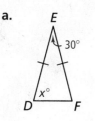

b.

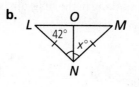

10. The measure of one base angle of an isosceles triangle is 23. What are the measures of the other two angles?

Do you UNDERSTAND?

11. What is the relationship between sides and angles for each type of triangle?

   a. isosceles

   b. equilateral

12. Error Analysis Claudia drew an isosceles triangle. She asked Sue to mark it. Explain why the marking of the diagram is incorrect.

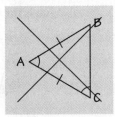

More Practice and Problem-Solving Exercises

B Apply

STEM **13. Architecture** Each face of the Great Pyramid at Giza is an isosceles triangle with a 76° vertex angle. What are the measures of the base angles?

14. Reasoning What are the measures of the base angles of a right isosceles triangle? Explain.

Given isosceles △JKL with base $\overline{JL}$, find each value.

15. If $m\angle L = 58$, then $m\angle LKJ = \underline{\ ?\ }$.

16. If $\overline{JL} = 5$, then $\overline{ML} = \underline{\ ?\ }$.

17. If $m\angle JKM = 48$, then $m\angle J = \underline{\ ?\ }$.

18. If $m\angle J = 55$, then $m\angle JKM = \underline{\ ?\ }$.

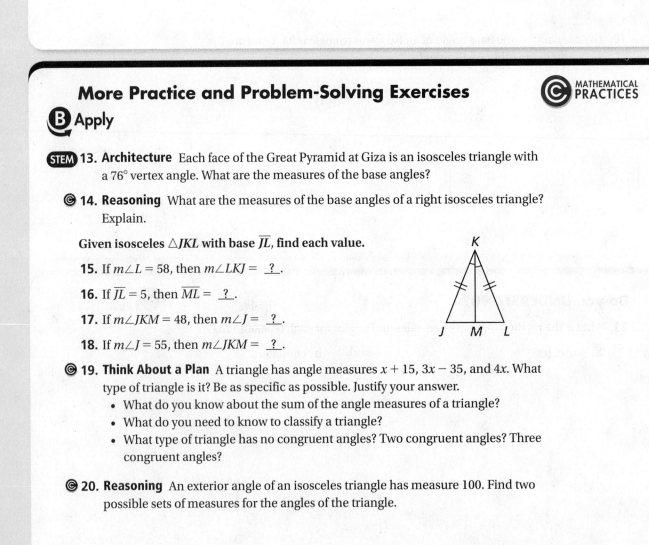

19. Think About a Plan A triangle has angle measures $x + 15$, $3x - 35$, and $4x$. What type of triangle is it? Be as specific as possible. Justify your answer.
- What do you know about the sum of the angle measures of a triangle?
- What do you need to know to classify a triangle?
- What type of triangle has no congruent angles? Two congruent angles? Three congruent angles?

20. Reasoning An exterior angle of an isosceles triangle has measure 100. Find two possible sets of measures for the angles of the triangle.

21. Developing Proof Here is another way to prove the Isosceles Triangle Theorem. Supply the missing information.

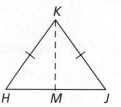

Begin with isosceles $\triangle HKJ$ with $\overline{KH} \cong \overline{KJ}$.

Draw **a.** ? , a bisector of the base $\overline{HJ}$.

Given: $\overline{KH} \cong \overline{KJ}$, **b.** ? bisects $\overline{HJ}$

Prove: $\angle H \cong \angle J$

Statements	Reasons
1) $\overline{KM}$ bisects $\overline{HJ}$.	1) **c.** ?
2) $\overline{HM} \cong \overline{JM}$	2) **d.** ?
3) $\overline{KH} \cong \overline{KJ}$	3) Given
4) $\overline{KM} \cong \overline{KM}$	4) **e.** ?
5) $\triangle KHM \cong \triangle KJM$	5) **f.** ?
6) $\angle H \cong \angle J$	6) **g.** ?

Proof **22.** Supply the missing information in this statement of the Converse of the Isosceles Triangle Theorem. Then write a proof.

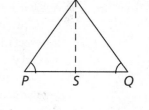

Begin with $\triangle PRQ$ with $\angle P \cong \angle Q$.

Draw **a.** ? , a bisector of $\angle PRQ$.

Given: $\angle P \cong \angle Q$, **b.** ? bisects $\angle PRQ$

Prove: $\overline{PR} \cong \overline{QR}$

23. Writing Explain how the corollaries to the Isosceles Triangle Theorem and its converse follow from the theorems.

Proof **24. Given:** $\overline{AE} \cong \overline{DE}$, $\overline{AB} \cong \overline{DC}$

Prove: $\triangle ABE \cong \triangle DCE$

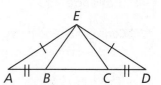

Proof **25.** Prove Theorem 22. Use the diagram given in the statement of the theorem.

STEM 26. a. Communications In the diagram at the right, what type of triangle is formed by the cables of the same height and the ground?

b. What are the two different base lengths of the triangles?

c. How is the tower related to each of the triangles?

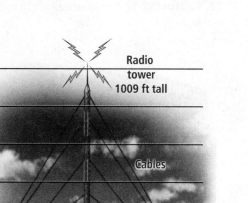

27. **Algebra** The length of the base of an isosceles triangle is x. The length of a leg is $2x - 5$. The perimeter of the triangle is 20. Find x.

28. **Constructions** Construct equiangular triangle ABC. Justify your method.

Algebra Find the values of m and n.

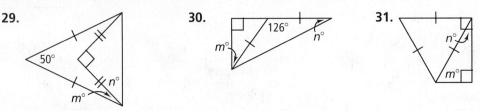

29.

30.

31.

32. **Constructions** A polygon is *inscribed in* a circle if the vertices of the polygon are on the circle. Given a circle and its center, construct a square inscribed in the circle. Justify your method by showing that the figure you inscribed is a quadrilateral with four right angles and four congruent sides.

33. **Constructions** Use a compass to draw a circle.
    a. Using the same compass setting, place the point of the compass on the circle and draw two arcs that intersect the circle.
    b. Again using the same compass setting, place the point of the compass on one of the two points of intersection from part (a) and draw two more arcs that intersect the original circle. Continue in this way until you have gone entirely around the original circle.
    c. Connect points of intersection of the arcs and the original circle. What regular polygon have you constructed? Explain.
    d. Use the construction from parts (a)–(c) to construct an equilateral triangle inscribed in a circle. Justify your construction.

Ⓒ Challenge

Coordinate Geometry For each pair of points, there are six points that could be the third vertex of an isosceles right triangle. Find the coordinates of each point.

34. $(4, 0)$ and $(0, 4)$ 35. $(0, 0)$ and $(5, 5)$ 36. $(2, 3)$ and $(5, 6)$

Ⓖ 37. **Reasoning** What measures are possible for the base angles of an acute isosceles triangle?

Congruence in Right Triangles

G.SRT.5 Use congruence . . . criteria . . . to solve problems and to prove relationships in geometric figures.
Also G.CO.10

Objective   To prove right triangles congruent using the Hypotenuse-Leg Theorem

Solve It!   Write your solution to the Solve It in the space below.

In the diagram below, two sides and a nonincluded angle of one triangle are congruent to two sides and the nonincluded angle of another triangle.

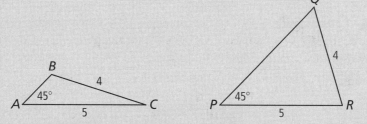

Notice that the triangles are not congruent. So, you can conclude that Side-Side-Angle is *not* a valid method for proving two triangles congruent. This method, however, works in the special case of right triangles, where the right angles are the nonincluded angles.

In a right triangle, the side opposite the right angle is called the **hypotenuse.** It is the longest side in the triangle. The other two sides are called **legs.**

> The right angle always "points" to the hypotenuse.

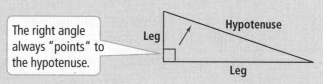

Essential Understanding You can prove that two triangles are congruent without having to show that *all* corresponding parts are congruent. In this lesson, you will prove right triangles congruent by using one pair of right angles, a pair of hypotenuses, and a pair of legs.

Theorem 23 Hypotenuse-Leg (HL) Theorem

Theorem	If . . .	Then . . .
If the hypotenuse and a leg of one right triangle are congruent to the hypotenuse and a leg of another right triangle, then the triangles are congruent.	$\triangle PQR$ and $\triangle XYZ$ are right $\triangle$, $\overline{PR} \cong \overline{XZ}$, and $\overline{PQ} \cong \overline{XY}$	$\triangle PQR \cong \triangle XYZ$

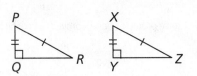

To prove the HL Theorem you will need to draw auxiliary lines to make a third triangle.

Proof Proof of Theorem 23: Hypotenuse-Leg Theorem

Given: $\triangle PQR$ and $\triangle XYZ$ are right triangles, with right angles Q and Y. $\overline{PR} \cong \overline{XZ}$ and $\overline{PQ} \cong \overline{XY}$.

Prove: $\triangle PQR \cong \triangle XYZ$

Proof: On $\triangle XYZ$, draw $\overrightarrow{ZY}$.

Mark point S so that $YS = QR$. Then, $\triangle PQR \cong \triangle XYS$ by SAS.

Since corresponding parts of congruent triangles are congruent, $\overline{PR} \cong \overline{XS}$. It is given that $\overline{PR} \cong \overline{XZ}$, so $\overline{XS} \cong \overline{XZ}$ by the Transitive Property of Congruence. By the Isosceles Triangle Theorem, $\angle S \cong \angle Z$, so $\triangle XYS \cong \triangle XYZ$ by AAS. Therefore, $\triangle PQR \cong \triangle XYZ$ by the Transitive Property of Congruence.

Key Concept Conditions for HL Theorem

To use the HL Theorem, the triangles must meet three conditions.

Conditions

- There are two right triangles.
- The triangles have congruent hypotenuses.
- There is one pair of congruent legs.

Problem 1 Using the HL Theorem

Got It? **a. Given:** ∠*PRS* and ∠*RPQ* are right angles, $\overline{SP} \cong \overline{QR}$

Prove: △*PRS* ≅ △*RPQ*

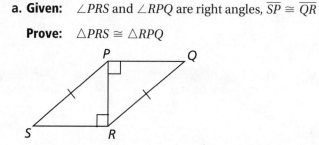

ⓒ b. Reasoning Your friend says, "Suppose you have two right triangles with congruent hypotenuses and one pair of congruent legs. It does not matter which leg in the first triangle is congruent to which leg in the second triangle. The triangles will be congruent." Is your friend correct? Explain.

A Practice   **1. Developing Proof** Complete the flow proof.

Given: $\overline{PS} \cong \overline{PT}$, $\angle PRS \cong \angle PRT$

Prove: $\triangle PRS \cong \triangle PRT$

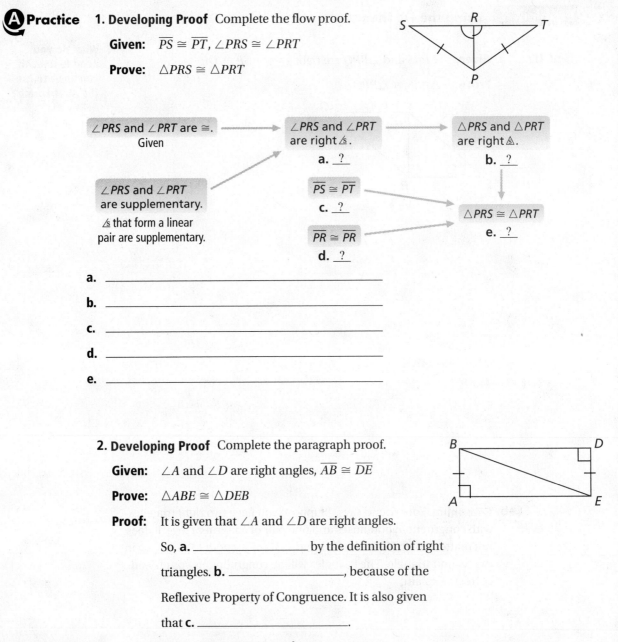

| ∠PRS and ∠PRT are ≅. Given |

| ∠PRS and ∠PRT are right ∡. a. _?_ |

| △PRS and △PRT are right ▲. b. _?_ |

| ∠PRS and ∠PRT are supplementary. ∡ that form a linear pair are supplementary. |

| $\overline{PS} \cong \overline{PT}$ c. _?_ |

| $\overline{PR} \cong \overline{PR}$ d. _?_ |

| △PRS ≅ △PRT e. _?_ |

a. _____

b. _____

c. _____

d. _____

e. _____

2. Developing Proof Complete the paragraph proof.

Given: $\angle A$ and $\angle D$ are right angles, $\overline{AB} \cong \overline{DE}$

Prove: $\triangle ABE \cong \triangle DEB$

Proof: It is given that $\angle A$ and $\angle D$ are right angles.

So, **a.** _____ by the definition of right

triangles. **b.** _____, because of the

Reflexive Property of Congruence. It is also given

that **c.** _____.

So, $\triangle ABE \cong \triangle DEB$ by **d.** _____.

Problem 2   **Writing a Proof Using the HL Theorem**

Got It?   **Given:** $\overline{CD} \cong \overline{EA}$, $\overline{AD}$ is the perpendicular bisector of $\overline{CE}$

Prove: $\triangle CBD \cong \triangle EBA$

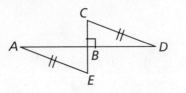

Think

What can you conclude if $\overline{AD}$ is the perpendicular bisector of $\overline{CE}$?

A Practice 3. **Given:** $\overline{HV} \perp \overline{GT}$, $\overline{GH} \cong \overline{TV}$, I is the midpoint of $\overline{HV}$

Proof **Prove:** $\triangle IGH \cong \triangle ITV$

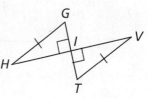

Proof 4. **Given:** $\overline{PM} \cong \overline{RJ}$, $\overline{PT} \perp \overline{TJ}$, $\overline{RM} \perp \overline{TJ}$, M is the midpoint of $\overline{TJ}$.

Prove: $\triangle PTM \cong \triangle RMJ$

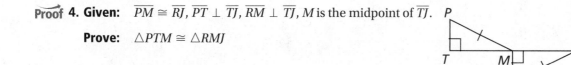

Lesson Check

Do you know HOW?

For Exercises 5–8, determine whether the two triangles are congruent. If so, write the congruence statement.

5.

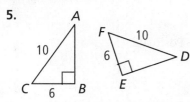

6.

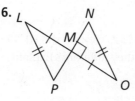

7.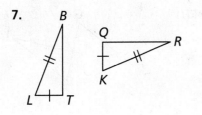

8.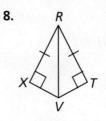

Do you UNDERSTAND?

 MATHEMATICAL PRACTICES

© **9. Vocabulary** A right triangle has side lengths of 5 cm, 12 cm, and 13 cm. What is the length of the hypotenuse? How do you know?

© **10. Compare and Contrast** How do the HL Theorem and the SAS Postulate compare? How are they different? Explain.

11. Error Analysis Your classmate says that there is not enough information to determine whether the two triangles at the right are congruent. Is your classmate correct? Explain.

More Practice and Problem-Solving Exercises

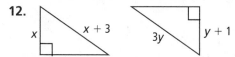

B Apply

Algebra For what values of x and y are the triangles congruent by HL?

12. x, $x + 3$, $3y$, $y + 1$

13. $3y + x$, $y - x$, $x + 5$, $y + 5$

14. Study Exercise 1. Can you prove that $\triangle PRS \cong \triangle PRT$ without using the HL Theorem? Explain.

15. Think About a Plan $\triangle ABC$ and $\triangle PQR$ are right triangular sections of a fire escape, as shown. Is each story of the building the same height? Explain.
- What can you tell from the diagram?
- How can you use congruent triangles here?

16. Writing "A HA!" exclaims your classmate. "There must be an HA Theorem, sort of like the HL Theorem!" Is your classmate correct? Explain.

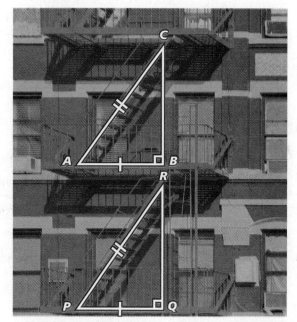

Proof 17. Given: $\overline{RS} \cong \overline{TU}$, $\overline{RS} \perp \overline{ST}$, $\overline{TU} \perp \overline{UV}$,
T is the midpoint of $\overline{RV}$

Prove: $\triangle RST \cong \triangle TUV$

Proof 18. Given: $\triangle LNP$ is isosceles with base $\overline{NP}$,
$\overline{MN} \perp \overline{NL}$, $\overline{QP} \perp \overline{PL}$, $\overline{ML} \cong \overline{QL}$

Prove: $\triangle MNL \cong \triangle QPL$

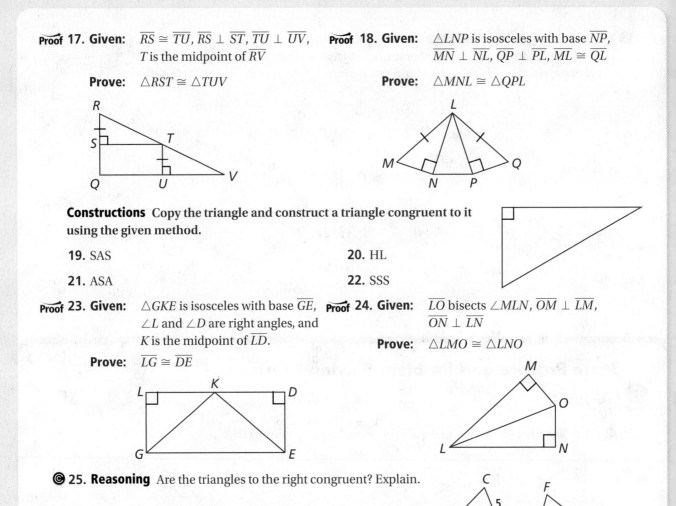

Constructions Copy the triangle and construct a triangle congruent to it using the given method.

19. SAS

20. HL

21. ASA

22. SSS

Proof 23. Given: $\triangle GKE$ is isosceles with base $\overline{GE}$,
$\angle L$ and $\angle D$ are right angles, and
K is the midpoint of $\overline{LD}$.

Prove: $\overline{LG} \cong \overline{DE}$

Proof 24. Given: $\overline{LO}$ bisects $\angle MLN$, $\overline{OM} \perp \overline{LM}$,
$\overline{ON} \perp \overline{LN}$

Prove: $\triangle LMO \cong \triangle LNO$

© **25. Reasoning** Are the triangles to the right congruent? Explain.

26. a. Coordinate Geometry Graph the points
$A(-5, 6)$, $B(1, 3)$, $D(-8, 0)$, and $E(-2, -3)$.
Draw $\overline{AB}$, $\overline{AE}$, $\overline{BD}$, and $\overline{DE}$. Label point C,
the intersection of $\overline{AE}$ and $\overline{BD}$.
  b. Find the slopes of $\overline{AE}$ and $\overline{BD}$. How would you
  describe $\angle ACB$ and $\angle ECD$?
  c. Algebra Write equations for $\overleftrightarrow{AE}$ and $\overleftrightarrow{BD}$. What are the coordinates of C?
  d. Use the Distance Formula to find AB, BC, DC, and DE.
  e. Write a paragraph to prove that $\triangle ABC \cong \triangle EDC$.

© **Challenge**

Geometry in 3 Dimensions For Exercises 27 and 28, use the figure at the right.

Proof 27. Given: $\overline{BE} \perp \overline{EA}$, $\overline{BE} \perp \overline{EC}$, $\triangle ABC$ is equilateral

Prove: $\triangle AEB \cong \triangle CEB$

28. Given: $\triangle AEB \cong \triangle CEB$, $\overline{BE} \perp \overline{EA}$, $\overline{BE} \perp \overline{EC}$
Can you prove that $\triangle ABC$ is equilateral? Explain.

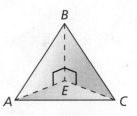

Congruence in Overlapping Triangles

G.SRT.5 Use congruence . . . criteria . . . to solve problems and to prove relationships in geometric figures. Also **G.CO.10**

Objectives To identify congruent overlapping triangles
To prove two triangles congruent using other congruent triangles

 Solve It! Write your solution to the Solve It in the space below.

In the Solve It, you located individual triangles among a jumble of triangles. Some triangle relationships are difficult to see because the triangles overlap.

Essential Understanding You can sometimes use the congruent corresponding parts of one pair of congruent triangles to prove another pair of triangles congruent. This often involves overlapping triangles.

Overlapping triangles may have a common side or angle. You can simplify your work with overlapping triangles by separating and redrawing the triangles.

Problem 1 **Identifying Common Parts**

Got It? **a.** What is the common side in △ABD and △DCA?

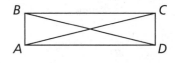

b. What is the common side in △ABD and △BAC?

Practice   **1.** In the diagram, the red and blue triangles are congruent. Identify the common side or angle.

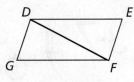

2. Separate and redraw $\triangle JKL$ and $\triangle MLK$. Identify any common angles or sides.

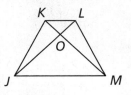

Problem 2   **Using Common Parts**

Got It?   **Given:** $\triangle CAB \cong \triangle BDC$

Prove: $\overline{CE} \cong \overline{BE}$

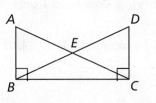

3. Developing Proof Complete the flow proof.

Given: $\angle T \cong \angle R$, $\overline{PQ} \cong \overline{PV}$

Prove: $\angle PQT \cong \angle PVR$

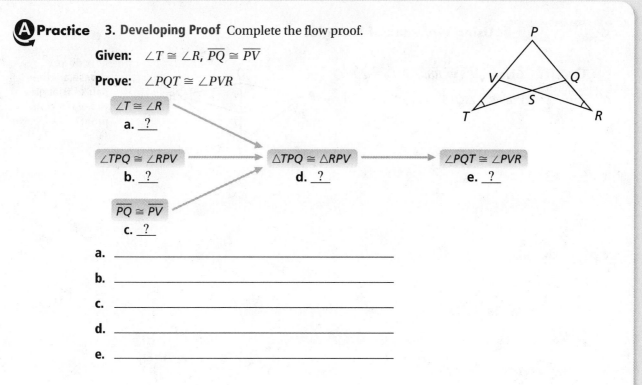

$\angle T \cong \angle R$
a. ?

$\angle TPQ \cong \angle RPV$ $\triangle TPQ \cong \triangle RPV$ $\angle PQT \cong \angle PVR$
b. ?   d. ?   e. ?

$\overline{PQ} \cong \overline{PV}$
c. ?

a. _____

b. _____

c. _____

d. _____

e. _____

Proof 4. Given: $\overline{QD} \cong \overline{UA}$, $\angle QDA \cong \angle UAD$

Prove: $\triangle QDA \cong \triangle UAD$

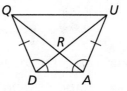

Problem 3 Using Two Pairs of Triangles

Got It? **Given:** $\overline{PS} \cong \overline{RS}$, $\angle PSQ \cong \angle RSQ$

Prove: $\triangle QPT \cong \triangle QRT$

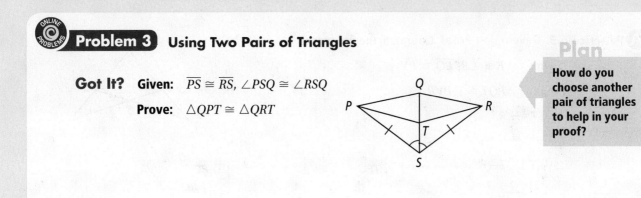

Plan

How do you choose another pair of triangles to help in your proof?

Ⓐ **Practice** **5. Given:** $\overline{AD} \cong \overline{ED}$, D is the midpoint of $\overline{BF}$

Proof **Prove:** $\triangle ADC \cong \triangle EDG$

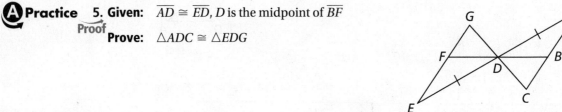

When several triangles overlap and you need to use one pair of congruent triangles to prove another pair congruent, you may find it helpful to draw a diagram of each pair of triangles.

Problem 4 **Separating Overlapping Triangles**

Got It? **Given:** $\angle CAD \cong \angle EAD$, $\angle C \cong \angle E$

Prove: $\overline{BD} \cong \overline{FD}$

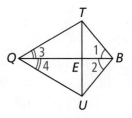

Plan

Which triangles are useful here?

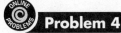**Practice** **6. Given:** $\angle 1 \cong \angle 2$, $\angle 3 \cong \angle 4$

Proof **Prove:** $\triangle QET \cong \triangle QEU$

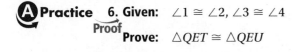

Lesson Check

Do you know HOW?

Identify any common angles or sides.

7. △MKJ and △LJK

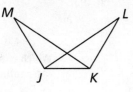

8. △DEH and △DFG

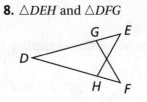

Separate and redraw the overlapping triangles. Label the vertices.

9.

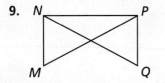

10.

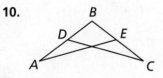

Do you UNDERSTAND?

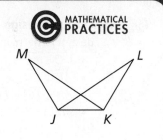

11. Reasoning In Exercise 7, both triangles have vertices *J* and *K*. Are $\angle J$ and $\angle K$ common angles for $\triangle MKJ$ and $\triangle LJK$? Explain.

12. Error Analysis In the diagram, $\triangle PSY \cong \triangle SPL$. Based on that fact, your friend claims that $\triangle PRL$ is not congruent to $\triangle SRY$. Explain why your friend is incorrect.

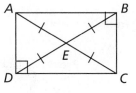

13. In the figure at the right, which pair of triangles could you prove congruent first in order to prove that $\triangle ACD \cong \triangle CAB$? Explain.

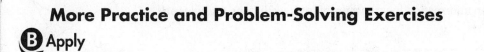

More Practice and Problem-Solving Exercises

B Apply

14. Think About a Plan In the diagram at the right, $\angle V \cong \angle S$, $\overline{VU} \cong \overline{ST}$, and $\overline{PS} \cong \overline{QV}$. Which two triangles are congruent by SAS? Explain.
- How can you use a new diagram to help you identify the triangles?
- What do you need to prove triangles congruent by SAS?

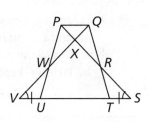

STEM **15. Clothing Design** The figure at the right is part of a clothing design pattern, and it has the following relationships.

- $\overline{GC} \perp \overline{AC}$
- $\overline{AB} \perp \overline{BC}$
- $\overline{AB} \parallel \overline{DE} \parallel \overline{FG}$
- $m\angle A = 50$
- $\triangle DEC$ is isosceles with base $\overline{DC}$.

a. Find the measures of all the numbered angles in the figure.
b. Suppose $\overline{AB} \cong \overline{FC}$. Name two congruent triangles and explain how you can prove them congruent.

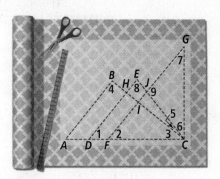

Proof **16. Given:** $\overline{AC} \cong \overline{EC}$, $\overline{CB} \cong \overline{CD}$

Prove: $\angle A \cong \angle E$

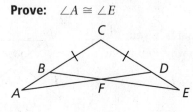

Proof **17. Given:** $\overline{QT} \perp \overline{PR}$, $\overline{QT}$ bisects $\overline{PR}$, $\overline{QT}$ bisects $\angle VQS$

Prove: $\overline{VQ} \cong \overline{SQ}$

@ **Open-Ended** Draw the diagram described.

18. Draw a vertical segment on your paper. On the right side of the segment draw two triangles that share the vertical segment as a common side.

19. Draw two triangles that have a common angle.

Proof **20. Given:** $\overline{TE} \cong \overline{RI}$, $\overline{TI} \cong \overline{RE}$, $\angle TDI$ and $\angle ROE$ are right $\triangle$

Prove: $\overline{TD} \cong \overline{RO}$

Proof **21. Given:** $\overline{AB} \perp \overline{BC}$, $\overline{DC} \perp \overline{BC}$, $\overline{AC} \cong \overline{DB}$

Prove: $\overline{AE} \cong \overline{DE}$

C Challenge

22. Identify a pair of overlapping congruent triangles in the diagram at the right. Then use the given information to write a proof to show that the triangles are congruent.

Given: $\overline{AC} \cong \overline{BC}$, $\angle A \cong \angle B$

@ **23. Reasoning** Draw a quadrilateral $ABCD$ with $\overline{AB} \parallel \overline{DC}$, $\overline{AD} \parallel \overline{BC}$, and diagonals $\overline{AC}$ and $\overline{DB}$ intersecting at E. Label your diagram to indicate the parallel sides.
a. List all the pairs of congruent segments in your diagram.
b. **Writing** Explain how you know that the segments you listed are congruent.

LESSON LAB

Use With Lesson 3-8

Review of Transformations

G.CO.6 Use geometric descriptions of rigid motions to transform figures . . .

Recall that a transformation of a geometric figure is a function, or *mapping*, that results in a change in the position, shape, or size of the figure. The original figure is called the *preimage* and the result of the transformation is the *image*. A special kind of transformation that preserves distance is a *rigid motion*, or *isometry*. Translations, reflections, and rotations are examples of rigid motions.

Example 1

What is a rule that describes the transformation that maps $\triangle ABC$ onto $\triangle A'B'C'$?

Find the vertices of the preimage $\triangle ABC$ and the image $\triangle A'B'C'$.

Preimage:	$A(-6, 2)$	Image:	$A'(2, 0)$
	$B(-4, -3)$		$B'(4, -5)$
	$C(-2, 1)$		$C'(6, -1)$

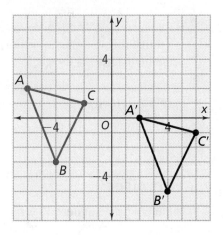

If you add 8 to each x-coordinate of the preimage and subtract 2 from each y-coordinate, the results are of the vertices of the image. This is an example of a translation. A translation is a transformation that maps all points of a figure the same distance in the same direction.

This translation is written using the function notation $T_{<8,-2>}(\triangle ABC) = \triangle A'B'C'$.

Example 2

What is a rule that describes the transformation that maps trapezoid $STUV$ onto trapezoid $S'T'U'V'$?

Find the vertices of the preimage $STUV$ and the image $S'T'U'V'$.

Preimage:	$S(7, 6)$	Image:	$S'(7, -6)$
	$T(8, 2)$		$T'(8, -2)$
	$U(1, 2)$		$U'(1, -2)$
	$V(3, 6)$		$V'(3, -6)$

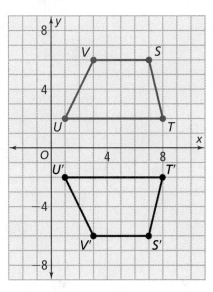

The vertices of the preimage and image have the same x-coordinates and opposite y-coordinates. Each vertex of the preimage is the same distance from the x-axis as the corresponding vertex of the image. This is an example of a reflection.

This reflection is written using function notation as $R_{x\text{-axis}}(STUV) = S'T'U'V'$.

Example 3

What is a rule that describes the transformation that maps △MNP onto △M'N'P'?

Find the vertices of the preimage △MNP and the image △M'N'P'.

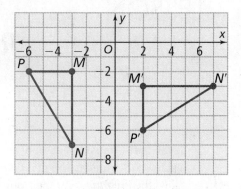

Preimage: $M(-3, -2)$ Image: $M'(2, -3)$
             $N(-3, -7)$ $N'(7, -3)$
             $P(-6, -2)$ $P'(2, -6)$

Each vertex (x, y) of the preimage is mapped to $(-y, x)$. Notice that the distance from the origin to each vertex of the preimage and each corresponding vertex of the image is the same. △MNP has been *turned* about the origin to form △M'N'P'. A rotation is a transformation that turns the preimage about a fixed point, called the center of rotation, to form the image.

In this Example, △MNP has been rotated 90° counterclockwise about the origin to form △M'N'P'. This rotation is written using function notation as $r_{(90°, O)}(△MNP) = △M'N'P'$.

Exercises

What is a rule that describes the transformation from each preimage onto each image?

1.
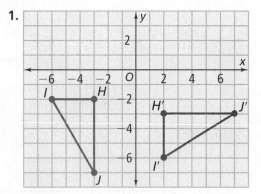

2.
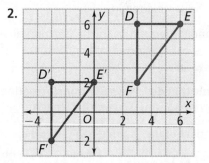

Sketch each preimage and image.

3. △*ABC* has vertices *A*(3, −6), *B*(1, 0), *C*(5, 2); $T_{<-5, 4>}(\triangle ABC)$

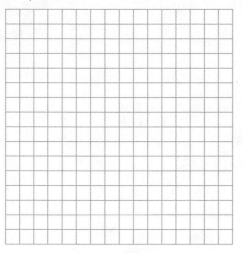

4. △*DEF* has vertices *D*(−7, 2), *E*(−2, 5), *F*(−3, −3); $R_{y\text{-axis}}(\triangle DEF)$

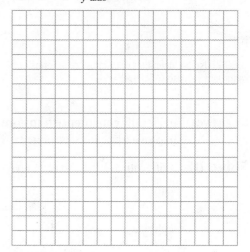

5. △*GHI* has vertices *G*(2, −4), *H*(4, −3), *I*(7, −6); $r_{(270°, O)}(\triangle GHI)$

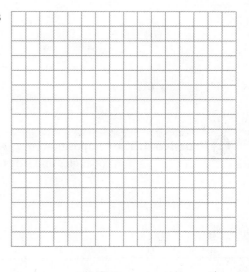

6. Recall that you can write the composition of rigid motions that describes a translation of quadrilateral *GHJK* 2 units left and 3 units up, followed by a reflection across the *x*-axis as $(R_{x\text{-axis}} \circ T_{<-2,3>})(GHJK)$. *GHJK* has vertices *G*(0, 2), *H*(1, −1), *J*(3, −3), and *K*(3, 1). Sketch *GHJK* and $(R_{x\text{-axis}} \circ T_{<-2,3>})(GHJK)$.

G.CO.7 Use the definition of congruence in terms of rigid motions to show that two triangles are congruent . . . Also **G.CO.6, G.CO.8**

Objectives To identify congruence transformations
To prove triangle congruence using isometries

Solve It! Write your solution to the Solve It in the space below.

In the Solve It, you may have used the properties of rigid motions to describe why the wings are identical.

Essential Understanding You can use compositions of rigid motions to understand congruence.

Problem 1 Identifying Equal Measures

Got It? The composition $(R_t \circ T_{<2,\,3>})(\triangle ABC) = \triangle XYZ$. List all of the pairs of angles and sides with equal measures.

Practice 1. The composition $(r_{(180°,O)} \circ T_{<-4,-6>})(\triangle HJK) = \triangle PRS$. List all of the pairs of angles and sides with equal measures.

In Problem 1 you saw that compositions of rigid motions preserve corresponding side lengths and angle measures. This suggests another way to define congruence.

take note

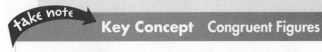

Key Concept Congruent Figures

Two figures are **congruent** if and only if there is a sequence of one or more rigid motions that maps one figure onto the other.

Problem 2 Identifying Congruent Figures

Got It? Which pairs of figures in the grid are congruent? For each pair, what is a sequence of rigid motions that maps one figure to the other?

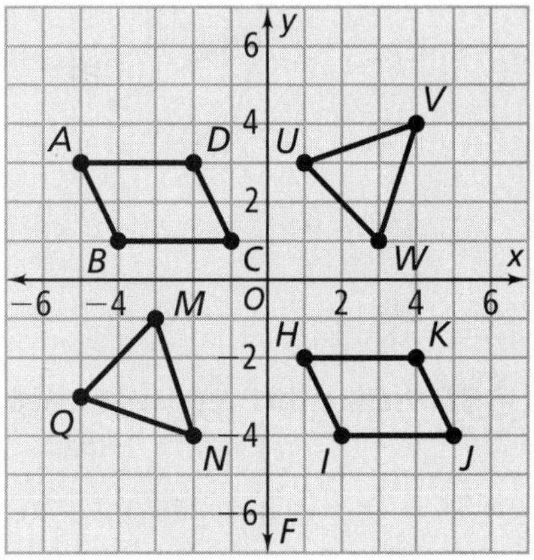

Practice For each coordinate grid, identify a pair of congruent figures. Then determine a congruence transformation that maps the preimage to the congruent image.

2.

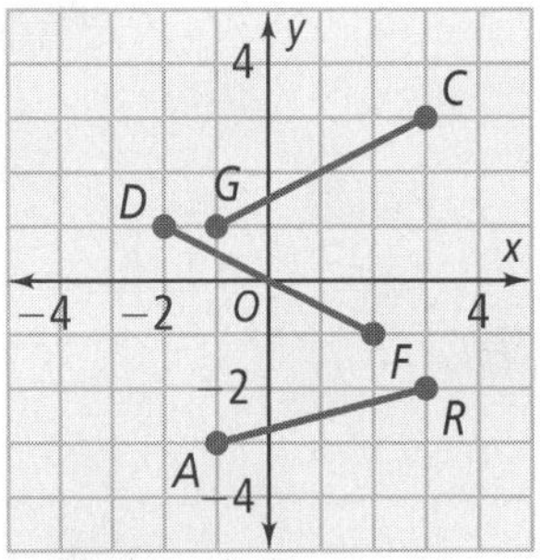

3.

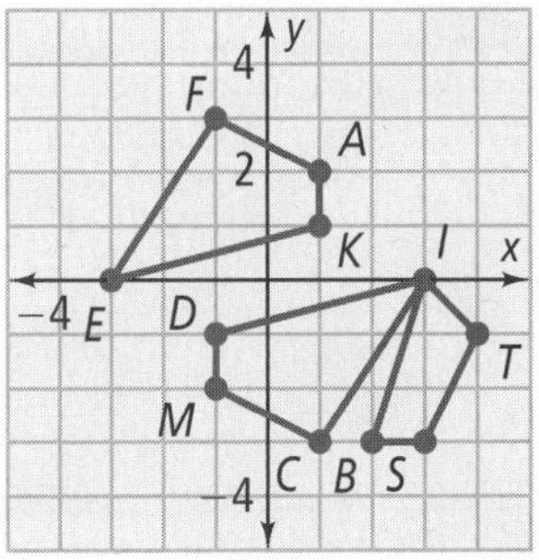

Because compositions of rigid motions take figures to congruent figures, they are also called **congruence transformations**.

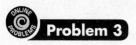

Problem 3 Identifying Congruence Transformations

Got It? What is a congruence transformation that maps △NAV to △BCY?

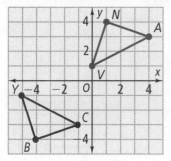

Think
What does the orientation of the triangles tell you?

Ⓐ Practice In Exercises 4 and 5, find a congruence transformation that maps △LMN to △RST.

4.

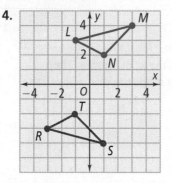

5.

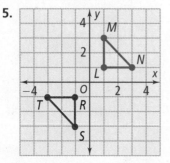

Earlier in this chapter, you studied triangle congruence postulates and theorems. You can use congruence transformations to justify criteria for determining triangle congruence.

Problem 4   Verifying the SAS Postulate

Think

How do you show that the two triangles are congruent?

Got It?   Verify the SSS postulate.

Given: $\overline{TD} = \overline{EN}$, $\overline{YT} = \overline{SE}$, $\overline{YD} = \overline{SN}$
Prove: $\triangle YDT \cong \triangle SNE$

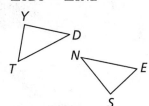

Ⓐ Practice   6. Verify the ASA Postulate for triangle congruence by using congruence
Proof transformations.

Given: $\overline{EK} \cong \overline{LH}$ **Prove:** $\triangle EKS \cong \triangle HLA$
$\quad\quad\quad\angle E \cong \angle H$
$\quad\quad\quad\angle K \cong \angle L$

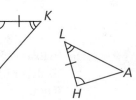

Proof 7. Verify the AAS Postulate for triangle congruence by using congruence transformations.

Given: $\angle I \cong \angle V$
$\angle C \cong \angle N$
$\overline{QC} \cong \overline{NZ}$

Prove: $\triangle NVZ \cong \triangle CIQ$

In Problem 4, you used the transformational approach to prove triangle congruence. Because this approach is more general, you can use what you know about congruence transformations to determine whether any two figures are congruent.

Problem 5 Determining Congruence

Got It? Are the figures shown at the right congruent? Explain.

Practice In Exercises 8 and 9, determine whether the figures are congruent. If so, describe a congruence transformation that maps one to the other. If not, explain.

8.

9.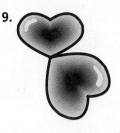

Lesson Check

Do you know HOW?

Use the graph for Exercises 10 and 11.

10. Identify a pair of congruent figures and write a congruence statement.

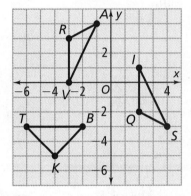

11. What is a congruence transformation that relates two congruent figures?

Do you UNDERSTAND?

12. How can the definition of congruence in terms of rigid motions be more useful than a definition of congruence that relies on corresponding angles and sides?

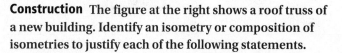

13. Reasoning Is a composition of a rotation followed by a glide reflection a congruence transformation? Explain.

14. Open-Ended What is an example of a board game in which a game piece is moved by using a congruence transformation?

More Practice and Problem-Solving Exercises

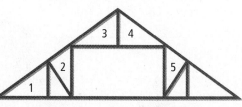

B Apply

Construction The figure at the right shows a roof truss of a new building. Identify an isometry or composition of isometries to justify each of the following statements.

15. Triangle 1 is congruent to triangle 3.

16. Triangle 1 is congruent to triangle 4.

17. Triangle 2 is congruent to triangle 5.

18. Vocabulary If two figures are ___?___, then there is an isometry that maps one figure onto the other.

19. Think About a Plan The figure at the right shows two congruent, isosceles triangles. What are four different isometries that map the top triangle onto the bottom triangle?
- How can you use the three basic rigid motions to map the top triangle onto the bottom triangle?
- What other isometries can you use?

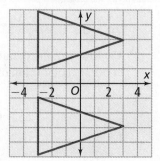

20. **Graphic Design** Most companies have a logo that is used on company letterhead and signs. A graphic designer sketched the logo at the right. What congruence transformations might she have used to draw this logo?

21. **Art** Artists frequently use congruence transformations in their work. The artworks shown below are called *tessellations*. What types of congruence transformations can you identify in the tessellations?

a.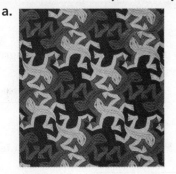

b.

22. In the footprints shown below, what congruence transformations can you use to extend the footsteps?

Proof 23. Prove the statements in parts (a) and (b) to show congruence in terms of transformations is equivalent to the criteria for triangle congruence you learned earlier in this chapter.

a. If there is a congruence transformation that maps $\triangle ABC$ to $\triangle DEF$ then corresponding pairs of sides and corresponding pairs of angles are congruent.

b. In $\triangle ABC$ and $\triangle DEF$, if corresponding pairs of sides and corresponding pairs of angles are congruent, then there is a congruence transformation that maps $\triangle ABC$ to $\triangle DEF$.

24. **Baking** Cookie makers often use a cookie press so that the cookies all look the same. The baker fills a cookie sheet for baking in the pattern shown. What types of congruence transformations are being used to set each cookie on the sheet?

Proof 25. Use congruence transformations to prove the Isosceles Triangle Theorem.
   Given: $\overline{FG} \cong \overline{FH}$
   Prove: $\angle G \cong \angle H$

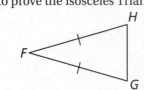

C Challenge

26. **Reasoning** You project an image for viewing in a large classroom. Is the projection of the image an example of a congruence transformation? Explain your reasoning.

MathXL® for School
Go to pearsonsuccessnet.com

3-1 Congruent Figures

Quick Review

Congruent polygons have congruent corresponding parts. When you name congruent polygons, always list corresponding vertices in the same order.

Example

HIJK ≅ PQRS. Write all possible congruence statements.

The order of the parts in the congruence statement tells you which parts correspond.

Sides: $\overline{HI} \cong \overline{PQ}$, $\overline{IJ} \cong \overline{QR}$, $\overline{JK} \cong \overline{RS}$, $\overline{KH} \cong \overline{SP}$

Angles: $\angle H \cong \angle P$, $\angle I \cong \angle Q$, $\angle J \cong \angle R$, $\angle K \cong \angle S$

Exercises

RSTUV ≅ KLMNO. Complete the congruence statements.

1. $\overline{TS} \cong$ _?_
2. $\angle N \cong$ _?_
3. $\overline{LM} \cong$ _?_
4. *VUTSR ≅* _?_

WXYZ ≅ PQRS. Find each measure or length.

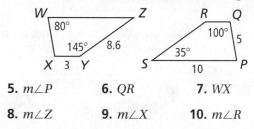

5. $m\angle P$
6. QR
7. WX
8. $m\angle Z$
9. $m\angle X$
10. $m\angle R$

3-2 and 3-3 Triangle Congruence by SSS, SAS, ASA, and AAS

Quick Review

You can prove triangles congruent with limited information about their congruent sides and angles.

Postulate or Theorem	You Need
Side-Side-Side (SSS)	three sides
Side-Angle-Side (SAS)	two sides and an included angle
Angle-Side-Angle (ASA)	two angles and an included side
Angle-Angle-Side (AAS)	two angles and a nonincluded side

Example

What postulate would you use to prove the triangles congruent?

You know that three pairs of sides are congruent. Use SSS.

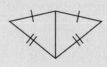

Exercises

11. In △HFD, what angle is included between $\overline{DH}$ and $\overline{DF}$?

12. In △OMR, what side is included between $\angle M$ and $\angle R$?

Which postulate or theorem, if any, could you use to prove the two triangles congruent? If there is not enough information to prove the triangles congruent, write *not enough information*.

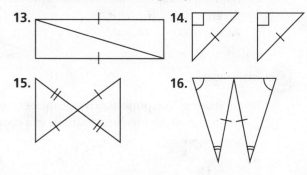

13.
14.
15.
16.

3-4 Using Corresponding Parts of Congruent Triangles

Quick Review

Once you know that triangles are congruent, you can make conclusions about corresponding sides and angles because, by definition, corresponding parts of congruent triangles are congruent. You can use congruent triangles in the proofs of many theorems.

Example

How can you use congruent triangles to prove $\angle Q \cong \angle D$?

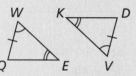

Since $\triangle QWE \cong \triangle DVK$ by AAS, you know that $\angle Q \cong \angle D$ because corresponding parts of congruent triangles are congruent.

Exercises

How can you use congruent triangles to prove the statement true?

17. $\overline{TV} \cong \overline{YW}$

18. $\overline{BE} \cong \overline{DE}$

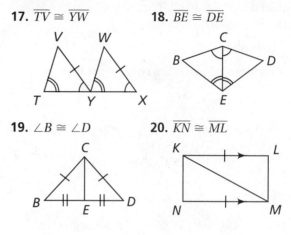

19. $\angle B \cong \angle D$

20. $\overline{KN} \cong \overline{ML}$

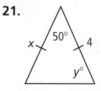
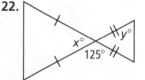

3-5 Isosceles and Equilateral Triangles

Quick Review

If two sides of a triangle are congruent, then the angles opposite those sides are also congruent by the **Isosceles Triangle Theorem.** If two angles of a triangle are congruent, then the sides opposite the angle are congruent by the **Converse of the Isosceles Triangle Theorem.**

Equilateral triangles are also equiangular.

Example

What is $m\angle G$?

Since $\overline{EF} \cong \overline{EG}$, $\angle F \cong \angle G$ by the Isosceles Triangle Theorem. So $m\angle G = 30$.

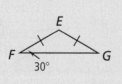

Exercises

Algebra Find the values of x and y.

21.

22.

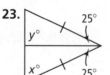

23.

24.

3-6 Congruence in Right Triangles

Quick Review

If the hypotenuse and a leg of one right triangle are congruent to the hypotenuse and a leg of another right triangle, then the triangles are congruent by the **Hypotenuse-Leg (HL) Theorem.**

Example

Which two triangles are congruent? Explain.

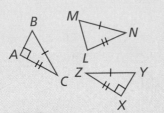

Since $\triangle ABC$ and $\triangle XYZ$ are right triangles with congruent legs, and $\overline{BC} \cong \overline{YZ}$, $\triangle ABC \cong \triangle XYZ$ by HL.

Exercises

Write a proof for each of the following.

25. Given: $\overline{LN} \perp \overline{KM}$, $\overline{KL} \cong \overline{ML}$
Prove: $\triangle KLN \cong \triangle MLN$

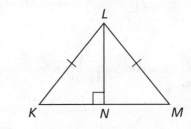

26. Given: $\overline{PS} \perp \overline{SQ}$, $\overline{RQ} \perp \overline{QS}$,
$\overline{PQ} \cong \overline{RS}$
Prove: $\triangle PSQ \cong \triangle RQS$

3-7 Congruence in Overlapping Triangles

Quick Review

To prove overlapping triangles congruent, you look for the common or shared sides and angles.

Example

Separate and redraw the overlapping triangles. Label the vertices.

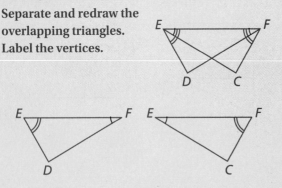

Exercises

Name a pair of overlapping congruent triangles in each diagram. State whether the triangles are congruent by SSS, SAS, ASA, AAS, or HL.

27.   28.

29.

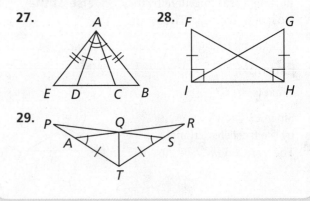

3-8 Congruence Transformations

Quick Review

Two figures are congruent if and only if there is a sequence of rigid motions that maps one figure onto the other.

Example

$R_{y\text{-axis}}(TGMB) = KWAV$. What are all of the congruent angles and all of the congruent sides?

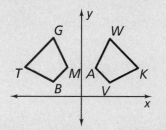

A reflection is a congruence transformation, so $TGMB \cong KWAV$, and corresponding angles and corresponding sides are congruent.

$\angle T \cong \angle K$, $\angle G \cong \angle W$, $\angle M \cong \angle A$, and $\angle B \cong \angle V$
$TG = KW$, $GM = WA$, $MB = AV$, and $TB = KV$

Exercises

30. In the diagram below, $\triangle LMN \cong \triangle XYZ$. Identify a congruence transformation that maps $\triangle LMN$ onto $\triangle XYZ$.

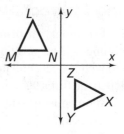

31. Fonts Graphic designers use some fonts because they have pleasing proportions or are easy to read from far away. The letters p and d above are used on a sign using a special font. Are the letters congruent? If so, describe a congruence transformation that maps one onto the other. If not, explain why not.

Pull It **All Together**

ASSESSMENT

Applying Indirect Measurement

Jamal wants to estimate the distance across a canyon, shown below. He locates a tree directly opposite his position at point *Y* and labels it point *X*. He then walks west along the canyon 500 feet and marks point *A*. After walking another 500 feet in the same direction, he turns 90° and walks south, perpendicular to the canyon. He stops when his location appears to form a straight line with points *A* and *X*. He measures the distance *BC* as 327 feet.

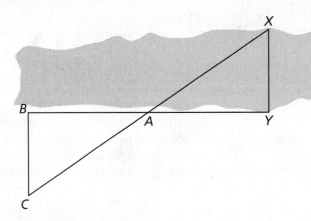

Task Description

Label the diagram above using the information given. Then estimate the distance across the canyon. Justify your answer.

- What part of the diagram represents the distance across the canyon?

- How are triangles *ABC* and *AYX* related?

Get Ready!

Basic Constructions

Use a compass and straightedge for each construction.

1. Construct the perpendicular bisector of a segment.

2. Construct the bisector of an angle.

The Midpoint Formula and Distance Formula

Find the coordinates of the midpoints of the sides of $\triangle ABC$. Then find the lengths of the three sides of the triangle.

3. $A(5, 1), B(-3, 3), C(1, -7)$

4. $A(-1, 2), B(9, 2), C(-1, 8)$

5. $A(-2, -3), B(2, -3), C(0, 3)$

Finding the Negation

Write the negation of each statement.

6. The team won.　　　**7.** It is not too late.　　　**8.** $m\angle R > 60$

Slope

Find the slope of the line passing through the given points.

9. $A(9, 6), B(8, 12)$　　　**10.** $C(3, -2), D(0, 6)$　　　**11.** $E(-3, 7), F(-3, 12)$

Looking Ahead Vocabulary

12. The *distance* between your home and your school is the length of the shortest path connecting them. How might you define the *distance between a point and a line* in geometry?

13. Consider the *midpoint* of a segment. What do you think a *midsegment* of a triangle is?

14. If two parties are happening at the same time, they are *concurrent*. What would it mean for three lines to be *concurrent*?

Proving Theorems About Triangles

Big Ideas

1 Coordinate Geometry
Essential Question How do you use coordinate geometry to find relationships within triangles?

2 Measurement
Essential Question How do you solve problems that involve measurements of triangles?

3 Reasoning and Proof
Essential Question How do you write indirect proofs?

ⓒ Domains

- Congruence
- Similarity, Right Triangles, and Trigonometry
- Mathematical Practice: Construct viable arguments

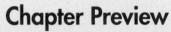

Interactive Digital Path

 Log in to **pearsonsuccessnet.com** and click on Interactive Digital Path to access the Solve Its and animated Problems.

Chapter Preview

Vocabulary

English/Spanish Vocabulary Audio Online:

English	Spanish
altitude of a triangle, *p. 225*	altura de un triángulo
centroid, *p. 223*	centroid
circumcenter, *p. 215*	circuncentro
concurrent, *p. 215*	concurrente
equidistant, *p. 207*	equidistante
incenter, *p. 218*	incentro
indirect proof, *p. 232*	prueba indirecta
median, *p. 223*	mediana
midsegment of a triangle, *p. 199*	segmento medio de un triángulo
orthocenter, *p. 226*	ortocentro

Midsegments of Triangles

G.CO.10 Prove theorems about triangles . . . the segment joining midpoints of two sides of a triangle is parallel to the third side and half the length . . . Also **G.SRT.5**

Objective To use properties of midsegments to solve problems

Solve It! Write your solution to the Solve It in the space below.

In the Solve It, $\overline{LN}$ is a midsegment of $\triangle ABC$. A **midsegment of a triangle** is a segment connecting the midpoints of two sides of the triangle.

Essential Understanding There are two special relationships between a midsegment of a triangle and the third side of the triangle.

take note

Theorem 24 Triangle Midsegment Theorem

Theorem	**If . . .**	**Then . . .**
If a segment joins the midpoints of two sides of a triangle, then the segment is parallel to the third side and is half as long.	D is the midpoint of $\overline{CA}$ and E is the midpoint of $\overline{CB}$	$\overline{DE} \parallel \overline{AB}$ and $DE = \frac{1}{2}AB$

You will prove Theorem 24 in Lesson 5-8.

Here's Why It Works You can verify that the Triangle Midsegment Theorem works for a particular triangle. Use the following steps to show that $\overline{DE} \parallel \overline{AB}$ and that $DE = \frac{1}{2}AB$ for a triangle with vertices at $A(4, 6)$, $B(6, 0)$, and $C(0, 0)$, where D and E are the midpoints of $\overline{CA}$ and $\overline{CB}$.

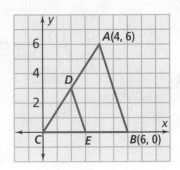

Step 1 Use the Midpoint Formula, $M = \left(\frac{x_1 + x_2}{2}, \frac{y_1 + y_2}{2} \right)$, to find the coordinates of D and E.

The midpoint of $\overline{CA}$ is $D\left(\frac{0 + 4}{2}, \frac{0 + 6}{2} \right) = D(2, 3)$.

The midpoint of $\overline{CB}$ is $E\left(\frac{0 + 6}{2}, \frac{0 + 0}{2} \right) = E(3, 0)$.

Step 2 To show that the midsegment $\overline{DE}$ is parallel to the side $\overline{AB}$, find the slope, $m = \frac{y_2 - y_1}{x_2 - x_1}$, of each segment.

slope of $\overline{DE} = \frac{0 - 3}{3 - 2}$ slope of $\overline{AB} = \frac{0 - 6}{6 - 4}$

$\quad\quad\quad\quad = \frac{-3}{1}$ $\quad\quad\quad\quad = \frac{-6}{2}$

$\quad\quad\quad\quad = -3$ $\quad\quad\quad\quad = -3$

The slopes of $\overline{DE}$ and $\overline{AB}$ are equal, so $\overline{DE}$ and $\overline{AB}$ are parallel.

Step 3 To show $DE = \frac{1}{2}AB$, use the Distance Formula, $d = \sqrt{(x_2 - x_1)^2 + (y_2 - y_1)^2}$, to find DE and AB.

$DE = \sqrt{(3 - 2)^2 + (0 - 3)^2}$ $AB = \sqrt{(6 - 4)^2 + (0 - 6)^2}$

$\quad\quad = \sqrt{1 + 9}$ $\quad\quad = \sqrt{4 + 36}$

$\quad\quad = \sqrt{10}$ $\quad\quad = \sqrt{40}$

$\quad\quad\quad\quad\quad\quad\quad\quad\quad\quad\quad\quad\quad = 2\sqrt{10}$

Since $\sqrt{10} = \frac{1}{2}(2\sqrt{10})$, you know that $DE = \frac{1}{2}AB$.

Problem 1 **Identifying Parallel Segments**

Got It? **a.** In $\triangle XYZ$, A is the midpoint of $\overline{XY}$, B is the midpoint of $\overline{YZ}$, and C is the midpoint of $\overline{ZX}$. What are the three pairs of parallel segments?

b. Reasoning What is $m\angle VUO$ in the figure below? Explain your reasoning.

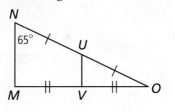

Think

What is the relationship between the 65° angle and $\angle VUO$?

 Practice

1. Identify three pairs of parallel segments in the diagram.

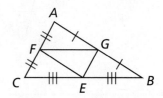

2. Name the segment that is parallel to $\overline{GE}$.

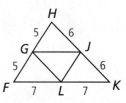

Got It? In the figure at the right, $AD = 6$ and $DE = 7.5$. What are the lengths of $\overline{DC}$, $\overline{AC}$, $\overline{EF}$, and $\overline{AB}$?

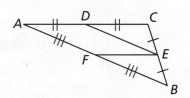

A Practice **Algebra** Find the value of x.

3.

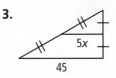

4.

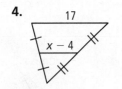

You can use the Triangle Midsegment Theorem to find lengths of segments that might be difficult to measure directly.

ONLINE PROBLEMS

Problem 3 Using a Midsegment of a Triangle

Got It? $\overline{CD}$ is a bridge being built over a lake, as shown in the figure below. What is the length of the bridge?

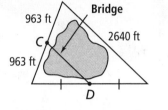

963 ft

Bridge

2640 ft

C

963 ft

D

Think

Which theorem will help you solve this problem?

Ⓐ Practice **5. Surveying** A surveyor needs to measure the distance PQ across the lake. Beginning at point S, she locates the midpoints of $\overline{SQ}$ and $\overline{SP}$ at M and N. She then measures $\overline{NM}$. What is PQ?

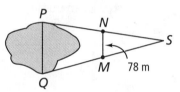

P

N

S

M   78 m

Q

✓ **Lesson Check**

Do you know HOW?

Use the figure at the right for Exercises 6–8.

6. Which segment is parallel to $\overline{JK}$?

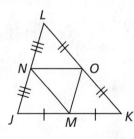

L

N   O

J   M   K

7. If $LK = 46$, what is NM?

8. If $JK = 5x + 20$ and $NO = 20$, what is the value of x?

Do you UNDERSTAND?

9. Vocabulary How does the term *midsegment* describe the segments discussed in this lesson?

10. Reasoning If two noncollinear segments in the coordinate plane have slope 3, what can you conclude?

11. Error Analysis A student sees this figure and concludes that $\overline{PL} \parallel \overline{NO}$. What is the error in the student's reasoning?

More Practice and Problem-Solving Exercises

Ⓑ Apply

12. **Kayaking** You want to paddle your kayak across a lake. To determine how far you must paddle, you pace out a triangle, counting the number of strides, as shown.
    a. If your strides average 3.5 ft, what is the length of the longest side of the triangle?
    b. What distance must you paddle across the lake?

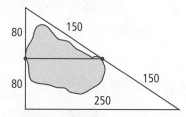

13. **Architecture** The triangular face of the Rock and Roll Hall of Fame in Cleveland, Ohio, is isosceles. The length of the base is 229 ft 6 in. Each leg is divided into four congruent parts by the red segments. What is the length of the white segment? Explain your reasoning.

Ⓒ 14. **Think About a Plan** Draw △ABC. Construct another triangle so that the three sides of △ABC are the midsegments of the new triangle.
    • Can you visualize or sketch the final figure?
    • Which segments in your final construction will be parallel?

Ⓒ 15. **Writing** In the figure at the right, $m\angle QST = 40$. What is $m\angle QPR$? Explain how you know.

16. **Coordinate Geometry** The coordinates of the vertices of a triangle are $E(1, 2)$, $F(5, 6)$, and $G(3, -2)$.
    a. Find the coordinates of H, the midpoint of $\overline{EG}$, and J, the midpoint of $\overline{FG}$.
    b. Show that $\overline{HJ} \parallel \overline{EF}$.
    c. Show that $HJ = \frac{1}{2}EF$.

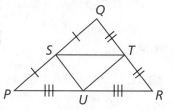

X is the midpoint of $\overline{UV}$. Y is the midpoint of $\overline{UW}$.

17. If $m\angle UXY = 60$, find $m\angle V$.

18. If $m\angle W = 45$, find $m\angle UYX$.

19. If $XY = 50$, find VW.

20. If $VW = 110$, find XY.

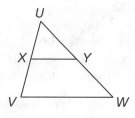

$\overline{IJ}$ is a midsegment of △FGH. $IJ = 7$, $FH = 10$, and $GH = 13$. Find the perimeter of each triangle.

21. △IJH

22. △FGH

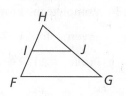

23. Kite Design You design a kite to look like the one at the right. Its diagonals measure 64 cm and 90 cm. You plan to use ribbon, represented by the rectangle, to connect the midpoints of its sides. How much ribbon do you need?

Ⓐ 77 cm   Ⓒ 154 cm

Ⓑ 122 cm   Ⓓ 308 cm

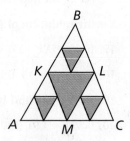

Algebra Find the value of each variable.

24.

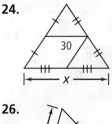

25.

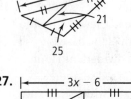

26.

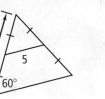

27.

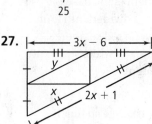

Use the figure at the right for Exercises 28–30.

28. $DF = 24$, $BC = 6$, and $DB = 8$. Find the perimeter of $\triangle ADF$.

29. **Algebra** If $BE = 2x + 6$ and $DF = 5x + 9$, find DF.

30. **Algebra** If $EC = 3x - 1$ and $AD = 5x + 7$, find EC.

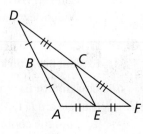

◎ 31. **Open-Ended** Explain how you could use the Triangle Midsegment Theorem as the basis for this construction: Draw $\overline{CD}$. Draw point A not on $\overline{CD}$. Construct $\overline{AB}$ so that $\overline{AB} \parallel \overline{CD}$ and $AB = \frac{1}{2}CD$.

Ⓒ Challenge

◎ 32. **Reasoning** In the diagram at the right, K, L, and M are the midpoints of the sides of $\triangle ABC$. The vertices of the three small red triangles are the midpoints of the sides of $\triangle KBL$, $\triangle AKM$, and $\triangle MLC$. The perimeter of $\triangle ABC$ is 24 cm. What is the perimeter of the shaded region?

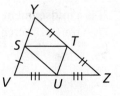

33. **Coordinate Geometry** In $\triangle GHJ$, $K(2, 3)$ is the midpoint of $\overline{GH}$, $L(4, 1)$ is the midpoint of $\overline{HJ}$, and $M(6, 2)$ is the midpoint of $\overline{GJ}$. Find the coordinates of G, H, and J.

Proof 34. Complete the Prove statement and then write a proof.

     Given: In $\triangle VYZ$, S, T, and U are midpoints.

     Prove: $\triangle YST \cong \triangle TUZ \cong \triangle SVU \cong \underline{\ ?\ }$

Perpendicular and Angle Bisectors

G.CO.9 Prove theorems about lines and angles . . . points on a perpendicular bisector of a line segment are exactly those equidistant from the segment's endpoints. Also **G.CO.12, G.SRT.5**

Objective To use properties of perpendicular bisectors and angle bisectors

Solve It! Write your solution to the Solve It in the space below.

In the Solve It, you thought about the relationships that must exist in order for a bulletin board to hang straight. You will explore these relationships in this lesson.

Essential Understanding There is a special relationship between the points on the perpendicular bisector of a segment and the endpoints of the segment.

In the diagram below, $\overleftrightarrow{CD}$ is the perpendicular bisector of $\overline{AB}$. $\overleftrightarrow{CD}$ is perpendicular to $\overline{AB}$ at its midpoint. In the diagram on the right, $\overline{CA}$ and $\overline{CB}$ are drawn to complete $\triangle CAD$ and $\triangle CBD$.

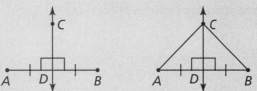

You should recognize from your work in Chapter 3 that $\triangle CAD \cong \triangle CBD$. So you can conclude that $\overline{CA} \cong \overline{CB}$, or that $CA = CB$. A point is **equidistant** from two objects if it is the same distance from the objects. So point C is equidistant from points A and B.

This suggests a proof of Theorem 25, the Perpendicular Bisector Theorem. Its converse is also true and is stated as Theorem 26.

Theorem 25   Perpendicular Bisector Theorem

Theorem	**If . . .**	**Then . . .**
If a point is on the perpendicular bisector of a segment, then it is equidistant from the endpoints of the segment.	$\overleftrightarrow{PM} \perp \overline{AB}$ and $MA = MB$	$PA = PB$

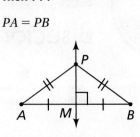

You will prove Theorem 25 in Exercise 26.

Theorem 26   Converse of the Perpendicular Bisector Theorem

Theorem	**If . . .**	**Then . . .**
If a point is equidistant from the endpoints of a segment, then it is on the perpendicular bisector of the segment.	$PA = PB$	$\overleftrightarrow{PM} \perp \overline{AB}$ and $MA = MB$

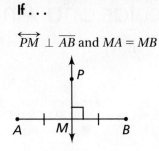

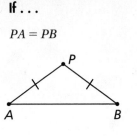

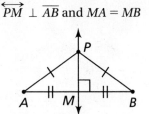

You will prove Theorem 26 in Exercise 27.

Problem 1   **Using the Perpendicular Bisector Theorem**

Got It?   What is the length of $\overline{QR}$?

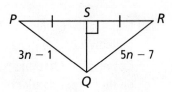

**Practice**   Use the figure at the right for Exercises 1 and 2.

1. What is the relationship between $\overline{MB}$ and $\overleftrightarrow{JK}$?

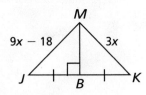

2. Find JM.

Got It?   **a.** Suppose the director from Problem 2 wants the T-shirt stand to be equidistant from the paddle boats and the Spaceship Shoot. What are the possible locations?

Plan

How do you find points that are equidistant from two given points?

ⓒ **b. Reasoning** Can you place the T-shirt stand so that it is equidistant from the paddle boats, the Spaceship Shoot, and the Rollin' Coaster? Explain.

Ⓐ **Practice**   **3. Reading Maps** Use the map of a part of Manhattan. Is St. Vincent's Hospital equidistant from Village Kids Nursery School and Legacy School? How do you know?

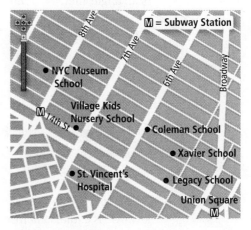

ⓒ **4. Writing** On a piece of paper, mark a point *H* for home and a point *S* for school. Describe how to find the set of points equidistant from *H* and *S*.

Essential Understanding There is a special relationship between the points on the bisector of an angle and the sides of the angle.

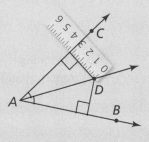

The **distance from a point to a line** is the length of the perpendicular segment from the point to the line. This distance is also the length of the shortest segment from the point to the line. You will prove this in Lesson 4-6. In the figure at the right, the distances from A to ℓ and from B to ℓ are represented by the red segments.

In the diagram, $\overrightarrow{AD}$ is the bisector of $\angle CAB$. If you measure the lengths of the perpendicular segments from D to the two sides of the angle, you will find that the lengths are equal. Point D is equidistant from the sides of the angle.

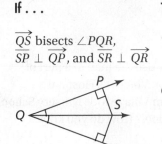

take note

Theorem 27   Angle Bisector Theorem

Theorem	**If . . .**	**Then . . .**
If a point is on the bisector of an angle, then the point is equidistant from the sides of the angle.	$\overrightarrow{QS}$ bisects $\angle PQR$, $\overline{SP} \perp \overrightarrow{QP}$, and $\overline{SR} \perp \overrightarrow{QR}$	$SP = SR$

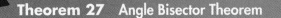

You will prove Theorem 27 in Exercise 28.

Theorem 28   Converse of the Angle Bisector Theorem

Theorem	**If . . .**	**Then . . .**
If a point in the interior of an angle is equidistant from the sides of the angle, then the point is on the angle bisector.	$\overline{SP} \perp \overrightarrow{QP}$, $\overline{SR} \perp \overrightarrow{QR}$, and $SP = SR$	$\overrightarrow{QS}$ bisects $\angle PQR$

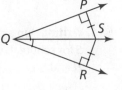
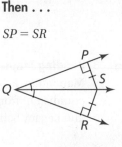

You will prove Theorem 28 in Exercise 29.

Problem 3 **Using the Angle Bisector Theorem**

Think

How can you use the expression for *FD* to check your answer?

Got It? What is the length of $\overline{FB}$?

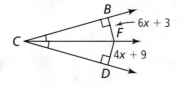

A **Practice** **5.** Find $m\angle KHL$ and $m\angle FHL$.

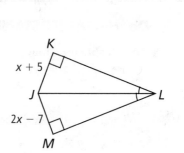

6. Algebra Find *x*, *JK*, and *JM*.

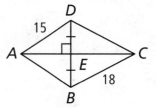

Lesson Check

Do you know HOW?

Use the figure at the right for Exercises 7–9.

7. What is the relationship between $\overline{AC}$ and $\overline{BD}$?

8. What is the length of $\overline{AB}$?

9. What is the length of $\overline{DC}$?

Do you UNDERSTAND?

10. Vocabulary Draw a line and a point not on the line. Draw the segment that represents the distance from the point to the line.

11. Writing Point P is in the interior of $\angle LOX$. Describe how you can determine whether P is on the bisector of $\angle LOX$ without drawing the angle bisector.

More Practice and Problem-Solving Exercises

Ⓑ Apply

Algebra Use the figure at the right for Exercises 12–16.

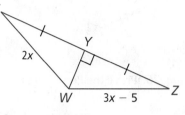

12. Find the value of x.

13. Find TW.

14. Find WZ.

15. What kind of triangle is $\triangle TWZ$? Explain.

16. If R is on the perpendicular bisector of $\overline{TZ}$, then R is ____?____ from T and Z, or ____?____ = ____?____.

Ⓒ **17. Think About a Plan** In the diagram at the right, the soccer goalie will prepare for a shot from the player at point P by moving out to a point on $\overline{XY}$. To have the best chance of stopping the ball, should the goalie stand at the point on $\overline{XY}$ that lies on the perpendicular bisector of $\overline{GL}$ or at the point on $\overline{XY}$ that lies on the bisector of $\angle GPL$? Explain your reasoning.

- How can you draw a diagram to help?
- Would the goalie want to be the same distance from G and L or from $\overline{PG}$ and $\overline{PL}$?

Ⓒ **18. a. Constructions** Draw $\angle CDE$. Construct the angle bisector of the angle.
  b. Reasoning Use the converse of the Angle Bisector Theorem to justify your construction.

Ⓒ **19. a. Constructions** Draw $\overline{QR}$. Construct the perpendicular bisector of $\overline{QR}$ to construct $\triangle PQR$.
  b. Reasoning Use the Perpendicular Bisector Theorem to justify that your construction is an isosceles triangle.

20. Write Theorems 25 and 26 as a single biconditional statement.

21. Write Theorems 27 and 28 as a single biconditional statement.

Ⓒ **22. Error Analysis** To prove that $\triangle PQR$ is isosceles, a student began by stating that since Q is on the segment perpendicular to $\overline{PR}$, Q is equidistant from the endpoints of $\overline{PR}$. What is the error in the student's reasoning?

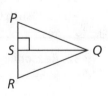

Writing Determine whether *A* must be on the bisector of ∠*TXR*. Explain.

23.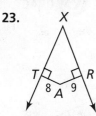

24.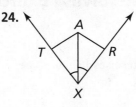

25.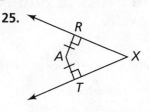

Proof 26. Prove the Perpendicular Bisector Theorem.

Given: $\overleftrightarrow{PM} \perp \overline{AB}$, $\overleftrightarrow{PM}$ bisects $\overline{AB}$

Prove: $AP = BP$

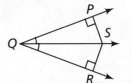

Proof 27. Prove the Converse of the Perpendicular Bisector Theorem.

Given: $PA = PB$, with $\overleftrightarrow{PM} \perp \overline{AB}$ at *M*.

Prove: *P* is on the perpendicular bisector of $\overline{AB}$.

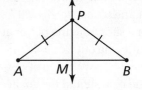

Proof 28. Prove the Angle Bisector Theorem.

Given: $\overrightarrow{QS}$ bisects ∠*PQR*, $\overline{SP} \perp \overrightarrow{QP}$, $\overline{SR} \perp \overrightarrow{QR}$

Prove: $SP = SR$

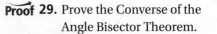

Proof 29. Prove the Converse of the Angle Bisector Theorem.

Given: $\overline{SP} \perp \overrightarrow{QP}$, $\overline{SR} \perp \overrightarrow{QR}$, $SP = SR$

Prove: $\overrightarrow{QS}$ bisects ∠*PQR*.

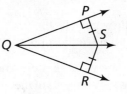

30. **Coordinate Geometry** Use points *A*(6, 8), *O*(0, 0), and *B*(10, 0).
   a. Write equations of lines ℓ and *m* such that $\ell \perp \overleftrightarrow{OA}$ at *A* and $m \perp \overleftrightarrow{OB}$ at *B*.
   b. Find the intersection *C* of lines ℓ and *m*.
   c. Show that $CA = CB$.
   d. Explain why *C* is on the bisector of ∠*AOB*.

C Challenge

31. *A*, *B*, and *C* are three noncollinear points. Describe and sketch a line in plane *ABC* such that points *A*, *B*, and *C* are equidistant from the line. Justify your response.

32. **Reasoning** *M* is the intersection of the perpendicular bisectors of two sides of △*ABC*. Line ℓ is perpendicular to plane *ABC* at *M*. Explain why a point *E* on ℓ is equidistant from *A*, *B*, and *C*. (*Hint:* See Lesson 1-1, Exercise 30. Explain why △*EAM* ≅ △*EBM* ≅ △*ECM*.)

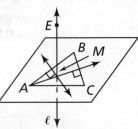

4-3 Bisectors in Triangles

G.CO.10 Prove theorems about triangles . . . Also G.C.3

Objective To identify properties of perpendicular bisectors and angle bisectors

Solve It! Write your solution to the Solve It in the space below.

In the Solve It, the three lines you drew intersect at one point, the center of the circle. When three or more lines intersect at one point, they are **concurrent.** The point at which they intersect is the **point of concurrency.**

Essential Understanding For any triangle, certain sets of lines are always concurrent. Two of these sets of lines are the perpendicular bisectors of the triangle's three sides and the bisectors of the triangle's three angles.

take note

Theorem 29 Concurrency of Perpendicular Bisectors Theorem

Theorem	Diagram	Symbols
The perpendicular bisectors of the sides of a triangle are concurrent at a point equidistant from the vertices.	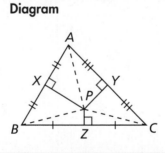	Perpendicular bisectors $\overline{PX}$, $\overline{PY}$, and $\overline{PZ}$ are concurrent at P. $PA = PB = PC$

The point of concurrency of the perpendicular bisectors of a triangle is called the **circumcenter of the triangle.**

Since the circumcenter is equidistant from the vertices, you can use the circumcenter as the center of the circle that contains each vertex of the triangle. You say the circle is **circumscribed about** the triangle.

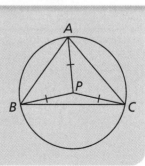

Proof **Proof of Theorem 29**

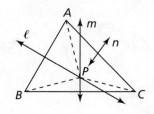

Given: Lines ℓ, m, and n are the perpendicular bisectors of the sides of $\triangle ABC$. P is the intersection of lines ℓ and m.

Prove: Line n contains point P, and $PA = PB = PC$.

Proof: A point on the perpendicular bisector of a segment is equidistant from the endpoints of the segment. Point P is on ℓ, which is the perpendicular bisector of $\overline{AB}$, so $PA = PB$. Using the same reasoning, since P is on m, and m is the perpendicular bisector of $\overline{BC}$, $PB = PC$. Thus, $PA = PC$ by the Transitive Property. Since $PA = PC$, P is equidistant from the endpoints of $\overline{AC}$. Then, by the Converse of the Perpendicular Bisector Theorem, P is on line n, the perpendicular bisector of $\overline{AC}$.

The circumcenter of a triangle can be inside, on, or outside a triangle.

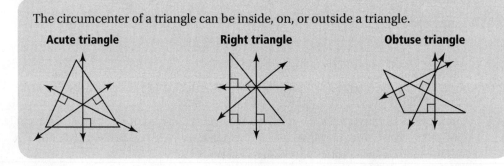

| Acute triangle | Right triangle | Obtuse triangle |

Problem 1 **Finding the Circumcenter of a Triangle**

Got It? What are the coordinates of the circumcenter of the triangle with vertices $A(2, 7)$, $B(10, 7)$, and $C(10, 3)$?

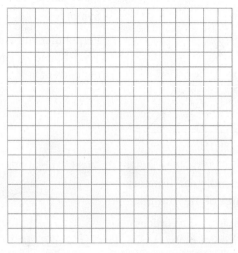

Practice   1. **Coordinate Geometry** Find the coordinates of the
circumcenter of the triangle.

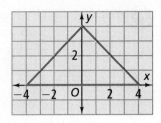

2. **Coordinate Geometry** Find the coordinates of the circumcenter of
the triangle with vertices $A(-4, 5)$, $B(-2, 5)$, and $C(-2, -2)$.

Problem 2   **Using a Circumcenter**

Got It?   In Problem 2, the town planner wants to place a bench
equidistant from the three trees in the park. Where should
he place the bench?

Think

How do you
find a point
equidistant from
three points?

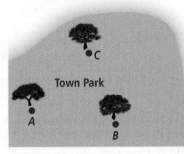

Town Park

A Practice **3. City Planning** Show where town officials should place a recycling barrel so that it is equidistant from the lifeguard chair, the snack bar, and the volleyball court. Explain.

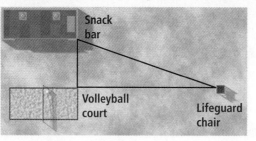

Snack bar

Volleyball court

Lifeguard chair

Theorem 30 Concurrency of Angle Bisectors Theorem

Theorem	**Diagram**	**Symbols**
The bisectors of the angles of a triangle are concurrent at a point equidistant from the sides of the triangle.	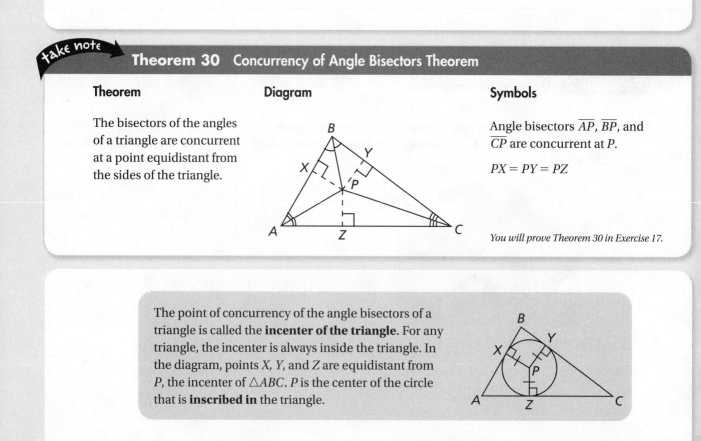	Angle bisectors $\overline{AP}$, $\overline{BP}$, and $\overline{CP}$ are concurrent at P. $$PX = PY = PZ$$ *You will prove Theorem 30 in Exercise 17.*

The point of concurrency of the angle bisectors of a triangle is called the **incenter of the triangle**. For any triangle, the incenter is always inside the triangle. In the diagram, points X, Y, and Z are equidistant from P, the incenter of $\triangle ABC$. P is the center of the circle that is **inscribed in** the triangle.

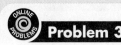

Problem 3 **Identifying and Using the Incenter of a Triangle**

Think

Which segments in the diagram are congruent?

Got It? **a.** $QN = 5x + 36$ and $QM = 2x + 51$. What is QO?

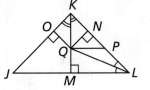

b. Reasoning Is it possible for QP to equal 50? Explain.

 Practice **4.** Name the point of concurrency of the angle bisectors.

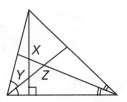

5. Find the value of x.

$RS = 4(x - 3) + 6$ and $RT = 5(2x - 6)$.

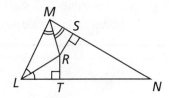

Lesson Check

Do you know HOW?

6. What are the coordinates of the circumcenter of the triangle at the right?

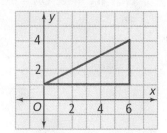

7. In the figure at the right, $TV = 3x - 12$ and $TU = 5x - 24$. What is the value of x?

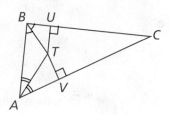

Do you UNDERSTAND?

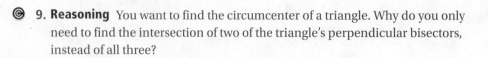

MATHEMATICAL PRACTICES

8. Vocabulary A triangle's circumcenter is outside the triangle. What type of triangle is it?

9. Reasoning You want to find the circumcenter of a triangle. Why do you only need to find the intersection of two of the triangle's perpendicular bisectors, instead of all three?

10. Error Analysis Your friend sees the triangle at the right and concludes that $CT = CP$. What is the error in your friend's reasoning?

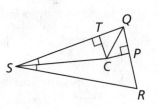

11. Compare and Contrast How are the circumcenter and incenter of a triangle alike? How are they different?

More Practice and Problem-Solving Exercises

B Apply

12. Think About a Plan In the figure at the right, P is the incenter of isosceles $\triangle RST$. What type of triangle is $\triangle RPT$? Explain.
- What segments determine the incenter of a triangle?
- What do you know about the base angles of an isosceles triangle?

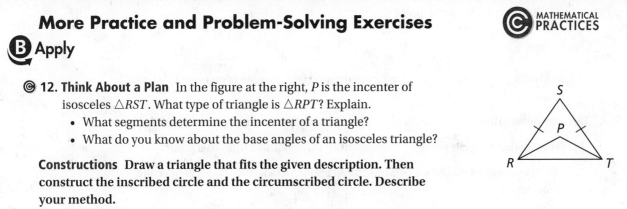

Constructions Draw a triangle that fits the given description. Then construct the inscribed circle and the circumscribed circle. Describe your method.

13. right triangle, $\triangle DEF$ **14.** obtuse triangle, $\triangle STU$

15. Algebra In the diagram at the right, G is the incenter of $\triangle DEF$, $m\angle DEF = 60$, and $m\angle EFD = 2 \cdot m\angle EDF$. What are $m\angle DGE$, $m\angle DGF$, and $m\angle EGF$?

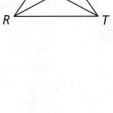

16. Writing Ivars found an old piece of paper inside an antique book.

It read,

From the spot I buried Olaf's treasure, equal sets of paces did I measure; each of three directions in a line, there to plant a seedling Norway pine. I could not return for failing health; now the hounds of Haiti guard my wealth.   —*Karl*

After searching Caribbean islands for five years, Ivars found an island with three tall Norway pines. How might Ivars find where Karl buried Olaf's treasure?

Proof 17. Use the diagram at the right to prove the Concurrrency of Angle Bisectors Theorem.

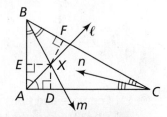

Given: Rays ℓ, m, and n are bisectors of the angles of $\triangle ABC$. X is the intersection of rays ℓ and m, $\overline{XD} \perp \overline{AC}$, $\overline{XE} \perp \overline{AB}$, and $\overline{XF} \perp \overline{BC}$.

Prove: Ray n contains point X, and $XD = XE = XF$.

18. Noise Control You are trying to talk to a friend on the phone in a busy bus station. The buses are so loud that you can hardly hear. Referring to the figure at the right, should you stand at P or C to be as far as possible from all the buses? Explain.

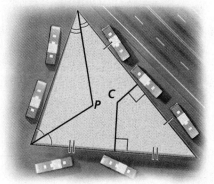

Reasoning Determine whether each statement is *true* or *false*. If the statement is false, give a counterexample.

19. The incenter of a triangle is equidistant from all three vertices.

20. The incenter of a triangle always lies inside the triangle.

21. You can circumscribe a circle about any three points in a plane.

22. If point C is the circumcenter of $\triangle PQR$ and the circumcenter of $\triangle PQS$, then R and S must be the same point.

Challenge

23. Reasoning Explain why the circumcenter of a right triangle is on one of the triangle's sides.

Determine whether each statement is *always*, *sometimes*, or *never* true. Explain.

24. It is possible to find a point equidistant from three parallel lines in a plane.

25. The circles inscribed in and circumscribed about an isosceles triangle have the same center.

4-4   Medians and Altitudes

G.CO.10 Prove theorems about triangles . . . the medians of a triangle meet at a point. Also G.SRT.5

Objective   To identify properties of medians and altitudes of a triangle

Solve It!   Write your solution to the Solve It in the space below.

In the Solve It, the last set of segments you drew are the triangle's medians. A **median of a triangle** is a segment whose endpoints are a vertex and the midpoint of the opposite side.

Essential Understanding   A triangle's three medians are always concurrent.

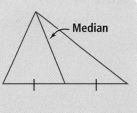

Median

take note

Theorem 31   Concurrency of Medians Theorem

The medians of a triangle are concurrent at a point that is two thirds the distance from each vertex to the midpoint of the opposite side.

$$DC = \frac{2}{3}DJ \qquad EC = \frac{2}{3}EG \qquad FC = \frac{2}{3}FH$$

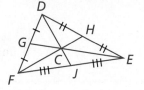

You will prove Theorem 31 in Lesson 5–8.

In a triangle, the point of concurrency of the medians is the **centroid of the triangle**. The point is also called the *center of gravity* of a triangle because it is the point where a triangular shape will balance. For any triangle, the centroid is always inside the triangle.

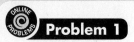
Got It? **a.** If $ZA = 9$, what is the length of $\overline{ZC}$?

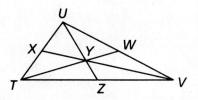

◎ b. Reasoning What is the ratio of ZA to AC? Explain.

 Practice In $\triangle TUV$, Y is the centroid.

1. If $YU = 3.6$, find ZY and ZU.

2. If $VX = 9$, find VY and YX.

An **altitude of a triangle** is the perpendicular segment from a vertex of the triangle to the line containing the opposite side. An altitude of a triangle can be inside or outside the triangle, or it can be a side of the triangle.

ONLINE PROBLEMS **Problem 2** Identifying Medians and Altitudes

Got It? For △ABC, is each segment a *median*, an *altitude*, or *neither*? Explain.

a. $\overline{AD}$

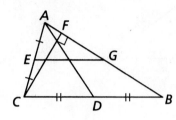

Plan

How do you determine whether a segment is an altitude or a median?

b. $\overline{EG}$

c. $\overline{CF}$

Practice For △ABC, is the red segment a *median*, an *altitude*, or *neither*? Explain.

3.

4.

Theorem 32 Concurrency of Altitudes Theorem

The lines that contain the altitudes of a triangle are concurrent.

You will prove Theorem 32 in Lesson 5–8.

The lines that contain the altitudes of a triangle are concurrent at the **orthocenter of the triangle**. The orthocenter of a triangle can be inside, on, or outside the triangle.

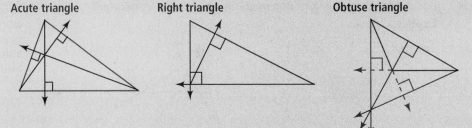

Acute triangle   Right triangle   Obtuse triangle

 Problem 3   **Finding the Orthocenter**

Got It? $\triangle DEF$ has vertices $D(1, 2)$, $E(1, 6)$, and $F(4, 2)$. What are the coordinates of the orthocenter of $\triangle DEF$?

> **Think**
>
> Which two altitudes of $\triangle DEF$ should you choose?

Practice   **Coordinate Geometry**   In Exercises 5 and 6, find the coordinates of the orthocenter of $\triangle ABC$ with the given vertices.

     5. $A(0, 0)$, $B(4, 0)$, and $C(4, 2)$

6. $A(0, -2)$, $B(4, -2)$, and $C(-2, -8)$

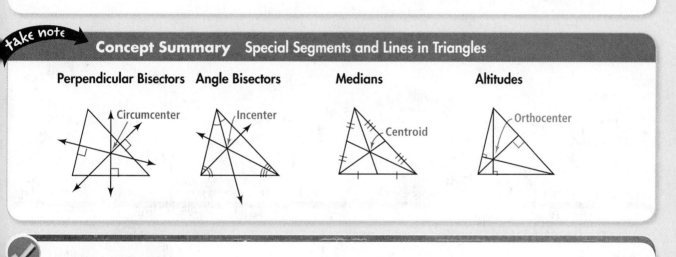

Concept Summary Special Segments and Lines in Triangles

Perpendicular Bisectors **Angle Bisectors** **Medians** **Altitudes**

Circumcenter   Incenter   Centroid   Orthocenter

Lesson Check

Do you know HOW?

Use △*ABC* for Exercises 7–10.

7. Is $\overline{AP}$ a *median* or an *altitude*?

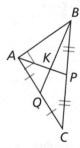

8. If $AP = 18$, what is KP?

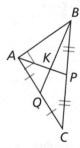

9. If $BK = 15$, what is KQ?

10. Which two segments are altitudes?

Do you UNDERSTAND?

11. Error Analysis Your classmate says she drew $\overline{HJ}$ as an altitude of $\triangle ABC$. What error did she make?

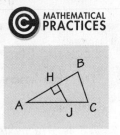

12. Reasoning Does it matter which two altitudes you use to locate the orthocenter of a triangle? Explain.

© **13. Reasoning** The orthocenter of △ABC lies at vertex A. What can you conclude about $\overline{BA}$ and $\overline{AC}$? Explain.

More Practice and Problem-Solving Exercises

Ⓑ **Apply**

Name the centroid.

14.

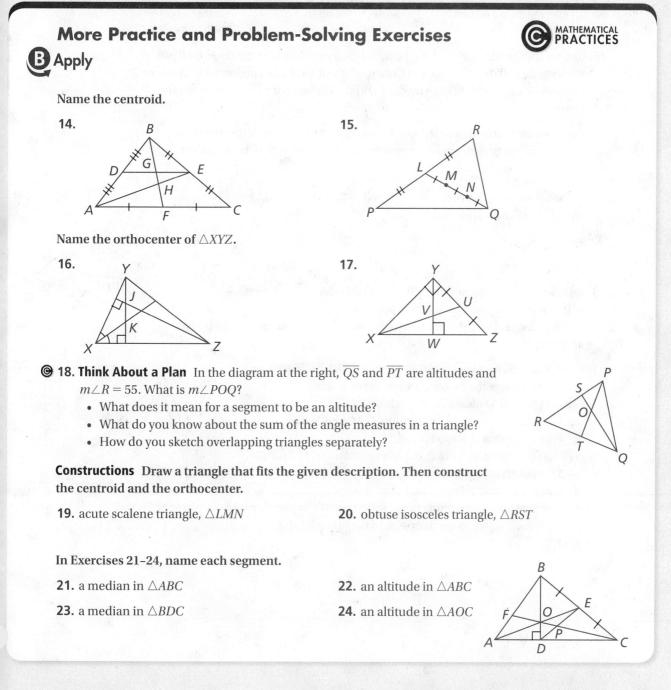

15.

Name the orthocenter of △XYZ.

16.

17.

© **18. Think About a Plan** In the diagram at the right, $\overline{QS}$ and $\overline{PT}$ are altitudes and $m\angle R = 55$. What is $m\angle POQ$?
  - What does it mean for a segment to be an altitude?
  - What do you know about the sum of the angle measures in a triangle?
  - How do you sketch overlapping triangles separately?

Constructions Draw a triangle that fits the given description. Then construct the centroid and the orthocenter.

19. acute scalene triangle, △LMN

20. obtuse isosceles triangle, △RST

In Exercises 21–24, name each segment.

21. a median in △ABC

22. an altitude in △ABC

23. a median in △BDC

24. an altitude in △AOC

25. Reasoning A centroid separates a median into two segments. What is the ratio of the length of the shorter segment to the length of the longer segment?

Paper Folding The figures below show how to construct altitudes and medians by paper folding. Refer to them for Exercises 26 and 27.

Folding an Altitude

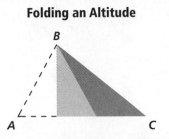

Fold the triangle so that a side $\overline{AC}$ overlaps itself and the fold contains the opposite vertex B.

Folding a Median

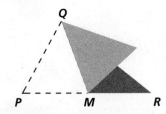

Fold one vertex R to another vertex P. This locates the midpoint M of a side.

Unfold the triangle. Then fold it so that the fold contains the midpoint M and the opposite vertex Q.

26. Cut out a large triangle. Fold the paper carefully to construct the three medians of the triangle and demonstrate the Concurrency of Medians Theorem. Use a ruler to measure the length of each median and the distance of each vertex from the centroid.

27. Cut out a large acute triangle. Fold the paper carefully to construct the three altitudes of the triangle and demonstrate the Concurrency of Altitudes Theorem.

28. In the figure at the right, C is the centroid of $\triangle DEF$. If $GF = 12x^2 + 6y$, which expression represents CF?

Ⓐ $6x^2 + 3y$　　　　　　　　　　Ⓒ $4x^2 + 2y$

Ⓑ $8x^2 + 4y$　　　　　　　　　　Ⓓ $8x^2 + 3y$

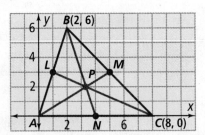

29. Reasoning What type of triangle has its orthocenter on the exterior of the triangle? Draw a sketch to support your answer.

30. Writing Explain why the median to the base of an isosceles triangle is also an altitude.

31. Coordinate Geometry $\triangle ABC$ has vertices $A(0, 0)$, $B(2, 6)$, and $C(8, 0)$. Complete the following steps to verify the Concurrency of Medians Theorem for $\triangle ABC$.
  a. Find the coordinates of midpoints L, M, and N.
  b. Find equations of $\overleftrightarrow{AM}$, $\overleftrightarrow{BN}$, and $\overleftrightarrow{CL}$.
  c. Find the coordinates of P, the intersection of $\overleftrightarrow{AM}$ and $\overleftrightarrow{BN}$. This point is the centroid.
  d. Show that point P is on $\overleftrightarrow{CL}$.
  e. Use the Distance Formula to show that point P is two-thirds of the distance from each vertex to the midpoint of the opposite side.

Challenge

32. Constructions A, B, and O are three noncollinear points. Construct point C such that O is the orthocenter of $\triangle ABC$. Describe your method.

33. Reasoning In an isosceles triangle, show that the circumcenter, incenter, centroid, and orthocenter can be four different points, but all four must be collinear.

A, B, C, **and** *D* **are points of concurrency for the triangle. Determine whether each point is a** *circumcenter, incenter, centroid,* **or** *orthocenter.* **Explain.**

34.

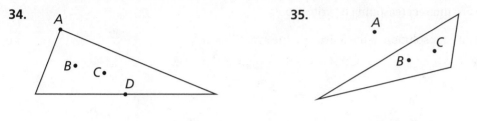

35.

36. **History** In 1765, Leonhard Euler proved that, for any triangle, three of the four points of concurrency are collinear. The line that contains these three points is known as Euler's Line. Use Exercises 34 and 35 to determine which point of concurrency does not necessarily lie on Euler's Line.

4-5 Indirect Proof

G.CO.10 Prove theorems about triangles . . .

Objective To use indirect reasoning to write proofs

 Solve It! Write your solution to the Solve It in the space below.

In the Solve It, you can conclude that a square must contain a certain number if you can eliminate the other three numbers as possibilities. This type of reasoning is called indirect reasoning. In **indirect reasoning,** all possibilities are considered and then all but one are proved false. The remaining possibility must be true.

Essential Understanding You can use indirect reasoning as another method of proof.

A proof involving indirect reasoning is an **indirect proof.** Often in an indirect proof, a statement and its negation are the only possibilities. When you see that one of these possibilities leads to a conclusion that contradicts a fact you know to be true, you can eliminate that possibility. For this reason, indirect proof is sometimes called *proof by contradiction.*

take note

Key Concept   Writing an Indirect Proof

Step 1 State as a temporary assumption the opposite (negation) of what you want to prove.

Step 2 Show that this temporary assumption leads to a contradiction.

Step 3 Conclude that the temporary assumption must be false and that what you want to prove must be true.

In the first step of an indirect proof you assume as true the opposite of what you want to prove.

Got It? Suppose you want to write an indirect proof of each statement. As the first step of the proof, what would you assume?

    a. $\triangle BOX$ is not acute.

    b. At least one pair of shoes you bought cost more than $25.

Ⓐ Practice Write the first step of an indirect proof of the given statement.

    1. At least one angle is obtuse.

    2. $m\angle 2 > 90$

To write an indirect proof, you have to be able to identify a contradiction.

Problem 2 Identifying Contradictions

Got It?   **a.** Which two statements contradict each other?

   I. △XYZ is acute.

   II. △XYZ is scalene.

   III. △XYZ is equiangular.

> **Think**
>
> How do you know that two statements contradict each other?

b. Reasoning Statements I and II below contradict each other.
Statement III is the negation of Statement I. Are Statements II and
III equivalent? Explain your reasoning.

   I. △ABC is scalene.

   II. △ABC is equilateral.

   III. △ABC is not scalene.

Practice Identify the two statements that contradict each other.

   3. **I.** Each of the two items that Val bought costs more than $10.

   II. Val spent $34 for the two items.

   III. Neither of the two items that Val bought costs more than $15.

   4. **I.** In right △ABC, $m\angle A = 60$.

   II. In right △ABC, $\angle A \cong \angle C$.

   III. In right △ABC, $m\angle B = 90$.

Got It? **Given:** $7(x + y) = 70$ and $x \neq 4$.

Prove: $y \neq 6$

Plan

What statement should be negated to begin the proof?

Practice **5. Developing Proof** Fill in the blanks to prove the following statement. If the Yoga Club and Go Green Club together have fewer than 20 members and the Go Green Club has 10 members, then the Yoga Club has fewer than 10 members.

Given: The total membership of the Yoga Club and the Go Green Club is fewer than 20. The Go Green Club has 10 members.

Prove: The Yoga Club has fewer than 10 members.

Proof: Assume temporarily that the Yoga Club has 10 or more members.

This means that together the two clubs have

a. _____ members. This contradicts the given

information that **b.** _____.

The temporary assumption is false. Therefore, it is true that

c. _____.

Ⓖ **6. Developing Proof** Fill in the blanks to prove the following statement.
In a given triangle, $\triangle LMN$, there is at most one right angle.

Given: $\triangle LMN$

Prove: $\triangle LMN$ has at most one right angle.

Proof: Assume temporarily that $\triangle LMN$ has more than one

a. _____. That is, assume that both $\angle M$ and

$\angle N$ are b. _____. If $\angle M$ and $\angle N$ are both right

angles, then $m\angle M = m\angle N =$ c. _____. By

the Triangle Angle-Sum Theorem, $m\angle L + m\angle M + m\angle N =$

d. _____. Use substitution to write the equation

$m\angle L +$ e. _____ $+$ f. _____ $= 180$. When you solve

for $m\angle L$, you find that $m\angle L =$ g. _____. This means

that there is no $\triangle LMN$, which contradicts the given

statement. So the temporary assumption that $\triangle LMN$ has

h. _____ must be false. Therefore, $\triangle LMN$ has

i. _____.

Lesson Check

Do you know HOW?

7. Suppose you want to write an indirect proof of the following statement. As the
first step of the proof, what would you assume?

Quadrilateral $ABCD$ has four right angles.

8. Write a statement that contradicts the following statement. Draw a diagram to
support your answer.

Lines a and b are parallel.

Do you UNDERSTAND?

MATHEMATICAL PRACTICES

@ **9. Error Analysis** A classmate began an indirect proof as shown at the right. Explain and correct your classmate's error.

> Given: △ABC
> Prove: ∠A is obtuse
> ~~Assume temporarily that ∠A is acute.~~

More Practice and Problem-Solving Exercises

MATHEMATICAL PRACTICES

B Apply

10. History Use indirect reasoning to eliminate all but one of the following answers. In what year was George Washington born?

  Ⓐ 1492   Ⓑ 1732   Ⓒ 1902   Ⓓ 2002

@ **11. Think About a Plan** Write an indirect proof.

Given: $\angle 1 \not\cong \angle 2$

Prove: $\ell \not\parallel p$

- What assumption should be the first step of your proof?
- In the figure, what type of angle pair do $\angle 1$ and $\angle 2$ form?

Write the first step of an indirect proof of the given statement.

12. If a number n ends in 5, then it is not divisible by 2.

13. If point X is on the perpendicular bisector of $\overline{AB}$, then $\overline{XB} \cong \overline{XA}$.

14. If a transversal intersects two parallel lines, then alternate exterior angles are congruent.

@ **15. Reasoning** Identify the two statements that contradict each other.

  I. The orthocenter of $\triangle JRK$ is on the triangle.

  II. The centroid of $\triangle JRK$ is inside the triangle.

  III. $\triangle JRK$ is an obtuse triangle.

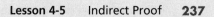

Write an indirect proof.

Proof **16.** Use the figure at the right.

      Given: $\triangle ABC$ with $BC > AC$

      Prove: $\angle A \not\cong \angle B$

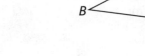

Proof **17. Given:** $\triangle XYZ$ is isosceles.

      Prove: Neither base angle is a right angle.

Ⓖ **Writing** For Exercises 18 and 19, write a convincing argument that uses indirect reasoning.

STEM **18. Chemistry** Ice is forming on the sidewalk in front of Toni's house. Show that the temperature of the sidewalk surface must be 32°F or lower.

19. Show that an obtuse triangle cannot contain a right angle.

Ⓖ **20. Error Analysis** Your friend wants to prove indirectly that $\triangle ABC$ is equilateral. For a first step, he writes, "Assume temporarily that $\triangle ABC$ is scalene." What is wrong with your friend's statement? How can he correct himself?

21. Literature In Arthur Conan Doyle's story "The Sign of the Four," Sherlock Holmes talks to his friend Watson about how a culprit enters a room that has only four entrances: a door, a window, a chimney, and a hole in the roof.

> "You will not apply my precept," he said, shaking his head. "How often have I said to you that when you have eliminated the impossible, whatever remains, however improbable, must be the truth? We know that he did not come through the door, the window, or the chimney. We also know that he could not have been concealed in the room, as there is no concealment possible. Whence, then, did he come?"

How did the culprit enter the room? Explain.

Proof **22.** Prove Theorem 9, the Converse of the Corresponding Angles Theorem. (*Hint:* Use the Triangle Angle-Sum Theorem.)

Ⓒ **Challenge**

Use the figure at the right for Exercises 23 and 24.

Proof **23. Given:** $\triangle ABC$ is scalene, $m\angle ABX = 36$, $m\angle CBX = 36$
      Prove: $\overline{XB}$ is not perpendicular to $\overline{AC}$.

Proof **24. Given:** $\triangle ABC$ is scalene, $m\angle ABX = 36$, $m\angle CBX = 36$
      Prove: $\overline{AX} \not\cong \overline{XC}$

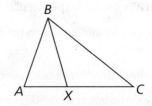

4-6 Inequalities in One Triangle

G.CO.10 Prove theorems about triangles . . .

Objective To use inequalities involving angles and sides of triangles

Solve It! Write your solution to the Solve It in the space below.

In the Solve It, you explored triangles formed by various lengths of board. You may have noticed that changing the angle formed by two sides of the sandbox changes the length of the third side.

Essential Understanding The angles and sides of a triangle have special relationships that involve inequalities.

take note

Property Comparison Property of Inequality

If $a = b + c$ and $c > 0$, then $a > b$.

Proof **Proof of the Comparison Property of Inequality**

Given: $a = b + c, c > 0$
Prove: $a > b$

Statements	Reasons
1) $c > 0$	1) Given
2) $b + c > b + 0$	2) Addition Property of Inequality
3) $b + c > b$	3) Identity Property of Addition
4) $a = b + c$	4) Given
5) $a > b$	5) Substitution

The Comparison Property of Inequality allows you to prove the following corollary to the Triangle Exterior Angle Theorem (Theorem 17).

Corollary   Corollary to the Triangle Exterior Angle Theorem

Corollary	If . . .	Then . . .
The measure of an exterior angle of a triangle is greater than the measure of each of its remote interior angles.	$\angle 1$ is an exterior angle. 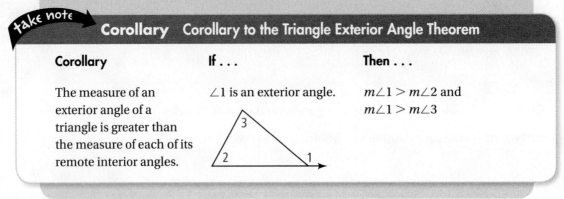	$m\angle 1 > m\angle 2$ and $m\angle 1 > m\angle 3$

Proof Proof of the Corollary

Given: $\angle 1$ is an exterior angle of the triangle.

Prove: $m\angle 1 > m\angle 2$ and $m\angle 1 > m\angle 3$.

Proof: By the Triangle Exterior Angle Theorem, $m\angle 1 = m\angle 2 + m\angle 3$. Since $m\angle 2 > 0$ and $m\angle 3 > 0$, you can apply the Comparison Property of Inequality and conclude that $m\angle 1 > m\angle 2$ and $m\angle 1 > m\angle 3$.

Problem 1   Applying the Corollary

Got It? Why is $m\angle 5 > m\angle C$?

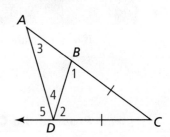

A Practice Explain why $m\angle 1 > m\angle 2$.

1.

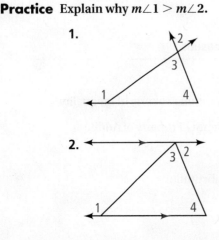

2.

You can use the corollary to Theorem 17 to prove the following theorem.

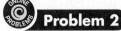

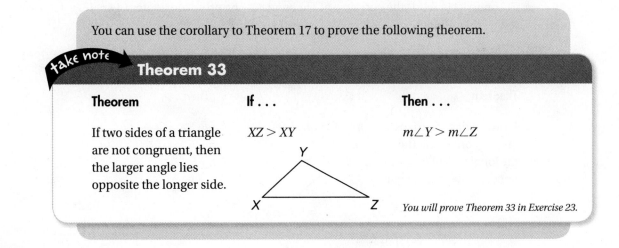

Theorem 33

Theorem	If . . .	Then . . .
If two sides of a triangle are not congruent, then the larger angle lies opposite the longer side.	$XZ > XY$	$m\angle Y > m\angle Z$

You will prove Theorem 33 in Exercise 23.

Problem 2 Using Theorem 33

Got It? Suppose the landscape architect from Problem 2 wants to place a drinking fountain at the corner with the second-largest angle. Which two streets form the corner with the second-largest angle?

Practice For Exercises 3 and 4, list the angles of each triangle in order from smallest to largest.

3.
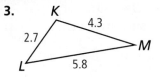

4. $\triangle ABC$, where $AB = 8$, $BC = 5$, and $CA = 7$

Theorem 34 below is the converse of Theorem 33. The proof of Theorem 34 relies on indirect reasoning.

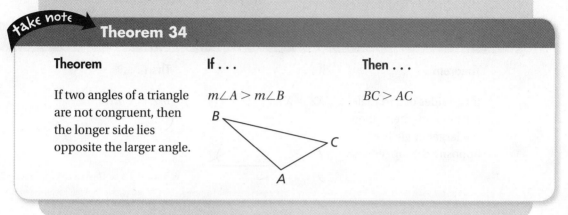

take note

Theorem 34

Theorem	If . . .	Then . . .
If two angles of a triangle are not congruent, then the longer side lies opposite the larger angle.	$m\angle A > m\angle B$	$BC > AC$

Proof **Indirect Proof of Theorem 34**

Given: $m\angle A > m\angle B$
Prove: $BC > AC$

Step 1 Assume temporarily that BC is not greater than AC. That is, assume temporarily that either $BC < AC$ or $BC = AC$.

Step 2 If $BC < AC$, then $m\angle A < m\angle B$ (Theorem 33). This contradicts the given fact that $m\angle A > m\angle B$. Therefore, $BC < AC$ must be false.

If $BC = AC$, then $m\angle A = m\angle B$ (Isosceles Triangle Theorem). This also contradicts $m\angle A > m\angle B$. Therefore, $BC = AC$ must be false.

Step 3 The temporary assumption $BC \not> AC$ is false, so $BC > AC$.

ONLINE PROBLEMS

Problem 3 **Using Theorem 34**

Ⓔ Got It? **Reasoning** In the figure below, $m\angle S = 24$ and $m\angle O = 130$. Which side of $\triangle SOX$ is the shortest side? Explain your reasoning.

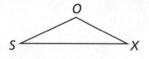

Plan

How do you use the angle measures to order the side lengths?

A Practice For Exercises 5 and 6, list the sides of each triangle in order from shortest to longest.

5.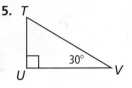

6. $\triangle DEF$, with $m\angle D = 20$, $m\angle E = 120$, and $m\angle F = 40$

For three segments to form a triangle, their lengths must be related in a certain way. Notice that only one of the sets of segments below can form a triangle. The sum of the smallest two lengths must be greater than the greatest length.

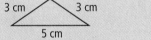

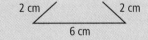

take note

Theorem 35 Triangle Inequality Theorem

The sum of the lengths of any two sides of a triangle is greater than the length of the third side.

$XY + YZ > XZ \qquad YZ + XZ > XY \qquad XZ + XY > YZ$

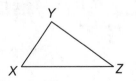

You will prove Theorem 35 in Exercise 28.

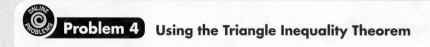

Problem 4   **Using the Triangle Inequality Theorem**

Got It?   Can a triangle have sides with the given lengths? Explain.

   a. 2 m, 6 m, and 9 m

> **Think**
>
> **How can you determine if the lengths can form a triangle?**

   b. 4 yd, 6 yd, and 9 yd

Ⓐ Practice   Can a triangle have sides with the given lengths? Explain.

   7. 2 in., 3 in., 6 in.

   8. 11 cm, 12 cm, 15 cm

Problem 5 Finding Possible Side Lengths

Got It? A triangle has side lengths of 4 in. and 7 in. What is the range of possible lengths for the third side?

Practice **Algebra** **The lengths of two sides of a triangle are given. Find the range of possible lengths for the third side.**

9. 18 m, 23 m

10. 20 km, 35 km

Lesson Check

Do you know HOW?

Use △*ABC* for Exercises 11 and 12.

11. Which side is the longest?

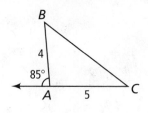

12. Which angle is the smallest?

13. Can a triangle have sides of lengths 4, 5, and 10? Explain.

Do you UNDERSTAND?

MATHEMATICAL
PRACTICES

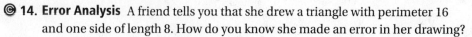
14. Error Analysis A friend tells you that she drew a triangle with perimeter 16 and one side of length 8. How do you know she made an error in her drawing?

15. Reasoning Is it possible to draw a right triangle with an exterior angle measuring 88? Explain your reasoning.

More Practice and Problem-Solving Exercises

Ⓑ Apply

Ⓒ **16. Think About a Plan** You are setting up a study area where you will do your homework each evening. It is triangular with an entrance on one side. You want to put your computer in the corner with the largest angle and a bookshelf on the longest side. Where should you place your computer? On which side should you place the bookshelf? Explain.

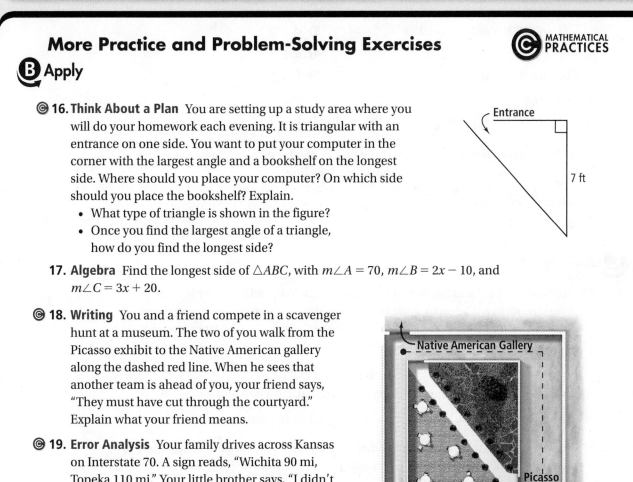

- What type of triangle is shown in the figure?
- Once you find the largest angle of a triangle, how do you find the longest side?

17. Algebra Find the longest side of $\triangle ABC$, with $m\angle A = 70$, $m\angle B = 2x - 10$, and $m\angle C = 3x + 20$.

Ⓒ **18. Writing** You and a friend compete in a scavenger hunt at a museum. The two of you walk from the Picasso exhibit to the Native American gallery along the dashed red line. When he sees that another team is ahead of you, your friend says, "They must have cut through the courtyard." Explain what your friend means.

Ⓒ **19. Error Analysis** Your family drives across Kansas on Interstate 70. A sign reads, "Wichita 90 mi, Topeka 110 mi." Your little brother says, "I didn't know that it was only 20 miles from Wichita to Topeka." Explain why the distance between the two cities does not have to be 20 mi.

Ⓒ **Reasoning** Determine which segment is shortest in each diagram.

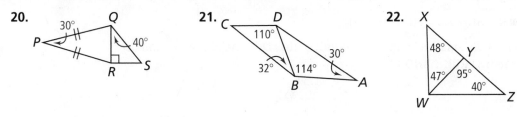

20.

21.

22.

23. Developing Proof Fill in the blanks for a proof of Theorem 33:
If two sides of a triangle are not congruent, then the larger angle
lies opposite the longer side.

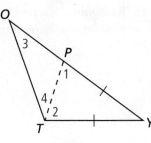

Given: $\triangle TOY$, with $YO > YT$

Prove: **a.** __?__ > **b.** __?__

Mark P on $\overline{YO}$ so that $\overline{YP} \cong \overline{YT}$. Draw $\overline{TP}$.

Statements	Reasons
1) $\overline{YP} \cong \overline{YT}$	1) Ruler Postulate
2) $m\angle 1 = m\angle 2$	2) **c.** __?__
3) $m\angle OTY = m\angle 4 + m\angle 2$	3) **d.** __?__
4) $m\angle OTY > m\angle 2$	4) **e.** __?__
5) $m\angle OTY > m\angle 1$	5) **f.** __?__
6) $m\angle 1 > m\angle 3$	6) **g.** __?__
7) $m\angle OTY > m\angle 3$	7) **h.** __?__

Proof 24. Prove this corollary to Theorem 34: The perpendicular segment from a point to a
line is the shortest segment from the point to the line.

Given: $\overline{PT} \perp \overline{TA}$

Prove: $PA > PT$

Challenge

25. Probability A student has two straws. One is 6 cm long and the other is 9 cm
long. She picks a third straw at random from a group of four straws whose lengths
are 3 cm, 5 cm, 11 cm, and 15 cm. What is the probability that the straw she picks
will allow her to form a triangle? Justify your answer.

For Exercises 26 and 27, x and y are integers such that $1 < x < 5$ and $2 < y < 9$.

26. The sides of a triangle are 5 cm, x cm, and y cm. List all possible (x, y) pairs.

27. Probability What is the probability that you can draw an isosceles triangle that
has sides 5 cm, x cm, and y cm, with x and y chosen at random?

Proof 28. Prove the Triangle Inequality Theorem: The sum of the lengths of any two sides
of a triangle is greater than the length of the third side.

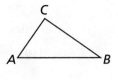

Given: $\triangle ABC$

Prove: $AC + CB > AB$

(*Hint:* On $\overrightarrow{BC}$, mark a point D not on $\overline{BC}$, so that $DC = AC$. Draw $\overline{DA}$ and use
Theorem 34 with $\triangle ABD$.)

4-7   Inequalities in Two Triangles

G.CO.10   Prove theorems about triangles . . .

Objective   To apply inequalities in two triangles

Solve It!   Write your solution to the Solve It in the space below.

In the Solve It, the hands of the clock and the segment labeled x form a triangle. As the time changes, the shape of the triangle changes, but the lengths of two of its sides do not change.

Essential Understanding   In triangles that have two pairs of congruent sides, there is a relationship between the included angles and the third pair of sides.

When you close a door, the angle between the door and the frame (at the hinge) gets smaller. The relationship between the measure of the hinge angle and the length of the opposite side is the basis for the SAS Inequality Theorem, also known as the Hinge Theorem.

 take note

Theorem 36   The Hinge Theorem (SAS Inequality Theorem)

Theorem	If . . .	Then . . .
If two sides of one triangle are congruent to two sides of another triangle, and the included angles are not congruent, then the longer third side is opposite the larger included angle.	$m\angle A > m\angle X$	$BC > YZ$

You will prove Theorem 36 in Exercise 21.

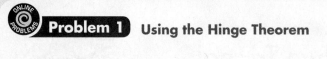

Problem 1 **Using the Hinge Theorem**

Got It? **a.** What inequality relates *LN* and *OQ* in the figure at the right?

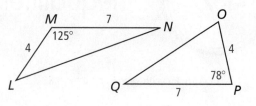

b. Reasoning In △*ABC*, *AB* = 3, *BC* = 4, and *CA* = 6. In △*PQR*, *PQ* = 3, *QR* = 5, and *RP* = 6. How can you use indirect reasoning to explain why *m*∠*P* > *m*∠*A*?

Ⓐ **Practice** Write an inequality relating the given side lengths. If there is not enough information to reach a conclusion, write *no conclusion*.

1. *LM* and *KL*

2. *YZ* and *UV*

Problem 2 **Applying the Hinge Theorem**

Think

What does not change about both pairs of scissors in the diagram?

Got It? The diagram below shows a pair of scissors in two different positions. In which position is the distance between the tips of the two blades greater? Use the Hinge Theorem to justify your answer.

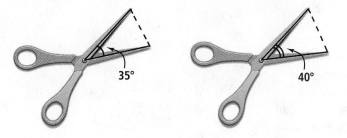

Practice 3. The diagram below shows a robotic arm in two different positions. In which position is the tip of the robotic arm closer to the base? Use the Hinge Theorem to justify your answer.

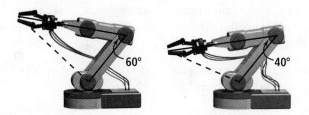

The Converse of the Hinge Theorem is also true. The proof of the converse is an indirect proof.

take note

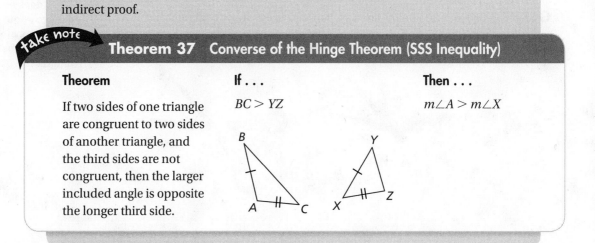

Theorem 37   Converse of the Hinge Theorem (SSS Inequality)

Theorem

If two sides of one triangle are congruent to two sides of another triangle, and the third sides are not congruent, then the larger included angle is opposite the longer third side.

If . . .

$BC > YZ$

Then . . .

$m\angle A > m\angle X$

Proof Indirect Proof of the Converse of the Hinge Theorem (SSS Inequality)

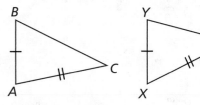

Given: $\overline{AB} \cong \overline{XY}$, $\overline{AC} \cong \overline{XZ}$, $BC > YZ$
Prove: $m\angle A > m\angle X$

Step 1 Assume temporarily that $m\angle A \not> m\angle X$. This means either $m\angle A < m\angle X$ or $m\angle A = m\angle X$.

Step 2 If $m\angle A < m\angle X$, then $BC < YZ$ by the Hinge Theorem. This contradicts the given information that $BC > YZ$. Therefore, the assumption that $m\angle A < m\angle X$ must be false.

If $m\angle A = m\angle X$, then $\triangle ABC \cong \triangle XYZ$ by SAS. If the two triangles are congruent, then $BC = YZ$ because corresponding parts of congruent triangles are congruent. This contradicts the given information that $BC > YZ$. Therefore, the assumption that $m\angle A = m\angle X$ must be false.

Step 3 The temporary assumption that $m\angle A \not> m\angle X$ is false. Therefore, $m\angle A > m\angle X$.

ONLINE PROBLEMS

Problem 3   Using the Converse of the Hinge Theorem

Got It? What is the range of possible values for x in the figure at the right?

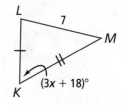
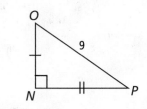

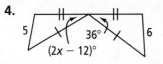 **Practice** **Algebra** Find the range of possible values for each variable.

4.

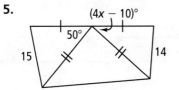

5.

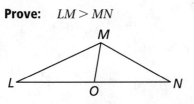

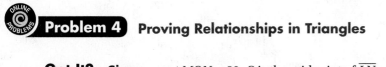 **Problem 4** **Proving Relationships in Triangles**

Got It? **Given:** $m\angle MON = 80$, O is the midpoint of $\overline{LN}$

Prove: $LM > MN$

Think
How can you
find the measure
of $\angle MOL$?

A Practice

6. Developing Proof Complete the following proof.

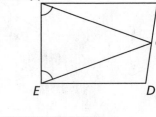

Given: C is the midpoint of $\overline{BD}$,
$m\angle EAC = m\angle AEC$,
$m\angle BCA > m\angle DCE$

Prove: $AB > ED$

Statements	Reasons
1) $m\angle EAC = m\angle AEC$	**1)** Given
2) $AC = EC$	**2) a.** _____
3) C is the midpoint of $\overline{BD}$.	**3) b.** _____
4) $\overline{BC} \cong \overline{CD}$	**4) c.** _____
5) d. _____	**5)** $\cong$ segments have $=$ length.
6) $m\angle BCA > m\angle DCE$	**6) e.** _____
7) $AB > ED$	**7) f.** _____

✓ Lesson Check

Do you know HOW?

Write an inequality relating the given side lengths or angle measures.

7. FD and BC

8. $m\angle UST$ and $m\angle VST$

Do you UNDERSTAND?

9. Vocabulary Explain why *Hinge Theorem* is an appropriate name for Theorem 36.

10. Error Analysis From the figure at the right, your friend concludes that $m\angle BAD > m\angle BCD$. How would you correct your friend's mistake?

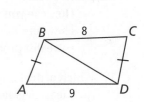

11. Compare and Contrast How are the Hinge Theorem and the SAS Congruence Postulate similar?

More Practice and Problem-Solving Exercises

Ⓑ Apply

Copy and complete with > or <. Explain your reasoning.

12. $PT \blacksquare QR$

13. $m\angle QTR \blacksquare m\angle RTS$

14. $PT \blacksquare RS$

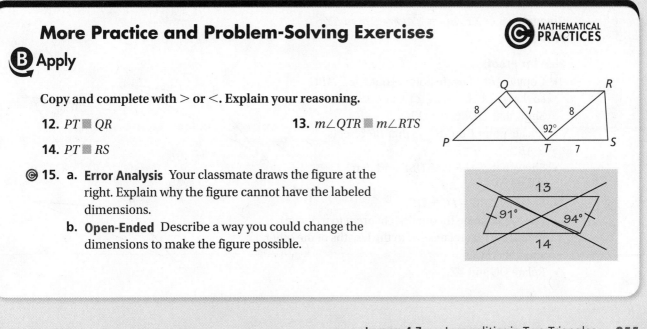

15. a. Error Analysis Your classmate draws the figure at the right. Explain why the figure cannot have the labeled dimensions.

  b. Open-Ended Describe a way you could change the dimensions to make the figure possible.

16. Reasoning The legs of a right isosceles triangle are congruent to the legs of an isosceles triangle with an 80° vertex angle. Which triangle has a greater perimeter? How do you know?

17. Think About a Plan Ship A and Ship B leave from the same point in the ocean. Ship A travels 150 mi due west, turns 65° toward north, and then travels another 100 mi. Ship B travels 150 mi due east, turns 70° toward south, and then travels another 100 mi. Which ship is farther from the starting point? Explain.

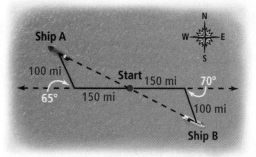

- How can you use the given angle measures?
- How does the Hinge Theorem help you to solve this problem?

18. Which of the following lists the segment lengths in order from least to greatest?

Ⓐ CD, AB, DE, BC, EF   Ⓒ BC, DE, EF, AB, CD

Ⓑ EF, DE, AB, BC, CD   Ⓓ EF, BC, DE, AB, CD

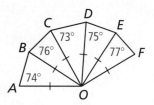

Proof **19.** Use the figure at the right.

Given: △ABE is isosceles with vertex ∠B,
△ABE ≅ △CBD,
m∠EBD > m∠ABE

Prove: ED > AE

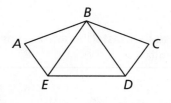

Ⓒ Challenge

20. Coordinate Geometry △ABC has vertices A(0, 7), B(−1, −2), C(2, −1), and O(0, 0). Show that m∠AOB > m∠AOC.

Proof **21.** Use the plan below to complete a proof of the Hinge Theorem: If two sides of one triangle are congruent to two sides of another triangle and the included angles are not congruent, then the longer third side is opposite the larger included angle.

Given: $\overline{AB} \cong \overline{XY}$, $\overline{BC} \cong \overline{YZ}$, m∠B > m∠Y
Prove: AC > XZ

Plan for proof:
- Copy △ABC. Locate point D outside △ABC so that m∠CBD = m∠ZYX and BD = YX. Show that △DBC ≅ △XYZ.
- Locate point F on $\overline{AC}$, so that $\overline{BF}$ bisects ∠ABD.
- Show that △ABF ≅ △DBF and that $\overline{AF} \cong \overline{DF}$.
- Show that AC = FC + DF.
- Use the Triangle Inequality Theorem to write an inequality that relates DC to the lengths of the other sides of △FCD.
- Relate DC and XZ.

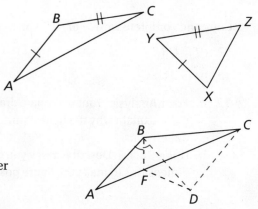

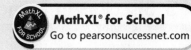
4-1 Midsegments of Triangles

Quick Review

A **midsegment of a triangle** is a segment that connects the midpoints of two sides. A midsegment is parallel to the third side and is half as long.

Example

Algebra Find the value of x.

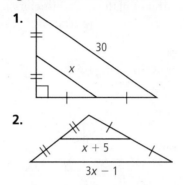

$\overline{DE}$ is a midsegment because D and E are midpoints.

$DE = \frac{1}{2}BC$ △ Midsegment Theorem

$2x = \frac{1}{2}(x + 12)$ Substitute.

$4x = x + 12$ Multiply each side by 2.

$3x = 12$ Subtract x from each side.

$x = 4$ Divide each side by 3.

Exercises

Algebra Find the value of x.

1.

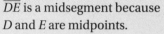

2.

3. △ABC has vertices $A(0, 0)$, $B(2, 2)$, and $C(5, -1)$. Find the coordinates of L, the midpoint of $\overline{AC}$, and M, the midpoint of $\overline{BC}$. Verify that $\overline{LM} \parallel \overline{AB}$ and $LM = \frac{1}{2}AB$.

4-2 Perpendicular and Angle Bisectors

Quick Review

The **Perpendicular Bisector Theorem** together with its converse states that P is equidistant from A and B if and only if P is on the perpendicular bisector of $\overline{AB}$.

The **distance from a point to a line** is the length of the perpendicular segment from the point to the line.

The **Angle Bisector Theorem** together with its converse states that P is equidistant from the sides of an angle if and only if P is on the angle bisector.

Example

In the figure, $QP = 4$ and $AB = 8$. Find QR and CB.

Q is on the bisector of $\angle ABC$, so $QR = QP = 4$.
B is on the perpendicular bisector of $\overline{AC}$, so $CB = AB = 8$.

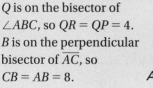

Exercises

4. **Writing** Describe how to find all the points on a baseball field that are equidistant from second base and third base.

In the figure, $m\angle DBE = 50$. Find each of the following.

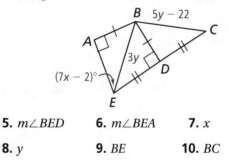

5. $m\angle BED$ 6. $m\angle BEA$ 7. x

8. y 9. BE 10. BC

4-3 Bisectors in Triangles

Quick Review

When three or more lines intersect in one point, they are **concurrent**.

- The point of concurrency of the perpendicular bisectors of a triangle is the **circumcenter of the triangle**.
- The point of concurrency of the angle bisectors of a triangle is the **incenter of the triangle**.

Example

Identify the incenter of the triangle.

The incenter of a triangle is the point of concurrency of the angle bisectors. $\overline{MR}$ and $\overline{LQ}$ are angle bisectors that intersect at Z. So, Z is the incenter.

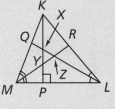

Exercises

Find the coordinates of the circumcenter of $\triangle DEF$.

11. $D(6, 0)$, $E(0, 6)$, $F(-6, 0)$

12. $D(0, 0)$, $E(6, 0)$, $F(0, 4)$

13. $D(5, -1)$, $E(-1, 3)$, $F(3, -1)$

14. $D(2, 3)$, $E(8, 3)$, $F(8, -1)$

P is the incenter of $\triangle XYZ$. Find the indicated angle measure.

15. $m\angle PXY$

16. $m\angle XYZ$

17. $m\angle PZX$

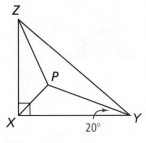

4-4 Medians and Altitudes

Quick Review

A **median of a triangle** is a segment from a vertex to the midpoint of the opposite side. An **altitude of a triangle** is a perpendicular segment from a vertex to the line containing the opposite side.

- The point of concurrency of the medians of a triangle is the **centroid of the triangle**. The centroid is two thirds the distance from each vertex to the midpoint of the opposite side.
- The point of concurrency of the altitudes of a triangle is the **orthocenter of the triangle**.

Example

If $PB = 6$, what is SB?

S is the centroid because $\overline{AQ}$ and $\overline{CR}$ are medians. So, $SB = \frac{2}{3}PB = \frac{2}{3}(6) = 4$.

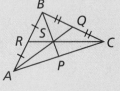

Exercises

Determine whether $\overline{AB}$ is a *median*, an *altitude*, or *neither*. Explain.

18.

19.

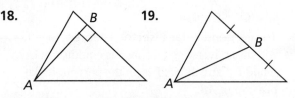

20. $\triangle PQR$ has medians $\overline{QM}$ and $\overline{PN}$ that intersect at Z. If $ZM = 4$, find QZ and QM.

$\triangle ABC$ has vertices $A(2, 3)$, $B(-4, -3)$, and $C(2, -3)$. Find the coordinates of each point of concurrency.

21. centroid

22. orthocenter

4-5 Indirect Proof

Quick Review

In an **indirect proof**, you first assume temporarily the opposite of what you want to prove. Then you show that this temporary assumption leads to a contradiction.

Example

Which two statements contradict each other?

 I. The perimeter of $\triangle ABC$ is 14.
 II. $\triangle ABC$ is isosceles.
 III. The side lengths of $\triangle ABC$ are 3, 5, and 6.

An isosceles triangle can have a perimeter of 14.

The perimeter of a triangle with side lengths 3, 5, and 6 is 14.

An isosceles triangle must have two sides of equal length. Statements II and III contradict each other.

Exercises

Write a convincing argument that uses indirect reasoning.

23. The product of two numbers is even. Show that at least one of the numbers must be even.

24. Two lines in the same plane are not parallel. Show that a third line in the plane must intersect at least one of the two lines.

25. Show that a triangle can have at most one obtuse angle.

26. Show that an equilateral triangle cannot have an obtuse angle.

27. The sum of three integers is greater than 9. Show that one of the integers must be greater than 3.

4-6 and 4-7 Inequalities in Triangles

Quick Review

For any triangle,

- the measure of an exterior angle is greater than the measure of each of its remote interior angles
- if two sides are not congruent, then the larger angle lies opposite the longer side
- if two angles are not congruent, then the longer side lies opposite the larger angle
- the sum of any two side lengths is greater than the third

The **Hinge Theorem** states that if two sides of one triangle are congruent to two sides of another triangle, and the included angles are not congruent, then the longer third side is opposite the larger included angle.

Example

Which is greater, BC or AD?

$\overline{BA} \cong \overline{CD}$ and $\overline{BD} \cong \overline{DB}$, so $\triangle ABD$ and $\triangle CDB$ have two pairs of congruent corresponding sides. Since $60 > 45$, you know $BC > AD$ by the Hinge Theorem.

Exercises

28. In $\triangle RST$, $m\angle R = 70$ and $m\angle S = 80$. List the sides of $\triangle RST$ in order from shortest to longest.

Is it possible for a triangle to have sides with the given lengths? Explain.

29. 5 in., 8 in., 15 in.

30. 10 cm, 12 cm, 20 cm

31. The lengths of two sides of a triangle are 12 ft and 13 ft. Find the range of possible lengths for the third side.

Use the figure below. Complete each statement with $>$, $<$, or $=$.

32. $m\angle BAD \ \blacksquare \ m\angle ABD$

33. $m\angle CBD \ \blacksquare \ m\angle BCD$

34. $m\angle ABD \ \blacksquare \ m\angle CBD$

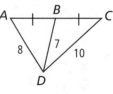

Pull It **All Together**

Estimating the Length of a Hiking Trail

ASSESSMENT

A group of hikers plan to hike from the campground lookout tower to the hut. To challenge the group, the leader gives them the diagram below. (All distances are given in kilometers.) The dashed line shows the trail they will take, but the distances along the trail are unknown.

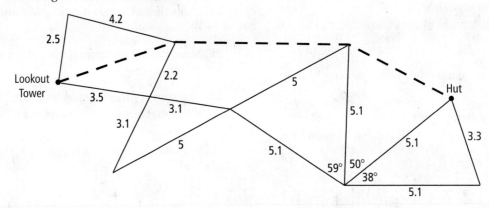

The group must determine the best lower bound and the best upper bound for the length of the trail. To do this, they are allowed to use the Triangle Inequality Theorem and the Hinge Theorem.

Task Description

Find a range in kilometers for the length of the trail.

- Do you need to draw any additional segments in the diagram to help you estimate the length of the trail?

- The trail from the lookout tower to the hut includes three segments. How can you find a range for each segment? How do these ranges lead you to determine the lower and upper bounds for the length of the trail?

Get Ready!

Properties of Parallel Lines

Algebra Use properties of parallel lines to find the value of *x*.

1.
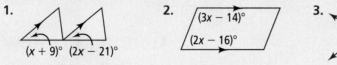
$(x + 9)°$ $(2x - 21)°$

2.
$(3x - 14)°$
$(2x - 16)°$

3.
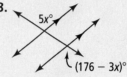
$5x°$
$(176 - 3x)°$

Proving Lines Parallel

Algebra Determine whether $\overline{AB}$ is parallel to $\overline{CD}$.

4.
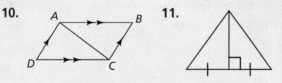
A   B
C   D

5.
B
D $3x°$
$4x°$ F
C $2x°$
A $(3x + 18)°$

6.
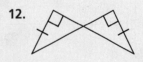
$(2x + 11)°$ $(3x - 9)°$ B
A
$(6x + 9)°$
C   D

Using Slope to Determine Parallel and Perpendicular Lines

Algebra Determine whether each pair of lines is *parallel*, *perpendicular*, or *neither*.

7. $y = -2x; y = -2x + 4$ **8.** $y = -\frac{3}{5}x + 1; y = \frac{5}{3}x - 3$ **9.** $2x - 3y = 1; 3x - 2y = 8$

Proving Triangles Congruent

Determine the postulate or theorem that makes each pair of triangles congruent.

10.
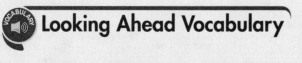
A   B
D   C

11.

12.

Looking Ahead Vocabulary

13. You know the meaning of *equilateral*. What do you think an *equiangular* polygon is?

14. When a team wins two *consecutive* gold medals, it means they have won two gold medals in a row. What do you think two *consecutive* angles in a quadrilateral means?

Proving Theorems About Quadrilaterals

Big Ideas

1 Measurement
Essential Question How can you find the sum of the measures of polygon angles?

2 Reasoning and Proof
Essential Question How can you classify quadrilaterals?

3 Coordinate Geometry
Essential Question How can you use coordinate geometry to prove general relationships?

ⓒ Domains

- Congruence
- Similarity, Right Triangles, and Trigonometry
- Expressing Geometric Properties with Equations

Interactive Digital Path

🖑 Log in to **pearsonsuccessnet.com** and click on Interactive Digital Path to access the Solve Its and animated Problems.

Chapter Preview

🔊 Vocabulary

English/Spanish Vocabulary Audio Online:

English	Spanish
coordinate proof, *p. 319*	prueba de coordenadas
equiangular polygon, *p. 264*	polígono equiángulo
equilateral polygon, *p. 264*	polígono equilátero
isosceles trapezoid, *p. 306*	trapecio isósceles
kite, *p. 310*	cometa
midsegment of a trapezoid, *p. 308*	segmento medio de un trapecio
parallelogram, *p. 270*	paralelogramo
rectangle, *p. 289*	rectángulo
regular polygon, *p. 264*	polígono regular
rhombus, *p. 289*	rombo
trapezoid, *p. 306*	trapecio

5-1 The Polygon Angle-Sum Theorems

G.CO.9 Prove theorems about lines and angles . . . Also G.SRT.5

Objectives To find the sum of the measures of the interior angles of a polygon
To find the sum of the measures of the exterior angles of a polygon

Solve It! Write your solution to the Solve It in the space below.

The Solve It is related to a formula for the sum of the interior angle measures of a polygon. (In this textbook, a polygon is convex unless otherwise stated.)

Essential Understanding The sum of the interior angle measures of a polygon depends on the number of sides the polygon has.

By dividing a polygon with n sides into $(n - 2)$ triangles, you can show that the sum of the interior angle measures of any polygon is a multiple of 180.

Theorem 38 Polygon Angle-Sum Theorem

The sum of the measures of the interior angles of an n-gon is $(n - 2)180$.

Problem 1 Finding a Polygon Angle Sum

Got It? **a.** What is the sum of the interior angle measures of a 17-gon?

© **b. Reasoning** The sum of the interior angle measures of a polygon is 1980. How can you find the number of sides in the polygon?

Ⓐ Practice Find the sum of the interior angle measures of each polygon.

1. 35-gon **2.** 20-gon

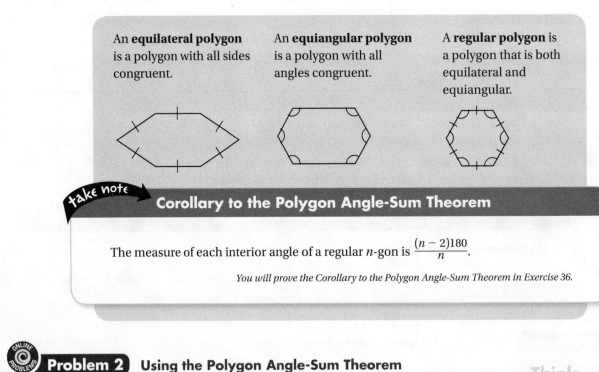

An **equilateral polygon** is a polygon with all sides congruent.

An **equiangular polygon** is a polygon with all angles congruent.

A **regular polygon** is a polygon that is both equilateral and equiangular.

take note

Corollary to the Polygon Angle-Sum Theorem

The measure of each interior angle of a regular n-gon is $\dfrac{(n-2)180}{n}$.

You will prove the Corollary to the Polygon Angle-Sum Theorem in Exercise 36.

Problem 2 **Using the Polygon Angle-Sum Theorem**

Got It? What is the measure of each interior angle in a regular nonagon?

Think

How does the word *regular* help you answer the question?

A **Practice** Find the measure of one interior angle in each regular polygon.

3.

4.

 Problem 3 **Using the Polygon Angle-Sum Theorem**

Got It? What is $m\angle G$ in quadrilateral *EFGH*?

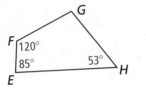

> **Think**
>
> What is the sum of the measures of the angles of a quadrilateral?

A **Practice** **Algebra** In Exercises 5 and 6, find the missing angle measures.

5.

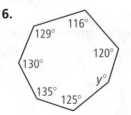

6.

You can draw exterior angles at any vertex of a polygon. The figures below show that the sum of the measures of the exterior angles, one at each vertex, is 360.

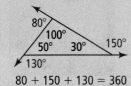

80 + 150 + 130 = 360

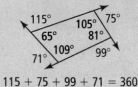

115 + 75 + 99 + 71 = 360

 take note

Theorem 39 Polygon Exterior Angle-Sum Theorem

The sum of the measures of the exterior angles of a polygon, one at each vertex, is 360.

For the pentagon, $m\angle 1 + m\angle 2 + m\angle 3 + m\angle 4 + m\angle 5 = 360$.

You will prove Theorem 39 in Exercise 32.

Problem 4 **Finding an Exterior Angle Measure**

Got It? What is the measure of an exterior angle of a regular nonagon?

Ⓐ Practice Find the measure of an exterior angle of each regular polygon.

7. 36-gon

8. 100-gon

Lesson Check

Do you know HOW?

9. What is the sum of the interior angle measures of an 11-gon?

10. What is the sum of the measures of the exterior angles of a 15-gon?

11. Find the measures of an interior angle and an exterior angle of a regular decagon.

Do you UNDERSTAND?

Ⓒ **12. Vocabulary** Can you draw an equiangular polygon that is not equilateral? Explain.

© 13. **Reasoning** Which angles are the exterior angles for $\angle 1$? What do you know about their measures? Explain.

© 14. **Error Analysis** Your friend says that she measured an interior angle of a regular polygon as 130. Explain why this result is impossible.

More Practice and Problem-Solving Exercises

© MATHEMATICAL PRACTICES

Ⓑ Apply

The sum of the interior angle measures of a polygon with n sides is given. Find n.

15. 180   **16.** 1080   **17.** 1980   **18.** 2880

© 19. **Open-Ended** Sketch an equilateral polygon that is not equiangular.

20. **Stage Design** A theater-in-the-round allows for a play to have an audience on all sides. The diagram at the right shows a platform constructed for a theater-in-the-round stage. What type of regular polygon is the largest platform? Find the measure of each numbered angle.

© 21. **Think About a Plan** A triangle has two congruent interior angles and an exterior angle that measures 100. Find two possible sets of interior angle measures for the triangle.
   • How can a diagram help you?
   • What is the sum of the angle measures in a triangle?

Algebra Find the value of each variable.

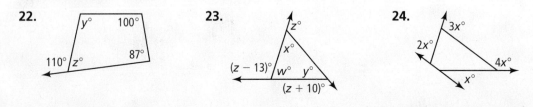

22.
$y°$ $100°$
$110°$ $z°$ $87°$

23.
$z°$
$x°$
$(z - 13)°$ $w°$ $y°$
$(z + 10)°$

24.
$3x°$
$2x°$
$4x°$
$x°$

The measure of an exterior angle of a regular polygon is given. Find the measure of an interior angle. Then find the number of sides.

25. 72   **26.** 36   **27.** 18   **28.** 30   **29.** x

Packaging The gift package at the right contains fruit and cheese. The fruit is in a container that has the shape of a regular octagon. The fruit container fits in a square box. A triangular cheese wedge fills each corner of the box.

30. Find the measure of each interior angle of a cheese wedge.

Ⓖ **31. Reasoning** Show how to rearrange the four pieces of cheese to make a regular polygon. What is the measure of each interior angle of the polygon?

32. Algebra A polygon has n sides. An interior angle of the polygon and an adjacent exterior angle form a straight angle.
  a. What is the sum of the measures of the n straight angles?
  b. What is the sum of the measures of the n interior angles?
  c. Using your answers above, what is the sum of the measures of the n exterior angles?
  d. What theorem do the steps above prove?

Ⓖ **33. Reasoning** Your friend says she has another way to find the sum of the interior angle measures of a polygon. She picks a point inside the polygon, draws a segment to each vertex, and counts the number of triangles. She multiplies the total by 180, and then subtracts 360 from the product. Does her method work? Explain.

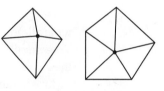

34. Algebra The measure of an interior angle of a regular polygon is three times the measure of an exterior angle of the same polygon. What is the name of the polygon?

Ⓒ **Challenge**

35. Probability Find the probability that the measure of an interior angle of a regular n-gon is a positive integer when n is an integer and $3 \leq n \leq 12$.

36. a. In the Corollary to the Polygon Angle-Sum Theorem, explain why the measure of an interior angle of a regular n-gon is given by the formulas $\frac{180(n-2)}{n}$ and $180 - \frac{360}{n}$.

  b. Use the second formula to explain what happens to the measures of the interior angles of regular n-gons as n becomes a large number. Explain also what happens to the polygons.

37. *ABCDEFGHJK* is a regular decagon. A ray bisects $\angle C$, and another ray bisects $\angle D$. The two rays intersect in the decagon's interior. Find the measure of the acute angles formed by the intersecting rays.

5-2 Properties of Parallelograms

G.CO.11 Prove theorems about parallelograms. Theorems include: opposite sides are congruent, opposite angles are congruent, the diagonals of a parallelogram bisect each other . . . Also **G.SRT.5**

Objectives To use relationships among sides and angles of parallelograms
To use relationships among diagonals of parallelograms

Solve It! Write your solution to the Solve It in the space below.

A **parallelogram** is a quadrilateral with both pairs of opposite sides parallel. In the Solve It, you made some conjectures about the characteristics of a parallelogram. In this lesson, you will verify whether your conjectures are correct.

Essential Understanding Parallelograms have special properties regarding their sides, angles, and diagonals.

In a quadrilateral, **opposite sides** do not share a vertex and **opposite angles** do not share a side.

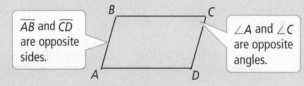

$\overline{AB}$ and $\overline{CD}$ are opposite sides.

∠A and ∠C are opposite angles.

You can abbreviate *parallelogram* with the symbol ▱ and *parallelograms* with the symbol ▱. You can use what you know about parallel lines and transversals to prove some theorems about parallelograms.

take note

Theorem 40

Theorem	If . . .	Then . . .
If a quadrilateral is a parallelogram, then its opposite sides are congruent.	*ABCD* is a ▱ 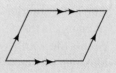	$\overline{AB} \cong \overline{CD}$ and $\overline{BC} \cong \overline{DA}$

Proof **Proof of Theorem 40**

Given: ▱ABCD

Prove: $\overline{AB} \cong \overline{CD}$ and $\overline{BC} \cong \overline{DA}$

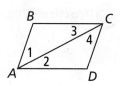

Statements	Reasons
1) ABCD is a parallelogram.	**1)** Given
2) $\overline{AB} \parallel \overline{CD}$ and $\overline{BC} \parallel \overline{DA}$	**2)** Definition of parallelogram
3) $\angle 1 \cong \angle 4$ and $\angle 3 \cong \angle 2$	**3)** If lines are $\parallel$, then alt. int. ⦞ are ≅.
4) $\overline{AC} \cong \overline{AC}$	**4)** Reflexive Property of ≅
5) $\triangle ABC \cong \triangle CDA$	**5)** ASA
6) $\overline{AB} \cong \overline{CD}$ and $\overline{BC} \cong \overline{DA}$	**6)** Corresp. parts of ≅▲ are ≅.

Angles of a polygon that share a side are **consecutive angles**. In the diagram, $\angle A$ and $\angle B$ are consecutive angles because they share side $\overline{AB}$.

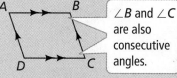

∠B and ∠C are also consecutive angles.

The theorem below uses the fact that consecutive angles of a parallelogram are same-side interior angles of parallel lines.

Theorem 41

Theorem	If . . .	Then . . .
If a quadrilateral is a parallelogram, then its consecutive angles are supplementary.	ABCD is a ▱	$m\angle A + m\angle B = 180$ $m\angle B + m\angle C = 180$ $m\angle C + m\angle D = 180$ $m\angle D + m\angle A = 180$

You will prove Theorem 41 in Exercise 23.

Problem 1 **Using Consecutive Angles**

Got It? Suppose you adjust the lamp in Problem 1 so that $m\angle S = 86$. What is $m\angle R$ in ▱PQRS?

Think

What is the relationship between ∠R and ∠S?

1.

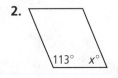

2.

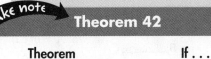

Parallelograms have some other special properties.

take note

Theorem 42

Theorem	If . . .	Then . . .
If a quadrilateral is a parallelogram, then its opposite angles are congruent.	*ABCD* is a ▱	∠A ≅ ∠C and ∠B ≅ ∠D

Theorem 43

Theorem	If . . .	Then . . .
If a quadrilateral is a parallelogram, then its diagonals bisect each other.	*ABCD* is a ▱	$\overline{AE} \cong \overline{CE}$ and $\overline{BE} \cong \overline{DE}$

You will prove Theorem 43 in Exercise 3.

A proof of Theorem 42 in Problem 2 uses the consecutive angles of a parallelogram and the fact that supplements of the same angle are congruent.

Problem 2 **Using Properties of Parallelograms in a Proof**

Got It? Use the diagram at the right.

Given: □*ABCD*, $\overline{AK} \cong \overline{MK}$
Prove: ∠*BCD* ≅ ∠*CMD*

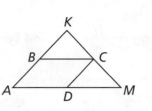

> **Think**
> What kind
> of triangle is
> △*AKM*?

Ⓐ Practice **3. Developing Proof** Complete this two-column proof of Theorem 43.

Given: □*ABCD*
Prove: $\overline{AC}$ and $\overline{BD}$ bisect each other at *E*.

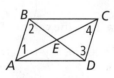

Statements	**Reasons**
1) *ABCD* is a parallelogram.	**1)** Given
2) $\overline{AB} \parallel \overline{DC}$	**2) a.** _____
3) ∠1 ≅ ∠4; ∠2 ≅ ∠3	**3) b.** _____
4) $\overline{AB} \cong \overline{DC}$	**4) c.** _____
5) d. _____	**5)** ASA
6) $\overline{AE} \cong \overline{CE}; \overline{BE} \cong \overline{DE}$	**6) e.** _____
7) f. _____	**7)** Definition of bisector

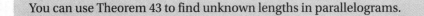

You can use Theorem 43 to find unknown lengths in parallelograms.

Problem 3 **Using Algebra to Find Lengths**

Got It? **a.** Find the values of x and y in $\square PQRS$ at the right. What are PR and SQ?

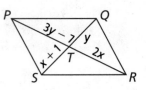

ⓒ **b. Reasoning** In Problem 3, does it matter which variable you solve for first? Explain.

Ⓐ **Practice Algebra** Find the values of x and y in $\square PQRS$.

4. $PT = 2x$, $TR = y + 4$, $QT = x + 2$, $TS = y$

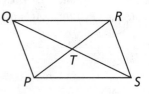

5. $PT = x + 2$, $TR = y$, $QT = 2x$, $TS = y + 3$

You will use parallelograms to prove the following theorem.

take note

Theorem 44

Theorem	If . . .	Then . . .
If three (or more) parallel lines cut off congruent segments on one transversal, then they cut off congruent segments on every transversal.	$\overleftrightarrow{AB} \parallel \overleftrightarrow{CD} \parallel \overleftrightarrow{EF}$ and $\overline{AC} \cong \overline{CE}$ 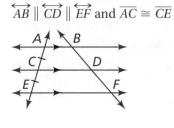	$\overline{BD} \cong \overline{DF}$ 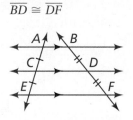

You will prove Theorem 44 in Exercise 34.

Problem 4 — Using Parallel Lines and Transversals

Got It? Use the figure in Problem 4, shown at the right. If $EF = FG = GH = 6$ and $AD = 15$, what is CD?

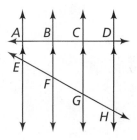

Ⓐ **Practice** In the figure, $PQ = QR = RS$. Find each length.

6. ZU

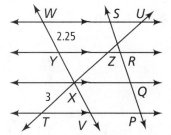

7. WV

Lesson Check

Do you know HOW?

For Exercises 8–11, use the diagram of $\square ABCD$ to find each value.

8. $m\angle A$

9. $m\angle D$

10. x

11. AB

12. What are ED and FD in the figure at the right?

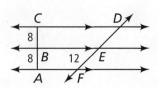

Do you UNDERSTAND?

13. Reasoning If you know one angle measure of a parallelogram, how do you find the other three angle measures? Explain.

14. Compare and Contrast What is the difference between a quadrilateral and a parallelogram?

15. Error Analysis Your classmate says that $QV = 10$. Explain why the statement may not be correct.

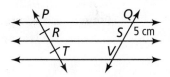

More Practice and Problem-Solving Exercises

Ⓑ Apply

Algebra Find the value(s) of the variable(s) in each parallelogram.

16.
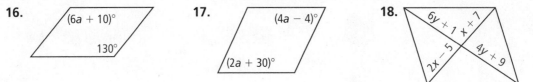
$(6a + 10)°$
$130°$

17.
$(4a - 4)°$
$(2a + 30)°$

18.
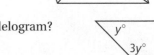
$6y + 1$ $x + 7$
$2x - 5$ $4y + 9$

Ⓖ **19. Think About a Plan** What are the values of x and y in the parallelogram?
- How are the angles related?
- Which variable should you solve for first?

$y°$
$3y°$ $3x°$

Algebra Find the value of a. Then find each side length or angle measure.

20.
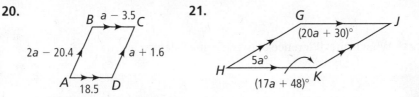
B $a - 3.5$ C
$2a - 20.4$ $a + 1.6$
A 18.5 D

21.
G $(20a + 30)°$ J
H $5a°$
$(17a + 48)°$ K

22. Studio Lighting A pantograph is an expandable device shown at the right. Pantographs are used in the television industry in positioning lighting and other equipment. In the photo, points D, E, F, and G are the vertices of a parallelogram. $\square DEFG$ is one of many parallelograms that change shape as the pantograph extends and retracts.

a. If $DE = 2.5$ ft, what is FG?
b. If $m\angle E = 129$, what is $m\angle G$?
c. What happens to $m\angle D$ as $m\angle E$ increases or decreases? Explain.

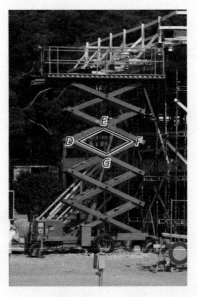

Proof 23. Prove Theorem 41.

Given: $\square ABCD$
Prove: $\angle A$ is supplementary to $\angle B$.
$\angle A$ is supplementary to $\angle D$.

B C
A D

Proof In the figure at the right, $\overline{GS}$ and $\overline{EH}$ intersect at point N. Use the diagram at the right to complete Exercises 24–26.

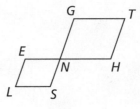
G T
E
N H
L S

24. Given: $\square LENS$ and $\square NGTH$
Prove: $\angle L \cong \angle T$

25. Given: $\square LENS$ and $\square NGTH$
Prove: $\overline{LS} \parallel \overline{GT}$

26. Given: $\square LENS$ and $\square NGTH$
Prove: $\angle E$ is supplementary to $\angle T$.

Proof In the figure at the right, points *S*, *Y*, and *T* are collinear, and points *T*, *Z*, and *W* are collinear. Use the figure for Exercises 27 and 28.

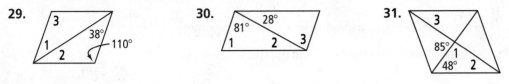

27. **Given:** ▱*RSTW* and ▱*XYTZ*
    Prove: ∠*R* ≅ ∠*X*

28. **Given:** ▱*RSTW* and ▱*XYTZ*
    Prove: $\overline{XY} \parallel \overline{RS}$

Find the measures of the numbered angles for each parallelogram.

29.
30.
31.

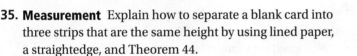

32. **Algebra** The perimeter of ▱*ABCD* is 92 cm. *AD* is 7 cm more than twice *AB*. Find the lengths of all four sides of ▱*ABCD*.

C Challenge

33. **Writing** Is there an SSSS congruence theorem for parallelograms? Explain.

Proof 34. Prove Theorem 44. Use the diagram at the right.

Given: $\overleftrightarrow{AB} \parallel \overleftrightarrow{CD} \parallel \overleftrightarrow{EF}$, $\overline{AC} \cong \overline{CE}$
Prove: $\overline{BD} \cong \overline{DF}$
(*Hint:* Draw lines through *B* and *D* parallel to $\overleftrightarrow{AE}$ and intersecting $\overleftrightarrow{CD}$ at *G* and $\overleftrightarrow{EF}$ at *H*.)

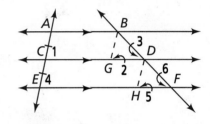

35. **Measurement** Explain how to separate a blank card into three strips that are the same height by using lined paper, a straightedge, and Theorem 44.

5-3 Proving That a Quadrilateral Is a Parallelogram

G.CO.11 Prove theorems about parallelograms . . . the diagonals of a parallelogram bisect each other . . .
Also **G.SRT.5**

Objective To determine whether a quadrilateral is a parallelogram

 Solve It! Write your solution to the Solve It in the space below.

In the Solve It, you used angle properties to show that lines are parallel. In this lesson, you will apply the same properties to show that a quadrilateral is a parallelogram.

Essential Understanding You can decide whether a quadrilateral is a parallelogram if its sides, angles, and diagonals have certain properties.

In Lesson 5-2, you learned theorems about the properties of parallelograms. In this lesson, you will learn the converses of those theorems. That is, if a quadrilateral has certain properties, then it must be a parallelogram. Theorem 45 is the converse of Theorem 40.

Theorem 45

Theorem	If . . .	Then . . .
If both pairs of opposite sides of a quadrilateral are congruent, then the quadrilateral is a parallelogram.	$\overline{AB} \cong \overline{CD}$ $\overline{BC} \cong \overline{DA}$	$ABCD$ is a $\square$

You will prove Theorem 45 in Exercise 15.

Theorems 46 and 47 are the converses of Theorems 41 and 42, respectively. They use angle relationships to conclude that a quadrilateral is a parallelogram.

Theorem 46

Theorem	If . . .	Then . . .
If an angle of a quadrilateral is supplementary to both of its consecutive angles, then the quadrilateral is a parallelogram.	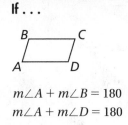 $m\angle A + m\angle B = 180$ $m\angle A + m\angle D = 180$	$ABCD$ is a $\square$

You will prove Theorem 46 in Exercise 16.

Theorem 47

Theorem	If . . .	Then . . .
If both pairs of opposite angles of a quadrilateral are congruent, then the quadrilateral is a parallelogram.	$\angle A \cong \angle C$ $\angle B \cong \angle D$	$ABCD$ is a $\square$

You will prove Theorem 47 in Exercise 13.

You can use algebra together with Theorems 45, 46, and 47 to find segment lengths and angle measures that assume that a quadrilateral is a parallelogram.

Problem 1 **Finding Values for Parallelograms**

Plan

What theorem should you use?

Got It? Use the diagram below. For what values of x and y must $EFGH$ be a parallelogram?

Algebra In Exercises 1 and 2, for what values of x and y must
ABCD be a parallelogram?

1.

B   C
$3x°$ $(y + 78)°$
$3y°$ $(4x − 21)°$
A   D

2.

D $5x − 8$ C
A $2x + 7$ B

You know that the converses of Theorems 40, 41, and 42 are true. Using what you
have learned, you can show that the converse of Theorem 43 is also true.

take note

Theorem 48

Theorem	**If . . .**	**Then . . .**
If the diagonals of a quadrilateral bisect each other, then the quadrilateral is a parallelogram.	$\overline{AE} = \overline{CE}$ $\overline{BE} = \overline{DE}$	*ABCD* is a $\square$

Proof **Proof of Theorem 48**

Given: $\overline{AC}$ and $\overline{BD}$ bisect each other at *E*.

Prove: *ABCD* is a parallelogram.

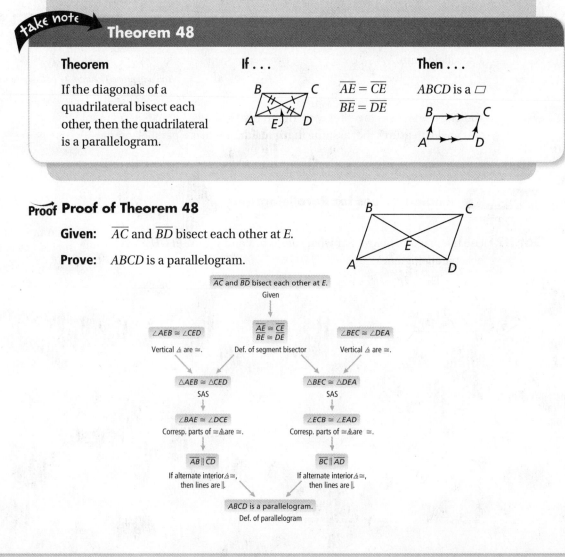

$\overline{AC}$ and $\overline{BD}$ bisect each other at *E*.
Given

∠*AEB* ≅ ∠*CED*
Vertical ∡ are ≅.

$\overline{AE} ≅ \overline{CE}$
$\overline{BE} ≅ \overline{DE}$
Def. of segment bisector

∠*BEC* ≅ ∠*DEA*
Vertical ∡ are ≅.

△*AEB* ≅ △*CED*
SAS

△*BEC* ≅ △*DEA*
SAS

∠*BAE* ≅ ∠*DCE*
Corresp. parts of ≅△are ≅.

∠*ECB* ≅ ∠*EAD*
Corresp. parts of ≅△are ≅.

$\overline{AB} \parallel \overline{CD}$
If alternate interior∡≅, then lines are ∥.

$\overline{BC} \parallel \overline{AD}$
If alternate interior∡≅, then lines are ∥.

ABCD is a parallelogram.
Def. of parallelogram

Theorem 49 suggests that if you keep two objects of the same length parallel, such as cross-country skis, then the quadrilateral formed by connecting their endpoints is always a parallelogram.

Theorem 49

Theorem	If . . .	Then . . .
If one pair of opposite sides of a quadrilateral is both congruent and parallel, then the quadrilateral is a parallelogram.	$\overline{BC} \cong \overline{DA}$ $\overline{BC} \parallel \overline{DA}$	$ABCD$ is a ▱ 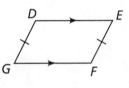

You will prove Theorem 49 in Exercise 14.

Problem 2 **Deciding Whether a Quadrilateral Is a Parallelogram**

> **Think**
>
> How do you decide if you have enough information?

Got It? Can you prove that the quadrilateral is a parallelogram based on the given information? Explain.

a. Given: $\overline{EF} \cong \overline{GD}, \overline{DE} \parallel \overline{FG}$

   Prove: *DEFG* is a parallelogram.

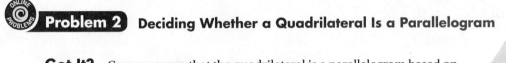

b. Given: $\angle ALN \cong \angle DNL, \angle ANL \cong \angle DLN$

   Prove: *LAND* is a parallelogram.

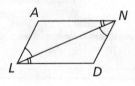

Practice **Algebra** Can you prove that the quadrilateral is a parallelogram based on the given information? Explain.

3.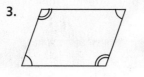

4.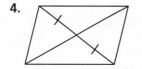

Problem 3 **Identifying Parallelograms**

© **Got It?** **Reasoning** What is the maximum height that the vehicle lift can elevate the truck? Explain.

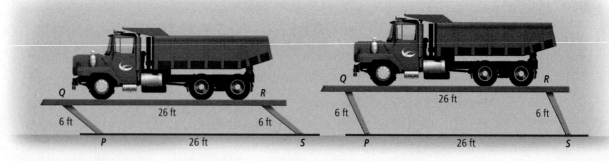

Ⓐ Practice

5. Fishing Quadrilaterals are formed on the side of this fishing tackle box by the adjustable shelves and connecting pieces. Explain why the shelves are always parallel to each other no matter what their position is.

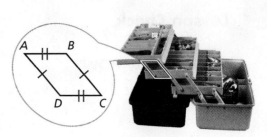

---

take note

Concept Summary   Proving That a Quadrilateral Is a Parallelogram

Method	Source	Diagram
Prove that both pairs of opposite sides are parallel.	Definition of parallelogram	
Prove that both pairs of opposite sides are congruent.	Theorem 45	
Prove that an angle is supplementary to both of its consecutive angles.	Theorem 46	75° / 75° 105°
Prove that both pairs of opposite angles are congruent.	Theorem 47	
Prove that the diagonals bisect each other.	Theorem 48	
Prove that one pair of opposite sides is congruent and parallel.	Theorem 49	

Lesson Check

Do you know HOW?

6. For what value of *y* must *LMNP* be a parallelogram?

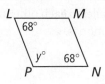

For Exercises 7 and 8, is the given information enough to prove that *ABCD* is a parallelogram? Explain.

7.

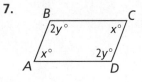

8.

Do you UNDERSTAND?

9. Vocabulary Explain why you can now write a biconditional statement regarding opposite sides of a parallelogram.

10. **Compare and Contrast** How is Theorem 48 in this lesson different from Theorem 43 in the previous lesson? In what situations should you use each theorem? Explain.

11. **Error Analysis** Your friend says, "If a quadrilateral has a pair of opposite sides that are congruent and a pair of opposite sides that are parallel, then it is a parallelogram." What is your friend's error? Explain.

More Practice and Problem-Solving Exercises

B Apply

12. **Writing** Combine each of Theorems 40, 41, 42, and 43 with its converse from this lesson into biconditional statements.

13. **Developing Proof** Complete this two-column proof of Theorem 47.

Given: $\angle A \cong \angle C, \angle B \cong \angle D$

Prove: $ABCD$ is a parallelogram.

Statements	Reasons
1) $x + y + x + y = 360$	1) The sum of the measures of the angles of a quadrilateral is 360.
2) $2(x + y) = 360$	2) a. ___?___
3) $x + y = 180$	3) b. ___?___
4) $\angle A$ and $\angle B$ are supplementary. $\angle A$ and $\angle D$ are supplementary.	4) Definition of supplementary
5) c. ___?___ ∥ ___?___, ___?___ ∥ ___?___	5) d. ___?___
6) $ABCD$ is a parallelogram.	6) e. ___?___

14. Think About a Plan Prove Theorem 49.

Proof **Given:** $\overline{BC} \parallel \overline{DA}$, $\overline{BC} \cong \overline{DA}$

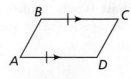

Prove: ABCD is a parallelogram.
- How can drawing diagonals help you?
- How can you use triangles in this proof?

Proof **15.** Prove Theorem 45.

Given: $\overline{AB} \cong \overline{CD}$, $\overline{BC} \cong \overline{DA}$

Prove: ABCD is a parallelogram.

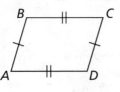

Proof **16.** Prove Theorem 46.

Given: $\angle A$ is supplementary to $\angle B$.
$\angle A$ is supplementary to $\angle D$.

Prove: ABCD is a parallelogram.

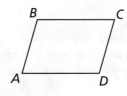

Algebra For what values of the variables must ABCD be a parallelogram?

17.
18.
19.

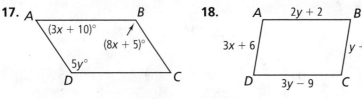

Proof **20. Given:** $\triangle TRS \cong \triangle RTW$

Prove: RSTW is a parallelogram.

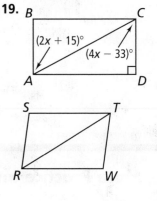

21. Open-Ended Sketch two noncongruent parallelograms ABCD and EFGH such that $\overline{AC} \cong \overline{EG}$ and $\overline{BD} \cong \overline{FH}$.

Challenge

Proof **22. Construction** In the figure at the right, point D is constructed by drawing two arcs. One has center C and radius AB. The other has center B and radius AC. Prove that $\overline{AM}$ is a median of $\triangle ABC$.

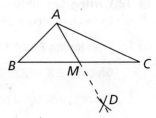

23. Probability If two opposite angles of a quadrilateral measure 120 and the measures of the other angles are multiples of 10, what is the probability that the quadrilateral is a parallelogram?

5-4 Properties of Rhombuses, Rectangles, and Squares

G.CO.11 Prove theorems about parallelograms . . . rectangles are parallelograms with congruent diagonals.
Also **G.SRT.5**

Objectives To define and classify special types of parallelograms
To use properties of diagonals of rhombuses and rectangles

Solve It! Write your solution to the Solve It in the space below.

In the Solve It, you formed a special type of parallelogram with characteristics that you will study in this lesson.

Essential Understanding The parallelograms in the Take Note box below have basic properties about their sides and angles that help identify them. The diagonals of these parallelograms also have certain properties.

take note

Key Concept   Special Parallelograms

Definition	Diagram
A **rhombus** is a parallelogram with four congruent sides.	
A **rectangle** is a parallelogram with four right angles.	
A **square** is a parallelogram with four congruent sides and four right angles.	

The Venn diagram at the right shows the relationships among special parallelograms.

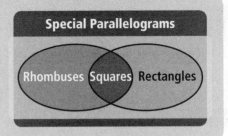

Special Parallelograms

Rhombuses Squares Rectangles

Problem 1 Classifying Special Parallelograms

Got It? Is □*EFGH* in Problem 1 a rhombus, a rectangle, or a square? Explain.

Think

How do you decide whether *EFGH* is a rhombus, rectangle, or square?

A Practice Decide whether the parallelogram is a rhombus, a rectangle, or a square. Explain.

1.

2.

Theorem 50

Theorem	If . . .	Then . . .
If a parallelogram is a rhombus, then its diagonals are perpendicular.	ABCD is a rhombus	$\overline{AC} \perp \overline{BD}$

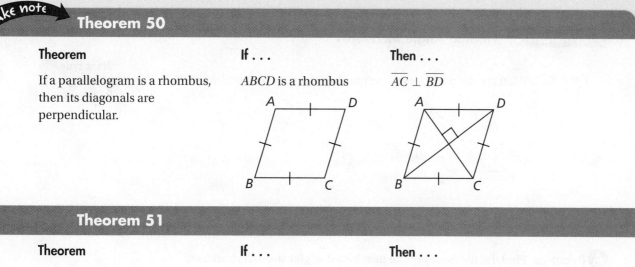

Theorem 51

Theorem	If . . .	Then . . .
If a parallelogram is a rhombus, then each diagonal bisects a pair of opposite angles.	ABCD is a rhombus	$\angle 1 \cong \angle 2$ $\angle 3 \cong \angle 4$ $\angle 5 \cong \angle 6$ $\angle 7 \cong \angle 8$

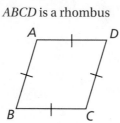
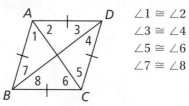

You will prove Theorem 51 in Exercise 34.

Proof Proof of Theorem 50

Given: ABCD is a rhombus.

Prove: The diagonals of ABCD are perpendicular.

Statements	Reasons
1) A and C are equidistant from B and D; B and D are equidistant from A and C.	1) All sides of a rhombus are ≅.
2) A and C are on the perpendicular bisector of $\overline{BD}$; B and D are on the perpendicular bisector of $\overline{AC}$.	2) Converse of the Perpendicular Bisector Theorem
3) $\overline{AC} \perp \overline{BD}$	3) Through two points, there is one unique line perpendicular to a given line.

You can use Theorems 50 and 51 to find angle measures in a rhombus.

Problem 2 Finding Angle Measures

Got It? What are the measures of the numbered angles in rhombus *PQRS*?

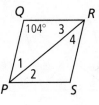

Think

What type of triangle is △*PQR*?

Ⓐ Practice Find the measures of the numbered angles in each rhombus.

3.

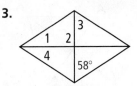

4.

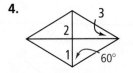

The diagonals of a rectangle also have a special property.

take note

Theorem 52

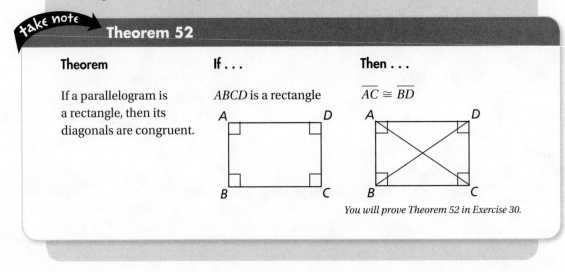

Theorem	**If . . .**	**Then . . .**
If a parallelogram is a rectangle, then its diagonals are congruent.	*ABCD* is a rectangle	$\overline{AC} \cong \overline{BD}$

You will prove Theorem 52 in Exercise 30.

Problem 3 **Finding Diagonal Length**

Got It? **a.** If $LN = 4x - 17$ and $MO = 2x + 13$, what are the lengths of the diagonals of rectangle $LMNO$?

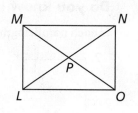

@ **b. Reasoning** What type of triangle is $\triangle PMN$? Explain.

Practice **Algebra** $LMNP$ is a rectangle. Find the value of x and the length of each diagonal.

5. $LN = 5x - 8$ and $MP = 2x + 1$

6. $LN = 3x + 1$ and $MP = 8x - 4$

Lesson Check

Do you know HOW?

Is each parallelogram a rhombus, rectangle, or square? Explain.

7.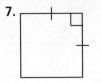

8.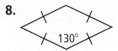

9. What are the measures of the numbered angles in the rhombus?

10. **Algebra** *JKLM* is a rectangle. If *JL* = 4*x* − 12 and *MK* = *x*, what is the value of *x*? What is the length of each diagonal?

Do you UNDERSTAND?

Ⓒ **11. Vocabulary** Which special parallelograms are equiangular? Which special parallelograms are equilateral?

Ⓒ **12. Error Analysis** Your class needs to find the value of x for which □$DEFG$ is a rectangle. A classmate's work is shown at the right. What is the error? Explain.

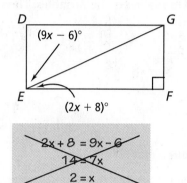

More Practice and Problem-Solving Exercises

Ⓑ **Apply**

Determine the most precise name for each quadrilateral.

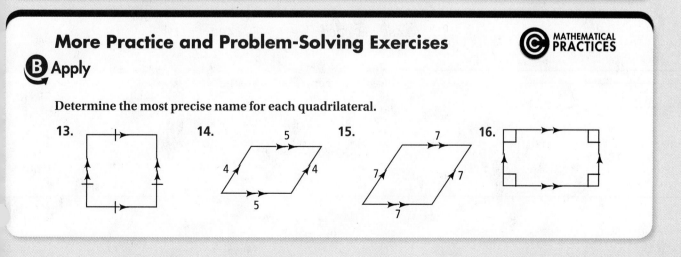

13.

14.

15.

16.

List the quadrilaterals that have the given property. Choose among *parallelogram,* *rhombus, rectangle,* **and** *square.*

17. All sides are ≅.

18. Opposite sides are ≅.

19. Opposite sides are ∥.

20. Opposite ∠ are ≅.

21. All ∠ are right ∠.

22. Consecutive ∠ are supplementary.

23. Diagonals bisect each other.

24. Diagonals are ≅.

25. Diagonals are ⊥.

26. Each diagonal bisects opposite ∠.

Algebra **Find the values of the variables. Then find the side lengths.**

27. rhombus

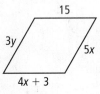

15

3y

5x

4x + 3

28. square

2x − 7

y − 1

2y − 5

3y − 9

🄖 **29. Think About a Plan** Write a proof.

Proof

Given: Rectangle *PLAN*

Prove: △*LTP* ≅ △*NTA*

- What do you know about the diagonals of rectangles?
- Which triangle congruence postulate or theorem can you use?

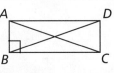

🄖 **30. Developing Proof** Complete the flow proof of Theorem 52.

Given: *ABCD* is a rectangle.

Prove: $\overline{AC} \cong \overline{BD}$

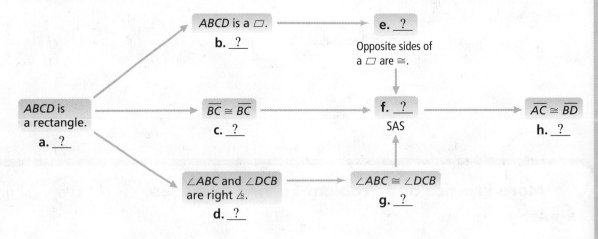

ABCD is a ▱.
b. __?__

e. __?__
Opposite sides of a ▱ are ≅.

ABCD is a rectangle.
a. __?__

$\overline{BC} \cong \overline{BC}$
c. __?__

f. __?__
SAS

$\overline{AC} \cong \overline{BD}$
h. __?__

∠ABC and ∠DCB are right ∠.
d. __?__

∠ABC ≅ ∠DCB
g. __?__

Algebra Find the value(s) of the variable(s) for each parallelogram.

31. $RZ = 2x + 5$,
$SW = 5x - 20$

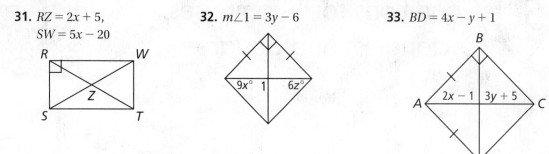

32. $m\angle 1 = 3y - 6$

33. $BD = 4x - y + 1$

34. Prove Theorem 51.

Proof

    Given: *ABCD* is a rhombus.

    Prove: $\overline{AC}$ bisects $\angle BAD$ and $\angle BCD$.

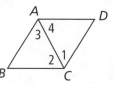

Ⓖ 35. Writing Summarize the properties of squares that follow from a square being (a) a parallelogram, (b) a rhombus, and (c) a rectangle.

36. Algebra Find the angle measures and the side lengths of the rhombus at the right.

Ⓖ 37. Open-Ended On graph paper, draw a parallelogram that is neither a rectangle nor a rhombus.

Algebra *ABCD* is a rectangle. Find the length of each diagonal.

38. $AC = 2(x - 3)$ and $BD = x + 5$

39. $AC = 2(5a + 1)$ and $BD = 2(a + 1)$

40. $AC = \dfrac{3y}{5}$ and $BD = 3y - 4$

41. $AC = \dfrac{3c}{9}$ and $BD = 4 - c$

Ⓒ Challenge

Algebra Find the value of *x* in the rhombus.

42.

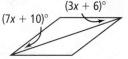

43.

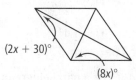

5-5 Conditions for Rhombuses, Rectangles, and Squares

G.CO.11 Prove theorems about parallelograms . . . rectangles are parallelograms with congruent diagonals. Also **G.SRT.5**

Objective To determine whether a parallelogram is a rhombus or rectangle

Solve It! Write your solution to the Solve It in the space below.

Essential Understanding You can determine whether a parallelogram is a rhombus or a rectangle based on the properties of its diagonals.

take note

Theorem 53

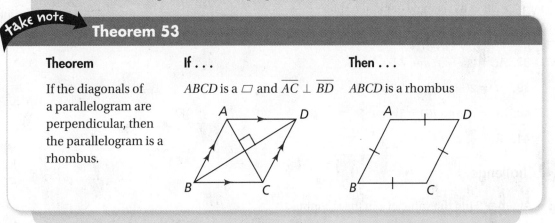

Theorem	If . . .	Then . . .
If the diagonals of a parallelogram are perpendicular, then the parallelogram is a rhombus.	$ABCD$ is a $\square$ and $\overline{AC} \perp \overline{BD}$	$ABCD$ is a rhombus

Proof **Proof of Theorem 53**

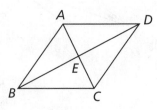

Given: $ABCD$ is a parallelogram, $\overline{AC} \perp \overline{BD}$
Prove: $ABCD$ is a rhombus.

Since $ABCD$ is a parallelogram, $\overline{AC}$ and $\overline{BD}$ bisect each other, so $\overline{BE} \cong \overline{DE}$. Since $\overline{AC} \perp \overline{BD}$, $\angle AED$ and $\angle AEB$ are congruent right angles. By the Reflexive Property of Congruence, $\overline{AE} \cong \overline{AE}$.

So $\triangle AEB \cong \triangle AED$ by SAS. Corresponding parts of congruent triangles are congruent, so $\overline{AB} \cong \overline{AD}$. Since opposite sides of a parallelogram are congruent, $\overline{AB} \cong \overline{DC} \cong \overline{BC} \cong \overline{AD}$. By definition, $ABCD$ is a rhombus.

Theorem 54

Theorem	**If . . .**	**Then . . .**
If one diagonal of a parallelogram bisects a pair of opposite angles, then the parallelogram is a rhombus.	$ABCD$ is a $\square$, $\angle 1 \cong \angle 2$, and $\angle 3 \cong \angle 4$ 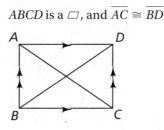	$ABCD$ is a rhombus 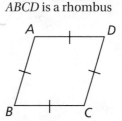 *You will prove Theorem 54 in Exercise 21.*

Theorem 55

Theorem	**If . . .**	**Then . . .**
If the diagonals of a parallelogram are congruent, then the parallelogram is a rectangle.	$ABCD$ is a $\square$, and $\overline{AC} \cong \overline{BD}$ 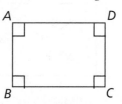	$ABCD$ is a rectangle 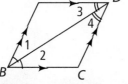 *You will prove Theorem 55 in Exercise 22.*

You can use Theorems 53, 54, and 55 to classify parallelograms. Notice that if a parallelogram is both a rectangle and a rhombus, then it is a square.

Problem 1 Identifying Special Parallelograms

Got It?   **a.** A parallelogram has angle measures of 20, 160, 20, and 160. Can you conclude that it is a rhombus, a rectangle, or a square? Explain.

Think
How can you determine whether a figure is a special parallelogram?

© b. Reasoning Suppose the diagonals of a quadrilateral bisect each other. Can you conclude that it is a rhombus, a rectangle, or a square? Explain.

Ⓐ Practice Can you conclude that the parallelogram is a rhombus, a rectangle, or a square? Explain.

1.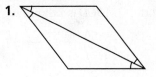

2.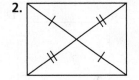

Problem 2 **Using Properties of Special Parallelograms**

Got It?   For what value of *y* is ▱*DEFG* a rectangle?

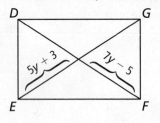

Think

What do you know about the diagonals of a rectangle?

Practice For what value of x is the figure the given special parallelogram?

3. rhombus

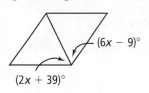

$(6x - 9)°$

$(2x + 39)°$

4. rectangle

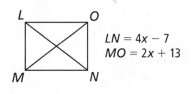

$LN = 4x - 7$
$MO = 2x + 13$

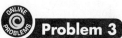 **Problem 3** **Using Properties of Parallelograms**

Got It? Can you adapt the method described in Problem 3 to stake off a square play area? Explain.

 Practice **5. Carpentry** A carpenter is building a bookcase. How can the carpenter use a tape measure to check that the bookshelf is rectangular? Justify your answer and name any theorems used.

Lesson Check

Do you know HOW?

Can you conclude that the parallelogram is a rhombus, a rectangle, or a square? Explain.

6.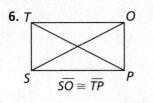

$\overline{SO} \cong \overline{TP}$

7.

For what value of x is the figure the given special parallelogram?

8. rhombus

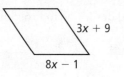

$3x + 9$

$8x - 1$

9. rectangle

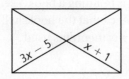

$3x - 5$ $x + 1$

Do you UNDERSTAND?

10. Name all of the special parallelograms that have each property.

    a. Diagonals are perpendicular.

    b. Diagonals are congruent.

    c. Diagonals are angle bisectors.

    d. Diagonals bisect each other.

    e. Diagonals are perpendicular bisectors of each other.

© **11. Error Analysis** Your friend says, "A parallelogram with perpendicular diagonals is a rectangle." What is your friend's error? Explain.

© **12. Reasoning** When you draw a circle and two of its diameters and connect the endpoints of the diameters, what quadrilateral do you get? Explain.

More Practice and Problem-Solving Exercises

MATHEMATICAL
PRACTICES

B Apply

13. Hardware You can use a simple device called a turnbuckle to "square up" structures that are parallelograms. For the gate pictured at the right, you tighten or loosen the turnbuckle on the diagonal cable so that the rectangular frame will keep the shape of a parallelogram when it sags. What are two ways you can make sure that the turnbuckle works? Explain.

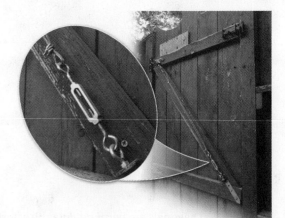

© **14. Reasoning** Suppose the diagonals of a parallelogram are both perpendicular and congruent. What type of special quadrilateral is it? Explain your reasoning.

Algebra For what value of *x* is the figure the given special parallelogram?

15. rectangle

(5x + 2)°
3x°

16. rhombus

(3x + 6)°
(8x + 7)°

17. rectangle

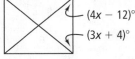
(4x − 12)°
(3x + 4)°

◉ **Open-Ended** Given two segments with lengths *a* and *b* (*a* ≠ *b*), what special parallelograms meet the given conditions? Show each sketch.

18. Both diagonals have length *a*.

19. The two diagonals have lengths *a* and *b*.

20. One diagonal has length *a*, and one side of the quadrilateral has length *b*.

Proof **21.** Prove Theorem 54.

> **Given:** *ABCD* is a parallelogram.
> $\overline{AC}$ bisects ∠*BAD* and ∠*BCD*.
>
> **Prove:** *ABCD* is a rhombus.

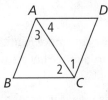

Proof **22.** Prove Theorem 55.

> **Given:** □*ABCD*, $\overline{AC} \cong \overline{BD}$
>
> **Prove:** *ABCD* is a rectangle.

◉ **Think About a Plan** Explain how to construct each figure given its diagonals.
- What do you know about the diagonals of each figure?
- How can you apply constructions to what you know about the diagonals?

23. parallelogram   **24.** rectangle   **25.** rhombus

ⒸChallenge

Determine whether the quadrilateral can be a parallelogram. Explain.

26. The diagonals are congruent, but the quadrilateral has no right angles.

27. Each diagonal is 3 cm long and two opposite sides are 2 cm long.

28. Two opposite angles are right angles, but the quadrilateral is not a rectangle.

Proof **29.** In Theorem 54, replace "a pair of opposite angles" with "one angle." Write a paragraph that proves this new statement to be true, or give a counterexample to prove it to be false.

G.SRT.5 Use congruence . . . criteria . . . to solve problems and to prove relationships in geometric figures.
Also G.CO.9

Objective   To verify and use properties of trapezoids and kites

Solve It!   Write your solution to the Solve It in the space below.

In the Solve It, the orange and green regions are trapezoids. The entire figure is a kite. In this lesson, you will learn about these special quadrilaterals that are not parallelograms.

Essential Understanding   The angles, sides, and diagonals of a trapezoid have certain properties.

A **trapezoid** is a quadrilateral with exactly one pair of parallel sides. The parallel sides of a trapezoid are called **bases**. The nonparallel sides are called **legs**. The two angles that share a base of a trapezoid are called **base angles**. A trapezoid has two pairs of base angles.

An **isosceles trapezoid** is a trapezoid with legs that are congruent. *ABCD* at the right is an isosceles trapezoid. The angles of an isosceles trapezoid have some unique properties.

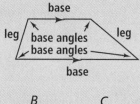

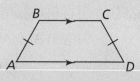

take note

Theorem 56

Theorem	**If . . .**	**Then . . .**
If a quadrilateral is an isosceles trapezoid, then each pair of base angles is congruent.	*TRAP* is an isosceles trapezoid with bases $\overline{RA}$ and $\overline{TP}$	$\angle T \cong \angle P, \angle R \cong \angle A$

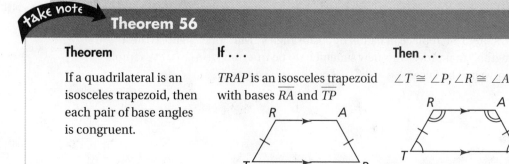

You will prove Theorem 56 in Exercise 35.

Problem 1 **Finding Angle Measures in Trapezoids**

Got It?   **a.** In the diagram, *PQRS* is an isosceles trapezoid and $m\angle R = 106$. What are $m\angle P$, $m\angle Q$, and $m\angle S$?

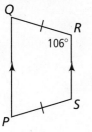

What do you know about the angles of an isosceles trapezoid?

b. Reasoning In Problem 1, if *CDEF* were not an isosceles trapezoid, would $\angle C$ and $\angle D$ still be supplementary? Explain.

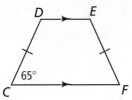

Practice Find the measures of the numbered angles in each isosceles trapezoid.

1.

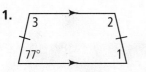

2.

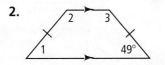

Problem 2 Finding Angle Measures in Isosceles Trapezoids

Got It? A fan like the one in Problem 2 has 15 angles meeting at the center. What are the measures of the base angles of the trapezoids in its second ring?

Practice Find the measures of the numbered angles in each isosceles trapezoid.

3.

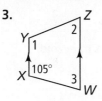

4.

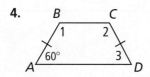

take note

Theorem 57

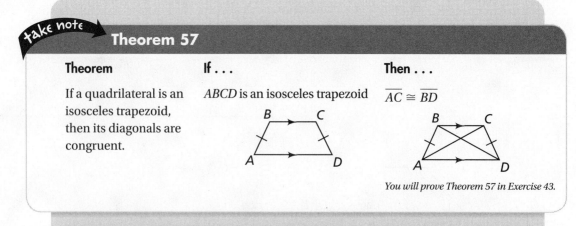

Theorem	If . . .	Then . . .
If a quadrilateral is an isosceles trapezoid, then its diagonals are congruent.	*ABCD* is an isosceles trapezoid	$\overline{AC} \cong \overline{BD}$

You will prove Theorem 57 in Exercise 43.

In Lesson 4–1, you learned about midsegments of triangles. Trapezoids also have midsegments. The **midsegment of a trapezoid** is the segment that joins the midpoints of its legs. The midsegment has two unique properties.

Theorem 58   Trapezoid Midsegment Theorem

Theorem	If . . .	Then . . .

Theorem

If a quadrilateral is a trapezoid, then
(1) the midsegment is parallel to the bases, and
(2) the length of the midsegment is half the sum of the lengths of the bases.

If . . .

TRAP is a trapezoid with midsegment $\overline{MN}$

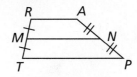

Then . . .

(1) $\overline{MN} \parallel \overline{TP}$, $\overline{MN} \parallel \overline{RA}$, and

(2) $MN = \frac{1}{2}\left(TP + RA\right)$

You will prove Theorem 58 in Lesson 5-8.

Problem 3   Using the Midsegment of a Trapezoid

Got It?   **a. Algebra** $\overline{MN}$ is the midsegment of trapezoid *PQRS*. What is *x*? What is *MN*?

Q 10 R
2x + 11
M   N
P   8x − 12   S

Think

How can you check your answer?

b. Reasoning How many midsegments can a triangle have? How many midsegments can a trapezoid have? Explain.

A Practice Find *EF* in each trapezoid.

5.

A 4 D
E   F
3x + 5
B   7x + 4   C

6.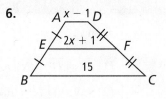

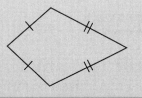

A **kite** is a quadrilateral with two pairs of consecutive sides congruent and no opposite sides congruent.

Essential Understanding The angles, sides, and diagonals of a kite have certain properties.

take note

Theorem 59

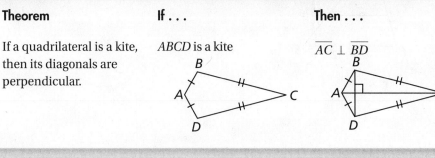

Theorem	If . . .	Then . . .
If a quadrilateral is a kite, then its diagonals are perpendicular.	*ABCD* is a kite	$\overline{AC} \perp \overline{BD}$

Proof **Proof of Theorem 59**

Given: Kite *ABCD* with $\overline{AB} \cong \overline{AD}$ and $\overline{CB} \cong \overline{CD}$

Prove: $\overline{AC} \perp \overline{BD}$

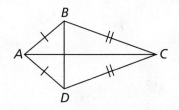

Statements	Reasons
1) Kite *ABCD* with $\overline{AB} \cong \overline{AD}$ and $\overline{CB} \cong \overline{CD}$	**1)** Given
2) *A* and *C* lie on the perpendicular bisector of $\overline{BD}$.	**2)** Converse of Perpendicular Bisector Theorem
3) $\overline{AC}$ is the perpendicular bisector of $\overline{BD}$.	**3)** Two points determine a line.
4) $\overline{AC} \perp \overline{BD}$	**4)** Definition of perpendicular bisector

Got It? Quadrilateral *KLMN* is a kite. What are $m\angle 1$, $m\angle 2$, and $m\angle 3$?

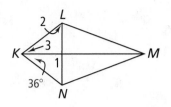

Ⓐ **Practice** Find the measures of the numbered angles in each kite.

7.

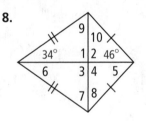

8.

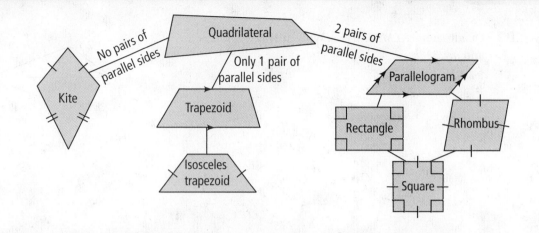

Lesson Check

Do you know HOW?

What are the measures of the numbered angles?

9.
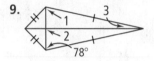

10.
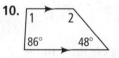

11. What is the length of the midsegment of a trapezoid with bases of lengths 14 and 26?

Do you UNDERSTAND?

12. Vocabulary Is a kite a parallelogram? Explain.

13. Compare and Contrast How is a kite similar to a rhombus? How is it different? Explain.

14. Error Analysis Since a parallelogram has two pairs of parallel sides, it certainly has one pair of parallel sides. Therefore, a parallelogram must also be a trapezoid. What is the error in this reasoning? Explain.

More Practice and Problem-Solving Exercises

B Apply

15. Open-Ended Sketch two noncongruent kites such that the diagonals of one are congruent to the diagonals of the other.

16. Think About a Plan The perimeter of a kite is 66 cm. The length of one of its sides is 3 cm less than twice the length of another. Find the length of each side of the kite.
- Can you draw a diagram?
- How can you write algebraic expressions for the lengths of the sides?

17. Reasoning If $KLMN$ is an isosceles trapezoid, is it possible for $\overline{KM}$ to bisect $\angle LMN$ and $\angle LKN$? Explain.

Algebra Find the value of the variable in each isosceles trapezoid.

18.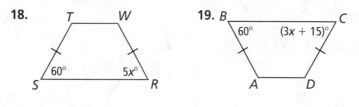

19.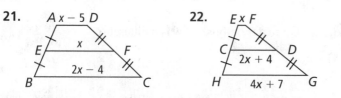

20.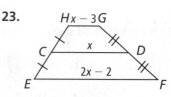

$QS = x + 5$
$RP = 3x + 3$

Algebra Find the lengths of the segments with variable expressions.

21.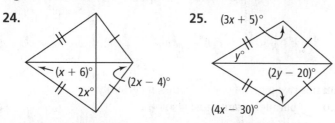

22.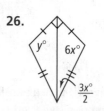

23.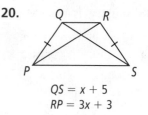

Algebra Find the value(s) of the variable(s) in each kite.

24.

25. $(3x + 5)°$ ... $y°$ ... $(2y - 20)°$ ... $(4x - 30)°$

26. $y°$ ... $6x°$ ... $\dfrac{3x°}{2}$

24. $(x + 6)°$ ... $2x°$ ... $(2x - 4)°$

STEM **Bridge Design** The beams of the bridge at the right form quadrilateral $ABCD$. $\triangle AED \cong \triangle CDE \cong \triangle BEC$ and $m\angle DCB = 120$.

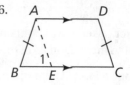

27. Classify the quadrilateral. Explain your reasoning.

28. Find the measures of the other interior angles of the quadrilateral.

Ⓖ Reasoning Can two angles of a kite be as follows? Explain.

29. opposite and acute

30. consecutive and obtuse

31. opposite and supplementary

32. consecutive and supplementary

33. opposite and complementary

34. consecutive and complementary

Ⓖ 35. Developing Proof The plan suggests a proof of Theorem 56. Write a proof that follows the plan.

Given: Isosceles trapezoid $ABCD$ with $\overline{AB} \cong \overline{DC}$

Prove: $\angle B \cong \angle C$ and $\angle BAD \cong \angle D$

Plan: Begin by drawing $\overline{AE} \parallel \overline{DC}$ to form parallelogram $AECD$ so that $\overline{AE} \cong \overline{DC} \cong \overline{AB}$. $\angle B \cong \angle C$ because $\angle B \cong \angle 1$ and $\angle 1 \cong \angle C$. Also, $\angle BAD \cong \angle D$ because they are supplements of the congruent angles, $\angle B$ and $\angle C$.

Proof 36. Prove the converse of Theorem 56: If a trapezoid has a pair of congruent base angles, then the trapezoid is isosceles.

Name each type of special quadrilateral that can meet the given condition. Make sketches to support your answers.

37. exactly one pair of congruent sides

38. two pairs of parallel sides

39. four right angles

40. adjacent sides that are congruent

41. perpendicular diagonals

42. congruent diagonals

Proof 43. Prove Theorem 57.

Given: Isosceles trapezoid $ABCD$ with $\overline{AB} \cong \overline{DC}$

Prove: $\overline{AC} \cong \overline{DB}$

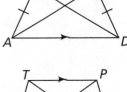

Proof 44. Prove the converse of Theorem 57: If the diagonals of a trapezoid are congruent, then the trapezoid is isosceles.

Proof 45. Given: Isosceles trapezoid $TRAP$ with $\overline{TR} \cong \overline{PA}$

Prove: $\angle RTA \cong \angle APR$

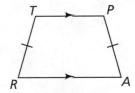

Proof 46. Prove that the angles formed by the noncongruent sides of a kite are congruent. (*Hint:* Draw a diagonal of the kite.)

Determine whether each statement is *true* or *false*. Justify your response.

47. All squares are rectangles.

48. A trapezoid is a parallelogram.

49. A rhombus can be a kite.

50. Some parallelograms are squares.

51. Every quadrilateral is a parallelogram.

52. All rhombuses are squares.

Challenge

Proof 53. Given: Isosceles trapezoid $TRAP$ with $\overline{TR} \cong \overline{PA}$; $\overline{BI}$ is the perpendicular bisector of $\overline{RA}$, intersecting $\overline{RA}$ at B and $\overline{TP}$ at I.

Prove: $\overline{BI}$ is the perpendicular bisector of $\overline{TP}$.

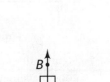

For a trapezoid, consider the segment joining the midpoints of the two given segments. How are its length and the lengths of the two parallel sides of the trapezoid related? Justify your answer.

54. the two nonparallel sides

55. the diagonals

56. $\overleftrightarrow{BN}$ is the perpendicular bisector of $\overline{AC}$ at N. Describe the set of points, D, for which $ABCD$ is a kite.

5-7 Applying Coordinate Geometry

G.CO.11 Prove theorems about parallelograms. Theorems include: opposite sides are congruent . . . Also **G.CO.10**

Objective To name coordinates of special figures by using their properties

Solve It! Write your solution to the Solve It in the space below.

In the Solve It, you found coordinates of a point and named it using numbers for the *x*- and *y*-coordinates. In this lesson, you will learn to use variables for the coordinates.

Essential Understanding You can use variables to name the coordinates of a figure. This allows you to show that relationships are true for a general case.

In Chapter 4, you learned about the segment joining the midpoints of two sides of a triangle. Here are three possible ways to place a triangle and its midsegment.

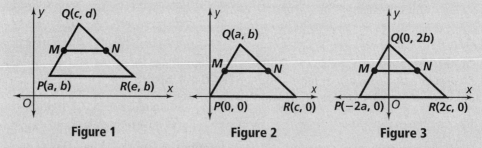

Figure 1 does not use the axes, so it requires more variables. Figures 2 and 3 have good placement. In Figure 2, the midpoint coordinates are $M\left(\frac{a}{2}, \frac{b}{2}\right)$ and $N\left(\frac{a+c}{2}, \frac{b}{2}\right)$. In Figure 3, the coordinates are $M(-a, b)$ and $N(c, b)$. You can see that Figure 3 is the easiest to work with.

To summarize, to place a figure in the coordinate plane, it is usually helpful to place at least one side on an axis or to center the figure at the origin. For the coordinates, try to anticipate what you will need to do in the problem. Then multiply the coordinates by the appropriate number to make your work easier.

Figure 1 Figure 2 Figure 3

Got It? What are the coordinates of the vertices of each figure?

a. *RECT* is a rectangle with height *a* and length 2*b*. The *y*-axis bisects $\overline{EC}$ and $\overline{RT}$.

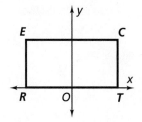

b. *KITE* is a kite where $IE = 2a$, $KO = b$, and $OT = c$. The *x*-axis bisects $\overline{IE}$.

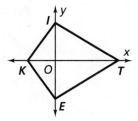

Ⓐ Practice **Algebra** What are the coordinates of the vertices of each figure?

1. parallelogram where *S* is *a* units from the origin and *Z* is *b* units from the origin

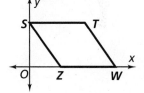

2. isosceles trapezoid with base centered at the origin, with base 2*a* and $OR = c$

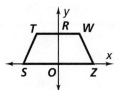

Got It?   **a. Reasoning** In Problem 2, explain why the *x*-coordinate of *B* is the sum of 2*a* and 2*b*.

b. The diagram below shows a trapezoid with the base centered at the origin. Is the trapezoid isosceles? Explain.

Plan

Which formula should you use to show that the trapezoid is isosceles?

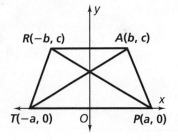

Practice **3.** The diagram at the right shows a parallelogram. Without using the Distance Formula, determine whether the parallelogram is a rhombus. How do you know?

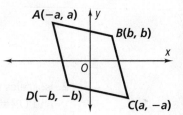

You can use coordinate geometry and algebra to prove theorems in geometry. This kind of proof is called a **coordinate proof.** Sometimes it is easier to show that a theorem is true by using a coordinate proof rather than a standard deductive proof. It is useful to write a plan for a coordinate proof. Problem 3 shows you how.

 **Problem 3** **Planning a Coordinate Proof**

Got It? Plan a coordinate proof of the Triangle Midsegment Theorem (Theorem 24).

Think

What conditions must be proved for the Triangle Midsegment Theorem?

 Practice 4. Plan a coordinate proof to show that the midpoints of the sides of an isosceles trapezoid form a rhombus.

a. Name the coordinates of isosceles trapezoid *TRAP* at the right, with bottom base length 4*a*, top base length 4*b*, and *EG* = 2*c*. The *y*-axis bisects the bases.

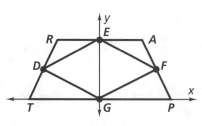

b. Write the *Given* and *Prove* statements.

c. How will you find the coordinates of the midpoints of each side?

d. How will you determine whether *DEFG* is a rhombus?

Lesson Check

Do you know HOW?

Use the diagram at the right.

5. In □*KLMO*, *OM* = 2*a*. What are the coordinates of *K* and *M*?

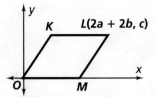

6. What are the slopes of the diagonals of *KLMO*?

7. What are the coordinates of the point of intersection of $\overline{KM}$ and $\overline{OL}$?

Do you UNDERSTAND?

8. Reasoning How do variable coordinates generalize figures in the coordinate plane?

9. Reasoning A vertex of a quadrilateral has coordinates (a, b). The x-coordinates of the other three vertices are a or $-a$, and the y-coordinates are b or $-b$. What kind of quadrilateral is the figure?

@ **10. Error Analysis** A classmate says the endpoints of the midsegment of the trapezoid in Problem 3 are $\left(\frac{b}{2}, \frac{c}{2}\right)$ and $\left(\frac{d+a}{2}, \frac{c}{2}\right)$. What is your classmate's error? Explain.

More Practice and Problem-Solving Exercises

Ⓑ Apply

@ **11. Open-Ended** Place a general quadrilateral in the coordinate plane.

@ **12. Reasoning** A rectangle *LMNP* is centered at the origin with $M(r, -s)$. What are the coordinates of *P*?

Give the coordinates for point *P* without using any new variables.

13. isosceles trapezoid   **14.** trapezoid with a right ∠   **15.** kite

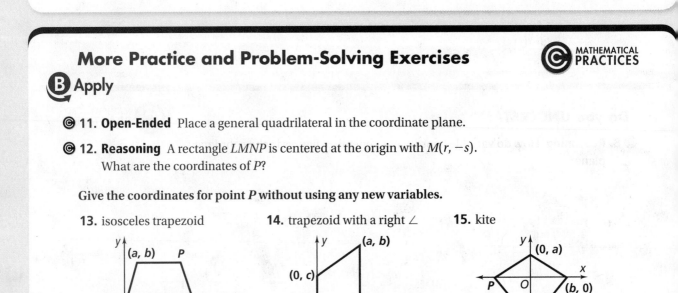

@ **16. a.** Draw a square whose diagonals of length 2*b* lie on the *x*- and *y*-axes.
   b. Give the coordinates of the vertices of the square.
   c. Compute the length of a side of the square.
   d. Find the slopes of two adjacent sides of the square.
   e. Writing Do the slopes show that the sides are perpendicular? Explain.

17. Make two drawings of an isosceles triangle with base length 2*b* and height 2*c*.
   a. In one drawing, place the base on the *x*-axis with a vertex at the origin.
   b. In the second, place the base on the *x*-axis with its midpoint at the origin.
   c. Find the lengths of the legs of the triangle as placed in part (a).
   d. Find the lengths of the legs of the triangle as placed in part (b).
   e. How do the results of parts (c) and (d) compare?

18. W and Z are the midpoints of $\overline{OR}$ and $\overline{ST}$, respectively. In parts (a)–(c), find the coordinates of W and Z.

a. 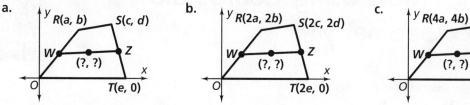 **b.** **c.**

d. You are to plan a coordinate proof involving the midpoint of $\overline{WZ}$. Which of the figures (a)–(c) would you prefer to use? Explain.

Plan the coordinate proof of each statement.

19. Think About a Plan The opposite sides of a parallelogram are congruent (Theorem 40).
- How will you place the parallelogram in a coordinate plane?
- What formulas will you need to use?

20. The diagonals of a rectangle bisect each other.

21. The consecutive sides of a square are perpendicular.

Classify each quadrilateral as precisely as possible.

22. $A(b, 2c)$, $B(4b, 3c)$, $C(5b, c)$, $D(2b, 0)$

23. $E(a, b)$, $F(2a, 2b)$, $G(3a, b)$, $H(2a, -b)$

24. $O(0, 0)$, $P(t, 2s)$, $Q(3t, 2s)$, $R(4t, 0)$

25. $O(0, 0)$, $L(-e, f)$, $M(f - e, f + e)$, $N(f, e)$

26. What property of a rhombus makes it convenient to place its diagonals on the x- and y-axes?

STEM **27. Marine Archaeology** Marine archaeologists sometimes use a coordinate system on the ocean floor. They record the coordinates of points where artifacts are found. Assume that each diver searches a square area and can go no farther than b units from the starting point. Draw a model for the region one diver can search. Assign coordinates to the vertices without using any new variables.

© Challenge

Here are coordinates for eight points in the coordinate plane ($q > p > 0$).
$A(0, 0)$, $B(p, 0)$, $C(q, 0)$, $D(p + q, 0)$, $E(0, q)$, $F(p, q)$, $G(q, q)$, $H(p + q, q)$.
Which four points, if any, are the vertices for each type of figure?

28. parallelogram   **29.** rhombus   **30.** rectangle

31. square   **32.** trapezoid   **33.** isosceles trapezoid

5-8 Proofs Using Coordinate Geometry

G.CO.11 Prove theorems about parallelograms . . . Also G.CO.10

Objective To prove theorems using figures in the coordinate plane

 Solve It! Write your solution to the Solve It in the space below.

In the Solve It, the coordinates of the points include variables. In this lesson, you will use coordinates with variables to write coordinate proofs.

Essential Understanding You can prove geometric relationships using variable coordinates for figures in the coordinate plane.

Problem 1 Writing a Coordinate Proof

Got It? **Reasoning** Refer to the proof in Problem 1. What is the advantage of using coordinates $O(0, 0)$, $E(0, 2b)$, and $F(2a, 0)$ rather than $O(0, 0)$, $E(0, b)$, and $F(a, 0)$?

Think

What is the advantage of placing the legs of the right triangle on the axes?

Developing Proof Complete the following coordinate proof.

1. The medians drawn to the congruent sides of an isosceles triangle are congruent.

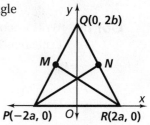

Given: $\triangle PQR$ with $\overline{PQ} \cong \overline{RQ}$, M is the midpoint of $\overline{PQ}$, N is the midpoint of $\overline{RQ}$

Prove: $\overline{PN} \cong \overline{RM}$

a. What are the coordinates of M and N?

b. What are PN and RM?

c. Explain why $\overline{PN} \cong \overline{RM}$.

In the previous lesson, you wrote a plan for the proof of the Trapezoid Midsegment Theorem. Now you will write the full coordinate proof.

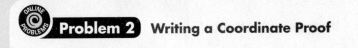

Problem 2 Writing a Coordinate Proof

Got It? Write a coordinate proof of the Triangle Midsegment Theorem (Theorem 24).

Think

How will you place the triangle in the coordinate plane and assign coordinates?

 Practice Developing Proof Complete the following coordinate proof.

2. The diagonals of an isosceles trapezoid are congruent.

Given: Trapezoid *EFGH* with $\overline{EF} \cong \overline{GH}$

Prove: $\overline{EG} \cong \overline{FH}$

a. Find *EG*.

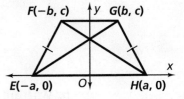

b. Find *FH*.

c. Explain why $\overline{EG} \cong \overline{FH}$.

Lesson Check

Do you know HOW?

3. Use coordinate geometry to prove that the diagonals of a rectangle are congruent.

  a. Place rectangle *PQRS* in the coordinate plane with *P* at (0, 0).

  b. What are the coordinates of *Q, R,* and *S*?

  c. Write the *Given* and *Prove* statements.

  d. Write a coordinate proof.

Do you UNDERSTAND?

MATHEMATICAL
PRACTICES

4. Reasoning Describe a good strategy for placing the vertices of a rhombus for a coordinate proof.

5. Error Analysis Your classmate places a trapezoid on the coordinate plane. What is the error?

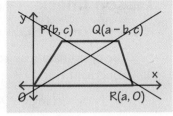

More Practice and Problem-Solving Exercises

MATHEMATICAL PRACTICES

Ⓑ Apply

Tell whether you can reach each type of conclusion below using coordinate methods. Give a reason for each answer.

6. $\overline{AB} \cong \overline{CD}$

7. $\overline{AB} \parallel \overline{CD}$

8. $\overline{AB} \perp \overline{CD}$

9. $\overline{AB}$ bisects $\overline{CD}$.

10. $\overline{AB}$ bisects $\angle CAD$.

11. $\angle A \cong \angle B$

12. $\angle A$ is a right angle.

13. $AB + BC = AC$

14. $\triangle ABC$ is isosceles.

15. Quadrilateral $ABCD$ is a rhombus.

16. $\overline{AB}$ and $\overline{CD}$ bisect each other.

17. $\angle A$ is the supplement of $\angle B$.

18. $\overline{AB}$, $\overline{CD}$, and $\overline{EF}$ are concurrent.

Proof **19. Flag Design** The flag design at the right is made by connecting the midpoints of the sides of a rectangle. Use coordinate geometry to prove that the quadrilateral formed is a rhombus.

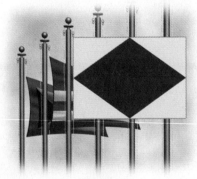

20. Open-Ended Give an example of a statement that you think is easier to prove with a coordinate geometry proof than with a proof method that does not require coordinate geometry. Explain your choice.

Use coordinate geometry to prove each statement.

21. Think About a Plan If a parallelogram is a rhombus, its diagonals are perpendicular (Theorem 50).
- How will you place the rhombus in a coordinate plane?
- What formulas will you need to use?

22. The altitude to the base of an isosceles triangle bisects the base.

23. If the midpoints of a trapezoid are joined to form a quadrilateral, then the quadrilateral is a parallelogram.

24. One diagonal of a kite divides the kite into two congruent triangles.

Proof **25.** You learned in Theorem 31 that the centroid of a triangle is two thirds the distance from each vertex to the midpoint of the opposite side. Complete the steps to prove this theorem.

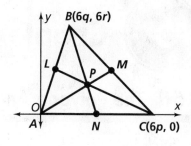

   a. Find the coordinates of points L, M, and N, the midpoints of the sides of $\triangle ABC$.

   b. Find equations of $\overleftrightarrow{AM}$, $\overleftrightarrow{BN}$, and $\overleftrightarrow{CL}$.

   c. Find the coordinates of point P, the intersection of $\overleftrightarrow{AM}$ and $\overleftrightarrow{BN}$.

   d. Show that point P is on $\overleftrightarrow{CL}$.

   e. Use the Distance Formula to show that point P is two thirds the distance from each vertex to the midpoint of the opposite side.

Proof **26.** Complete the steps to prove Theorem 32. You are given $\triangle ABC$ with altitudes p, q, and r. Show that p, q, and r intersect at a point (called the orthocenter of the triangle).

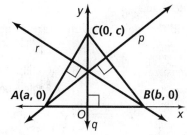

   a. The slope of $\overline{BC}$ is $\frac{c}{-b}$. What is the slope of line p?

   b. Show that the equation of line p is $y = \frac{b}{c}(x - a)$.

   c. What is the equation of line q?

   d. Show that lines p and q intersect at $\left(0, \frac{-ab}{c}\right)$.

   e. The slope of $\overline{AC}$ is $\frac{c}{-a}$. What is the slope of line r?

   f. Show that the equation of line r is $y = \frac{a}{c}(x - b)$.

   g. Show that lines r and q intersect at $\left(0, \frac{-ab}{c}\right)$.

   h. What are the coordinates of the orthocenter of $\triangle ABC$?

Ⓒ Challenge

27. Multiple Representations Use the diagram at the right.

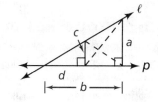

   a. Explain using area why $\frac{1}{2}ad = \frac{1}{2}bc$ and therefore $ad = bc$.

   b. Find two ratios for the slope of ℓ. Use these two ratios to show that $ad = bc$.

Proof **28. Prove:** If two lines are perpendicular, the product of their slopes is -1.

   a. Two nonvertical lines, ℓ_1 and ℓ_2, intersect as shown at the right. Find the coordinates of C.

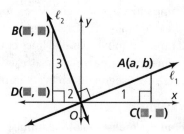

   b. Choose coordinates for D and B. (*Hint:* Find the relationship between $\angle 1$, $\angle 2$, and $\angle 3$. Then use congruent triangles.)

   c. Complete the proof that the product of slopes is -1.

5-1 The Polygon Angle-Sum Theorems

Quick Review

The sum of the measures of the interior angles of an n-gon is $(n-2)180$. The measure of one interior angle of a regular n-gon is $\frac{(n-2)180}{n}$. The sum of the measures of the exterior angles of a polygon, one at each vertex, is 360.

Example

Find the measure of an interior angle of a regular 20-gon.

$\begin{aligned} \text{Measure} &= \frac{(n-2)180}{n} & \text{Corollary to the Polygon} \\ & & \text{Angle-Sum Theorem} \\ &= \frac{(20-2)180}{20} & \text{Substitute.} \\ &= \frac{18 \cdot 180}{20} & \text{Simplify.} \\ &= 162 \end{aligned}$

The measure of an interior angle is 162.

Exercises

Find the measure of an interior angle and an exterior angle of each regular polygon.

1. hexagon

2. 16-gon

3. pentagon

4. What is the sum of the exterior angles for each polygon in Exercises 1–3?

Find the measure of the missing angle.

5.
6.

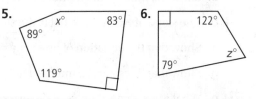

5-2 Properties of Parallelograms

Quick Review

Opposite sides and **opposite angles** of a **parallelogram** are congruent. **Consecutive angles** in a parallelogram are supplementary. The diagonals of a parallelogram bisect each other. If three (or more) parallel lines cut off congruent segments on one transversal, then they cut off congruent segments on every transversal.

Example

Find the measures of the numbered angles in the parallelogram.

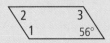

Since consecutive angles are supplementary, $m\angle 1 = 180 - 56$, or 124. Since opposite angles are congruent, $m\angle 2 = 56$ and $m\angle 3 = 124$.

Exercises

Find the measures of the numbered angles for each parallelogram.

7.
8.
9.
10.

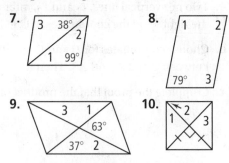

Find the values of x and y in $\square\,ABCD$.

11. $AB = 2y$, $BC = y + 3$, $CD = 5x - 1$, $DA = 2x + 4$

12. $AB = 2y + 1$, $BC = y + 1$, $CD = 7x - 3$, $DA = 3x$

5-3 Proving That a Quadrilateral Is a Parallelogram

Quick Review

A quadrilateral is a parallelogram if any one of the following is true.

- Both pairs of opposite sides are parallel.
- Both pairs of opposite sides are congruent.
- Consecutive angles are supplementary.
- Both pairs of opposite angles are congruent.
- The diagonals bisect each other.
- One pair of opposite sides is both congruent and parallel.

Example

Must the quadrilateral be a parallelogram?

Yes, both pairs of opposite angles are congruent.

Exercises

Determine whether the quadrilateral must be a parallelogram.

13.   **14.**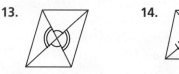

Algebra Find the values of the variables for which *ABCD* must be a parallelogram.

15. 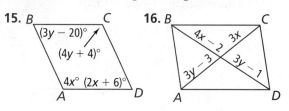   **16.**

5-4 Properties of Rhombuses, Rectangles, and Squares

Quick Review

A **rhombus** is a parallelogram with four congruent sides.

A **rectangle** is a parallelogram with four right angles.

A **square** is a parallelogram with four congruent sides and four right angles.

The diagonals of a rhombus are perpendicular. Each diagonal bisects a pair of opposite angles.

The diagonals of a rectangle are congruent.

Example

What are the measures of the numbered angles in the rhombus?

$m\angle 1 = 60$ Each diagonal of a rhombus bisects a pair of opposite angles.

$m\angle 2 = 90$ The diagonals of a rhombus are $\perp$.

$60 + m\angle 2 + m\angle 3 = 180$ Triangle Angle-Sum Thm.

$60 + 90 + m\angle 3 = 180$ Substitute.

$m\angle 3 = 30$ Simplify.

Exercises

Find the measures of the numbered angles in each special parallelogram.

17.   **18.**

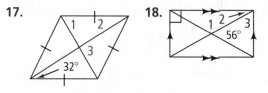

Determine whether each statement is *always, sometimes,* or *never* true.

19. A rhombus is a square.

20. A square is a rectangle.

21. A rhombus is a rectangle.

22. The diagonals of a parallelogram are perpendicular.

23. The diagonals of a parallelogram are congruent.

24. Opposite angles of a parallelogram are congruent.

5-5 Conditions for Rhombuses, Rectangles, and Squares

Quick Review

If one diagonal of a parallelogram bisects two angles of the parallelogram, then the parallelogram is a rhombus. If the diagonals of a parallelogram are perpendicular, then the parallelogram is a rhombus. If the diagonals of a parallelogram are congruent, then the parallelogram is a rectangle.

Example

Can you conclude that the parallelogram is a rhombus, rectangle, or square? Explain.

Yes, the diagonals are perpendicular, so the parallelogram is a rhombus.

Exercises

Can you conclude that the parallelogram is a rhombus, rectangle, or square? Explain.

25. 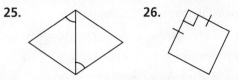   26.

For what value of x is the figure the given parallelogram? Justify your answer.

27. **Rhombus**   28. **Rectangle**

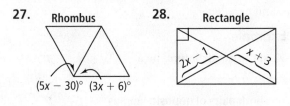

$(5x - 30)°$ $(3x + 6)°$

5-6 Trapezoids and Kites

Quick Review

The parallel sides of a **trapezoid** are its **bases** and the nonparallel sides are its **legs**. Two angles that share a base of a trapezoid are **base angles** of the trapezoid. The **midsegment of a trapezoid** joins the midpoints of its legs.

The base angles of an isosceles trapezoid are congruent.

The diagonals of an isosceles trapezoid are congruent.

The diagonals of a kite are perpendicular.

Example

ABCD is an isosceles trapezoid. What is $m\angle C$?

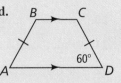

Since $\overline{BC} \parallel \overline{AD}$, $\angle C$ and $\angle D$ are same-side interior angles.

$m\angle C + m\angle D = 180$ Same-side interior angles are supplementary.

$m\angle C + 60 = 180$ Substitute.

$m\angle C = 120$ Subtract 60 from each side.

Exercises

Find the measures of the numbered angles in each isosceles trapezoid.

29.   30.

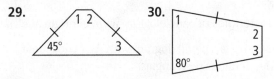

Find the measures of the numbered angles in each kite.

31.   32.

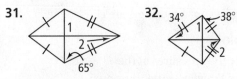

33. **Algebra** A trapezoid has base lengths of $(6x - 1)$ units and 3 units. Its midsegment has a length of $(5x - 3)$ units. What is the value of x?

5-7 and 5-8
Applying Coordinate Geometry and Proofs Using Coordinate Geometry

Quick Review

When placing a figure in the coordinate plane, it is usually helpful to place at least one side on an axis. Use variables when naming the coordinates of a figure in order to show that relationships are true for a general case.

Example

Rectangle *PQRS* has length *a* and width 4*b*. The *x*-axis bisects $\overline{PS}$ and $\overline{QR}$. What are the coordinates of the vertices?

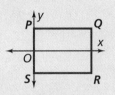

Since the width of *PQRS* is 4*b* and the *x*-axis bisects $\overline{PS}$ and $\overline{QR}$, all the vertices are 2*b* units from the *x*-axis. $\overline{PS}$ is on the *y*-axis, so $P = (0, 2b)$ and $S = (0, -2b)$. The length of *PQRS* is *a*, so $Q = (a, 2b)$ and $R = (a, -2b)$.

Exercises

34. In rhombus *FLPS*, the axes form the diagonals. If $SL = 2a$ and $FP = 4b$, what are the coordinates of the vertices?

35. The figure at the right is a parallelogram. Give the coordinates of point *P* without using any new variables.

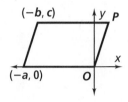

36. Use coordinate geometry to prove that the quadrilateral formed by connecting the midpoints of a kite is a rectangle.

Pull It All Together

Building a Kite

Charles is building a paper kite. He needs another dowel to make the vertical support for the frame. He gives his friend Amy the measurements below but neglects to include the length of the support.

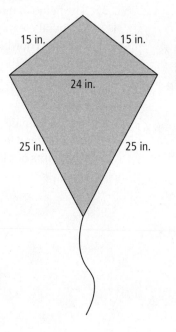

Task Description

Find the length of the vertical support for this kite and the area of the paper used to make the kite.

- What is true about the diagonals of a kite? How can you use this information to find the length of the vertical support?

- How can you find the kite's area by decomposing the kite into smaller figures?

Get Ready!

Properties of Parallel Lines

Use the diagram at the right. Find the measure of each angle. Justify your answer.

1. ∠1   **2.** ∠2   **3.** ∠3   **4.** ∠4

Naming Congruent Parts

$\triangle PAC \cong \triangle DHL$. **Complete each congruence statement.**

5. $\overline{PC} \cong$?   **6.** $\angle H \cong$?   **7.** $\angle PCA \cong$?   **8.** $\triangle HDL \cong$?

Triangle Congruence

Write a congruence statement for each pair of triangles. Explain why the triangles are congruent.

9. 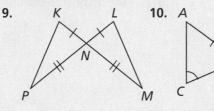   **10.** 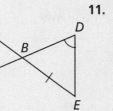   **11.**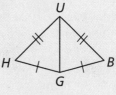

Midsegments of Triangles

Use the diagram at the right for Exercises 12–13.

12. If $BC = 12$, then $BF =$? and $DE =$? .

13. If $EF = 4.7$, then $AD =$? and $AC =$? .

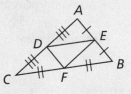

Looking Ahead Vocabulary

14. An artist sketches a person. She is careful to draw the different parts of the person's body in *proportion*. What does *proportion* mean in this situation?

15. Siblings often look *similar* to each other. How might two geometric figures be *similar*?

16. A road map has a *scale* on it that tells you how many miles are equivalent to a distance of 1 inch on the map. How would you use the *scale* to estimate the distance between two cities on the map?

Similarity

Big Ideas

1 Similarity

Essential Question How do you use proportions to find side lengths in similar polygons?

2 Reasoning and Proof

Essential Question How do you show two triangles are similar?

3 Visualization

Essential Question How do you identify corresponding parts of similar triangles?

© Domains

- Similarity, Right Triangles, and Trigonometry
- Expressing Geometric Properties with Equations
- Mathematical Practice: Construct viable arguments

Interactive Digital Path

Log in to **pearsonsuccessnet.com** and click on Interactive Digital Path to access the Solve Its and animated Problems.

Chapter Preview

Vocabulary

English/Spanish Vocabulary Audio Online:

6-1 Ratios and Proportions

Prepares for **G.SRT.5** Use . . . similarity criteria for triangles to solve problems and to prove relationships in geometric figures. Also **N.Q.2**

Objective   To write ratios and solve proportions

Solve It!   Write your solution to the Solve It in the space below.

In the Solve It, you compared two quantities for four years.

Essential Understanding   You can write a *ratio* to compare two quantities.

A **ratio** is a comparison of two quantities by division. You can write the ratio of two numbers a and b, where $b \neq 0$, in three ways: $\frac{a}{b}$, $a : b$, and a to b. You usually express a and b in the same unit and write the ratio in simplest form.

 **Problem 1**   **Writing a Ratio**

Got It?   A bonsai tree is 18 in. wide and stands 2 ft tall.
What is the ratio of the width of the bonsai to its height?

> **Think**
>
> How can you write the width and the height using the same units?

A Practice Write the ratio of the first measurement to the second measurement.

1. length of a tennis racket: 2 ft 4 in.

length of a table tennis paddle: 10 in.

2. diameter of a table tennis ball: 40 mm

diameter of a tennis ball: 6.8 cm

Problem 2 **Dividing a Quantity Into a Given Ratio**

Got It? The measures of two supplementary angles are in the ratio 1 : 4. What are the measures of the angles?

Practice

3. **Baseball** A baseball team played 154 regular season games. The ratio of the number of games they won to the number of games they lost was $\frac{5}{2}$. How many games did they win? How many games did they lose?

4. The measures of two supplementary angles are in the ratio 5 : 7. What is the measure of the larger angle?

An **extended ratio** compares three (or more) numbers. In the extended ratio $a : b : c$, the ratio of the first two numbers is $a : b$, the ratio of the last two numbers is $b : c$, and the ratio of the first and last numbers is $a : c$.

Problem 3 Using an Extended Ratio

Got It? The lengths of the sides of a triangle are in the extended ratio 4 : 7 : 9. The perimeter is 60 cm. What are the lengths of the sides?

Think

How do you use the extended ratio to write the equation?

5. The lengths of the sides of a triangle are in the extended ratio $6:7:9$. The perimeter of the triangle is 88 cm. What are the lengths of the sides?

6. The measures of the angles of a triangle are in the extended ratio $4:3:2$. What is the measure of the largest angle?

Essential Understanding If two ratios are equivalent, you can write an equation stating that the ratios are equal. If the equation contains a variable, you can solve the equation to find the value of the variable.

An equation that states that two ratios are equal is called a **proportion.** The first and last numbers in a proportion are the **extremes.** The middle two numbers are the **means.**

$$\overset{\displaystyle\lceil\text{extremes}\rceil}{2 : \underset{\underset{\text{means}}{\uparrow\ \ \uparrow}}{3 = 4} : 6} \qquad \begin{array}{l}\text{extremes} \rightarrow \\ \text{means} \rightarrow\end{array} \begin{array}{l}②\!\!\diagdown\!\!④ \\ ③\!\!\diagup\!\!⑥\end{array}$$

take note

Key Concept Cross Products Property

Words	Symbols	Example
In a proportion, the product of the extremes equals the product of the means.	If $\frac{a}{b} = \frac{c}{d}$, where $b \neq 0$ and $d \neq 0$, then $ad = bc$.	$\frac{2}{3} = \frac{4}{6}$ $2 \cdot 6 = 3 \cdot 4$ $12 = 12$

Here's Why It Works Begin with $\frac{a}{b} = \frac{c}{d}$, where $b \neq 0$ and $d \neq 0$.

$bd \cdot \dfrac{a}{b} = \dfrac{c}{d} \cdot bd$ Multiply each side of the proportion by bd.

$\dfrac{\cancel{b}d}{1} \cdot \dfrac{a}{\cancel{b}} = \dfrac{c}{\cancel{d}} \cdot \dfrac{b\cancel{d}}{1}$ Divide the common factors.

$\quad\quad ad = bc$ Simplify.

Problem 4 Solving a Proportion

Got It? What is the solution of each proportion?

a. $\frac{9}{2} = \frac{a}{14}$

b. $\frac{15}{m+1} = \frac{3}{m}$

Practice **Algebra** Solve each proportion.

7. $\frac{y}{10} = \frac{15}{25}$

8. $\frac{n+4}{8} = \frac{n}{4}$

Using the Properties of Equality, you can rewrite proportions in equivalent forms.

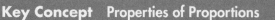

take note

Key Concept   Properties of Proportions

a, b, c, and d do not equal zero.

Property	**How to Apply It**

(1) $\frac{a}{b} = \frac{c}{d}$ is equivalent to $\frac{b}{a} = \frac{d}{c}$.

Write the reciprocal of each ratio.

$\left(\frac{2}{3} = \frac{4}{6} \right)$ becomes $\frac{3}{2} = \frac{6}{4}$.

(2) $\frac{a}{b} = \frac{c}{d}$ is equivalent to $\frac{a}{c} = \frac{b}{d}$.

Switch the means.

$\frac{2}{3} \diagup \frac{4}{6}$ becomes $\frac{2}{4} = \frac{3}{6}$.

(3) $\frac{a}{b} = \frac{c}{d}$ is equivalent to $\frac{a+b}{b} = \frac{c+d}{d}$.

In each ratio, add the denominator to the numerator.

$\frac{2}{3} = \frac{4}{6}$ becomes $\frac{2+3}{3} = \frac{4+6}{6}$.

ONLINE PROBLEMS

Problem 5   Writing Equivalent Proportions

Got It?   For parts (a) and (b), use the proportion $\frac{x}{6} = \frac{y}{7}$. What ratio completes the equivalent proportion? Justify your answer.

a. $\frac{6}{x} = \frac{\blacksquare}{\blacksquare}$

b. $\frac{\blacksquare}{\blacksquare} = \frac{y+7}{7}$

ⓒ c. **Reasoning**   Explain why $\frac{6}{x-6} = \frac{7}{y-7}$ is an equivalent proportion to $\frac{x}{6} = \frac{y}{7}$. (Assume $x \neq 6$ and $y \neq 7$.)

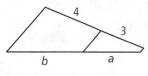

A Practice In the diagram, $\frac{a}{b} = \frac{3}{4}$. Complete each statement. Justify your answer.

9. $4a = \blacksquare$

10. $\dfrac{a+b}{b} = \blacksquare$

Lesson Check

Do you know HOW?

11. A cell phone is 84 mm long and 46 mm wide. What is the ratio of the width to the length?

12. Two angle measures are in the ratio 5 : 9. Write expressions for the two angle measures in terms of the variable x.

13. What is the solution of the proportion $\frac{20}{z} = \frac{5}{3}$?

14. For $\frac{a}{7} = \frac{13}{b}$ complete each equivalent proportion.

   a. $\frac{a}{\blacksquare} = \frac{7}{\blacksquare}$

   b. $\frac{a-7}{7} = \frac{\blacksquare}{\blacksquare}$

   c. $\frac{7}{a} = \frac{\blacksquare}{\blacksquare}$

Do you UNDERSTAND?

© **15. Vocabulary** What is the difference between a ratio and a proportion?

© **16. Open-Ended** The lengths of the sides of a triangle are in the extended ratio $3 : 6 : 7$. What are two possible sets of side lengths, in inches, for the triangle?

© **17. Error Analysis** What is the error in the solution of the proportion shown at the right?

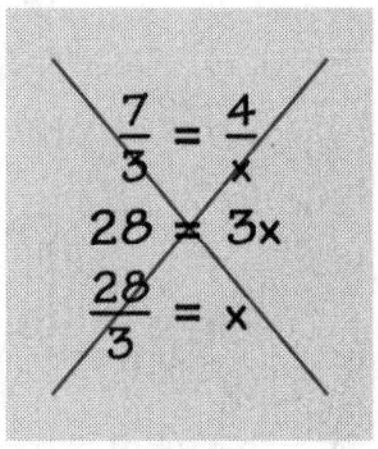

$$\frac{7}{3} = \frac{4}{x}$$
$$28 = 3x$$
$$\frac{28}{3} = x$$

18. What is a proportion that has means 6 and 18 and extremes 9 and 12?

B Apply

Coordinate Geometry Use the graph. Write each ratio in simplest form.

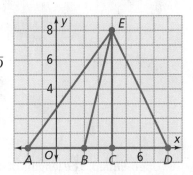

19. $\frac{AC}{BD}$ 20. $\frac{AE}{EC}$ 21. slope of $\overline{EB}$ 22. slope of $\overline{ED}$

23. **Think About a Plan** The area of a rectangle is 150 in.². The ratio of the length to the width is 3 : 2. Find the length and the width.
    - What is the formula for the area of a rectangle?
    - How can you use the given ratio to write expressions for the length and width?

Art To draw a face, you can sketch the head as an oval and then lightly draw horizontal lines to help locate the eyes, nose, and mouth. You can use the extended ratios shown in the diagrams to help you place the lines for an adult's face or for a baby's face.

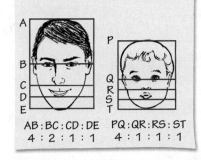

24. If $AE = 72$ cm in the diagram, find AB, BC, CD, and DE.

25. You draw a baby's head as an oval that is 21 in. from top to bottom.
    a. How far from the top should you place the line for the eyes?
    b. Suppose you decide to make the head an adult's head. How far up should you move the line for the eyes?

Algebra Solve each proportion.

26. $\frac{1}{7y - 5} = \frac{2}{9y}$

27. $\frac{4a + 1}{7} = \frac{2a}{3}$

28. $\frac{5}{x + 2} = \frac{3}{x + 1}$

29. $\frac{2b - 1}{4} = \frac{b - 2}{12}$

30. The ratio of the length to the width of a rectangle is 9 : 4. The width of the rectangle is 52 mm. Write and solve a proportion to find the length.

31. **Open-Ended** Draw a quadrilateral that satisfies this condition: The measures of the consecutive angles are in the extended ratio 4 : 5 : 4 : 7.

32. **Reasoning** The means of a proportion are 4 and 15. List all possible pairs of positive integers that could be the extremes of the proportion.

33. **Writing** Describe how to use the Cross Products Property to determine whether $\frac{10}{26} = \frac{16}{42}$ is a true proportion.

© 34. Reasoning Explain how to use two different properties of proportions to change the proportion $\frac{3}{4} = \frac{12}{16}$ into the proportion $\frac{12}{3} = \frac{16}{4}$.

Complete each statement. Justify your answer.

35. If $4m = 9n$, then $\frac{m}{n} = \blacksquare$.

36. If $\frac{30}{t} = \frac{18}{r}$, then $\frac{t}{r} = \blacksquare$.

37. If $\frac{a+5}{5} = \frac{b+2}{2}$, then $\frac{a}{5} = \blacksquare$.

38. If $\frac{a}{b} = \frac{c}{d}$, then $\frac{a+b}{c+d} = \blacksquare$.

39. If $\frac{a}{b} = \frac{c}{d}$, then $\frac{a+c}{b+d} = \blacksquare$.

40. If $\frac{a}{b} = \frac{c}{d}$, then $\frac{a+2b}{b} = \blacksquare$.

© Challenge

Algebra Use properties of equality to justify each property of proportions.

41. $\frac{a}{b} = \frac{c}{d}$ is equivalent to $\frac{b}{a} = \frac{d}{c}$.

42. $\frac{a}{b} = \frac{c}{d}$ is equivalent to $\frac{a}{c} = \frac{b}{d}$.

43. $\frac{a}{b} = \frac{c}{d}$ is equivalent to $\frac{a+b}{b} = \frac{c+d}{d}$.

6-2 Similar Polygons

G.SRT.5 Use . . . similarity criteria for triangles to solve problems and to prove relationships in geometric figures.

Objective To identify and apply similar polygons

 Solve It! Write your solution to the Solve It in the space below.

Similar figures have the same shape but not necessarily the same size. You can abbreviate *is similar to* with the symbol ~.

Essential Understanding You can use ratios and proportions to decide whether two polygons are similar and to find unknown side lengths of similar figures.

take note

Key Concept Similar Polygons

Define	**Diagram**	**Symbols**
Two polygons are **similar polygons** if corresponding angles are congruent and if the lengths of corresponding sides are proportional.	$ABCD \sim GHIJ$ 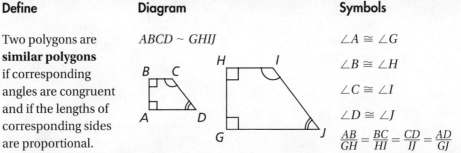	$\angle A \cong \angle G$ $\angle B \cong \angle H$ $\angle C \cong \angle I$ $\angle D \cong \angle J$ $\dfrac{AB}{GH} = \dfrac{BC}{HI} = \dfrac{CD}{IJ} = \dfrac{AD}{GJ}$

You write a similarity statement with corresponding vertices in order, just as you write a congruence statement. When three or more ratios are equal, you can write an **extended proportion.** The proportion $\frac{AB}{GH} = \frac{BC}{HI} = \frac{CD}{IJ} = \frac{AD}{GJ}$ is an extended proportion.

A **scale factor** is the ratio of corresponding linear measurements of two similar figures. The ratio of the lengths of corresponding sides $\overline{BC}$ and $\overline{YZ}$, or more simply stated, the ratio of corresponding sides, is $\frac{BC}{YZ} = \frac{20}{8} = \frac{5}{2}$. So the scale factor of $\triangle ABC$ to $\triangle XYZ$ is $\frac{5}{2}$, or $5 : 2$.

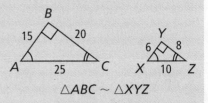

Problem 1 **Understanding Similarity**

Got It? *DEFG ~ HJKL*

    a. What are the pairs of congruent angles?

    b. What is the extended proportion for the ratios of the lengths
       of corresponding sides?

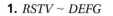

Think

How can you use
the similarity
statement to
write ratios of
corresponding
sides?

Practice List the pairs of congruent angles and the extended proportion that
relates the corresponding sides for the similar polygons.

    1. *RSTV ~ DEFG*

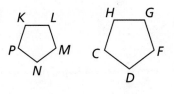

    2. *KLMNP ~ HGFDC*

Problem 2 **Determining Similarity**

Think

How do you identify corresponding sides?

Got It? Are the polygons similar? If they are, write a similarity statement and give the scale factor.

a.

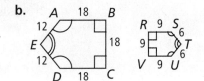

b.

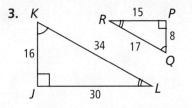

Ⓐ Practice Determine whether the polygons are similar. If so, write a similarity statement and give the scale factor. If not, explain.

3.

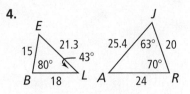

4.

Problem 3 **Using Similar Polygons**

Got It? Use the diagram in Problem 3. *ABCD* ~ *EFGD* What is the value of *y*?

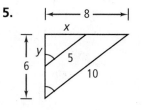

Practice **Algebra** The polygons are similar. Find the value of each variable.

5.

6.

Problem 4 **Using Similarity**

Got It? A poster design is 6 in. high by 10 in. wide. What are the dimensions of the largest enlarged poster that will fit in a space 3 ft high by 4 ft wide?

A 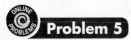 **Practice** **7. Web Page Design** The space allowed for the mascot on a school's

STEM Web page is 120 pixels wide by 90 pixels high. Its digital image is
500 pixels wide by 375 pixels high. What is the largest image of the
mascot that will fit on the Web page?

8. Art The design for a mural is 16 in. wide and 9 in. high. What are
the dimensions of the largest possible complete mural that can be
painted on a wall 24 ft wide by 14 ft high?

> In a **scale drawing**, all lengths are proportional to their corresponding actual lengths.
> The **scale** is the ratio that compares each length in the scale drawing to the actual
> length. The lengths used in a scale can be in different units. For example, a scale
> might be written as 1 cm to 50 km, 1 in. = 100 mi, or 1 in. : 10 ft.
>
> You can use proportions to find the actual dimensions represented in a scale drawing.

Problem 5 **Using a Scale Drawing**

Got It? **a.** Use the scale drawing in Problem 5. What is the actual height of the
towers above the roadway?

Ⓖ b. Reasoning The Space Needle in Seattle is 605 ft tall. A classmate wants to make a scale drawing of the Space Needle on an $8\frac{1}{2}$ in.-by-11 in. sheet of paper. He decides to use the scale 1 in. = 50 ft. Is this a reasonable scale? Explain.

9. Architecture You want to make a scale drawing of New York City's Empire State Building using the scale 1 in. = 250 ft. If the building is 1250 ft tall, how tall should you make the building in your scale drawing?

10. Cartography A cartographer is making a map of Pennsylvania. She uses the scale 1 in. = 10 mi. The actual distance between Harrisburg and Philadelphia is about 95 mi. How far apart should she place the two cities on the map?

Lesson Check

Do you know HOW?

JDRT ~ WHYX. Complete each statement.

11. $\angle D \cong$ _____

12. $\dfrac{RT}{YX} = \dfrac{\blacksquare}{WX}$

13. Are the polygons similar? If they are, write a similarity statement and give the scale factor.

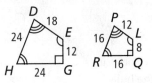

14. $\triangle FGH \sim \triangle MNP$. What is the value of *x*?

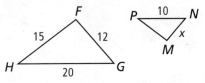

Do you UNDERSTAND?

15. Vocabulary What does the scale on a scale drawing indicate?

16. Error Analysis The polygons at the right are similar. Which similarity statement is *not* correct? Explain.

   A. *TRUV ~ NPQU*   **B.** *RUVT ~ QUNP*

17. Reasoning Is similarity reflexive? Transitive? Symmetric? Justify your reasoning.

18. The triangles at the right are similar. What are three similarity statements for the triangles?

More Practice and Problem-Solving Exercises

B Apply

In the diagram at the right, $\triangle DFG \sim \triangle HKM$. Find each of the following.

19. the scale factor of $\triangle HKM$ to $\triangle DFG$ **20.** $m\angle K$

21. $\frac{GD}{MH}$ **22.** MK **23.** GD

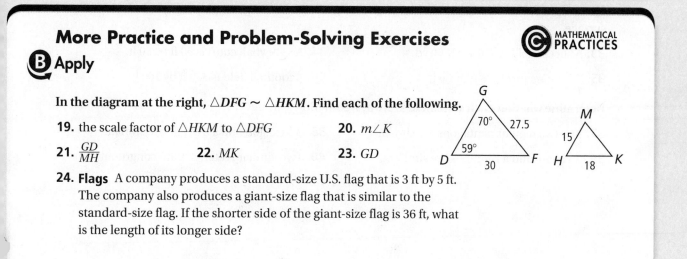

24. Flags A company produces a standard-size U.S. flag that is 3 ft by 5 ft. The company also produces a giant-size flag that is similar to the standard-size flag. If the shorter side of the giant-size flag is 36 ft, what is the length of its longer side?

25. **a. Coordinate Geometry** What are the measures of ∠A, ∠ABC, ∠BCD, ∠CDA, ∠E, ∠F, and ∠G? Explain.

   b. What are the lengths of $\overline{AB}$, $\overline{BC}$, $\overline{CD}$, $\overline{DA}$, $\overline{AE}$, $\overline{EF}$, $\overline{FG}$, and $\overline{AG}$?

   c. Is *ABCD* similar to *AEFG*? Justify your answer.

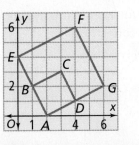

© 26. **Think About a Plan** The Davis family is planning to drive from San Antonio to Houston. About how far will they have to drive?

   • How can you find the distance between the two cities on the map?

   • What proportion can you set up to solve the problem?

© 27. **Reasoning** Two polygons have corresponding side lengths that are proportional. Can you conclude that the polygons are similar? Justify your reasoning.

© 28. **Writing** Explain why two congruent figures must also be similar. Include scale factor in your explanation.

29. △*JLK* and △*RTS* are similar. The scale factor of △*JLK* to △*RTS* is 3 : 1. What is the scale factor of △*RTS* to △*JLK*?

© 30. **Open-Ended** Draw and label two different similar quadrilaterals. Write a similarity statement for each and give the scale factor.

Algebra Find the value of *x*. Give the scale factor of the polygons.

31. △*WLJ* ~ △*QBV*

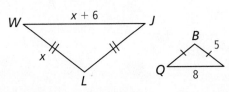

32. *GKNM* ~ *VRPT*

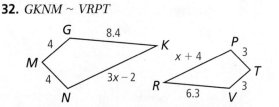

Sports Choose a scale and make a scale drawing of each rectangular playing surface.

33. A soccer field is 110 yd by 60 yd.

34. A volleyball court is 60 ft by 30 ft.

35. A tennis court is 78 ft by 36 ft.

36. A football field is 360 ft by 160 ft.

Determine whether each statement is always, sometimes, or never true.

37. Any two regular pentagons are similar.

38. A hexagon and a triangle are similar.

39. A square and a rhombus are similar.

40. Two similar rectangles are congruent.

STEM **41. Architecture** The scale drawing at the right is part of a floor plan for a home. The scale is 1 cm = 10 ft. What are the actual dimensions of the family room?

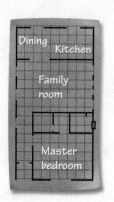

C Challenge

42. The lengths of the sides of a triangle are in the extended ratio 2 : 3 : 4. The perimeter of the triangle is 54 in.

   a. The length of the shortest side of a similar triangle is 16 in. What are the lengths of the other two sides of this triangle?

   b. Compare the ratio of the perimeters of the two triangles to their scale factor. What do you notice?

43. In rectangle *BCEG*, *BC* : *CE* = 2 : 3. In rectangle *LJAW*, *LJ* : *JA* = 2 : 3. Show that *BCEG* ~ *LJAW*.

44. Prove the following statement: If $\triangle ABC \sim \triangle DEF$ and $\triangle DEF \sim \triangle GHK$, then $\triangle ABC \sim \triangle GHK$.

6-3 Proving Triangles Similar

G.SRT.5 Use . . . similarity criteria for triangles to solve problems and to prove relationships in geometric figures.
Also **G.GPE.5**

Objectives To use the AA ~ Postulate and the SAS ~ and SSS ~ Theorems
To use similarity to find indirect measurements

Solve It! Write your solution to the Solve It in the space below.

In the Solve It, you determined whether the two triangles are similar. That is, you needed information about all three pairs of angles and all three pairs of sides. In this lesson, you'll learn an easier way to determine whether two triangles are similar.

Essential Understanding You can show that two triangles are similar when you know the relationships between only two or three pairs of corresponding parts.

take note

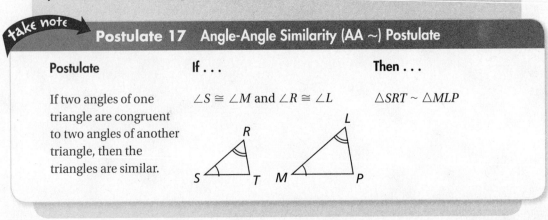

Postulate 17 Angle-Angle Similarity (AA ~) Postulate

Postulate	If . . .	Then . . .
If two angles of one triangle are congruent to two angles of another triangle, then the triangles are similar.	$\angle S \cong \angle M$ and $\angle R \cong \angle L$	$\triangle SRT \sim \triangle MLP$

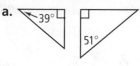 **Problem 1** **Using the AA ~ Postulate**

Got It? Are the two triangles similar? How do you know?

a.
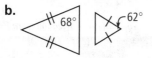

 Plan

What do you need to show that the triangles are similar?

b.
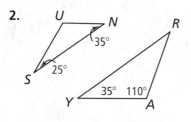

Ⓐ **Practice** Determine whether the triangles are similar. If so, write a similarity statement and name the postulate you used. If not, explain.

1.

2.

Here are two other ways to determine whether two triangles are similar.

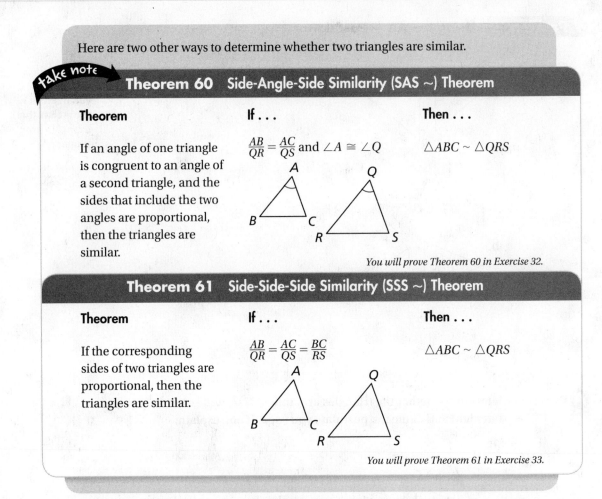

Theorem 60 Side-Angle-Side Similarity (SAS ~) Theorem

Theorem

If an angle of one triangle is congruent to an angle of a second triangle, and the sides that include the two angles are proportional, then the triangles are similar.

If . . .

$\frac{AB}{QR} = \frac{AC}{QS}$ and $\angle A \cong \angle Q$

Then . . .

$\triangle ABC \sim \triangle QRS$

You will prove Theorem 60 in Exercise 32.

Theorem 61 Side-Side-Side Similarity (SSS ~) Theorem

Theorem

If the corresponding sides of two triangles are proportional, then the triangles are similar.

If . . .

$\frac{AB}{QR} = \frac{AC}{QS} = \frac{BC}{RS}$

Then . . .

$\triangle ABC \sim \triangle QRS$

You will prove Theorem 61 in Exercise 33.

Proof **Proof of Theorem 60: Side-Angle-Side Similarity Theorem**

Given: $\frac{AB}{QR} = \frac{AC}{QS}$, $\angle A \cong \angle Q$

Prove: $\triangle ABC \sim \triangle QRS$

Plan for Proof: Choose X on $\overline{RQ}$ so that $QX = AB$. Draw $\overleftrightarrow{XY} \parallel \overline{RS}$. Show that $\triangle QXY \sim \triangle QRS$ by the AA ~ Postulate. Then use the proportion $\frac{QX}{QR} = \frac{QY}{QS}$ and the given proportion $\frac{AB}{QR} = \frac{AC}{QS}$ to show that $AC = QY$. Then prove that $\triangle ABC \cong \triangle QXY$. Finally, prove that $\triangle ABC \sim \triangle QRS$ by the AA ~ Postulate.

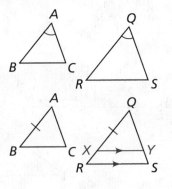

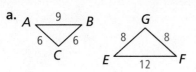
Got It? Are the triangles similar? If so, write a similarity statement for the triangles and explain how you know the triangles are similar.

a.
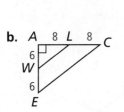

> **Plan**
>
> How can you make it easier to identify corresponding sides and angles?

b.
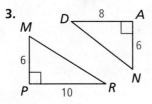

A Practice Determine whether the triangles are similar. If so, write a similarity statement and name the postulate or theorem you used. If not, explain.

3.

4.

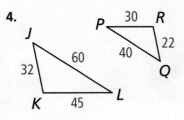

ONLINE
PROBLEMS

Problem 3 **Proving Triangles Similar**
Proof

Got It? **a. Given:** $\overline{MP} \parallel \overline{AC}$

Prove: $\triangle ABC \sim \triangle PBM$

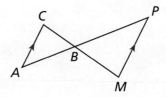

b. Reasoning For the figure above, suppose you are given only that $\frac{CA}{PM} = \frac{CB}{MB}$. Could you prove that the triangles are similar? Explain.

Proof 5. Given: $\angle ABC \cong \angle ACD$

Prove: $\triangle ABC \sim \triangle ACD$

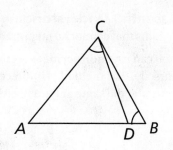

Proof 6. Given: $PR = 2NP, PQ = 2MP$

Prove: $\triangle MNP \sim \triangle QRP$

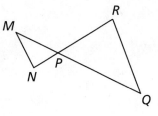

> **Essential Understanding** Sometimes you can use similar triangles to find
> lengths that cannot be measured easily using a ruler or other measuring device.
>
> You can use **indirect measurement** to find lengths that are difficult to measure
> directly. One method of indirect measurement uses the fact that light reflects off a
> mirror at the same angle at which it hits the mirror.

Problem 4   **Finding Lengths in Similar Triangles**

Ⓒ Got It?   **Reasoning** Why is it important that the ground be flat to use the method
of indirect measurement illustrated in Problem 4? Explain.

Ⓐ Practice   **7. Indirect Measurement** Explain why
the triangles are similar. Then find the
distance represented by *x*.

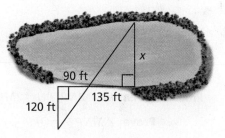

90 ft

135 ft

120 ft

x

8. Washington Monument At a certain time of day, a 1.8-m-tall person
standing next to the Washington Monument casts a 0.7-m shadow.
At the same time, the Washington Monument casts a 65.8-m shadow.
How tall is the Washington Monument?

Lesson Check

Do you know HOW?

Are the triangles similar? If yes, write a similarity statement and explain how you know they are similar.

9.

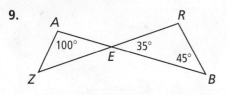

10.

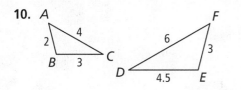

11.

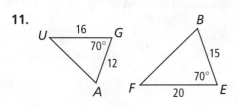

Do you UNDERSTAND?

12. Vocabulary How could you use indirect measurement to find the height of the flagpole at your school?

13. Error Analysis Which solution for the value of *x* in the figure at the right is *not* correct? Explain.

A.
$$\frac{4}{8} = \frac{8}{x}$$
$$4x = 72$$
$$x = 18$$

B.
$$\frac{8}{x} = \frac{4}{6}$$
$$48 = 4x$$
$$12 = x$$

14. a. Compare and Contrast How are the SAS Similarity Theorem and the SAS Congruence Postulate alike? How are they different?

b. How are the SSS Similarity Theorem and the SSS Congruence Postulate alike? How are they different?

More Practice and Problem-Solving Exercises

B Apply

Can you conclude that the triangles are similar? If so, state the postulate or theorem you used and write a similarity statement. If not, explain.

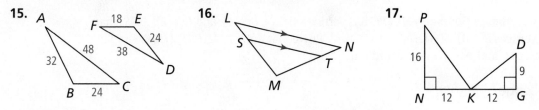

15.   **16.**   **17.**

18. a. Are two isosceles triangles always similar? Explain.
   b. Are two right isosceles triangles always similar? Explain.

19. Think About a Plan On a sunny day, a classmate uses indirect measurement to find the height of a building. The building's shadow is 12 ft long and your classmate's shadow is 4 ft long. If your classmate is 5 ft tall, what is the height of the building?
   • Can you draw and label a diagram to represent the situation?
   • What proportion can you use to solve the problem?

20. Indirect Measurement A 2-ft vertical post casts a 16-in. shadow at the same time a nearby cell phone tower casts a 120-ft shadow. How tall is the cell phone tower?

Algebra For each pair of similar triangles, find the value of x.

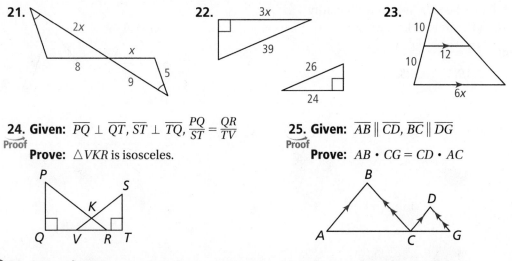

21.   **22.**   **23.**

24. Given: $\overline{PQ} \perp \overline{QT}$, $\overline{ST} \perp \overline{TQ}$, $\dfrac{PQ}{ST} = \dfrac{QR}{TV}$
Proof
   Prove: $\triangle VKR$ is isosceles.

25. Given: $\overline{AB} \parallel \overline{CD}$, $\overline{BC} \parallel \overline{DG}$
Proof
   Prove: $AB \cdot CG = CD \cdot AC$

26. Reasoning Does any line that intersects two sides of a triangle and is parallel to the third side of the triangle form two similar triangles? Justify your reasoning.

27. Constructions Draw any $\triangle ABC$ with $m\angle C = 30$. Use a straightedge and compass to construct $\triangle LKJ$ so that $\triangle LKJ \sim \triangle ABC$.

28. Reasoning In the diagram at the right, $\triangle PMN \sim \triangle SRW$. $\overline{MQ}$ and $\overline{RT}$ are altitudes. The scale factor of $\triangle PMN$ to $\triangle SRW$ is $4:3$. What is the ratio of $\overline{MQ}$ to $\overline{RT}$? Explain how you know.

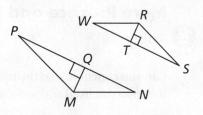

29. Coordinate Geometry $\triangle ABC$ has vertices $A(0, 0)$, $B(2, 4)$, and $C(4, 2)$. $\triangle RST$ has
Proof vertices $R(0, 3)$, $S(-1, 5)$, and $T(-2, 4)$. Prove that $\triangle ABC \sim \triangle RST$. (*Hint:* Graph $\triangle ABC$ and $\triangle RST$ in the coordinate plane.)

Challenge

30. Write a proof of the following: Any two
Proof nonvertical parallel lines have equal slopes.

> **Given:** Nonvertical lines ℓ_1 and ℓ_2, $\ell_1 \parallel \ell_2$, $\overline{EF}$ and $\overline{BC}$ are $\perp$ to the x-axis
>
> **Prove:** $\dfrac{BC}{AC} = \dfrac{EF}{DF}$

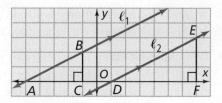

31. Use the diagram in Exercise 30. Prove: Any two nonvertical lines with equal
Proof slopes are parallel.

32. Prove the Side-Angle-Side Similarity Theorem
Proof (Theorem 60).

> **Given:** $\dfrac{AB}{QR} = \dfrac{AC}{QS}$, $\angle A \cong \angle Q$
>
> **Prove:** $\triangle ABC \sim \triangle QRS$

33. Proof Prove the Side-Side-Side Similarity
Proof Theorem (Theorem 61).

> **Given:** $\dfrac{AB}{QR} = \dfrac{AC}{QS} = \dfrac{BC}{RS}$
>
> **Prove:** $\triangle ABC \sim \triangle QRS$

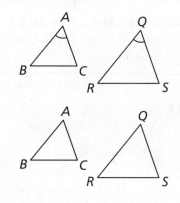

6-4 Similarity in Right Triangles

G.SRT.5 Use . . . similarity criteria for triangles to solve problems and to prove relationships in geometric figures. Also **G.GPE.5, G.GPE.6**

Objective   To find and use relationships in similar right triangles

Solve It!   Write your solution to the Solve It in the space below.

In the Solve It, you looked at three similar right triangles. In this lesson, you will learn new ways to think about the proportions that come from these similar triangles. You began with three separate, nonoverlapping triangles in the Solve It. Now you will see the two smaller right triangles fitting side by side to form the largest right triangle.

Essential Understanding   When you draw the *altitude to the hypotenuse* of a right triangle, you form three pairs of similar right triangles.

take note

Theorem 62

Theorem	**If . . .**	**Then . . .**
The altitude to the hypotenuse of a right triangle divides the triangle into two triangles that are similar to the original triangle and to each other.	$\triangle ABC$ is a right triangle with right $\angle ACB$, and $\overline{CD}$ is the altitude to the hypotenuse	$\triangle ABC \sim \triangle ACD$ $\triangle ABC \sim \triangle CBD$ $\triangle ACD \sim \triangle CBD$

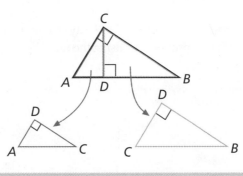

Proof **Proof of Theorem 62**

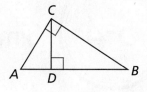

Given: Right △ABC with right ∠ACB and altitude $\overline{CD}$

Prove: △ACD ~ △ABC, △CBD ~ △ABC, △ACD ~ △CBD

Statements	Reasons
1) ∠ACB is a right angle.	**1)** Given
2) $\overline{CD}$ is an altitude.	**2)** Given
3) $\overline{CD} \perp \overline{AB}$	**3)** Definition of altitude
4) ∠ADC and ∠CDB are right angles.	**4)** Definition of ⊥
5) ∠ADC ≅ ∠ACB, ∠CDB ≅ ∠ACB	**5)** All right ⚟ are ≅.
6) ∠A ≅ ∠A, ∠B ≅ ∠B	**6)** Reflexive Property of ≅
7) △ACD ~ △ABC, △CBD ~ △ABC	**7)** AA ~ Postulate
8) ∠ACD ≅ ∠B	**8)** Corresponding ⚟ of ~ △ are ≅.
9) ∠ADC ≅ ∠CDB	**9)** All right ⚟ are ≅.
10) △ACD ~ △CBD	**10)** AA ~ Postulate

Problem 1 **Identifying Similar Triangles**

Got It? **a.** What similarity statement can you write relating the three triangles in the diagram?

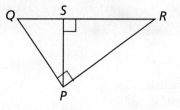

Plan

What will help you see the corresponding vertices?

b. Reasoning From the similarity statement in part (a), write two different proportions using the ratio $\frac{SR}{SP}$.

Ⓐ Practice Write a similarity statement relating the three triangles in each
diagram.

1.

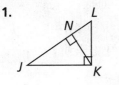

2.

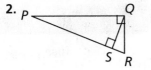

Proportions in which the means are equal occur frequently in geometry. For any two
positive numbers a and b, the **geometric mean** of a and b is the positive number x
such that $\frac{a}{x} = \frac{x}{b}$.

Problem 2 **Finding the Geometric Mean**

Got It? What is the geometric mean of 4 and 18?

> **Plan**
> **How do you use
> the definition of
> *geometric
> mean*?**

Ⓐ Practice **Algebra** Find the geometric mean of each pair of numbers.

3. 5 and 125 **4.** 4 and 49

In part (b) of the Got it for Problem 1, you used a pair of similar triangles to write a proportion with a geometric mean.

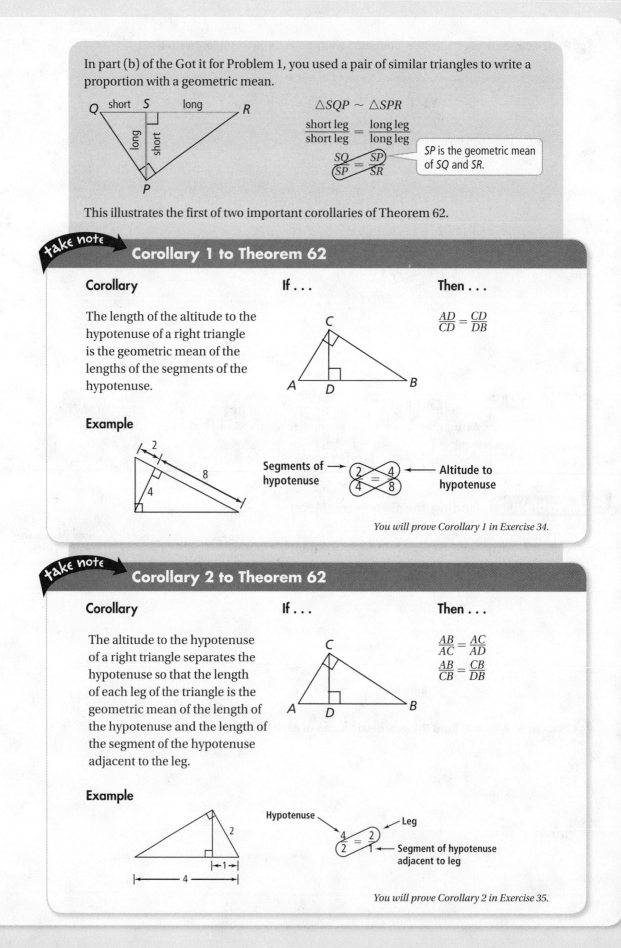

$\triangle SQP \sim \triangle SPR$

$$\frac{\text{short leg}}{\text{short leg}} = \frac{\text{long leg}}{\text{long leg}}$$

$$\frac{SQ}{SP} = \frac{SP}{SR}$$

SP is the geometric mean of *SQ* and *SR*.

This illustrates the first of two important corollaries of Theorem 62.

take note

Corollary 1 to Theorem 62

Corollary

The length of the altitude to the hypotenuse of a right triangle is the geometric mean of the lengths of the segments of the hypotenuse.

If . . .

Then . . .

$$\frac{AD}{CD} = \frac{CD}{DB}$$

Example

Segments of hypotenuse → $\frac{2}{4} = \frac{4}{8}$ ← Altitude to hypotenuse

You will prove Corollary 1 in Exercise 34.

take note

Corollary 2 to Theorem 62

Corollary

The altitude to the hypotenuse of a right triangle separates the hypotenuse so that the length of each leg of the triangle is the geometric mean of the length of the hypotenuse and the length of the segment of the hypotenuse adjacent to the leg.

If . . .

Then . . .

$$\frac{AB}{AC} = \frac{AC}{AD}$$

$$\frac{AB}{CB} = \frac{CB}{DB}$$

Example

Hypotenuse → $\frac{4}{2} = \frac{2}{1}$ ← Leg

← Segment of hypotenuse adjacent to leg

You will prove Corollary 2 in Exercise 35.

The corollaries to Theorem 62 give you ways to write proportions using lengths in right triangles without thinking through the similar triangles. To help remember these corollaries, consider the diagram and these properties.

Corollary 1

$$\frac{s_1}{a} = \frac{a}{s_2}$$

Corollary 2

$$\frac{h}{\ell_1} = \frac{\ell_1}{s_1}, \frac{h}{\ell_2} = \frac{\ell_2}{s_2}$$

Problem 3 Using the Corollaries

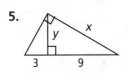

Got It? What are the values of x and y?

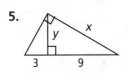

Plan

How do you decide which corollary to use?

ⓐ Practice **Algebra** Solve for x and y.

5.

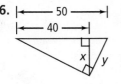

6. |◄—— 50 ——►|
   |◄—— 40 ——►|

Lesson Check

Do you know HOW?

Find the geometric mean of each pair of numbers.

7. 4 and 9

8. 4 and 12

Use the figure to complete each proportion.

9. $\dfrac{g}{e} = \dfrac{e}{\blacksquare}$

10. $\dfrac{j}{d} = \dfrac{d}{\blacksquare}$

11. $\dfrac{\blacksquare}{f} = \dfrac{f}{\blacksquare}$

12. $\dfrac{j}{\blacksquare} = \dfrac{\blacksquare}{g}$

Do you UNDERSTAND?

13. Vocabulary Identify the following in $\triangle RST$.

a. the hypotenuse

b. the segments of the hypotenuse

c. the segment of the hypotenuse adjacent to leg $\overline{ST}$

14. Error Analysis A classmate wrote an incorrect proportion to find x. Explain and correct the error.

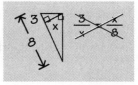

More Practice and Problem-Solving Exercises

B Apply

15. a. The altitude to the hypotenuse of a right triangle divides the hypotenuse into segments 2 cm and 8 cm long. Find the length of the altitude to the hypotenuse.

b. Use a ruler to make an accurate drawing of the right triangle in part (a).

c. Writing Describe how you drew the triangle in part (b).

Algebra Find the geometric mean of each pair of numbers.

16. 1 and 1000

17. 5 and 1.25

18. $\sqrt{8}$ and $\sqrt{2}$

19. $\frac{1}{2}$ and 2

20. $\sqrt{28}$ and $\sqrt{7}$

21. Reasoning A classmate says the following statement is true: The geometric mean of positive numbers a and b is $\sqrt{ab}$. Do you agree? Explain.

22. Think About a Plan The altitude to the hypotenuse of a right triangle divides the hypotenuse into segments with lengths in the ratio $1 : 2$. The length of the altitude is 8. How long is the hypotenuse?
- How can you use the given ratio to help you draw a sketch of the triangle?
- How can you use the given ratio to write expressions for the lengths of the segments of the hypotenuse?
- Which corollary to Theorem 62 applies to this situation?

23. Archaeology To estimate the height of a stone figure, Anya holds a small square up to her eyes and walks backward from the figure. She stops when the bottom of the figure aligns with the bottom edge of the square and the top of the figure aligns with the top edge of the square. Her eye level is 1.84 m from the ground. She is 3.50 m from the figure. What is the height of the figure to the nearest hundredth of a meter?

3.50 m

1.84 m

24. Reasoning Suppose the altitude to the hypotenuse of a right triangle bisects the hypotenuse. How does the length of the altitude compare with the lengths of the segments of the hypotenuse? Explain.

The diagram shows the parts of a right triangle with an altitude to the hypotenuse. For the two given measures, find the other four. Use simplest radical form.

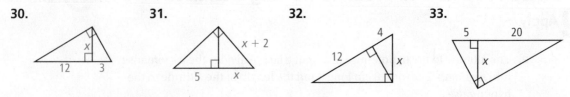

25. $h = 2$, $s_1 = 1$ **26.** $a = 6$, $s_1 = 6$ **27.** $h = 6$, $s_2 = 3$ **28.** $s_1 = 2$, $h = 4$

29. Coordinate Geometry $\overline{CD}$ is the altitude to the hypotenuse of right $\triangle ABC$. The coordinates of A, D, and B are $(4, 2)$, $(4, 6)$, and $(4, 7)$, respectively. Find all possible coordinates of point C.

Algebra Find the value of x.

30.

x

12   3

31.

$x + 2$

5   x

32.

4

12   x

33.

5   20

x

Use the figure at the right for Exercises 34 and 35.

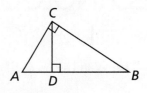

34. Prove Corollary 1 to
Proof Theorem 62.

> **Given:** Right $\triangle ABC$ with altitude
> to the hypotenuse $\overline{CD}$
>
> **Prove:** $\dfrac{AD}{CD} = \dfrac{CD}{DB}$

35. Prove Corollary 2 to
Proof Theorem 62.

> **Given:** Right $\triangle ABC$ with altitude
> to the hypotenuse $\overline{CD}$
>
> **Prove:** $\dfrac{AB}{AC} = \dfrac{AC}{AD}$, $\dfrac{AB}{BC} = \dfrac{BC}{DB}$

36. Given: Right $\triangle ABC$ with altitude $\overline{CD}$ to the
Proof hypotenuse $\overline{AB}$.

Prove: The product of the slopes of perpendicular
lines, where neither line is vertical is -1.

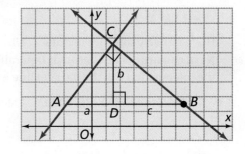

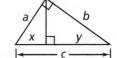 Challenge

37. a. Consider the following conjecture: The product of the lengths of the two legs
of a right triangle is equal to the product of the lengths of the hypotenuse and
the altitude to the hypotenuse. Draw a figure for the conjecture. Write the
Given information and what you are to *Prove*.

   b. Reasoning Is the conjecture true? Explain.

38. a. In the diagram, $c = x + y$. Use Corollary 2 to Theorem 62 to write two more
equations involving a, b, c, x, and y.

   b. The equations in part (a) form a system of three equations in five variables.
   Reduce the system to one equation in three variables by eliminating x and y.

   c. State in words what the one resulting equation tells you.

39. Given: In right $\triangle ABC$, $\overline{BD} \perp \overline{AC}$, and $\overline{DE} \perp \overline{BC}$.
Proof **Prove:** $\dfrac{AD}{DC} = \dfrac{BE}{EC}$

Exploring Proportions in Triangles

G.CO.12 Make formal geometric constructions with a variety of tools and methods . . . Also prepares for G.SRT.4

Activity 1

MATHEMATICAL
PRACTICES

Use geometry software to draw △ABC. Construct point D on $\overline{AB}$. Next, construct a line through D parallel to $\overline{AC}$. Then construct the intersection E of the parallel line with $\overline{BC}$.

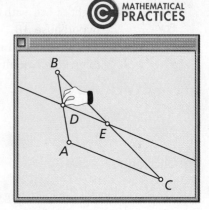

1. Measure $\overline{BD}$, $\overline{DA}$, $\overline{BE}$, and $\overline{EC}$. Calculate the ratios $\frac{BD}{DA}$ and $\frac{BE}{EC}$.

2. Manipulate △ABC and observe $\frac{BD}{DA}$ and $\frac{BE}{EC}$. What do you notice?

3. Make a conjecture about the four segments formed by a line parallel to one side of a triangle intersecting the other two sides.

Activity 2

Use geometry software to construct $\triangle ADE$ with vertices $A(3, 3)$, $D(-1, 0)$, and $E(5, 1)$.

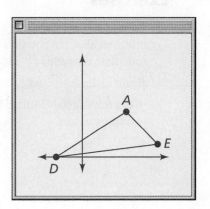

4. Measure $\overline{AD}$, $\overline{AE}$, and $\overline{DE}$.

5. Suppose you draw $\overline{BC}$ so that it partitions $\triangle ADE$ and $AB = \frac{2}{3}AD$ and $\overline{CB} \parallel \overline{DE}$. Describe how you could approximate the coordinates of points B and C.

6. Now use the geometry software to draw $\overline{BC}$ and manipulate the segment to most closely find the points B and C. What are the coordinates of points B and C?

Exercises

7. Construct $\overleftrightarrow{AB} \parallel \overleftrightarrow{CD} \parallel \overleftrightarrow{EF}$. Then construct two transversals that intersect all three parallel lines. Measure $\overline{AC}$, $\overline{CE}$, $\overline{BD}$, and $\overline{DF}$. Calculate the ratios $\frac{AC}{CE}$ and $\frac{BD}{DF}$. Manipulate the locations of A and B and observe $\frac{AC}{CE}$ and $\frac{BD}{DF}$. Make a conjecture about the segments of the transversals formed by the three parallel lines intersecting two transversals.

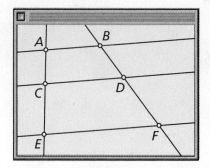

8. Suppose four or more parallel lines intersect two transversals. Make a conjecture about the segments of the transversals.

6-5 Proportions in Triangles

G.SRT.4 Prove theorems about triangles . . . a line parallel to one side of a triangle divides the other two proportionally . . .

Objective To use the Side-Splitter Theorem and the Triangle-Angle-Bisector Theorem

Solve It! Write your solution to the Solve It in the space below.

The Solve It involves parallel lines cut by two transversals that intersect. In this lesson, you will learn how to use proportions to find lengths of segments formed by parallel lines that intersect two or more transversals.

Essential Understanding When two or more parallel lines intersect other lines, proportional segments are formed.

take note

Theorem 63 Side-Splitter Theorem

Theorem	**If . . .**	**Then . . .**
If a line is parallel to one side of a triangle and intersects the other two sides, then it divides those sides proportionally.	$\overleftrightarrow{RS} \parallel \overleftrightarrow{XY}$	$\dfrac{XR}{RQ} = \dfrac{YS}{SQ}$

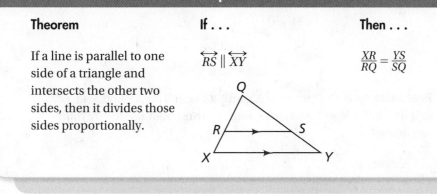

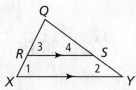

Proof **Proof of Theorem 63: Side-Splitter Theorem**

Given: $\triangle QXY$ with $\overleftrightarrow{RS} \parallel \overleftrightarrow{XY}$

Prove: $\dfrac{XR}{RQ} = \dfrac{YS}{SQ}$

Statements	Reasons
1) $\overleftrightarrow{RS} \parallel \overleftrightarrow{XY}$	1) Given
2) $\angle 1 \cong \angle 3,\ \angle 2 \cong \angle 4$	2) If lines are $\parallel$, then corresponding $\angle$s are $\cong$.
3) $\triangle QXY \sim \triangle QRS$	3) AA ~ Postulate
4) $\dfrac{XQ}{RQ} = \dfrac{YQ}{SQ}$	4) Corresponding sides of ~ $\triangle$s are proportional.
5) $XQ = XR + RQ,\ YQ = YS + SQ$	5) Segment Addition Postulate
6) $\dfrac{XR + RQ}{RQ} = \dfrac{YS + SQ}{SQ}$	6) Substitution Property
7) $\dfrac{XR}{RQ} = \dfrac{YS}{SQ}$	7) Property of Proportions (3)

 Problem 1 **Using the Side-Splitter Theorem**

Plan

How can you use the parallel lines in the diagram?

Got It? **a.** What is the value of a in the diagram below?

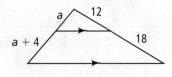

b. Reasoning In $\triangle XYZ$, $\overline{RS}$ joins $\overline{XY}$ and $\overline{YZ}$ with R on $\overline{XY}$ and S on $\overline{YZ}$, and $\overline{RS} \parallel \overline{XZ}$. If $\dfrac{YR}{RX} = \dfrac{YS}{SZ} = 1$, what must be true about RS? Justify your reasoning.

Practice Algebra Solve for *x*.

1.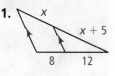
x
x + 5
8   12

2.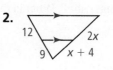
12
2*x*
9   *x* + 4

---

take note

Corollary   Corollary to the Side-Splitter Theorem

Corollary	**If . . .**	**Then . . .**
If three parallel lines intersect two transversals, then the segments intercepted on the transversals are proportional.	$a \parallel b \parallel c$ 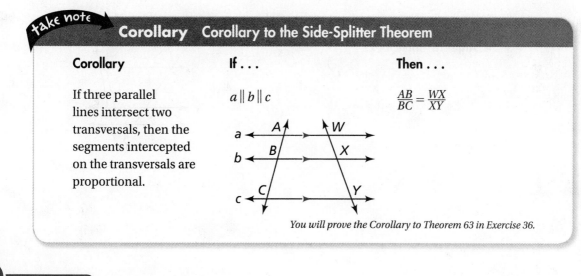	$\dfrac{AB}{BC} = \dfrac{WX}{XY}$

You will prove the Corollary to Theorem 63 in Exercise 36.

ONLINE PROBLEMS

Problem 2   Finding a Length

Got It?   In the figure in Problem 2, what is the length of Site C along the road?

Plan

What information does the diagram give you?

3. Marine Biology Use the information shown on the auger shell. What is the value of *y*?

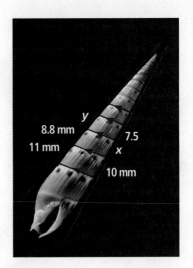

4. Algebra Solve for *x*.

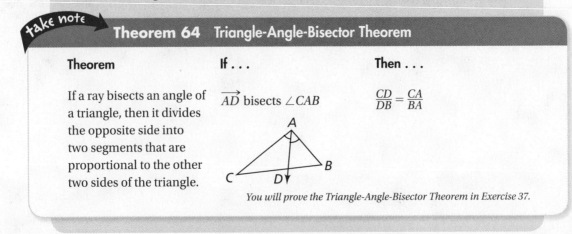

Essential Understanding The bisector of an angle of a triangle divides the opposite side into two segments with lengths proportional to the sides of the triangle that form the angle.

take note

Theorem 64 Triangle-Angle-Bisector Theorem

Theorem	**If . . .**	**Then . . .**
If a ray bisects an angle of a triangle, then it divides the opposite side into two segments that are proportional to the other two sides of the triangle.	$\overrightarrow{AD}$ bisects $\angle CAB$	$\dfrac{CD}{DB} = \dfrac{CA}{BA}$

You will prove the Triangle-Angle-Bisector Theorem in Exercise 37.

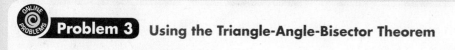

Problem 3 **Using the Triangle-Angle-Bisector Theorem**

Got It? What is the value of *y*?

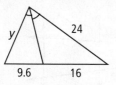

(A)Practice **5. Algebra** Solve for *x*.

6. The lengths of the sides of a triangle are 5 cm, 12 cm, and 13 cm. Find the lengths, to the nearest tenth, of the segments into which the bisector of each angle divides the opposite side.

Lesson Check

Do you know HOW?

Use the figure to complete each proportion.

7. $\dfrac{a}{b} = \dfrac{\blacksquare}{e}$

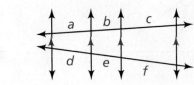

8. $\dfrac{b}{\blacksquare} = \dfrac{e}{f}$

9. $\dfrac{a}{b+c} = \dfrac{\blacksquare}{e+f}$

What is the value of x in each figure?

10.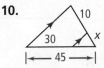

11.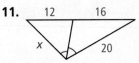

Do you UNDERSTAND?

12. Compare and Contrast How is the Corollary to the Side-Splitter Theorem related to Theorem 44: If three (or more) parallel lines cut off congruent segments on one transversal, then they cut off congruent segments on every transversal?

© **13. Compare and Contrast** How are the Triangle-Angle-Bisector Theorem and Corollary 1 to Theorem 62 alike? How are they different?

© **14. Error Analysis** A classmate says you can use the Side-Splitter Theorem to find both x and y in the diagram. Explain what is wrong with your classmate's statement.

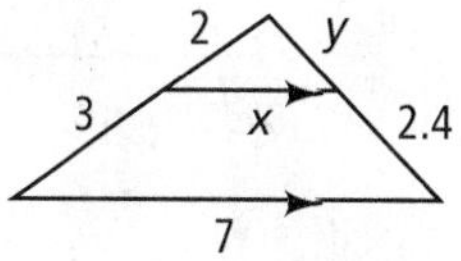

More Practice and Problem-Solving Exercises

Ⓑ Apply

Use the figure at the right to complete each proportion. Justify your answer.

15. $\dfrac{RS}{\blacksquare} = \dfrac{JR}{KJ}$

16. $\dfrac{KJ}{JP} = \dfrac{KS}{\blacksquare}$

17. $\dfrac{QL}{PM} = \dfrac{SQ}{\blacksquare}$

18. $\dfrac{PT}{\blacksquare} = \dfrac{TQ}{KQ}$

19. $\dfrac{KL}{LW} = \dfrac{\blacksquare}{MW}$

20. $\dfrac{\blacksquare}{KP} = \dfrac{LQ}{KQ}$

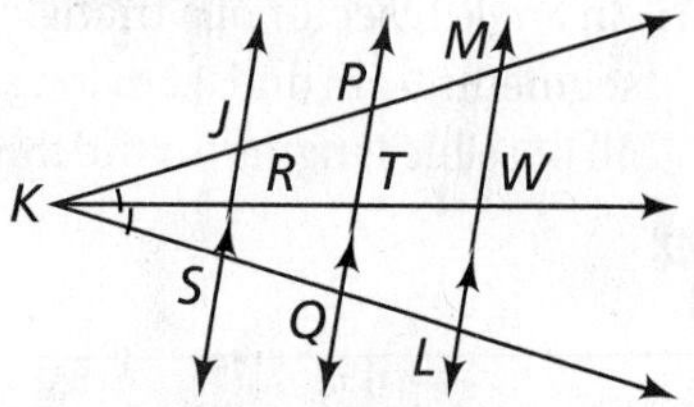

STEM Urban Design In Washington, D.C., E. Capitol Street, Independence Avenue, C Street, and D Street are parallel streets that intersect Kentucky Avenue and 12th Street.

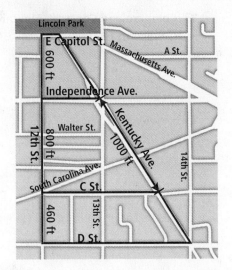

21. How long (to the nearest foot) is Kentucky Avenue between C Street and D Street?

22. How long (to the nearest foot) is Kentucky Avenue between E. Capitol Street and Independence Avenue?

Algebra Solve for x.

23.

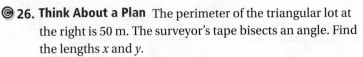

$4x$ $4x + 8$

$5x$ $6x - 10$

24.

$7x$ $10x - 4$

$5x$ $6x$

25.

12   8

14

$7x$

⊚ 26. Think About a Plan The perimeter of the triangular lot at the right is 50 m. The surveyor's tape bisects an angle. Find the lengths x and y.

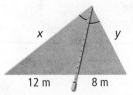

x   y

12 m   8 m

- How can you use the perimeter to write an equation in x and y?
- What other relationship do you know between x and y?

27. Prove the Converse of the Side-Splitter Theorem: If a line
Proof divides two sides of a triangle proportionally, then it is parallel to the third side.

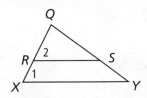

Q

R   2   S

1

X   Y

Given: $\dfrac{XR}{RQ} = \dfrac{YS}{SQ}$

Prove: $\overline{RS} \parallel \overline{XY}$

Determine whether the red segments are parallel. Explain each answer. You can use the theorem proved in Exercise 27.

28.

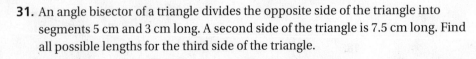

6   9

10   15

29.

10

24

12   28

30.

12

15

20   16

31. An angle bisector of a triangle divides the opposite side of the triangle into segments 5 cm and 3 cm long. A second side of the triangle is 7.5 cm long. Find all possible lengths for the third side of the triangle.

© **32. Open-Ended** In a triangle, the bisector of an angle divides the opposite side into two segments with lengths 6 cm and 9 cm. How long could the other two sides of the triangle be? (*Hint:* Make sure the three sides satisfy the Triangle Inequality Theorem.)

© **33. Reasoning** In $\triangle ABC$, the bisector of $\angle C$ bisects the opposite side. What type of triangle is $\triangle ABC$? Explain your reasoning.

Algebra Solve for x.

34.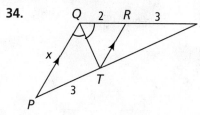

35.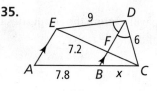

36. Prove the Corollary to the Side-Splitter Theorem. In the diagram
Proof from the statement of the theorem, draw the auxiliary line $\overleftrightarrow{CW}$ and label its intersection with b as point P.

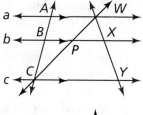

Given: $a \parallel b \parallel c$
Prove: $\dfrac{AB}{BC} = \dfrac{WX}{XY}$

37. Prove the Triangle-Angle-Bisector Theorem. In the diagram from
Proof the statement of the theorem, draw the auxiliary line $\overleftrightarrow{BE}$ so that $\overleftrightarrow{BE} \parallel \overline{DA}$. Extend $\overline{CA}$ to meet $\overleftrightarrow{BE}$ at point F.

Given: $\overleftrightarrow{AD}$ bisects $\angle CAB$.
Prove: $\dfrac{CD}{DB} = \dfrac{CA}{BA}$

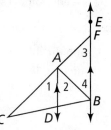

© **Challenge**

38. Use the definition in part (a) to prove the statements in parts (b) and (c).
   a. Write a definition for a midsegment of a parallelogram.
   b. A parallelogram midsegment is parallel to two sides of the parallelogram.
   c. A parallelogram midsegment bisects the diagonals of a parallelogram.

39. State the converse of the Triangle-Angle-Bisector Theorem. Give a convincing argument that the converse is true or a counterexample to prove that it is false.

40. In $\triangle ABC$, the bisectors of $\angle A$, $\angle B$, and $\angle C$ cut the opposite sides into lengths a_1 and a_2, b_1 and b_2, and c_1 and c_2, respectively, labeled in order counterclockwise around $\triangle ABC$. Find the perimeter of $\triangle ABC$ for each set of values.

   a. $b_1 = 16$, $b_2 = 20$, $c_1 = 18$

   b. $a_1 = \frac{5}{3}$, $a_2 = \frac{10}{3}$, $b_1 = \frac{15}{4}$

ACTIVITY LAB

Use With Lesson 6-6

Exploring Dilations

G.SRT.1.b The dilation of a line segment is . . . given by the scale factor.
Also **G.SRT.1.a**

In this activity, you will explore the properties of dilations. A dilation is defined by a center of dilation and a scale factor.

Activity 1

To dilate a segment by a scale factor n with center of dilation at the origin, you measure the distance from the origin to each point on the segment. The diagram at the right shows the dilation of $\overline{GH}$ by the scale factor 3 with center of dilation at the origin. To locate the dilation image of $\overline{GH}$, draw rays from the origin through points G and H. Then measure the distance from the origin to G. Next, find the point along the same ray that is 3 times that distance. Label the point G'. Now dilate the endpoint H similarly. Draw $\overline{G'H'}$.

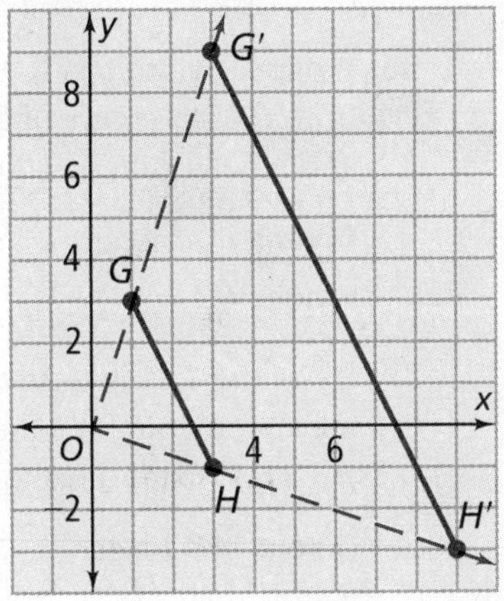

1. Graph $\overline{RS}$ with $R(1, 4)$ and $S(2, -1)$. What is the length of $\overline{RS}$?
2. Graph the dilations of the endpoints of $\overline{RS}$ by scale factor 2 and center of dilation at the origin. Label the dilated endpoints R' and S'.
3. What are the coordinates of R' and S'?
4. Graph $\overline{R'S'}$.

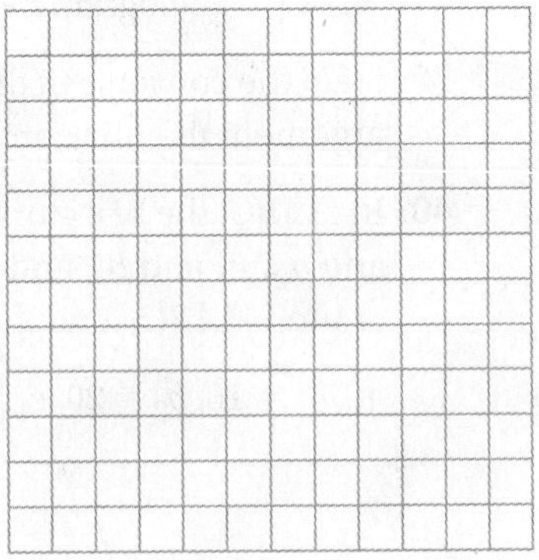

5. What is $R'S'$?
6. How do the lengths of $\overline{RS}$ and $\overline{R'S'}$ compare?

7. Graph the dilation of $\overline{RS}$ by scale factor $\frac{1}{2}$ with center of dilation at the origin. Label the dilation $\overline{R''S''}$.

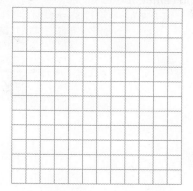

8. What is $R''S''$?

9. How do the lengths of $\overline{R'S'}$ and $\overline{R''S''}$ compare?

10. What can you conjecture about the length of a line segment that has been dilated by scale factor n?

11. Graph $L'M'N'P'$, the dilation of $LMNP$ with scale factor 3 and center of dilation at the origin. What are the coordinates of L', M', N', and P'?

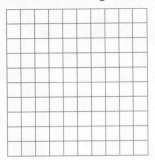

12. How are the coordinates of the vertices of $LMNP$ and $L'M'N'P'$ related?

13. Compare the shape, size, and orientation of the preimage $LMNP$ with the image $L'M'N'P'$. What conjecture can you make about the properties of dilations?

6-6 Dilations

G.SRT.1.a A dilation takes a line not passing through the center of the dilation to a parallel line . . .
Also **G.SRT.1.b**

Objective To understand dilation images of figures

 Solve It! Write your solution to the Solve It in the space below.

In the Solve It, you looked at how the pupil of an eye changes in size, or *dilates*. In this lesson, you will learn how to dilate geometric figures.

Essential Understanding You can use a scale factor to make a larger or smaller copy of a figure that is similar to the original figure.

take note

Key Concept Dilation

A **dilation** with **center of dilation** C and **scale factor** n, $n > 0$, can be written as $D_{(n, C)}$. A dilation is a transformation with the following properties.

- The image of C is itself (that is, $C' = C$).
- For any other point R, R' is on $\overrightarrow{CR}$ and $CR' = n \cdot CR$, or $n = \frac{CR'}{CR}$.
- Dilations preserve angle measure.

$CR' = n \cdot CR$

The scale factor n of a dilation is the ratio of a length of the image to the corresponding length in the preimage, with the image length always in the numerator. For the figure shown above, $n = \frac{CR'}{CR} = \frac{R'P'}{RP} = \frac{P'Q'}{PQ} = \frac{Q'R'}{QR}$.

A dilation is an **enlargement** if the scale factor n is greater than 1. The dilation is a **reduction** if the scale factor n is between 0 and 1.

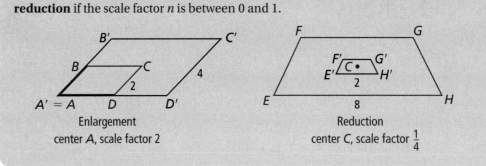

Enlargement
center A, scale factor 2

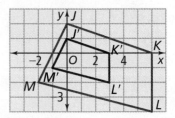

Reduction
center C, scale factor $\frac{1}{4}$

Problem 1 Finding a Scale Factor

Got It? Is $D_{(n, O)}(JKLM) = J'K'L'M'$ an enlargement or a reduction? What is the scale factor n of the dilation?

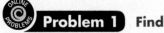

A Practice The red figure is a dilation image of the blue figure. The labeled point is the center of dilation. Tell whether the dilation is an enlargement or a reduction. Then find the scale factor of the dilation.

1.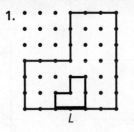

2.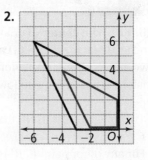

In the Got It for Problem 1, you looked at a dilation of a figure drawn in the coordinate plane. In this book, all dilations of figures in the coordinate plane have the origin as the center of dilation. So you can find the dilation image of a point $P(x, y)$ by multiplying the coordinates of P by the scale factor n. A dilation of scale factor n with center of dilation at the origin can be written as

$$D_n(x, y) = (nx, ny)$$

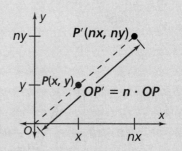

Finding a Dilation Image

Got It?   **a.** What are the coordinates of the vertices of $D_{\frac{1}{2}}(\triangle PZG)$?

Think

Will the vertices of the triangle move closer to (0, 0) or farther from (0, 0)?

© b. Reasoning How are $\overline{PZ}$ and $\overline{P'Z'}$ related? How are $\overline{PG}$ and $\overline{P'G'}$, and $\overline{GZ}$ and $\overline{G'Z'}$ related? Use these relationships to make a conjecture about the effects of dilations on lines.

Find the images of the vertices of △PQR for each dilation. Graph the image.

3. $D_3 (\triangle PQR)$

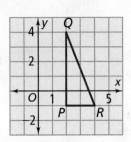

4. $D_{\frac{3}{4}} (\triangle PQR)$

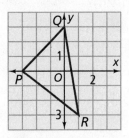

> Dilations and scale factors help you understand real-world enlargements and reductions, such as images seen through a microscope or on a computer screen.

ONLINE PROBLEMS

Problem 3 **Using a Scale Factor to Find a Length**

Got It? The height of a document on your computer screen is 20.4 cm. When you change the zoom setting on your screen from 100% to 25%, the new image of your document is a dilation of the previous image with scale factor 0.25. What is the height of the new image?

> **Think**
> What does a scale factor of 0.25 tell you?

Practice **Magnification** You look at each object described in Exercises 5 and 6 under a magnifying glass. Find the actual dimension of each object.

5. The image of an ant is 7 times the ant's actual size and has a length of 1.4 cm.

6. The image of a capital letter N is 6 times the letter's actual size and has a height of 1.68 cm.

Lesson Check

Do you know HOW?

7. The red figure is a dilation image of the blue figure with center of dilation *C*. Is the dilation an enlargement or a reduction? What is the scale factor of the dilation?

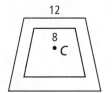

Find the image of each point.

8. $D_2\,(1, -5)$

9. $D_{\frac{1}{2}}\,(0, 6)$

10. $D_{10}\,(0, 0)$

Do you UNDERSTAND?

MATHEMATICAL
PRACTICES

© 11. Vocabulary Describe the scale factor of a reduction.

© 12. Error Analysis The red figure is a dilation image of the blue figure for a dilation with center *A*. Two students made errors when asked to find the scale factor. Explain and correct their errors.

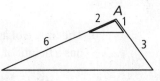

a.

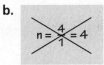

$$n = \frac{2}{6} = \frac{1}{3}$$

b.

$$n = \frac{4}{1} = 4$$

More Practice and Problem-Solving Exercises

MATHEMATICAL
PRACTICES

Ⓑ Apply

Find the image of each point for the given scale factor.

13. $L(-3, 0); D_5(L)$

14. $N(-4, 7); D_{0.2}(N)$

15. $A(-6, 2); D_{1.5}(A)$

16. $F(3, -2); D_{\frac{1}{3}}(F)$

17. $B\left(\frac{5}{4}, -\frac{3}{2}\right); D_{\frac{1}{10}}(B)$

18. $Q\left(6, \frac{\sqrt{3}}{2}\right); D_{\sqrt{6}}(Q)$

Use the graph at the right. Find the vertices of the image of *QRTW* **for a dilation with center (0, 0) and the given scale factor.**

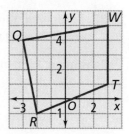

19. $\frac{1}{4}$ **20.** 0.6   **21.** 0.9   **22.** 10   **23.** 100

Ⓒ **24. Compare and Contrast** Compare the definition of scale factor of a dilation to the definition of scale factor of two similar polygons. How are they alike? How are they different?

Ⓒ **25. Think About a Plan** The diagram at the right shows $\triangle LMN$ and its image $\triangle L'M'N'$ for a dilation with center *P*. Find the values of *x* and *y*. Explain your reasoning.

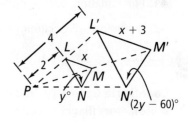

- What is the relationship between $\triangle LMN$ and $\triangle L'M'N'$?
- What is the scale factor of the dilation?
- Which variable can you find using the scale factor?

Ⓒ **26. Writing** An equilateral triangle has 4-in. sides. Describe its image for a dilation with center at one of the triangle's vertices and scale factor 2.5.

Coordinate Geometry Graph *MNPQ* and its image $M'N'P'Q'$ for a dilation with center (0, 0) and the given scale factor.

27. $M(1, 3), N(-3, 3), P(-5, -3), Q(-1, -3)$; 3

28. $M(2, 6), N(-4, 10), P(-4, -8), Q(-2, -12)$; $\frac{1}{4}$

Ⓒ **29. Open-Ended** Use the dilation command in geometry software or drawing software to create a design that involves repeated dilations, such as the one shown at the right. The software will prompt you to specify a center of dilation and a scale factor. Print your design and color it. Feel free to use other transformations along with dilations.

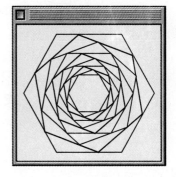

30. Copy Reduction Your picture of your family crest is 4.5 in. wide. You need a reduced copy for the front page of the family newsletter. The copy must fit in a space 1.8 in. wide. What scale factor should you use on the copy machine to adjust the size of your picture of the crest?

A dilation maps $\triangle HIJ$ onto $\triangle H'I'J'$. Find the missing values.

31. $HI = 8$ in. $H'I' = 16$ in.
   $IJ = 5$ in. $I'J' = \blacksquare$ in.
   $HJ = 6$ in. $H'J' = \blacksquare$ in.

32. $HI = 7$ cm $H'I' = 5.25$ cm
   $IJ = 7$ cm $I'J' = \blacksquare$ cm
   $HJ = \blacksquare$ cm $H'J' = 9$ cm

33. $HI = \blacksquare$ ft $H'I' = 8$ ft
   $IJ = 30$ ft $I'J' = \blacksquare$ ft
   $HJ = 24$ ft $H'J' = 6$ ft

Copy $\triangle TBA$ and point *O* for each of Exercises 34–37. Draw the dilation image $\triangle T'B'A'$.

34. $D_{(2, O)}(\triangle TBA)$ **35.** $D_{(3, B)}(\triangle TBA)$

36. $D_{(\frac{1}{3}, T)}(\triangle TBA)$ **37.** $D_{(\frac{1}{2}, O)}(\triangle TBA)$

38. Reasoning You are given $\overline{AB}$ and its dilation image $\overline{A'B'}$ with A, B, A', and B' noncollinear. Explain how to find the center of dilation and scale factor.

Reasoning Write *true* or *false* for Exercises 39–42. Explain your answers.

39. A dilation is an isometry.

40. A dilation with a scale factor greater than 1 is a reduction.

41. For a dilation, corresponding angles of the image and preimage are congruent.

42. A dilation image cannot have any points in common with its preimage.

Challenge

Coordinate Geometry In the coordinate plane, you can extend dilations to include scale factors that are negative numbers. For Exercises 43 and 44, use $\triangle PQR$ with vertices $P(1, 2)$, $Q(3, 4)$, and $R(4, 1)$.

43. Graph $D_{-3}(\triangle PQR)$.

44. a. Graph $D_{-1}(\triangle PQR)$.
   b. Explain why the dilation in part (a) may be called a *reflection through a point*. Extend your explanation to a new definition of point symmetry.

45. Shadows A flashlight projects an image of rectangle $ABCD$ on a wall so that each vertex of $ABCD$ is 3 ft away from the corresponding vertex of $A'B'C'D'$. The length of $\overline{AB}$ is 3 in. The length of $\overline{A'B'}$ is 1 ft. How far from each vertex of $ABCD$ is the light?

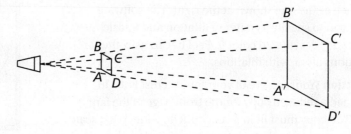

G.SRT.2 Given two figures, use the definition of similarity in terms of similarity transformations to decide if they are similar . . . Also **G.SRT.3**

Objective To identify similarity transformations and verify properties of similarity

Solve It! Write your solution to the Solve It in the space below.

In the Solve It, you used a composition of a rigid motion and a dilation to describe the mapping from $\triangle ABC$ to $\triangle A'B'C'$.

Essential Understanding You can use compositions of rigid motions and dilations to help you understand the properties of similarity.

Problem 1 Drawing Transformations

Got It? **Reasoning** $\triangle LMN$ has vertices $L(-4, 2)$, $M(-3, -3)$, and $N(-1, 1)$. Suppose the triangle is translated 4 units right and 2 units up and then dilated by a scale factor of 0.5 with center of dilation at the origin. Sketch the resulting image of the composition of transformations.

△*MAT* has vertices *M*(6, −2), *A*(4, −5), and *T*(1, −2). For each of the following, sketch the image of the composition of transformations.

1. rotation of 180° about the origin followed by a dilation by a scale factor of 1.5

2. translation 6 units up followed by a reflection across the *y*-axis and then a dilation by a scale factor of 2

Problem 2 **Describing Transformations**

Got It? What is a composition of rigid motions and a dilation that maps trapezoid *ABCD* to trapezoid *MNHP*?

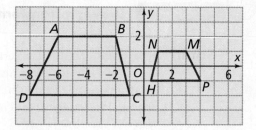

For each graph, describe the composition of transformations that maps △*FGH* to △*QRS*.

3.

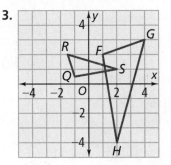

4.

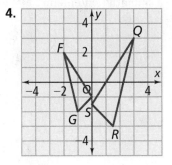

Notice that the figures in Problems 1 and 2 appear to have the same shape but different sizes. Compositions of rigid motions and dilations map preimages to similar images. For this reason, they are called **similarity transformations**. Similarity transformations give you another way to think about similarity.

take note

Key Concept Similar Figures

Two figures are **similar** if and only if there is a similarity transformation that maps one figure onto the other.

Here's Why It Works Consider the composition of a rigid motion and a dilation shown at the right.

Because rigid motions and dilations preserve angle measure, $m\angle P = m\angle P'$, $m\angle Q = m\angle Q'$, and $m\angle R = m\angle R'$. So corresponding angles are congruent.

Because there is a dilation, there is some scale factor k such that:

$$P'Q' = kPQ \qquad Q'R' = kQR \qquad P'R' = kPR$$

$$k = \frac{P'Q'}{PQ} \qquad\quad k = \frac{Q'R'}{QR} \qquad\quad k = \frac{P'R'}{PR}$$

So $\dfrac{P'Q'}{PQ} = \dfrac{Q'R'}{QR} = \dfrac{P'R'}{PR}$.

 Problem 3 **Finding Similarity Transformations**

Think

Does it matter what the center of dilation is?

Got It? Is there a similarity transformation that maps $\triangle JKL$ to $\triangle RST$? If so, identify the similarity transformation and write a similarity statement. If not, explain.

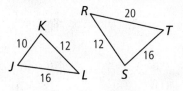

⒜ Practice For each pair of figures in Exercises 5 and 6, determine if there is a similarity transformation that maps one figure onto the other. If so, identify the similarity transformation and write a similarity statement. If not, explain.

5.

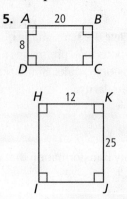

6.

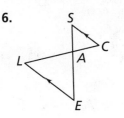

Similarity transformations provide a powerful general approach to similarity. In Problem 3, you used similarity transformations to verify the AA Postulate for triangle similarity. Another advantage to the transformational approach to similarity is that you can apply it to figures other than polygons.

 Problem 4 **Determining Similarity**

Got It? Are the figures below similar? Explain.

Think

How can you determine whether two figures are similar if you have no information about side lengths or angle measures?

Ⓐ Practice For each pair of figures in Exercises 7 and 8, determine whether or not the figures are similar. Explain your reasoning.

7.

8.

Lesson Check

Do you know HOW?

Use the diagram at the right for Exercises 9 and 10.

9. What is a similarity transformation that maps △*RST* to △*JKL*?

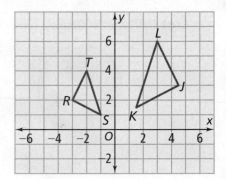

10. What are the coordinates of $(D_{\frac{1}{4}} \circ r_{(180°, O)})(\triangle RST)$?

Do you UNDERSTAND?

ⓒ **11. Vocabulary** Describe how the word *dilation* is used in areas outside of mathematics. How do these applications relate the mathematical definition?

ⓒ **12. Open-Ended** For △*TUV* at the right, give the vertices of a similar triangle after a similarity transformation that uses at least 1 rigid motion.

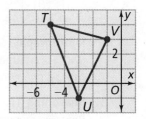

More Practice and Problem-Solving Exercises

Ⓑ **Apply**

ⓒ **13. Writing** Your teacher used geometry software program to plot △*ABC* with vertices *A*(2, 1), *B*(6, 1), and *C*(6, 4). Then he used a similarity transformation to plot △*DEF* with vertices *D*(−4, −2), *E*(−12, −2), and *F*(−12, −8). The corresponding angles of the two triangles are congruent. How can the Distance Formula be used to verify that the lengths of the corresponding sides are proportional? Verify that the figures are similar.

ⓒ **14. Think About a Plan** Suppose that △*JKL* is formed by connecting the midpoints of △*ABC*. Is △*AJL* similar to △*ABC*? Explain.
- How are the side lengths of △*AJL* related to the side lengths of △*ABC*?
- Can you find a similarity transformation that maps △*AJL* to △*ABC*? Explain.

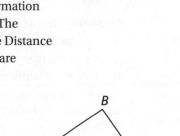

15. Writing What properties are preserved by rigid motions but not by similarity transformations?

Determine whether each statement is *always*, *sometimes*, or *never* true.

16. There is a similarity transformation between two rectangles.

17. There is a similarity transformation between two squares.

18. There is a similarity transformation between two circles.

19. There is a similarity transformation between a right triangle and an equilateral triangle.

20. Indirect Measurement A surveyor wants to use similar triangles to determine the distance across a lake as shown at the right.
  a. Are the two triangles in the figure similar? Justify your reasoning.
  b. What is the distance *d* across the lake?

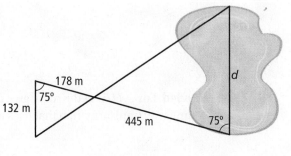

21. Photography A 4-in. by 6-in. rectangular photo is enlarged to fit an 8-in. by 10-in. frame. Are the two photographs similar? Explain.

22. Reasoning Is a rigid motion an example of a similarity transformation? Explain your reasoning and give an example.

23. Art A printing company enlarges a banner for a graduation party by a scale factor of 8.
  a. What are the dimensions of the larger banner?
  b. How can the printing company be sure that the enlarged banner is similar to the original?

13 in.

3 in.

Challenge

24. If △*ABC* has vertices given by *A*(*u*, *v*), *B*(*w*, *x*), and *C*(*y*, *z*), and △*NOP* has vertices given by *N*(5*u*, −4*v*), *O*(5*w*, −4*x*), and *P*(5*y*, −4*z*), is there a similarity transformation that maps △*ABC* to △*NOP*? Explain.

25. Overhead Projector When Mrs. Sheldon places a transparency on the screen of the overhead projector, the projector shows an enlargement of the transparency on the wall. Does this situation represent a similarity transformation? Explain.

26. Reasoning Tell whether each statement below is *true* or *false*.
  a. In order to show that two figures are similar, it is sufficient to show that there is a similarity transformation that maps one figure to the other.
  b. If there is a similarity transformation that maps one figure to another figure, then the figures are similar.
  c. If there is a similarity transformation that maps one figure to another figure, then the figures are congruent.

6-1 Ratios and Proportions

Quick Review

A **ratio** is a comparison of two quantities by division. A **proportion** is a statement that two ratios are equal. The **Cross Products Property** states that if $\frac{a}{b} = \frac{c}{d}$, where $b \neq 0$ and $d \neq 0$, then $ad = bc$.

Example

What is the solution of $\frac{x}{x+3} = \frac{4}{6}$?

$6x = 4(x + 3)$	Cross Products Property
$6x = 4x + 12$	Distributive Property
$2x = 12$	Subtract $4x$ from each side.
$x = 6$	Divide each side by 2.

Exercises

1. A high school has 16 math teachers for 1856 math students. What is the ratio of math teachers to math students?

2. The measures of two complementary angles are in the ratio $2 : 3$. What is the measure of the smaller angle?

Algebra Solve each proportion.

3. $\frac{x}{7} = \frac{18}{21}$

4. $\frac{6}{11} = \frac{15}{2x}$

5. $\frac{x}{3} = \frac{x+4}{5}$

6. $\frac{8}{x+9} = \frac{2}{x-3}$

6-2 and 6-3 Similar Polygons and Proving Triangles Similar

Quick Review

Similar polygons have congruent corresponding angles and proportional corresponding sides. You can prove triangles similar with limited information about congruent corresponding angles and proportional corresponding sides.

Postulate or Theorem	What You Need
Angle-Angle (AA ~)	two pairs of ≅ angles
Side-Angle-Side (SAS ~)	two pairs of proportional sides and the included angles ≅
Side-Side-Side (SSS ~)	three pairs of proportional sides

Example

Is △ABC similar to △RQP? How do you know?

You know that $\angle A \cong \angle R$. $\frac{AB}{RQ} = \frac{AC}{RP} = \frac{2}{1}$, so the triangles are similar by the SAS ~ Theorem.

Exercises

The polygons are similar. Write a similarity statement and give the scale factor.

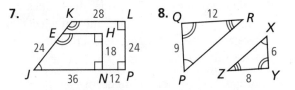

7.

8.

9. **City Planning** The length of a rectangular playground in a scale drawing is 12 in. If the scale is 1 in. = 10 ft, what is the actual length?

10. **Indirect Measurement** A 3-ft vertical post casts a 24-in. shadow at the same time a pine tree casts a 30-ft shadow. How tall is the pine tree?

Are the triangles similar? How do you know?

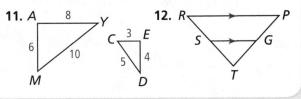

11.

12.

6-4 Similarity in Right Triangles

Quick Review

$\overline{CD}$ is the altitude to the
hypotenuse of right $\triangle ABC$.

- $\triangle ABC \sim \triangle ACD$,
  $\triangle ABC \sim \triangle CBD$, and
  $\triangle ACD \sim \triangle CBD$
- $\frac{AD}{CD} = \frac{CD}{DB}$, $\frac{AB}{AC} = \frac{AC}{AD}$, and $\frac{AB}{CB} = \frac{CB}{DB}$

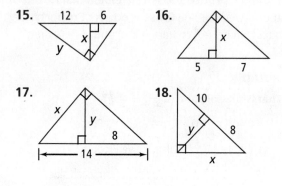

Example

What is the value of x?

$\frac{5+x}{10} = \frac{10}{5}$ Write a proportion.

$5(5 + x) = 100$ Cross Products Property

$25 + 5x = 100$ Distributive Property

$5x = 75$ Subtract 25 from each side.

$x = 15$ Divide each side by 5.

Exercises

Find the geometric mean of each pair of
numbers.

13. 9 and 16   **14.** 5 and 12

Algebra Find the value of each variable. Write
your answer in simplest radical form.

15. **16.**

17. **18.**

6-5 Proportions in Triangles

Quick Review

Side-Splitter Theorem and Corollary
If a line parallel to one side of a triangle intersects
the other two sides, then it divides those sides
proportionally. If three parallel lines intersect two
transversals, then the segments intercepted on the
transversals are proportional.

Triangle-Angle-Bisector Theorem
If a ray bisects an angle of a triangle, then it divides
the opposite side into two segments that are
proportional to the other two sides of the triangle.

Example

What is the value of x?

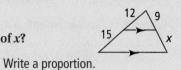

$\frac{12}{15} = \frac{9}{x}$ Write a proportion.

$12x = 135$ Cross Products Property

$x = 11.25$ Divide each side by 12.

Exercises

Algebra Find the value of x.

19. **20.**

21. **22.**

23. **24.**

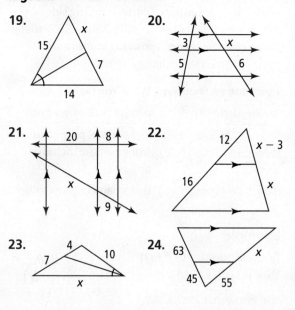

6-6 Dilations

Quick Review

The diagram shows a **dilation** with center C and scale factor n. The preimage and image are similar.

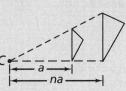

Example

The blue figure is a dilation image of the black figure. The center of dilation is A. Is the dilation an enlargement or a reduction? What is the scale factor?

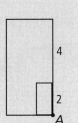

The image is smaller than the preimage, so the dilation is a reduction. The scale factor is

$$\frac{\text{image length}}{\text{original length}} = \frac{2}{2+4} = \frac{2}{6}, \text{ or } \frac{1}{3}.$$

Exercises

25. The red figure is a dilation image of the blue figure. The center of dilation is O. Tell whether the dilation is an enlargement or a reduction. Then find the scale factor.

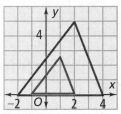

Graph the polygon with the given vertices. Then graph its image for a dilation with center $(0, 0)$ and the given scale factor.

26. $M(-3, 4)$, $A(-6, -1)$, $T(0, 0)$, $H(3, 2)$; scale factor 5

27. $F(-4, 0)$, $U(5, 0)$, $N(-2, -5)$; scale factor $\frac{1}{2}$

28. A dilation maps $\triangle LMN$ onto $\triangle L'M'N'$. $LM = 36$ ft, $LN = 26$ ft, $MN = 45$ ft, and $L'M' = 9$ ft. Find $L'N'$ and $M'N'$.

Lesson 6-7 Similarity Transformations

Quick Review

Two figures are similar if and only if there is a similarity transformation that maps one figure onto the other.

When a figure is transformed by a composition of rigid motions and dilations, the corresponding angles of the image and preimage are congruent, and the ratios of corresponding sides are proportional.

Example

Is $\triangle JKL$ similar to $\triangle DCX$? If so, write a similarity transformation rule. If not, explain why not.

$\triangle JKL$ can be rotated and then translated so that J and D coincide and $\overline{JK}$ and $\overline{CD}$ are collinear. Then if $\triangle JKL$ is dilated by scale factor $\frac{4}{5}$, then $\triangle JKL$ will coincide with $\triangle DCX$. So $\triangle JKL$ is similar to $\triangle DCX$, and the similarity transformation is a rotation, followed by a translation, followed by a dilation of scale factor $\frac{4}{5}$.

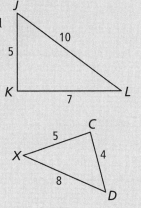

Exercises

29. $\square GHJK$ has vertices $G(-3, -1)$, $H(-3, 2)$ $J(4, 2)$, and $K(4, -1)$. Draw $\square GHJK$ and its image when you apply the composition $D_2 \circ R_{x\text{-axis}}$.

30. Writing Suppose that you have an 8-in. by 12-in. photo of your friends and a 2-in. by 6-in. copy of the same picture. Are the two photos similar figures? How do you know?

31. Reasoning A model airplane has an overall length that is $\frac{1}{20}$ the actual plane's length, and an overall height that is $\frac{1}{18}$ the actual plane's height. Are the model airplane and the actual airplane similar figures? Explain.

32. Determine whether the figures at the right are similar. If so, write the similarity transformation rule. If not, explain.

p d

Pull It **All Together**

Adjusting a Graphing Calculator Window

 ASSESSMENT

Lillian graphs the functions $y = 2x + 3$ and $y = -\frac{1}{2}x + 1$ on her graphing calculator. She knows the lines are perpendicular, but they do not appear to be on the screen.

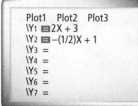

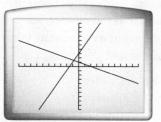

The screens above are the same shape as Lillian's graphing calculator screen. The **window** screen shows the interval of the x-axis (from **Xmin** to **Xmax**) and the y-axis (from **Ymin** to **Ymax**) for the viewing screen.

Lillian wants to adjust the values of **Xmin** and **Xmax** so that the graph of the lines is not skewed.

Task Description

Determine the values of **Xmin** and **Xmax** that Lillian should use for the viewing screen.

- What are the dimensions of the calculator screen in centimeters?

- How can similar figures help you solve the problem?

412 Chapter 6 Pull It All Together

Get Ready!

Solving Proportions

Algebra Solve for x. If necessary, round answers to the nearest thousandth.

1. $0.2734 = \frac{x}{17}$ **2.** $0.5858 = \frac{24}{x}$ **3.** $0.8572 = \frac{5271}{x}$ **4.** $0.5 = \frac{x}{3x + 5}$

Proving Triangles Similar

Name the postulate or theorem that proves each pair of triangles similar.

5. $\overline{CD} \parallel \overline{AB}$ **6.**   **7.** $\overline{JK} \perp \overline{ML}$

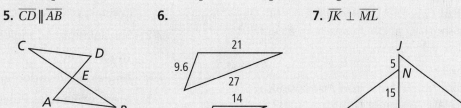

Similarity in Right Triangles

Algebra Find the value of x in $\triangle ABC$ with right $\angle C$ and altitude $\overline{CD}$.

8.   **9.**   **10.**   **11.**

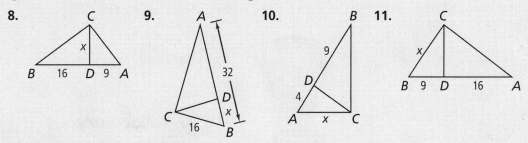

Looking Ahead Vocabulary

12. People often describe the height of a mountain as its *elevation*. How might you describe an *angle of elevation* in geometry?

13. You see the prefix *tri-* in many words, such as *triad, triathlon, trilogy,* and *trimester*. What does the prefix indicate in these words? What geometric figure do you think is associated with the phrase *trigonometric ratio*? Explain.

CHAPTER 7

Right Triangles and Trigonometry

Big Ideas

1 Measurement

Essential Question: How do you find a side length or angle measure in a right triangle?

2 Similarity

Essential Question: How do trigonometric ratios relate to similar right triangles?

© Domains

- Similarity, Right Triangles, and Trigonometry
- Modeling with Geometry

Interactive Digital Path

Log in to **pearsonsuccessnet.com** and click on Interactive Digital Path to access the Solve Its and animated Problems.

Chapter Preview

7-1 The Pythagorean Theorem and Its Converse

7-2 Special Right Triangles

7-3 Trigonometry

7-4 Angles of Elevation and Depression

7-5 Areas of Regular Polygons

Vocabulary

English/Spanish Vocabulary Audio Online:

English	Spanish
angle of depression, *p. 447*	ángulo de depresión
angle of elevation, *p. 447*	ángulo de elevación
apothem, *p. 454*	apotema
cosine, *p. 438*	coseno
Pythagorean triple, *p. 416*	tripleta de Pitágoras
radius of a regular polygon, *p. 454*	radio de un polígono regular
sine, *p. 438*	seno
tangent, *p. 438*	tangente

G.SRT.8 Use . . . the Pythagorean Theorem to solve right triangles in applied problems. Also **G.SRT.4**

Objective To use the Pythagorean Theorem and its converse

Solve It! Write your solution to the Solve It in the space below.

The equations in the Solve It demonstrate an important relationship in right triangles called the Pythagorean Theorem. This theorem is named for Pythagoras, a Greek mathematician who lived in the 500s B.C. We now know that the Babylonians, Egyptians, and Chinese were aware of this relationship before its discovery by Pythagoras. There are many proofs of the Pythagorean Theorem. You will see one proof in this lesson and others later in the book.

Essential Understanding If you know the lengths of any two sides of a right triangle, you can find the length of the third side by using the Pythagorean Theorem.

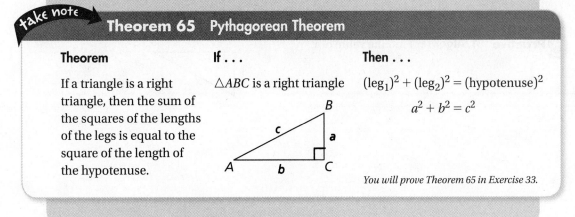

take note

Theorem 65 **Pythagorean Theorem**

Theorem	**If . . .**	**Then . . .**
If a triangle is a right triangle, then the sum of the squares of the lengths of the legs is equal to the square of the length of the hypotenuse.	$\triangle ABC$ is a right triangle	$(\text{leg}_1)^2 + (\text{leg}_2)^2 = (\text{hypotenuse})^2$ $$a^2 + b^2 = c^2$$

You will prove Theorem 65 in Exercise 33.

A **Pythagorean triple** is a set of nonzero whole numbers a, b, and c that satisfy the equation $a^2 + b^2 = c^2$. Below are some common Pythagorean triples.

3, 4, 5	5, 12, 13	8, 15, 17	7, 24, 25

If you multiply each number in a Pythagorean triple by the same whole number, the three numbers that result also form a Pythagorean triple. For example, the Pythagorean triples 6, 8, 10, and 9, 12, 15 each result from multiplying the numbers in the triple 3, 4, 5 by a whole number.

Problem 1 Finding the Length of the Hypotenuse

Got It? **a.** The legs of a right triangle have lengths 10 and 24. What is the length of the hypotenuse?

b. Do the side lengths in part (a) form a Pythagorean triple? Explain.

Ⓐ Practice **1. Algebra** Find the value of x.

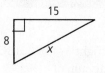

2. Do the numbers 4, 5, 6 form a Pythagorean triple? Explain.

 Problem 2 **Finding the Length of a Leg**

Got It? The hypotenuse of a right triangle has length 12. One leg has length 6. What is the length of the other leg? Express your answer in simplest radical form.

 Practice **Algebra** Find the value of x. Express your answer in simplest radical form.

3.

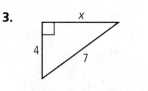

4.

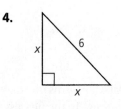

Got It? The size of a computer monitor is the length of its diagonal. You want to buy a 19-in. monitor that has a height of 11 in. What is the width of the monitor? Round to the nearest tenth of an inch.

Think

How do you know when to use a calculator?

 Practice 5. **Home Maintenance** A painter leans a 15-ft ladder against a house. The base of the ladder is 5 ft from the house. To the nearest tenth of a foot, how high on the house does the ladder reach?

6. A walkway forms one diagonal of a square playground. The walkway is 24 m long. To the nearest meter, how long is a side of the playground?

You can use the Converse of the Pythagorean Theorem to determine whether a triangle is a right triangle.

Theorem 66   Converse of the Pythagorean Theorem

Theorem	If . . .	Then . . .
If the sum of the squares of the lengths of two sides of a triangle is equal to the square of the length of the third side, then the triangle is a right triangle.	$a^2 + b^2 = c^2$ 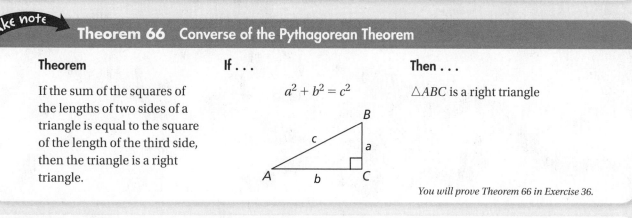	$\triangle ABC$ is a right triangle

You will prove Theorem 66 in Exercise 36.

Problem 4   **Identifying a Right Triangle**

Got It?   **a.** A triangle has side lengths 16, 48, and 50. Is the triangle a right triangle? Explain.

Plan
How do you know where each of the side lengths goes in the equation?

b. Reasoning Once you know which length represents the hypotenuse, does it matter which length you substitute for *a* and which length you substitute for *b*? Explain.

Practice Is the triangle a right triangle? Explain.

7.

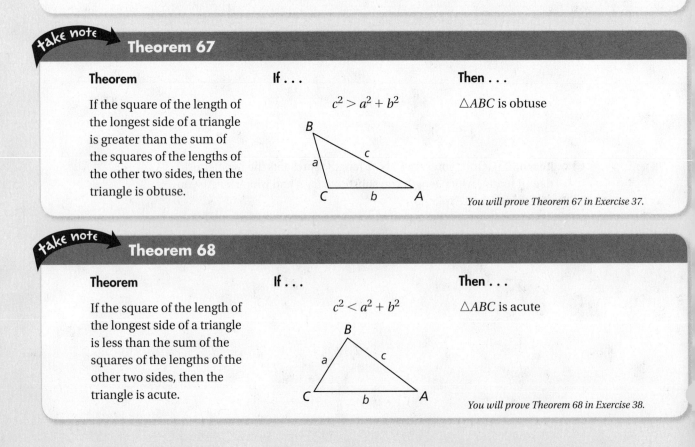

8.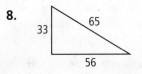

The theorems below allow you to determine whether a triangle is acute or obtuse. These theorems relate to the Hinge Theorem, which states that the longer side is opposite the larger angle and the shorter side is opposite the smaller angle.

take note

Theorem 67

Theorem	**If . . .**	**Then . . .**
If the square of the length of the longest side of a triangle is greater than the sum of the squares of the lengths of the other two sides, then the triangle is obtuse.	$c^2 > a^2 + b^2$	$\triangle ABC$ is obtuse

You will prove Theorem 67 in Exercise 37.

take note

Theorem 68

Theorem	**If . . .**	**Then . . .**
If the square of the length of the longest side of a triangle is less than the sum of the squares of the lengths of the other two sides, then the triangle is acute.	$c^2 < a^2 + b^2$	$\triangle ABC$ is acute

You will prove Theorem 68 in Exercise 38.

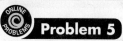

Problem 5 Classifying a Triangle

Got It? Is a triangle with side lengths 7, 8, and 9 *acute, obtuse,* or *right*?

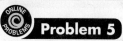 What information do you need?

A Practice The lengths of the sides of a triangle are given. Classify each triangle as *acute, obtuse,* or *right.*

9. 0.3, 0.4, 0.6

10. $\sqrt{11}, \sqrt{7}, 4$

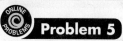

Lesson Check

Do you know HOW?

What is the value of x in simplest radical form?

11.

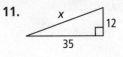

12.

13.

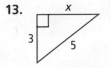

14.

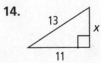

Do you UNDERSTAND?

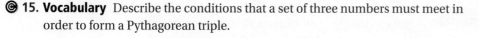

15. Vocabulary Describe the conditions that a set of three numbers must meet in order to form a Pythagorean triple.

16. Error Analysis A triangle has side lengths 16, 34, and 30. Your friend says it is not a right triangle. Look at your friend's work and describe the error.

$$16^2 + 34^2 \overset{?}{=} 30^2$$
$$256 + 1156 \overset{?}{=} 900$$
$$1412 \ne 900$$

More Practice and Problem-Solving Exercises

Ⓑ Apply

17. Think About a Plan You want to embroider a square design. You have an embroidery hoop with a 6 in. diameter. Find the largest value of x so that the entire square will fit in the hoop. Round to the nearest tenth.

- What does the diameter of the circle represent in the square?
- What do you know about the sides of a square?
- How do the side lengths of the square relate to the length of the diameter?

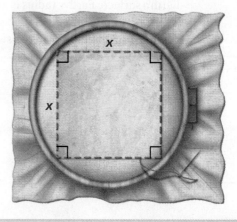

18. In parallelogram $RSTW$, $RS = 7$, $ST = 24$, and $RT = 25$. Is $RSTW$ a rectangle? Explain.

Proof **19. Coordinate Geometry** You can use the Pythagorean Theorem to prove the Distance Formula. Let points $P(x_1, y_1)$ and $Q(x_2, y_2)$ be the endpoints of the hypotenuse of a right triangle.

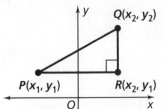

  a. Write an algebraic expression to complete each of the following:
     $PR = $ __?__ and $QR = $ __?__ .
  b. By the Pythagorean Theorem, $PQ^2 = PR^2 + QR^2$. Rewrite this statement by substituting the algebraic expressions you found for PR and QR in part (a).
  c. Complete the proof by taking the square root of each side of the equation that you wrote in part (b).

Algebra Find the value of x. If your answer is not an integer, express it in simplest radical form.

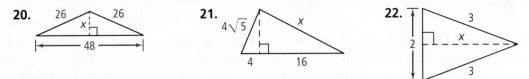

20. 26 x 26   48

21. $4\sqrt{5}$ x 4   16

22. 3   2 x 3

For each pair of numbers, find a third whole number such that the three numbers form a Pythagorean triple.

23. 20, 21   **24.** 14, 48   **25.** 13, 85   **26.** 12, 37

Open-Ended Find integers j and k such that (a) the two given integers and j represent the side lengths of an acute triangle and (b) the two given integers and k represent the side lengths of an obtuse triangle.

27. 4, 5   **28.** 2, 4   **29.** 6, 9

30. 5, 10   **31.** 6, 7   **32.** 9, 12

Proof **33.** Prove the Pythagorean Theorem.

  Given: $\triangle ABC$ is a right triangle.
  Prove: $a^2 + b^2 = c^2$
  (*Hint:* Begin with proportions suggested by Theorem 62 or its corollaries.)

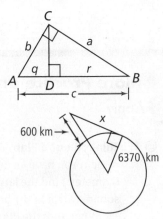

STEM **34. Astronomy** The Hubble Space Telescope orbits 600 km above Earth's surface. Earth's radius is about 6370 km. Use the Pythagorean Theorem to find the distance x from the telescope to Earth's horizon. Round your answer to the nearest ten kilometers. (Diagram is not to scale.)

35. Prove that if the slopes of two lines ℓ_1 and ℓ_2 have product -1, then the lines are perpendicular. Use parts (a)–(c) to write a coordinate proof.

 a. First, argue that neither line can be horizontal nor vertical.

 b. Then, tell why the lines must intersect. (*Hint:* Use indirect reasoning.)

 c. Place the lines in the coordinate plane. Choose a point on ℓ_1 and find a related point on ℓ_2. Complete the proof.

Ⓒ Challenge

Proof 36. Use the plan and write a proof of Theorem 66 (Converse of the Pythagorean Theorem).

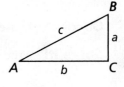

 Given: $\triangle ABC$ with sides of length a, b, and c, where $a^2 + b^2 = c^2$
 Prove: $\triangle ABC$ is a right triangle.
 Plan: Draw a right triangle (not $\triangle ABC$) with legs of lengths a and b. Label the hypotenuse x. By the Pythagorean Theorem, $a^2 + b^2 = x^2$. Use substitution to compare the lengths of the sides of your triangle and $\triangle ABC$. Then prove the triangles congruent.

Proof 37. Use the plan and write a proof of Theorem 67.

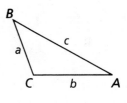

 Given: $\triangle ABC$ with sides of length a, b, and c, where $c^2 > a^2 + b^2$
 Prove: $\triangle ABC$ is an obtuse triangle.
 Plan: Draw a right triangle (not $\triangle ABC$) with legs of lengths a and b. Label the hypotenuse x. By the Pythagorean Theorem, $a^2 + b^2 = x^2$. Use substitution to compare lengths c and x. Then use the Converse of the Hinge Theorem to compare $\angle C$ to the right angle.

Proof 38. Prove Theorem 68.

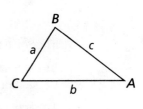

 Given: $\triangle ABC$ with sides of length a, b, and c, where $c^2 < a^2 + b^2$
 Prove: $\triangle ABC$ is an acute triangle.

7-2 Special Right Triangles

G.SRT.8 Use . . . the Pythagorean Theorem to solve right triangles in applied problems.

Objective To use the properties of 45°-45°-90° and 30°-60°-90° triangles

 Solve It! Write your solution to the Solve It in the space below.

The Solve It involves triangles with angles 45°, 45°, and 90°.

Essential Understanding Certain right triangles have properties that allow you to use shortcuts to determine side lengths without using the Pythagorean Theorem.

The acute angles of a right isosceles triangle are both 45° angles. Another name for an isosceles right triangle is a 45°-45°-90° triangle. If each leg has length x and the hypotenuse has length y, you can solve for y in terms of x.

$x^2 + x^2 = y^2$ Use the Pythagorean Theorem.

$2x^2 = y^2$ Simplify.

$x\sqrt{2} = y$ Take the positive square root of each side.

You have just proved the following theorem.

take note

Theorem 69   45°-45°-90° Triangle Theorem

In a 45°-45°-90° triangle, both legs are congruent and the length of the hypotenuse is $\sqrt{2}$ times the length of a leg.

hypotenuse $= \sqrt{2} \cdot$ leg

Problem 1 **Finding the Length of the Hypotenuse**

Got It? What is the length of the hypotenuse of a 45°-45°-90° triangle with leg length $5\sqrt{3}$?

Ⓐ Practice Find the value of each variable. If your answer is not an integer, express it in simplest radical form.

1.

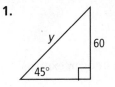

2.

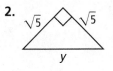

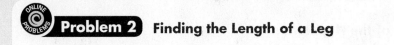

Problem 2 Finding the Length of a Leg

Got It? **a.** The length of the hypotenuse of a 45°-45°-90° triangle is 16. What is the length of one leg?

© **b. Reasoning** In Problem 2, why can you multiply $\frac{6}{\sqrt{2}}$ by $\frac{\sqrt{2}}{\sqrt{2}}$?

 Practice Find the value of each variable. If your answer is not an integer, express it in simplest radical form.

3.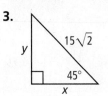

4.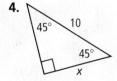

When you apply the 45°-45°-90° Triangle Theorem to a real-life example, you can use a calculator to evaluate square roots.

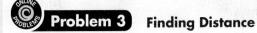 **Problem 3** **Finding Distance**

Got It? You plan to build a path along one diagonal of a 100 ft-by-100 ft square garden. To the nearest foot, how long will the path be?

 Practice 5. **Dinnerware Design** What is the side length of the smallest square plate on which a 20-cm chopstick can fit along a diagonal without any overhang? Round your answer to the nearest tenth of a centimeter.

6. **Aviation** The four blades of a helicopter meet at right angles and are all the same length. The distance between the tips of two adjacent blades is 36 ft. How long is each blade? Round your answer to the nearest tenth of a foot.

Another type of special right triangle is a 30°-60°-90° triangle.

Theorem 70   30°-60°-90° Triangle Theorem

In a 30°-60°-90° triangle, the length of the hypotenuse is twice
the length of the shorter leg. The length of the longer leg is $\sqrt{3}$
times the length of the shorter leg.

hypotenuse = 2 · shorter leg

longer leg = $\sqrt{3}$ · shorter leg

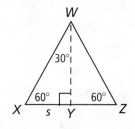

Proof **Proof of Theorem 70: 30°-60°-90° Triangle Theorem**

For equilateral $\triangle WXZ$, altitude $\overline{WY}$ bisects $\angle W$ and is the
perpendicular bisector of $\overline{XZ}$. So, $\overline{WY}$ divides $\triangle WXZ$ into two
congruent 30°-60°-90° triangles.

Thus, $XY = \frac{1}{2}XZ = \frac{1}{2}XW$, or $XW = 2XY = 2s$.

$XY^2 + YW^2 = XW^2$ Use the Pythagorean Theorem.

$s^2 + YW^2 = (2s)^2$ Substitute s for XY and $2s$ for XW.

$YW^2 = 4s^2 - s^2$ Subtract s^2 from each side.

$YW^2 = 3s^2$ Simplify.

$YW = s\sqrt{3}$ Take the positive square root of each side.

You can also use the 30°-60°-90° Triangle Theorem to find side lengths.

ONLINE
PROBLEMS
Problem 4   Using the Length of One Side

Got It?   What is the value of f in simplest radical form?

Think

How can
you write an
equation that
relates the
longer leg to the
hypotenuse?

Practice **Algebra** In Exercises 7–8, find the value of each variable. If your answer is not an integer, express it in simplest radical form.

7.

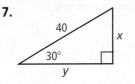

8.

Problem 5 **Applying the 30°-60°-90° Triangle Theorem**

Got It? Suppose the sides of the pendant, from Problem 5, are 18 mm long. What is the height of the pendant to the nearest tenth of a millimeter?

Plan

How does knowing the shape of the pendant help?

Practice

STEM

9. Architecture An escalator lifts people to the second floor of a building, 25 ft above the first floor. The escalator rises at a 30° angle. To the nearest foot, how far does a person travel from the bottom to the top of the escalator?

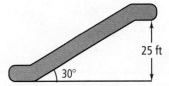

25 ft

30°

10. City Planning A rectangular park has a walkway that joins opposite corners. A triangle formed from two sides of the park and the walkway is a 30°-60°-90° triangle. If the shorter side of the park measures 150 feet, what is the length of the walkway?

Lesson Check

Do you know HOW?

What is the value of *x*? If your answer is not an integer, express it in simplest radical form.

11.

12.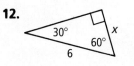

13.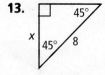

14.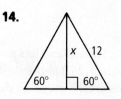

Do you UNDERSTAND?

15. Error Analysis Sandra drew the triangle at the right. Rika said that the labeled lengths are not possible. With which student do you agree? Explain.

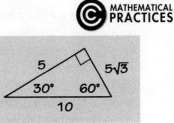

16. Reasoning A test question asks you to find two side lengths of a 45°-45°-90° triangle. You know that the length of one leg is 6, but you forgot the special formula for 45°-45°-90° triangles. Explain how you can still determine the other side lengths. What are they?

More Practice and Problem-Solving Exercises

Ⓑ Apply

Algebra Find the value of each variable. If your answer is not an integer, express it in simplest radical form.

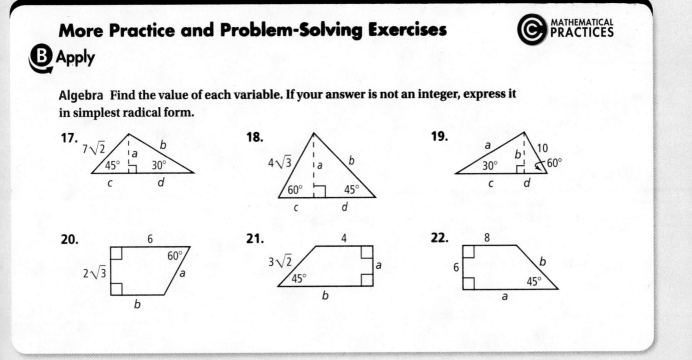

23. Think About a Plan A farmer's conveyor belt carries bales of hay from the ground to the barn loft. The conveyor belt moves at 100 ft/min. How many seconds does it take for a bale of hay to go from the ground to the barn loft?

- Which part of a right triangle does the conveyor belt represent?
- You know the speed. What other information do you need to find time?
- How are minutes and seconds related?

24. House Repair After heavy winds damaged a house, workers placed a 6-m brace against its side at a 45° angle. Then, at the same spot on the ground, they placed a second, longer brace to make a 30° angle with the side of the house.

a. How long is the longer brace? Round to the nearest tenth of a meter.

b. About how much higher does the longer brace reach than the shorter brace?

25. Open-Ended Write a real-life problem that you can solve using a 30°-60°-90° triangle with a 12-ft hypotenuse. Show your solution.

26. Constructions Construct a 30°-60°-90° triangle using a segment that is the given side.

a. the shorter leg   **b.** the hypotenuse   **c.** the longer leg

Ⓒ Challenge

27. Geometry in 3 Dimensions Find the length *d*, in simplest radical form, of the diagonal of a cube with edges of the given length.

a. 1 unit   **b.** 2 units   **c.** *s* units

Exploring Trigonometric Ratios

G.SRT.6 Understand that by similarity, side ratios in right triangles are properties of the angles in the triangle, . . .

Construct

Use geometry software to construct $\overrightarrow{AB}$ and $\overrightarrow{AC}$ so that $\angle A$ is acute. Through a point D on $\overrightarrow{AB}$, construct a line perpendicular to $\overrightarrow{AB}$ that intersects $\overrightarrow{AC}$ in point E.

Moving point D changes the size of $\triangle ADE$.
Moving point C changes the size of $\angle A$.

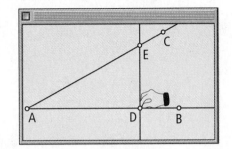

Exercises

1. • Measure $\angle A$ and find the lengths of the sides of $\triangle ADE$.

   • Calculate the ratio $\frac{\text{leg opposite } \angle A}{\text{hypotenuse}}$, which is $\frac{ED}{AE}$.

   • Move point D to change the size of $\triangle ADE$ without changing $m\angle A$.

   What do you observe about the ratio as the size of $\triangle ADE$ changes?

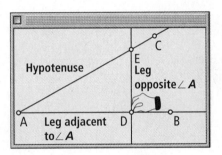

2. • Move point C to change $m\angle A$.

   a. What do you observe about the ratio as $m\angle A$ changes?

   b. What value does the ratio approach as $m\angle A$ approaches 0? As $m\angle A$ approaches 90?

3. • Make a table that shows values for $m\angle A$ and the ratio $\frac{\text{leg opposite } \angle A}{\text{hypotenuse}}$. In your table, include 10, 20, 30, ..., 80 for $m\angle A$.

• Compare your table with a table of trigonometric ratios.

Do your values for $\frac{\text{leg opposite } \angle A}{\text{hypotenuse}}$ match the values in one of the columns of the table? What is the name of this ratio in the table?

Extend

4. Repeat Exercises 1–3 for $\frac{\text{leg adjacent to } \angle A}{\text{hypotenuse}}$, which is $\frac{AD}{AE}$, and $\frac{\text{leg opposite } \angle A}{\text{leg adjacent to } \angle A}$, which is $\frac{ED}{AD}$.

5. • Choose a measure for $\angle A$ and determine the ratio $r = \dfrac{\text{leg opposite } \angle A}{\text{hypotenuse}}$. Record $m\angle A$ and this ratio.

• Manipulate the triangle so that $\dfrac{\text{leg adjacent to } \angle A}{\text{hypotenuse}}$ has the same value r. Record this $m\angle A$ and compare it with your first value of $m\angle A$.

• Repeat this procedure several times. Look for a pattern in the two measures of $\angle A$ that you found for different values of r.

Make a conjecture.

7-3 Trigonometry

G.SRT.8 Use trigonometric ratios . . . to solve right triangles in applied problems. Also **G.SRT.7, F.TF.8**

Objective To use the sine, cosine, and tangent ratios to determine side lengths and angle measures in right triangles

Solve It! Write your solution to the Solve It in the space below.

Essential Understanding If you know certain combinations of side lengths and angle measures of a right triangle, you can use ratios to find other side lengths and angle measures.

Any two right triangles that have a pair of congruent acute angles are similar by the AA Similarity Postulate. Similar right triangles have equivalent ratios for their corresponding sides called **trigonometric ratios**.

take note

Key Concept   Trigonometric Ratios

sine of $\angle A = \dfrac{\text{length of leg opposite } \angle A}{\text{length of hypotenuse}} = \dfrac{a}{c}$

cosine of $\angle A = \dfrac{\text{length of leg adjacent to } \angle A}{\text{length of hypotenuse}} = \dfrac{b}{c}$

tangent of $\angle A = \dfrac{\text{length of leg opposite } \angle A}{\text{length of leg adjacent to } \angle A} = \dfrac{a}{b}$

You can abbreviate the ratios as

$\sin A = \dfrac{\text{opposite}}{\text{hypotenuse}}, \cos A = \dfrac{\text{adjacent}}{\text{hypotenuse}}, \text{ and } \tan A = \dfrac{\text{opposite}}{\text{adjacent}}.$

Problem 1 Writing Trigonometric Ratios

Got It? What are the sine, cosine, and tangent ratios for ∠G?

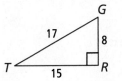

Think

How do the sides relate to ∠G?

Ⓐ Practice Write the ratios for sin *M*, cos *M*, and tan *M*.

1.

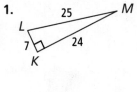

2.

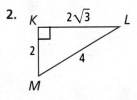

In Chapter 6, you used similar triangles to measure distances indirectly. You can also use trigonometry for indirect measurement.

Problem 2 **Using a Trigonometric Ratio to Find Distance**

Got It? For parts (a)–(c), find the value of *w* to the nearest tenth.

a.

54°

17   *w*

b.

w

1.0

28°

c.

w

33°

4.5

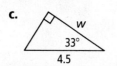

d. A section of Filbert Street in San Francisco rises at an angle of about 17°. If you walk 150 ft up this section, what is your vertical rise? Round to the nearest foot.

Practice 3. Find the value of *x*. Round to the nearest tenth.

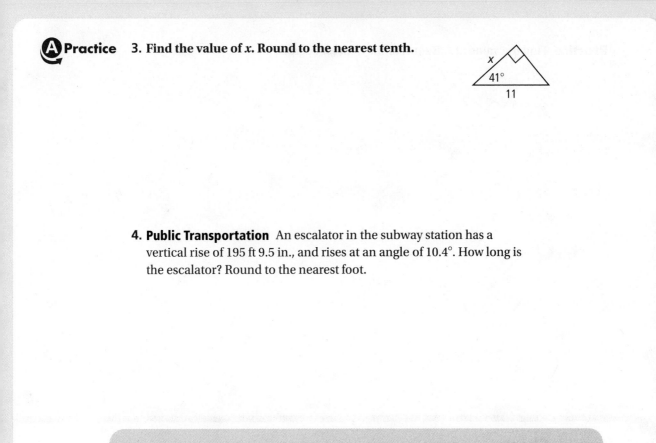

4. **Public Transportation** An escalator in the subway station has a vertical rise of 195 ft 9.5 in., and rises at an angle of 10.4°. How long is the escalator? Round to the nearest foot.

If you know the sine, cosine, or tangent ratio for an angle, you can use an inverse ($\sin^{-1}$, $\cos^{-1}$, or $\tan^{-1}$) to find the measure of the angle.

 **Problem 3** Using Inverses

Think
When should you use an inverse?

Got It? a. Use the figure below. What is $m\angle Y$ to the nearest degree?

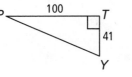

b. **Reasoning** Suppose you know the lengths of all three sides of a right triangle. Does it matter which trigonometric ratio you use to find the measure of any of the three angles? Explain.

Find the value of *x*. Round to the nearest degree.

5.

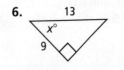

6.

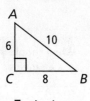

Lesson Check

Do you know HOW?

Write each ratio.

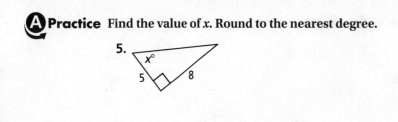

7. sin *A*

8. cos *A*

9. tan *A*

10. sin *B*

11. cos *B*

12. tan *B*

What is the value of *x*? Round to the nearest tenth.

13.

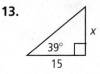

14.

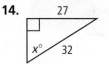

Do you UNDERSTAND?

MATHEMATICAL
PRACTICES

15. **Vocabulary** Some people use SOH-CAH-TOA to remember the trigonometric ratios for sine, cosine, and tangent. Why do you think that word might help? (*Hint*: Think of the first letters of the ratios.)

16. **Error Analysis** A student states that sin *A* > sin *X* because the lengths of the sides of △*ABC* are greater than the lengths of the sides of △*XYZ*. What is the student's error? Explain.

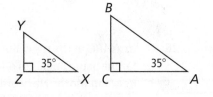

B **Apply**

17. The lengths of the diagonals of a rhombus are 2 in. and 5 in. Find the measures of the angles of the rhombus to the nearest degree.

© 18. **Think About a Plan** Carlos plans to build a grain bin with a radius of 15 ft. The recommended slant of the roof is 25°. He wants the roof to overhang the edge of the bin by 1 ft. What should the length *x* be? Give your answer in feet and inches.
   • What is the position of the side of length *x* in relation to the given angle?
   • What information do you need to find a side length of a right triangle?
   • Which trigonometric ratio could you use?

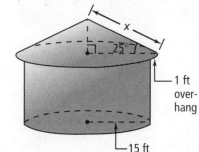

An *identity* is an equation that is true for all the allowed values of the variable. Use what you know about trigonometric ratios to show that each equation is an identity.

19. $\tan X = \dfrac{\sin X}{\cos X}$

20. $\sin X = \cos X \cdot \tan X$

21. $\cos X = \dfrac{\sin X}{\tan X}$

Find the values of *w* and then *x*. Round lengths to the nearest tenth and angle measures to the nearest degree.

22.

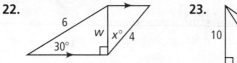

23.

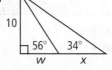

24.

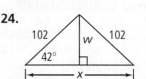

STEM 25. **Pyramids** All but two of the pyramids built by the ancient Egyptians have faces inclined at 52° angles. Suppose an archaeologist discovers the ruins of a pyramid. Most of the pyramid has eroded, but the archaeologist is able to determine that the length of a side of the square base is 82 m. How tall was the pyramid, assuming its faces were inclined at 52°? Round your answer to the nearest meter.

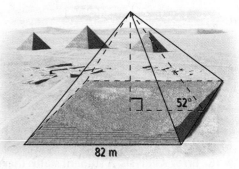

26. **a.** In △*ABC* at the right, how does sin *A* compare to cos *B*? Is this true for the acute angles of other right triangles?
   © **b.** **Reading Math** The word *cosine* is derived from the words *complement's sine*. Which angle in △*ABC* is the complement of ∠*A*? Of ∠*B*?
   c. Explain why the derivation of the word *cosine* makes sense.

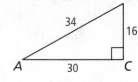

Proof 27. For right $\triangle ABC$ with right $\angle C$, prove each of the following.

   a. $\sin A < 1$　　　　　　　　　　　　**b.** $\cos A < 1$

© 28. a. Writing Explain why $\tan 60° = \sqrt{3}$. Include a diagram with your explanation.

   b. Make a Conjecture How are the sine and cosine of a 60° angle related? Explain.

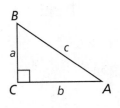

The sine, cosine, and tangent ratios each have a reciprocal ratio. The reciprocal ratios are cosecant (csc), secant (sec), and cotangent (cot). Use $\triangle ABC$ and the definitions below to write each ratio.

$$\csc X = \frac{1}{\sin X} \qquad \sec X = \frac{1}{\cos X} \qquad \cot X = \frac{1}{\tan X}$$

29. $\csc A$　　　　　　　　　**30.** $\sec A$　　　　　　　　　**31.** $\cot A$

32. $\csc B$　　　　　　　　　**33.** $\sec B$　　　　　　　　　**34.** $\cot B$

35. Graphing Calculator Use the ⟨table⟩ feature of your graphing calculator to study $\sin X$ as X gets close to (but not equal to) 90. In the ⟨y=⟩ screen, enter $Y1 = \sin X$.

   a. Use the ⟨tblset⟩ feature so that X starts at 80 and changes by 1. Access the ⟨table⟩. From the table, what is $\sin X$ for $X = 89$?

   b. Perform a "numerical zoom-in." Use the ⟨tblset⟩ feature, so that X starts with 89 and changes by 0.1. What is $\sin X$ for $X = 89.9$?

   c. Continue to zoom in numerically on values close to 90. What is the greatest value you can get for $\sin X$ on your calculator? How close is X to 90? Does your result contradict what you are asked to prove in Exercise 27a?

   d. Use right triangles to explain the behavior of $\sin X$ found above.

© 36. a. Reasoning Does $\tan A + \tan B = \tan(A + B)$ when $A + B < 90$? Explain.

   b. Does $\tan A - \tan B = \tan(A - B)$ when $A - B > 0$? Use part (a) and indirect reasoning to explain.

© Challenge

Verify that each equation is an identity by showing that each expression on the left simplifies to 1.

37. $(\sin A)^2 + (\cos A)^2 = 1$　　　　　　　**38.** $(\sin B)^2 + (\cos B)^2 = 1$

39. $\dfrac{1}{(\cos A)^2} - (\tan A)^2 = 1$　　　　　　**40.** $\dfrac{1}{(\sin A)^2} - \dfrac{1}{(\tan A)^2} = 1$

In Exercises 41–43, the value of one trigonometric ratio is given. Find the value of the other trigonometric ratio using the identities from Exercises 19 and 37.

41. $\sin x = \frac{12}{13}$; $\cos x$

42. $\cos x = \frac{3}{4}$; $\sin x$

43. $\sin x = \frac{3}{5}$; $\tan x$

44. Show that $(\tan A)^2 - (\sin A)^2 = (\tan A)^2 \cdot (\sin A)^2$ is an identity.

STEM **45.** **Astronomy** The Polish astronomer Nicolaus Copernicus devised a method for determining the sizes of the orbits of planets farther from the sun than Earth. His method involved noting the number of days between the times that a planet was in the positions labeled A and B in the diagram. Using this time and the number of days in each planet's year, he calculated c and d.

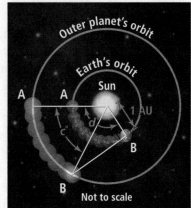

  a. For Mars, $c = 55.2$ and $d = 103.8$. How far is Mars from the sun in astronomical units (AU)? One astronomical unit is defined as the average distance from Earth to the center of the sun, about 93 million miles.

  b. For Jupiter, $c = 21.9$ and $d = 100.8$. How far is Jupiter from the sun in astronomical units?

7-4 Angles of Elevation and Depression

G.SRT.8 Use trigonometric ratios . . . to solve right triangles in applied problems.

Objective To use angles of elevation and depression to solve problems

Solve It! Write your solution to the Solve It in the space below.

The angles in the Solve It are formed below the horizontal black pipe. Angles formed above and below a horizontal line have specific names.

Suppose a person on the ground sees a hang glider at a 38° angle above a horizontal line. This angle is the **angle of elevation.**

At the same time, the person in the hang glider sees the person on the ground at a 38° angle below a horizontal line. This angle is the **angle of depression.**

Notice that the angle of elevation is congruent to the angle of depression because they are alternate interior angles.

Essential Understanding You can use the angles of elevation and depression as the acute angles of right triangles formed by a horizontal distance and a vertical height.

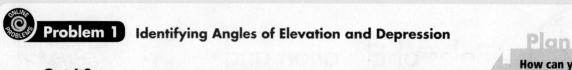

Got It? Use the diagram in Problem 1. What is a description of the angle as it relates to the situation shown?

a. ∠2   b. ∠3

Plan

How can you tell if it is an angle of elevation or depression?

Practice Describe each angle as it relates to the situation in the diagram.

1. ∠2

2. ∠5

Problem 2 **Using the Angle of Elevation**

Got It? You sight a rock climber on a cliff at a 32° angle of elevation. Your eye level is 6 ft above the ground and you are 1000 ft from the base of the cliff. What is the approximate height of the rock climber from the ground?

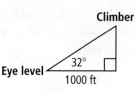

Climber

Eye level

32°

1000 ft

Think

Why does your eye level matter here?

Ⓐ Practice Find the value of *x*. Round to the nearest tenth of a unit.

3.

100 ft

x

20°

STEM **4. Meteorology** A meteorologist measures the angle of elevation of a weather balloon as 41°. A radio signal from the balloon indicates that it is 1503 m from his location. To the nearest meter, how high above the ground is the balloon?

Got It? An airplane pilot sights a life raft at a 26° angle of depression. The airplane's altitude is 3 km. What is the airplane's horizontal distance *d* from the raft?

Ⓐ Practice Find the value of *x*. Round to the nearest tenth of a unit.

5.

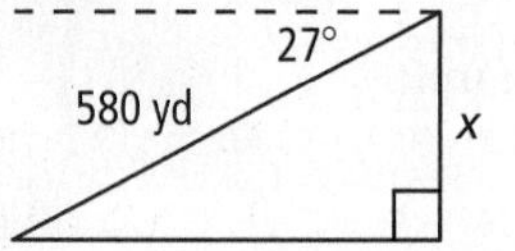

27°

580 yd

x

6. **Indirect Measurement** A tourist looks out from the crown of the Statue of Liberty, approximately 250 ft above the ground. The tourist sees a ship coming into the harbor and measures the angle of depression as 18°. Find the distance from the base of the statue to the ship to the nearest foot.

Lesson Check

Do you know HOW?

What is a description of each angle as it relates to the diagram?

7. ∠1

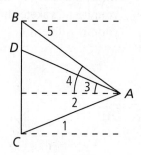

8. ∠2

9. ∠3

10. ∠4

11. ∠5

12. What are two pairs of congruent angles in the diagram? Explain why they are congruent.

Do you UNDERSTAND?

Ⓒ 13. **Vocabulary** How is an angle of elevation formed?

14. Error Analysis A homework question says that the angle of depression from the bottom of a house window to a ball on the ground is 20°. At the right is your friend's sketch of the situation. Describe your friend's error.

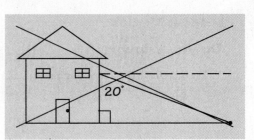

More Practice and Problem-Solving Exercises

MATHEMATICAL PRACTICES

Ⓑ Apply

15. Flagpole The world's tallest unsupported flagpole is a 282-ft-tall steel pole in Surrey, British Columbia. The shortest shadow cast by the pole during the year is 137 ft long. To the nearest degree, what is the angle of elevation of the sun when the flagpole casts its shortest shadow?

16. Think About a Plan Two office buildings are 51 m apart. The height of the taller building is 207 m. The angle of depression from the top of the taller building to the top of the shorter building is 15°. Find the height of the shorter building to the nearest meter.
   • How can a diagram help you?
   • How does the angle of depression from the top of the taller building relate to the angle of elevation from the top of the shorter building?

Algebra The angle of elevation *e* from *A* to *B* and the angle of depression *d* from *B* to *A* are given. Find the measure of each angle.

17. $e: (7x - 5)°, d: 4(x + 7)°$

18. $e: (3x + 1)°, d: 2(x + 8)°$

19. $e: (x + 21)°, d: 3(x + 3)°$

20. $e: 5(x - 2)°, d: (x + 14)°$

21. Writing A communications tower is located on a plot of flat land. The tower is supported by several guy wires. Assume that you are able to measure distances along the ground, as well as angles formed by the guy wires and the ground. Explain how you could estimate each of the following measurements.
   a. the length of any guy wire
   b. how high on the tower each wire is attached

Tower
Guy wires

Flying An airplane at a constant altitude a flies a horizontal distance d toward you at velocity v. You observe for time t and measure its angles of elevation $\angle E_1$ and $\angle E_2$ at the start and end of your observation. Find the missing information.

22. $a = $ ▇ mi, $v = 5$ mi/min, $t = 1$ min, $m\angle E_1 = 45$, $m\angle E_2 = 90$

23. $a = 2$ mi, $v = $ ▇ mi/min, $t = 15$ s, $m\angle E_1 = 40$, $m\angle E_2 = 50$

24. $a = 4$ mi, $d = 3$ mi, $v = 6$ mi/min, $t = $ ▇ min, $m\angle E_1 = 50$, $m\angle E_2 = $ ▇

25. **Aerial Television** A blimp provides aerial television views of a football game. The television camera sights the stadium at a 7° angle of depression. The altitude of the blimp is 400 m. What is the line-of-sight distance from the television camera to the base of the stadium? Round to the nearest hundred meters.

Not to scale

7°

400 m

Challenge

26. **Firefighting** A firefighter on the ground sees fire break through a window near the top of the building. The angle of elevation to the windowsill is 28°. The angle of elevation to the top of the building is 42°. The firefighter is 75 ft from the building and her eyes are 5 ft above the ground. What roof-to-windowsill distance can she report by radio to firefighters on the roof?

27. **Geography** For locations in the United States, the relationship between the latitude ℓ and the greatest angle of elevation a of the sun at noon on the first day of summer is $a = 90° - \ell + 23.5°$. Find the latitude of your town. Then determine the greatest angle of elevation of the sun for your town on the first day of summer.

42°

28°

75 ft

7-5 Areas of Regular Polygons

G.CO.13 Construct . . . a regular hexagon inscribed in a circle. Also **A.SSE.1.b**

Objective To find the area of a regular polygon

 Solve It! Write your solution to the Solve It in the space below.

The Solve It involves the area of a polygon. You can use trigonometric ratios and special right triangles to investigate properties of regular polygons.

Essential Understanding The area of a regular polygon is related to the distance from the center to a side.

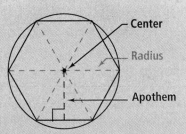

You can circumscribe a circle about any regular polygon. The center of a regular polygon is the center of the circumscribed circle. The **radius of a regular polygon** is the distance from the center to a vertex. The **apothem** is the perpendicular distance from the center to a side.

Problem 1 Finding Angle Measures

Got It? Below, a portion of a regular octagon has radii and an apothem drawn. What is the measure of each numbered angle?

Think

How do you know the radii make isosceles triangles?

Practice Each regular polygon has radii and apothem as shown. Find the measure of each numbered angle.

1.

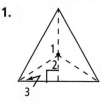

2.

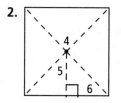

Postulate 18

If two figures are congruent, then their areas are equal.

Suppose you have a regular *n*-gon with side *s*. The radii divide the figure into *n* congruent isosceles triangles. By Postulate 17, the areas of the isosceles triangles are equal. Each triangle has a height of *a* and a base of length *s*, so the area of each triangle is $\frac{1}{2}as$.

Since there are *n* congruent triangles, the area of the *n*-gon is $A = n \cdot \frac{1}{2}as$. The perimeter *p* of the *n*-gon is the number of sides *n* times the length of a side *s*, or *ns*. By substitution, the area can be expressed as $A = \frac{1}{2}ap$.

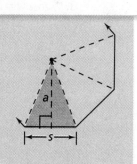

Theorem 71   Area of a Regular Polygon

The area of a regular polygon is half the product of the apothem and the perimeter.

$$A = \frac{1}{2}ap$$

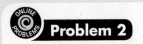

Problem 2 Finding the Area of a Regular Polygon

Plan

What do you know about the regular pentagon?

Got It? **a.** What is the area of a regular pentagon with an 8-cm apothem and 11.6-cm sides?

b. Reasoning If the side of a regular polygon is reduced to half its length, how does the perimeter of the polygon change? Explain.

Practice Find the area of each regular polygon with the given apothem *a* and side length *s*. Round to the nearest square unit.

3. 7-gon, $a = 29.1$ ft, $s = 28$ ft

4. nonagon, $a = 27.5$ in., $s = 20$ in.

Problem 3 **Using Special Triangles to Find Area**

Got It? The side of a regular hexagon is 16 ft. What is the area of the hexagon? Round your answer to the nearest square foot.

Practice **5. Art** You are painting a mural of colored equilateral triangles. The radius of each triangle is 12.7 in. What is the area of each triangle to the nearest square inch?

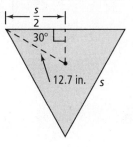

6. Find the area of the equilateral triangle. Leave your answer in simplest radical form.

Lesson Check

Do you know HOW?

What is the area of each regular polygon? Round your answer to the nearest tenth.

7.

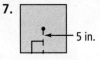

5 in.

8.

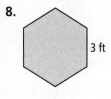

3 ft

9.

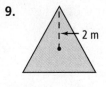

2 m

10.

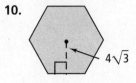

$4\sqrt{3}$

Do you UNDERSTAND?

ⓒ **11. Vocabulary** What is the difference between a radius and an apothem?

12. What is the relationship between the side length and the apothem in each figure?

   a. a square

   b. a regular hexagon

   c. an equilateral triangle

ⓒ **13. Error Analysis** Your friend says you can use special triangles to find the apothem of any regular polygon. What is your friend's error? Explain.

More Practice and Problem-Solving Exercises

B Apply

Find the measures of the angles formed by (a) two consecutive radii and (b) a radius and a side of the given regular polygon.

14. pentagon   **15.** octagon   **16.** nonagon   **17.** dodecagon

STEM **18. Satellites** One of the smallest space satellites ever developed has the shape of a pyramid. Each of the four faces of the pyramid is an equilateral triangle with sides about 13 cm long. What is the area of one equilateral triangular face of the satellite? Round your answer to the nearest whole number.

19. Think About a Plan The gazebo in the photo is built in the shape of a regular octagon. Each side is 8 ft long, and the enclosed area is about 309 ft². What is the length of the apothem?

- How can you *draw a diagram* to help you solve the problem?
- How can you use the area of a regular polygon formula?

20. A regular hexagon has perimeter 120 m. Find its area.

21. The area of a regular polygon is 36 in.². Find the length of a side if the polygon has the given number of sides. Round your answer to the nearest tenth.

a. 3   **b.** 4   **c.** 6

d. Estimation Suppose the polygon is a pentagon. What would you expect the length of a side to be? Explain.

22. A portion of a regular decagon has radii and an apothem drawn. Find the measure of each numbered angle.

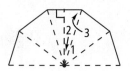

23. Writing Explain why the radius of a regular polygon is greater than the apothem.

24. Constructions Use a compass to draw a circle.
   a. Construct two perpendicular diameters of the circle.
   b. Construct diameters that bisect each of the four right angles.
   c. Connect the consecutive points where the diameters intersect the circle. What regular polygon have you constructed?
   d. Use your construction to construct a square inscribed in a circle.

Find the perimeter and area of each regular polygon. Round to the nearest tenth, as necessary.

25. a square with vertices at $(-1, 0)$, $(2, 3)$, $(5, 0)$ and $(2, -3)$

26. an equilateral triangle with two vertices at $(-4, 1)$ and $(4, 7)$

27. a hexagon with two adjacent vertices at $(-2, 1)$ and $(1, 2)$

28. To find the area of an equilateral triangle, you can use the formula $A = \frac{1}{2}bh$ or $A = \frac{1}{2}ap$. A third way to find the area of an equilateral triangle is to use the formula $A = \frac{1}{4}s^2\sqrt{3}$. Verify the formula $A = \frac{1}{4}s^2\sqrt{3}$ in two ways as follows:

    a. Find the area of Figure 1 using the formula $A = \frac{1}{2}bh$.

    b. Find the area of Figure 2 using the formula $A = \frac{1}{2}ap$.

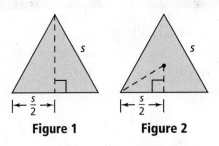

Figure 1   **Figure 2**

 **29.** For Problem 1 in this lesson, write a proof that the apothem bisects the vertex angle of an isosceles triangle formed by two radii.

C Challenge

 **30.** Prove that the bisectors of the angles of a regular polygon are concurrent and that they are, in fact, radii of the polygon. (*Hint:* For regular n-gon $ABCDE\ldots$, let P be the intersection of the bisectors of $\angle ABC$ and $\angle BCD$. Show that $\overline{DP}$ must be the bisector of $\angle CDE$.)

31. Coordinate Geometry A regular octagon with center at the origin and radius 4 is graphed in the coordinate plane.

    a. Since V_2 lies on the line $y = x$, its x- and y-coordinates are equal. Use the Distance Formula to find the coordinates of V_2 to the nearest tenth.

    b. Use the coordinates of V_2 and the formula $A = \frac{1}{2}bh$ to find the area of $\triangle V_1 OV_2$ to the nearest tenth.

    c. Use your answer to part (b) to find the area of the octagon to the nearest whole number.

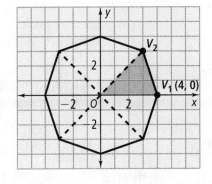

7-1 The Pythagorean Theorem and Its Converse

Quick Review

The **Pythagorean Theorem** holds true for any right triangle.

$$(\text{leg}_1)^2 + (\text{leg}_2)^2 = (\text{hypotenuse})^2$$
$$a^2 + b^2 = c^2$$

The Converse of the Pythagorean Theorem states that if $a^2 + b^2 = c^2$, where c is the greatest side length of a triangle, then the triangle is a right triangle.

Example

What is the value of x?

$a^2 + b^2 = c^2$	Pythagorean Theorem
$x^2 + 12^2 = 20^2$	Substitute.
$x^2 = 256$	Simplify.
$x = 16$	Take the positive square root.

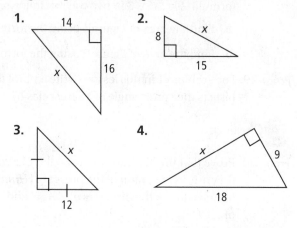

Exercises

Find the value of x. If your answer is not an integer, express it in simplest radical form.

1.

2.

3.

4.

7-2 Special Right Triangles

Quick Review

45°-45°-90° Triangle

$$\text{hypotenuse} = \sqrt{2} \cdot \text{leg}$$

30°-60°-90° Triangle

$$\text{hypotenuse} = 2 \cdot \text{shorter leg}$$
$$\text{longer leg} = \sqrt{3} \cdot \text{shorter leg}$$

Example

What is the value of x?

The triangle is a 30°-60°-90° triangle, and x represents the length of the longer leg.

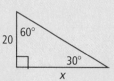

$$\text{longer leg} = \sqrt{3} \cdot \text{shorter leg}$$
$$x = 20\sqrt{3}$$

Exercises

Find the value of each variable. If your answer is not an integer, express it in simplest radical form.

5.

6.

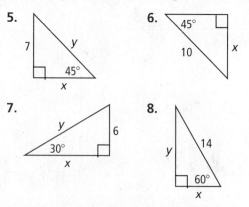

7.

8.

9. A square garden has sides 50 ft long. You stretch a hose from one corner of the garden to another corner along the garden's diagonal. To the nearest tenth, how long is the hose?

7-3 and 7-4
Trigonometry and Angles of Elevation and Depression

Quick Review

In right $\triangle ABC$, C is the right angle.

$\sin A = \dfrac{\text{leg opposite } \angle A}{\text{hypotenuse}}$

$\cos A = \dfrac{\text{leg adjacent to } \angle A}{\text{hypotenuse}}$

$\tan A = \dfrac{\text{leg opposite } \angle A}{\text{leg adjacent to } \angle A}$

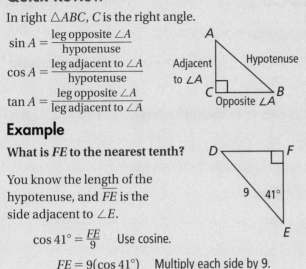

Example

What is FE to the nearest tenth?

You know the length of the hypotenuse, and $\overline{FE}$ is the side adjacent to $\angle E$.

$\cos 41° = \dfrac{FE}{9}$ Use cosine.

$FE = 9(\cos 41°)$ Multiply each side by 9.

$FE \approx 6.8$ Use a calculator.

Exercises

Express sin A, cos A, and tan A as ratios.

10.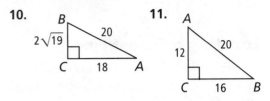

11.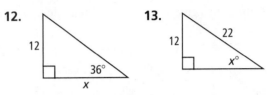

Find the value of x to the nearest tenth.

12.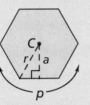

13.

14. While flying a kite, Linda lets out 45 ft of string and anchors it to the ground. She determines that the angle of elevation of the kite is 58°. What is the height of the kite from the ground? Round to the nearest tenth.

7-5 Areas of Regular Polygons

Quick Review

The **center of a regular polygon** C is the center of its circumscribed circle. The **radius** r is the distance from the center to a vertex. The **apothem** a is the perpendicular distance from the center to a side. The area of a regular polygon with apothem a and perimeter p is $A = \frac{1}{2}ap$.

Example

What is the area of a regular hexagon with apothem 17.3 mm and perimeter 120 mm?

$A = \frac{1}{2}ap$ Use the area formula.

$= \frac{1}{2}(17.3)(120) = 1038$ Substitute and simplify.

The area of the hexagon is 1038 mm².

Exercises

Find the area of each regular polygon. If your answer is not an integer, leave it in simplest radical form.

15. 6 in.

16. 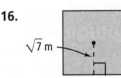 $\sqrt{7}$ m

17. What is the area of a regular hexagon with a perimeter of 240 cm?

18. What is the area of a square with radius 7.5 m?

Sketch each regular polygon with the given radius. Then find its area to the nearest tenth.

19. triangle; radius 4 in.

20. square; radius 8 mm

21. hexagon; radius 7 cm

Pull It **All Together**

Locating a Forest Fire

Rangers in the two lookout towers at a state forest notice a plume of smoke, as shown in the diagram. The towers are 2000 ft apart. One ranger observes the smoke at an angle of 54°. The other ranger observes it an angle of 30°. Both angles are measured from the line that connects the two towers. When the rangers call to report the fire, they must give the fire department the approximate distance from their lookout tower to the fire.

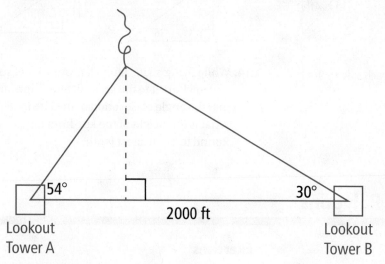

Task Description

Find the distance from each lookout tower to the fire.

- The dashed vertical line segment divides the distance between the lookout towers into two parts. What expressions can you use to represent the lengths of the parts?

- What expression represents the length of the dashed vertical line segment?

Get Ready!

Solving Equations

Algebra Solve for x.

1. $\frac{1}{2}(x + 42) = 62$

2. $(5 + 3)8 = (4 + x)6$

3. $(9 + x)2 = (12 + 4)3$

Isosceles and Equilateral Triangles

Algebra Find the value of x.

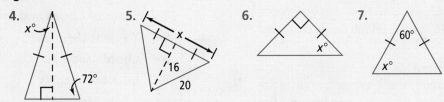

4. **5.** **6.** **7.**

The Pythagorean Theorem

Algebra Find the value of x. Leave your answer in simplest radical form.

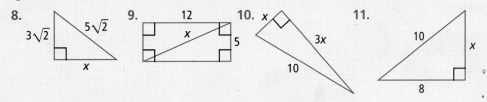

8. **9.** **10.** **11.**

Looking Ahead Vocabulary

12. When you are in a conversation and you go off on a *tangent*, you are leading the conversation away from the main topic. What do you think a line that is *tangent* to a circle might look like?

13. You learned how to *inscribe* a triangle in a circle in Chapter 4. What do you think an *inscribed* angle is?

14. A defensive player *intercepts* a pass when he catches the football before it reaches the intended receiver. On a circle, what might an *intercepted* arc of an angle be?

Circles

Big Ideas

1 Reasoning and Proof

Essential Question: How can you prove relationships between angles and arcs in a circle?

2 Measurement

Essential Question: When lines intersect a circle or within a circle, how do you find the measures of resulting angles, arcs, and segments?

© Domains

- Circles
- Modeling with Geometry

Interactive Digital Path

Log in to **pearsonsuccessnet.com** and click on Interactive Digital Path to access the Solve Its and animated Problems.

Chapter Preview

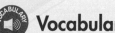

Vocabulary

English/Spanish Vocabulary Audio Online:

English	Spanish
central angle, *p. 467*	ángulo central
chord, *p. 498*	cuerda
concentric circles, *p. 470*	círculos concéntricos
diameter, *p. 467*	diámetro
inscribed angle, *p. 509*	ángulo inscrito
intercepted arc, *p. 509*	arco interceptor
major arc, *p. 467*	arco mayor
minor arc, *p. 467*	arco menor
secant, *p. 519*	secante
sector of a circle, *p. 479*	sector de un círculo
segment of a circle, *p. 480*	segmento de un círculo
tangent to a circle, *p. 488*	tagente de un círculo

G.C.1 Prove . . . all circles are similar. Also **G.C.2, G.C.5**

Objectives To find the measures of central angles and arcs
To find the circumference and arc length

Solve It! Write your solution to the Solve It in the space below.

In a plane, a **circle** is the set of all points equidistant from a given point called the **center**. You name a circle by its center. Circle P ($\odot P$) is shown below.

A **diameter** is a segment that contains the center of a circle and has both endpoints on the circle. A **radius** is a segment that has one endpoint at the center and the other endpoint on the circle. **Congruent circles** have congruent radii. A **central angle** is an angle whose vertex is the center of the circle.

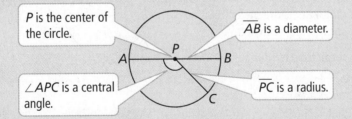

P is the center of the circle.

$\overline{AB}$ is a diameter.

$\angle APC$ is a central angle.

$\overline{PC}$ is a radius.

Essential Understanding You can find the length of part of a circle's circumference by relating it to an angle in the circle.

An arc is a part of a circle. One type of arc, a **semicircle**, is half of a circle. A **minor arc** is smaller than a semicircle. A **major arc** is larger than a semicircle. You name a minor arc by its endpoints and a major arc or a semicircle by its endpoints and another point on the arc.

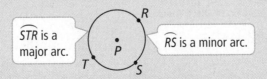

$\overset{\frown}{STR}$ is a major arc.

$\overset{\frown}{RS}$ is a minor arc.

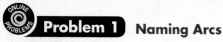

Problem 1 Naming Arcs

Got It? **a.** What are the minor arcs of ⊙A?

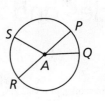

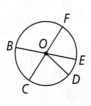

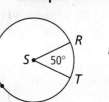

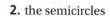

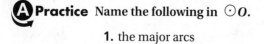

Think

How can you identify the minor arcs?

b. What are the semicircles of ⊙A?

c. What are the major arcs of ⊙A that contain point Q?

A Practice Name the following in ⊙O.

1. the major arcs

2. the semicircles

---

take note

Key Concept   Arc Measure

Arc Measure

The measure of a minor arc is equal to the measure of its corresponding central angle.

The measure of a major arc is the measure of the related minor arc subtracted from 360.

The measure of a semicircle is 180.

Example

$m \widehat{RT} = m\angle RST = 50$

$m \widehat{TQR} = 360 - m \widehat{RT}$

$= 310$

Adjacent arcs are arcs of the same circle that have exactly one point in common. You can add the measures of adjacent arcs just as you can add the measures of adjacent angles.

take note

Postulate 19   Arc Addition Postulate

The measure of the arc formed by two adjacent arcs is the sum of the measures of the two arcs.

$m \widehat{ABC} = m \widehat{AB} + m \widehat{BC}$

Problem 2 Finding the Measures of Arcs

Got It? What is the measure of each arc in ⊙C?

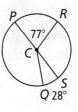

a. $m\widehat{PR}$

b. $m\widehat{RS}$

c. $m\widehat{PRQ}$

d. $m\widehat{PQR}$

 Practice Find the measure of each arc in ⊙P.

3. $\widehat{CBD}$

4. $\widehat{BCD}$

The **circumference** of a circle is the distance around the circle. The number **pi** (π) is the ratio of the circumference of a circle to its diameter.

Theorem 72 Circumference of a Circle

The circumference of a circle is π times the diameter.

$C = \pi d$ or $C = 2\pi r$

The number π is irrational, so you cannot write it as a terminating or repeating decimal. To approximate π, you can use 3.14, $\frac{22}{7}$, or the π key on your calculator.

Many properties of circles deal with ratios that stay the same no matter what size the circle is. This is because all circles are similar to each other. To see this, consider the circles at the right. There is a translation that maps circle O so that it shares the same center with circle P.

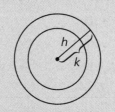

There also exists a dilation with scale factor $\frac{k}{h}$ that maps circle O to circle P. A translation followed by a dilation is a similarity transformation. Because a similarity transformation maps circle O to circle P, the two circles are similar.

Coplanar circles that have the same center are called **concentric circles**.

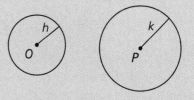

Concentric circles

Problem 3 Finding a Distance

Got It? **a.** A car has a circular turning radius of 16.1 ft. The distance between the two front tires is 4.7 ft. How much farther does a tire on the outside of the turn travel than a tire on the inside?

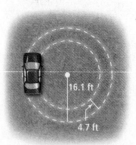

16.1 ft

4.7 ft

Plan

What do you need to find?

@ **b. Reasoning** Suppose the radius of $\odot A$ is equal to the diameter of $\odot B$. What is the ratio of the circumference of $\odot A$ to the circumference of $\odot B$? Explain.

 5. Find the circumference of this circle. Leave your answer in terms of π.

6. The wheel of a compact car has a 25-in. diameter. The wheel of a pickup truck has a 31-in. diameter. To the nearest inch, how much farther does the pickup truck wheel travel in one revolution than the compact car wheel?

The measure of an arc is in degrees, while the **arc length** is a fraction of the circumference.

Consider the arcs shown at the right. Since the circles are concentric, there is a dilation that maps C_1 to C_2. The same dilation maps the slice of the small circle to the slice of the large circle. Since corresponding lengths of similar figures are proportional,

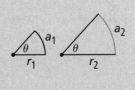

$$\frac{r_1}{r_2} = \frac{a_1}{a_2}$$
$$r_1 a_2 = r_2 a_1$$
$$a_1 = r_1 \cdot \frac{a_2}{r_2}$$

This means that the arc length a_1 is equal to the radius r_1 times some number. So for a given central angle, the length of the arc it intercepts depends only on the radius.

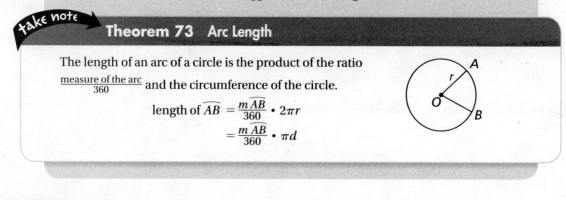

An arc of 60° represents $\frac{60}{360}$, or $\frac{1}{6}$, of the circle. So its arc length is $\frac{1}{6}$ of the circumference. This observation suggests the following theorem.

take note

Theorem 73 Arc Length

The length of an arc of a circle is the product of the ratio $\frac{\text{measure of the arc}}{360}$ and the circumference of the circle.

$$\text{length of } \widehat{AB} = \frac{m\widehat{AB}}{360} \cdot 2\pi r$$
$$= \frac{m\widehat{AB}}{360} \cdot \pi d$$

Problem 4 **Finding Arc Length**

Got It? What is the length of a semicircle with radius 1.3 m? Leave your answer in terms of π.

Practice Find the length of each arc shown in red. Leave your answer in terms of π.

7.

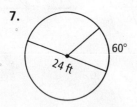

8.

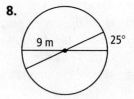

Lesson Check

Do you know HOW?

Use ⊙P at the right to answer each question. For Exercises 13 and 14, leave your answers in terms of π.

9. What is the name of a minor arc?

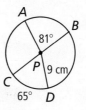

10. What is the name of a major arc?

11. What is the name of a semicircle?

12. What is $m\overarc{AB}$?

13. What is the circumference of ⊙P?

14. What is the length of $\overarc{BD}$?

Do you UNDERSTAND?

15. Vocabulary What is the difference between the measure of an arc and arc length? Explain.

16. Error Analysis Your class must find the length of $\overset{\frown}{AB}$. A classmate submits the following solution. What is the error?

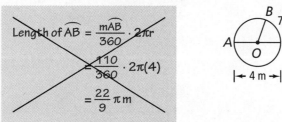

Length of $\overset{\frown}{AB} = \dfrac{m\overset{\frown}{AB}}{360} \cdot 2\pi r$

$= \dfrac{110}{360} \cdot 2\pi(4)$

$= \dfrac{22}{9}\pi$ m

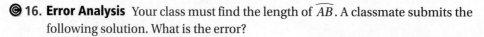

More Practice and Problem-Solving Exercises

Ⓑ Apply

17. Think About a Plan Nina designed a semicircular arch made of wrought iron for the top of a mall entrance. The nine segments between the two concentric semicircles are each 3 ft long. What is the total length of wrought iron used to make this structure? Round your answer to the nearest foot.
- What do you know from the diagram?
- What formula should you use to find the amount of wrought iron used in the semicircular arches?

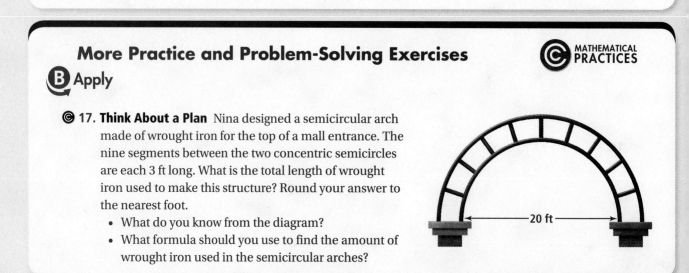

Find each indicated measure for ⊙O.

18. $m\angle EOF$ **19.** $m\,\widehat{EJH}$ **20.** $m\,\widehat{FH}$

21. $m\angle FOG$ **22.** $m\,\widehat{JEG}$ **23.** $m\,\widehat{HFJ}$

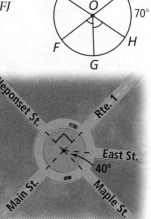

24. Pets A hamster wheel has a 7-in. diameter. How many feet will a hamster travel in 100 revolutions of the wheel?

STEM **25. Traffic** Five streets come together at a traffic circle, as shown at the right. The diameter of the circle traveled by a car is 200 ft. If traffic travels counterclockwise, what is the approximate distance from East St. to Neponset St.?

    Ⓐ 227 ft   Ⓒ 454 ft

    Ⓑ 244 ft   Ⓓ 488 ft

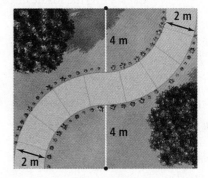

© 26. Writing Describe two ways to find the arc length of a major arc if you are given the measure of the corresponding minor arc and the radius of the circle.

27. Time Hands of a clock suggest an angle whose measure is continually changing. How many degrees does a minute hand move through during each time interval?
    a. 1 min   **b.** 5 min   **c.** 20 min

Algebra Find the value of each variable.

28.

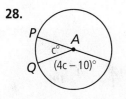

29.

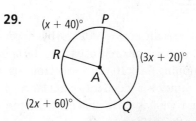

30. Landscape Design A landscape architect is constructing a curved path through a rectangular yard. The curved path consists of two 90° arcs. He plans to edge the two sides of the path with plastic edging. What is the total length of plastic edging he will need? Round your answer to the nearest meter.

© 31. Reasoning Suppose the radius of a circle is doubled. How does this affect the circumference of the circle? Explain.

32. A 60° arc of ⊙A has the same length as a 45° arc of ⊙B. What is the ratio of the radius of ⊙A to the radius of ⊙B?

Find the length of each arc shown in red. Leave your answer in terms of π.

33.

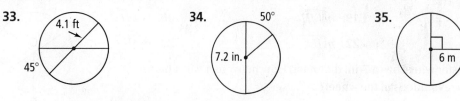

4.1 ft

45°

34. 50°

7.2 in.

35.

6 m

36. Coordinate Geometry Find the length of a semicircle with endpoints $(1, 3)$ and $(4, 7)$. Round your answer to the nearest tenth.

37. In $\odot O$, the length of $\overarc{AB}$ is 6π cm and $m\overarc{AB}$ is 120. What is the diameter of $\odot O$?

Challenge

38. The diagram below shows two concentric circles. $\overline{AR} \cong \overline{RW}$. Show that the length of $\overarc{ST}$ is equal to the length of $\overarc{QR}$.

V
Q
U
A
R
W
T
S

39. Given: $\odot P$ with $\overline{AB} \parallel \overline{PC}$
Proof Prove: $m\overarc{BC} = m\overarc{CD}$

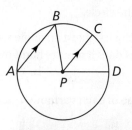

B
C
A
P
D

40. Sports An athletic field is a 100 yd-by-40 yd rectangle, with a semicircle at each of the short sides. A running track 10 yd wide surrounds the field. If the track is divided into eight lanes of equal width, what is the distance around the track along the inside edge of each lane?

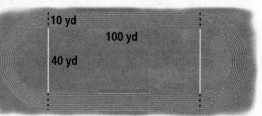

10 yd

100 yd

40 yd

Areas of Circles and Sectors

G.C.5 Derive using similarity the fact that the length of the arc intercepted by an angle is proportional to the radius . . . derive the formula for the area of a sector.

Objective To find the areas of circles, sectors, and segments of circles

Solve It! Write your solution to the Solve It in the space below.

In the Solve It, you explored the area of a circle.

Essential Understanding You can find the area of a circle when you know its radius. You can use the area of a circle to find the area of part of a circle formed by two radii and the arc the radii form when they intersect with the circle.

take note

Theorem 74 Area of a Circle

The area of a circle is the product of π and the square of the radius.

$A = \pi r^2$

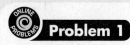 **Problem 1** **Finding the Area of a Circle**

Think

What do you
need in order
to use the area
formula?

Got It? **a.** What is the area of a circular wrestling region with
a 42-ft diameter?

 b. Reasoning If the radius of a circle is halved, how does its
area change? Explain.

 Practice Find the area of the circle. Leave your answer in terms of π.

1.

$\frac{2}{3}$ in.

STEM 2. Agriculture Some farmers use a circular irrigation method. An
irrigation arm acts as the radius of an irrigation circle. How much
land is covered with an irrigation arm of 300 ft?

A **sector of a circle** is a region bounded by an arc of the circle and the two radii to the arc's endpoints. You name a sector using one arc endpoint, the center of the circle, and the other arc endpoint.

The area of a sector is a fractional part of the area of a circle. The area of a sector formed by a 60° arc is $\frac{60}{360}$, or $\frac{1}{6}$, of the area of the circle.

Sector *RPS*

Theorem 75 Area of a Sector of a Circle

The area of a sector of a circle is the product of the ratio $\frac{\text{measure of the arc}}{360}$ and the area of the circle.

$$\text{Area of sector } AOB = \frac{m\widehat{AB}}{360} \cdot \pi r^2$$

Problem 2 Finding the Area of a Sector of a Circle

Got It? A circle has a radius of 4 in. What is the area of a sector bounded by a 45° minor arc? Leave your answer in terms of π.

Think

What fraction of a circle's area is the area of a sector formed by a 45° arc?

Practice 3. Find the area of each shaded sector of the circle. Leave your answer in terms of π.

4. Find the area of sector *TOP* in $\odot O$ using the given information. Leave your answer in terms of π.

$d = 16$ in., $m\widehat{PT} = 135$

A part of a circle bounded by an arc and the segment joining its endpoints is a **segment of a circle**.

To find the area of a segment for a minor arc, draw radii to form a sector. The area of the segment equals the area of the sector minus the area of the triangle formed.

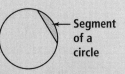
← Segment of a circle

take note

Key Concept   Area of a Segment

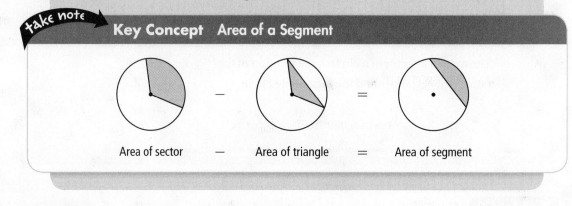

Area of sector   —   Area of triangle   =   Area of segment

Problem 3   **Finding the Area of a Segment of a Circle**

Got It?   What is the area of the shaded segment shown at the right? Round your answer to the nearest tenth.

Ⓐ Practice   Find the area of each shaded segment. Round your answer to the nearest tenth.

5.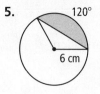

6.

Lesson Check

Do you know HOW?

7. What is the area of a circle with diameter 16 in.? Leave your answer in terms of π.

Find the area of the shaded region of the circle. Leave your answer in terms of π.

8.

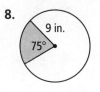

9 in.

75°

9.

2 m

120°

Do you UNDERSTAND?

MATHEMATICAL PRACTICES

⊙ 10. Vocabulary What is the difference between a sector of a circle and a segment of a circle?

© **11. Reasoning** Suppose a sector of ⊙*P* has the same area as a sector of ⊙*O*. Can you conclude that ⊙*P* and ⊙*O* have the same area? Explain.

© **12. Error Analysis** Your class must find the area of a sector of a circle determined by a 150° arc. The radius of the circle is 6 cm. What is your classmate's error? Explain.

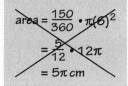

More Practice and Problem-Solving Exercises

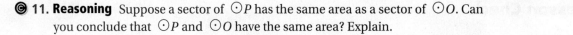

© **MATHEMATICAL PRACTICES**

B **Apply**

Find the area of the shaded region. Leave your answer in terms of π and in simplest radical form.

13.
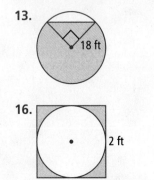
18 ft

14.
120°
9 cm

15.
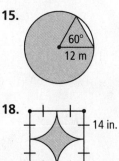
60°
12 m

16.
2 ft

17.
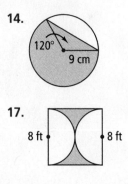
8 ft   8 ft

18.
14 in.

19. **Transportation** A town provides bus transportation to students living beyond 2 mi of the high school. What area of the town does *not* have the bus service? Round to the nearest tenth.

20. **Design** A homeowner wants to build a circular patio. If the diameter of the patio is 20 ft, what is its area to the nearest whole number?

Ⓒ 21. **Think About a Plan** A circular mirror is 24 in. wide and has a 4-in. frame around it. What is the area of the frame?
  - How can you *draw a diagram* to help solve the problem?
  - What part of a circle is the width?
  - Is there more than one area to consider?

STEM 22. **Industrial Design** Refer to the diagram of the regular hexagonal nut. What is the area of the hexagonal face to the nearest millimeter?

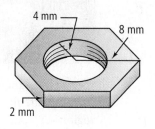

Ⓒ 23. **Reasoning** $\overline{AB}$ and $\overline{CD}$ are diameters of ⊙O. Is the area of sector AOC equal to the area of sector BOD? Explain.

24. A circle with radius 12 mm is divided into 20 sectors of equal area. What is the area of one sector to the nearest tenth?

25. The circumference of a circle is 26π in. What is its area? Leave your answer in terms of π.

26. In a circle, a 90° sector has area 36π in.^{2}. What is the radius of the circle?

Ⓒ 27. **Open-Ended** Draw a circle and a sector so that the area of the sector is 16π cm^2. Give the radius of the circle and the measure of the sector's arc.

Ⓒ 28. A method for finding the area of a segment determined by a minor arc is described in this lesson.
  a. **Writing** Describe two ways to find the area of a segment determined by a major arc.
  b. If $m\widehat{AB} = 90$ in a circle of radius 10 in., find the areas of the two segments determined by $\widehat{AB}$.

Find the area of the shaded segment to the nearest tenth.

29.
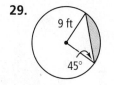
9 ft
45°

30.

7 m
300°

31.
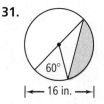
60°
|← 16 in. →|

Ⓒ **Challenge**

Find the area of the shaded region. Leave your answer in terms of π.

32.
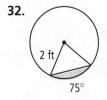
2 ft
75°

33.
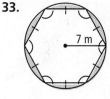
7 m

34.
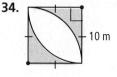
10 m

35. Recreation An 8 ft-by-10 ft floating dock is anchored in the middle of a pond. The bow of a canoe is tied to a corner of the dock with a 10-ft rope, as shown in the picture below.

  a. Sketch a diagram of the region in which the bow of the canoe can travel.

  b. What is the area of that region? Round your answer to the nearest square foot.

36. $\odot O$ at the right is inscribed in square $ABCD$ and circumscribed about square $PQRS$. Which is smaller, the blue region or the red region? Explain.

37. Circles T and U each have radius 10, and $TU = 10$. Find the area of the region that is contained inside both circles. (*Hint:* Think about where T and U must lie in a diagram of $\odot T$ and $\odot U$.)

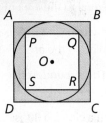

ACTIVITY LAB

Use With Lesson 8-2

Circles and Radians

G.C.5 Derive using similarity the fact that the length of the arc intercepted by an angle is proportional to the radius . . . derive the formula for the area of a sector.

Angles can be measured in degrees or *radians*. Radians are measures based on arc length.

Activity 1

Circle O has a radius of 12 cm and $m\angle POQ = 90$.

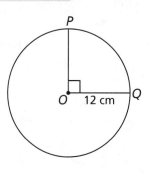

1. Find the length of $\overset{\frown}{PQ}$. Write your answer in terms of π.

2. Find the ratio of the arc length to the radius of circle P. This is the radian measure of $\angle POQ$.

The **radian measure** of a central angle of a circle is the ratio of the arc length of the intercepted arc to the radius of the circle.

$$\text{radian measure} = \frac{\text{arc length}}{\text{radius}}$$

One radian is equal to the measure of the central angle whose intercepted arc has a length equal to the radius of the circle.

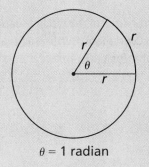

$\theta = 1$ radian

In Lesson 8-2, you learned how to find the area of the sector of a circle using proportions and the area of the circle. In Activity 2, you will derive a formula for the area of a sector when the central angle is given in radians.

Activity 2

Consider the circle below with a central angle of θ radians and radius r.

3. Write an expression for the area of the circle.

4. What is the angle measure, in radians, of a 360° central angle of the circle?

5. Write an expression for the ratio of θ to the radian measure of a 360° central angle.

6. The ratio of the area of the sector, x, to the area of the circle is equal to the ratio of the measure of the central angle θ to 2π radians. Write an equation that shows this proportional relationship. Then solve for x, the area of the sector.

Exercises

In Exercises 7–9, find the area of each sector with given radius and central angle.
Round to the nearest tenth.

7. $r = 9$ in., $m\angle\theta = 0.9$ radian

8. $r = 4.5$ ft, $m\angle\theta = 1.6$ radians

9. $r = 15$ mm, $m\angle\theta = 2$ radians

10. a. How many degrees are in 2π radians?

b. How many radians are in 180 degrees?

ⓒ **c. Reasoning** How can you convert angle measures from degrees to radians?
How can you convert angle measures from radians to degrees?

Tangent Lines

G.C.2 Identify and describe relationships among inscribed angles, radii, and chords . . . the radius of a circle is perpendicular to the tangent where the radius intersects the circle. Also **G.C.4**

Objective To use properties of a tangent to a circle

Solve It! Write your solution to the Solve It in the space below.

In the Solve It, you drew lines that touch a circle at only one point. These lines are called tangents. This use of the word *tangent* is related to, but different from, the tangent ratio in right triangles that you studied in Chapter 7.

A **tangent to a circle** is a line in the plane of the circle that intersects the circle in exactly one point.

The point where a circle and a tangent intersect is the **point of tangency**.

$\overrightarrow{BA}$ is a tangent ray and $\overline{BA}$ is a tangent segment.

Essential Understanding A radius of a circle and the tangent that intersects the endpoint of the radius on the circle have a special relationship.

take note

Theorem 76

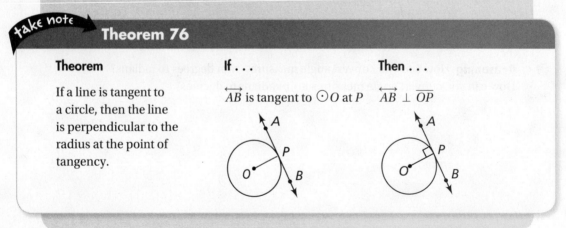

Theorem	**If . . .**	**Then . . .**
If a line is tangent to a circle, then the line is perpendicular to the radius at the point of tangency.	$\overleftrightarrow{AB}$ is tangent to $\odot O$ at P	$\overleftrightarrow{AB} \perp \overline{OP}$

Given: n is tangent to $\odot O$ at P.

Prove: $n \perp \overline{OP}$

Step 1 Assume that n is not perpendicular to $\overline{OP}$.

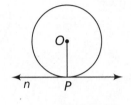

Step 2 If line n is not perpendicular to $\overline{OP}$, then, for some other point L on n, $\overline{OL}$ must be perpendicular to n. Also there is a point K on n such that $\overline{LK} \cong \overline{LP}$ because perpendicular lines form congruent adjacent angles. $\overline{OL} = \overline{OL}$. So, $\triangle OLK \cong \triangle OLP$ by SAS.

Since corresponding parts of congruent triangles are congruent, $\overline{OK} \cong \overline{OP}$. So K and P are both on $\odot O$ by the definition of a circle. For two points on n to also be on $\odot O$ contradicts the given fact that n is tangent to $\odot O$ at P. So the assumption that n is not perpendicular to $\overline{OP}$ must be false.

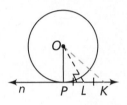

Step 3 Therefore, $n \perp \overline{OP}$ must be true.

Problem 1 Finding Angle Measures

Got It? **a.** $\overline{ED}$ is tangent to $\odot O$. What is the value of x?

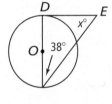

b. Reasoning Consider a quadrilateral like the one in Problem 1. Write a formula you could use to find the measure of any angle x formed by two tangents when you know the measure of the central angle c whose radii intersect the tangents.

Practice Algebra Lines that appear to be tangent are tangent. *O* is the center of each circle. What is the value of *x*?

1.

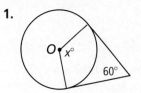

2.

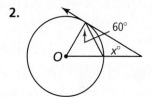

Problem 2   **Finding Distance**

Got It?   What is the distance to the horizon that a person can see on a clear day from an airplane 2 mi above Earth? Earth's radius is about 4000 mi.

A Practice **STEM** **Earth Science** The circle at the right represents Earth. The radius of Earth is about 6400 km. Find the distance d to the horizon that a person can see on a clear day from each of the following heights h above Earth. Round your answer to the nearest tenth of a kilometer.

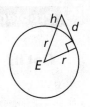

3. 1 km

4. 2500 m

Theorem 77 is the converse of Theorem 76. You can use it to prove that a line or segment is tangent to a circle. You can also use it to construct a tangent to a circle.

Theorem 77

Theorem	If . . .	Then . . .
If a line in the plane of a circle is perpendicular to a radius at its endpoint on the circle, then the line is tangent to the circle.	$\overleftrightarrow{AB} \perp \overline{OP}$ at P 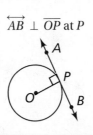	$\overleftrightarrow{AB}$ is tangent to $\odot O$

You will prove Theorem 77 in Exercise 26.

Problem 3 Finding a Radius

Got It? What is the radius of ⊙O?

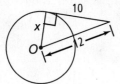

Think

Why does the value x appear on each side of the equation?

Ⓐ **Practice Algebra** In each circle, what is the value of x, to the nearest tenth?

5.

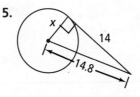

6.

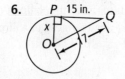

Problem 4 **Identifying a Tangent**

Got It? Is $\overline{ML}$ tangent to $\odot N$ at L? Explain.

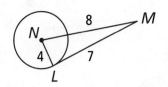

Ⓐ Practice Determine whether a tangent is shown in each diagram. Explain.

7.

8.

In the Solve It, you made a conjecture about the lengths of two tangents from a common endpoint outside a circle. Your conjecture may be confirmed by the following theorem.

take note

Theorem 78

Theorem	If . . .	Then . . .
If two tangent segments to a circle share a common endpoint outside the circle, then the two segments are congruent.	$\overline{BA}$ and $\overline{BC}$ are tangent to $\odot O$ 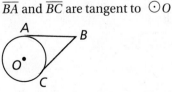	$\overline{BA} \cong \overline{BC}$

You will prove Theorem 78 in Exercise 19.

In the figure at the right, the sides of the triangle are tangent to the circle. The circle is *inscribed* in the triangle. The triangle is *circumscribed about* the circle.

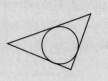

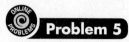

Problem 5   **Circles Inscribed in Polygons**

Got It? $\odot O$ is inscribed in $\triangle PQR$, which has a perimeter of 88 cm. What is the length of $\overline{QY}$?

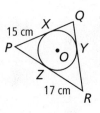

How does knowing the pairs of congruent segments help?

Practice   Each polygon circumscribes a circle. What is the perimeter of each polygon?

9.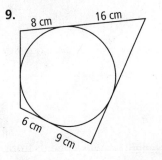

10.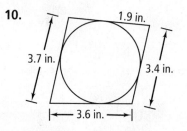

Lesson Check

Do you know HOW?

Use the figure at the right for Exercises 11–13.

11. If $m\angle A = 58$, what is $m\angle ACB$?

12. If $AC = 10$ and $BC = 8$, what is the radius?

13. If $AC = 12$ and $BC = 9$, what is the radius?

Do you UNDERSTAND?

14. **Vocabulary** How are the phrases *tangent ratio* and *tangent of a circle* used differently?

15. **Error Analysis** A classmate insists that $\overline{DF}$ is a tangent to $\odot E$. Explain how to show that your classmate is wrong.

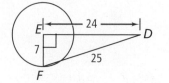

More Practice and Problem-Solving Exercises

B Apply

STEM 16. **Solar Eclipse** Common tangents to two circles may be *internal* or *external*. If you draw a segment joining the centers of the circles, a common internal tangent will intersect the segment. A common external tangent will not. For this cross-sectional diagram of the sun, moon, and Earth during a solar eclipse, use the terms above to describe the types of tangents of each color.

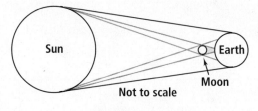

Not to scale

   a. red   **b.** blue   **c.** orange

   d. Which tangents show the extent on Earth's surface of total eclipse? Of partial eclipse?

17. **Reasoning** A nickel, a dime, and a quarter are touching as shown. Tangents are drawn from point A to both sides of each coin. What can you conclude about the four tangent segments? Explain.

@ **18. Think About a Plan** Leonardo da Vinci wrote, "When each of two squares touch the same circle at four points, one is double the other." Explain why the statement is true.
  - How will drawing a sketch help?
  - Are both squares inside the circle?

Proof **19.** Prove Theorem 78.
  Given: $\overline{BA}$ and $\overline{BC}$ are tangent to $\odot O$ at A and C, respectively.
  Prove: $\overline{BA} \cong \overline{BC}$

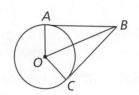

Proof **20. Given:** $\overline{BC}$ is tangent to $\odot A$ at D.
  $\overline{DB} \cong \overline{DC}$
  Prove: $\overline{AB} \cong \overline{AC}$

Proof **21. Given:** $\odot A$ and $\odot B$ with common tangents
  $\overline{DF}$ and $\overline{CE}$
  Prove: $\triangle GDC \sim \triangle GFE$

22. a. A belt fits snugly around the two circular pulleys. $\overline{CE}$ is an auxiliary line from E to $\overline{BD}$, and $\overline{CE} \parallel \overline{BA}$. What type of quadrilateral is $ABCE$? Explain.
  b. What is the length of $\overline{CE}$?
  c. What is the distance between the centers of the pulleys to the nearest tenth?

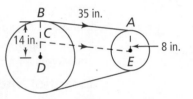

23. $\overline{BD}$ and $\overline{CK}$ at the right are diameters of $\odot A$. $\overline{BP}$ and $\overline{QP}$ are tangents to $\odot A$. What is $m\angle CDA$?

24. Constructions Draw a circle. Label the center T. Locate a point on the circle and label it R. Construct a tangent to $\odot T$ at R.

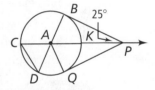

25. Coordinate Geometry Graph the equation $x^2 + y^2 = 9$. Then draw a segment from $(0, 5)$ tangent to the circle. Find the length of the segment.

ⒸChallenge

Proof **26.** Write an indirect proof of Theorem 77.
  Given: $\overleftrightarrow{AB} \perp \overline{OP}$ at P.
  Prove: $\overleftrightarrow{AB}$ is tangent to $\odot O$.

27. Two circles that have one point in common are *tangent circles*. Given any triangle, explain how to draw three circles that are centered at each vertex of the triangle and are tangent to each other.

G.C.2 Identify and describe relationships among inscribed angles, radii, and chords . . .

Objectives To use congruent chords, arcs, and central angles
To use perpendicular bisectors to chords

Solve It! Write your solution to the Solve It in the space below.

In the Solve It, you found the length of a **chord**, which is a segment whose endpoints are on a circle. The diagram shows the chord $\overline{PQ}$ and its related arc, $\overset{\frown}{PQ}$.

Essential Understanding You can use information about congruent parts of a circle (or congruent circles) to find information about other parts of the circle (or circles).

The following theorems and their converses confirm that if you know that chords, arcs, or central angles in a circle are congruent, then you know the other two parts are congruent.

Theorem 79 and Its Converse

Theorem

Within a circle or in congruent circles, congruent central angles have congruent arcs.

Converse

Within a circle or in congruent circles, congruent arcs have congruent central angles.

If $\angle AOB \cong \angle COD$, then $\overset{\frown}{AB} \cong \overset{\frown}{CD}$.
If $\overset{\frown}{AB} \cong \overset{\frown}{CD}$, then $\angle AOB \cong \angle COD$.

You will prove Theorem 79 and its converse in Exercises 17 and 33.

Theorem 80 and Its Converse

Theorem

Within a circle or in congruent circles, congruent central angles have congruent chords.

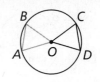

Converse

Within a circle or in congruent circles, congruent chords have congruent central angles.

If $\angle AOB \cong \angle COD$, then $\overline{AB} \cong \overline{CD}$.
If $\overline{AB} \cong \overline{CD}$, then $\angle AOB \cong \angle COD$.

You will prove Theorem 80 and its converse in Exercises 18 and 34.

Theorem 81 and Its Converse

Theorem

Within a circle or in congruent circles, congruent chords have congruent arcs.

Converse

Within a circle or in congruent circles, congruent arcs have congruent chords.

If $\overline{AB} \cong \overline{CD}$, then $\overset{\frown}{AB} \cong \overset{\frown}{CD}$.
If $\overset{\frown}{AB} \cong \overset{\frown}{CD}$, then $\overline{AB} \cong \overline{CD}$.

You will prove Theorem 81 and its converse in Exercises 19 and 35.

Problem 1 Using Congruent Chords

Got It? **Reasoning** Use the diagram in Problem 1, shown below. Suppose you are given $\odot O \cong \odot P$ and $\angle OBC \cong \angle PDF$. How can you show $\angle O \cong \angle P$? From this, what else can you conclude?

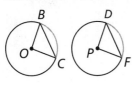

Think

Why is it important that the circles are congruent?

A **Practice** In Exercises 1 and 2, the circles are congruent. What can you conclude?

1.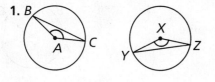

2.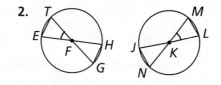

take note

Theorem 82 and Its Converse

Theorem

Within a circle or in congruent circles, chords equidistant from the center or centers are congruent.

Converse

Within a circle or in congruent circles, congruent chords are equidistant from the center (or centers).

If $OE = OF$, then $\overline{AB} \cong \overline{CD}$.
If $\overline{AB} \cong \overline{CD}$, then $OE = OF$.

You will prove the converse of Theorem 82 in Exercise 36.

Proof **Proof of Theorem 82**

Given: $\odot O$, $\overline{OE} \cong \overline{OF}$, $\overline{OE} \perp \overline{AB}$, $\overline{OF} \perp \overline{CD}$
Prove: $\overline{AB} \cong \overline{CD}$

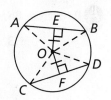

Statements	Reasons
1) $\overline{OA} \cong \overline{OB} \cong \overline{OC} \cong \overline{OD}$	1) Radii of a circle are congruent.
2) $\overline{OE} \cong \overline{OF}$, $\overline{OE} \perp \overline{AB}$, $\overline{OF} \perp \overline{CD}$	2) Given
3) $\angle AEO$ and $\angle CFO$ are right angles.	3) Def. of perpendicular segments
4) $\triangle AEO \cong \triangle CFO$	4) HL Theorem
5) $\angle A \cong \angle C$	5) Corres. parts of $\cong$ ⚠ are $\cong$.
6) $\angle B \cong \angle A$, $\angle C \cong \angle D$	6) Isosceles Triangle Theorem
7) $\angle B \cong \angle D$	7) Transitive Property of Congruence
8) $\angle AOB \cong \angle COD$	8) If two ⚞ of a $\triangle$ are $\cong$ to two ⚞ of another $\triangle$, then the third ⚞ are $\cong$.
9) $\overline{AB} \cong \overline{CD}$	9) $\cong$ central angles have $\cong$ chords.

Problem 2 **Finding the Length of a Chord**

Got It? What is the value of x? Justify your answer.

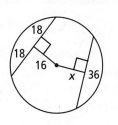

What information can you gather from the chords?

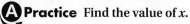

A Practice Find the value of *x*.

3.

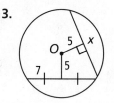

4.

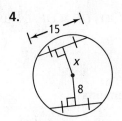

The Converse of the Perpendicular Bisector Theorem from Lesson 4-2 has special applications to a circle and its diameters, chords, and arcs.

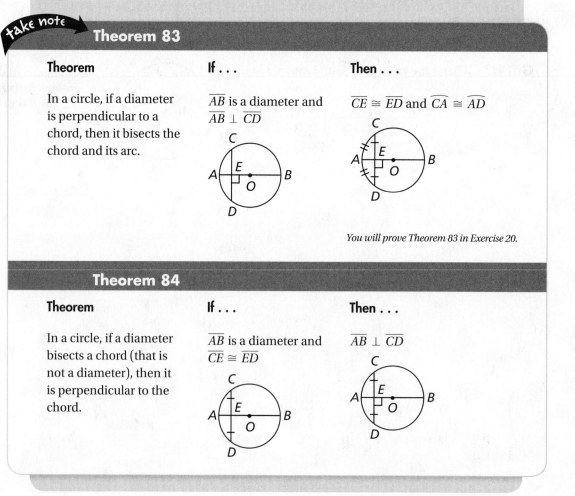

take note

Theorem 83

Theorem	If . . .	Then . . .
In a circle, if a diameter is perpendicular to a chord, then it bisects the chord and its arc.	$\overline{AB}$ is a diameter and $\overline{AB} \perp \overline{CD}$	$\overline{CE} \cong \overline{ED}$ and $\overset{\frown}{CA} \cong \overset{\frown}{AD}$

You will prove Theorem 83 in Exercise 20.

Theorem 84

Theorem	If . . .	Then . . .
In a circle, if a diameter bisects a chord (that is not a diameter), then it is perpendicular to the chord.	$\overline{AB}$ is a diameter and $\overline{CE} \cong \overline{ED}$	$\overline{AB} \perp \overline{CD}$

Theorem 85

Theorem	If . . .	Then . . .
In a circle, the perpendicular bisector of a chord contains the center of the circle.	$\overline{AB}$ is the perpendicular bisector of chord $\overline{CD}$ 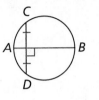	$\overline{AB}$ contains the center of $\odot O$ 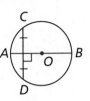

You will prove Theorem 85 in Exercise 31.

Proof **Proof of Theorem 84**

Given: $\odot O$ with diameter $\overline{AB}$ bisecting $\overline{CD}$ at E
Prove: $\overline{AB} \perp \overline{CD}$

Proof: $OC = OD$ because the radii of a circle are congruent.
$CE = ED$ by the definition of *bisect*. Thus, O and E are both
equidistant from C and D. By the Converse of the Perpendicular
Bisector Theorem, both O and E are on the perpendicular
bisector of $\overline{CD}$. Two points determine one line or segment, so
$\overline{OE}$ is the perpendicular bisector of $\overline{CD}$. Since $\overline{OE}$ is part of $\overline{AB}$,
$\overline{AB} \perp \overline{CD}$.

Problem 3   Using Diameters and Chords

Got It?   Trace a coin. What is its radius?

 **5.** In the diagram at the right, $\overline{GH}$ and $\overline{KM}$ are perpendicular bisectors of the chords they intersect. What can you conclude about the center of the circle? Justify your answer.

6. In ⊙O, $\overline{AB}$ is a diameter of the circle and $\overline{AB} \perp \overline{CD}$. What conclusions can you make?

Problem 4 **Finding Measures in a Circle**

© **Got It?** **Reasoning** In part (B) of Problem 4, how does the auxiliary $\overline{BA}$ make it simpler to solve for y?

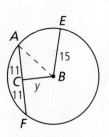

Practice Algebra Find the value of *x* to the nearest tenth.

7.
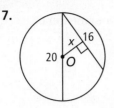

8.
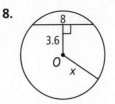

Lesson Check

Do you know HOW?

In ⊙*O*, $m\widehat{CD} = 50$ and $\overline{CA} \cong \overline{BD}$.

9. What is $m\,\widehat{AB}$? How do you know?

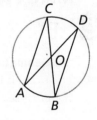

10. What is true of $\widehat{CA}$ and $\widehat{BD}$? Why?

11. Since $CA = BD$, what do you know about the distance of $\overline{CA}$ and $\overline{BD}$ from the center of ⊙*O*?

© **12. Vocabulary** Is a radius a chord? Is a diameter a chord? Explain your answers.

© **13. Error Analysis** What is the error in the diagram?

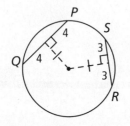

More Practice and Problem-Solving Exercises

 MATHEMATICAL
PRACTICES

B Apply

14. **Geometry in 3 Dimensions** In the figure at the right, sphere O with radius 13 cm is intersected by a plane 5 cm from center O. Find the radius of the cross section $\odot A$.

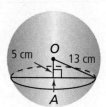

15. **Geometry in 3 Dimensions** A plane intersects a sphere that has radius 10 in., forming the cross section $\odot B$ with radius 8 in. How far is the plane from the center of the sphere?

© 16. **Think About a Plan** Two concentric circles have radii of 4 cm and 8 cm. A segment tangent to the smaller circle is a chord of the larger circle. What is the length of the segment to the nearest tenth?
   • How will you start the diagram?
   • Where is the best place to position the radius of each circle?

Proof **17.** Prove Theorem 79.

Given: $\odot O$ with $\angle AOB \cong \angle COD$
Prove: $\overset{\frown}{AB} \cong \overset{\frown}{CD}$

Proof **18.** Prove Theorem 80.

Given: $\odot O$ with $\angle AOB \cong \angle COD$
Prove: $\overline{AB} \cong \overline{CD}$

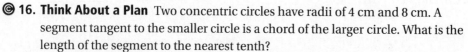

Proof 19. Prove Theorem 81.

Given: $\odot O$ with $\overline{AB} \cong \overline{CD}$
Prove: $\overset{\frown}{AB} \cong \overset{\frown}{CD}$

Proof 20. Prove Theorem 83.

Given: $\odot O$ with diameter $\overline{ED} \perp \overline{AB}$ at C
Prove: $\overset{\frown}{AC} \cong \overset{\frown}{BC}$, $\overset{\frown}{AD} \cong \overset{\frown}{BD}$

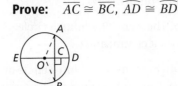

$\odot A$ and $\odot B$ are congruent. $\overline{CD}$ is a chord of both circles.

21. If $AB = 8$ in. and $CD = 6$ in., how long is a radius?

22. If $AB = 24$ cm and a radius $= 13$ cm, how long is $\overline{CD}$?

23. If a radius $= 13$ ft and $CD = 24$ ft, how long is $\overline{AB}$?

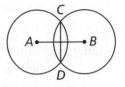

24. Construction Use Theorem 80 to construct a regular octagon.

25. In the diagram at the right, the endpoints of the chord are the points where the line $x = 2$ intersects the circle $x^2 + y^2 = 25$. What is the length of the chord? Round your answer to the nearest tenth.

26. Construction Use a circular object such as a can or a saucer to draw a circle. Construct the center of the circle.

Ⓖ 27. Writing Theorems 79 and 80 both begin with the phrase "within a circle or in congruent circles." Explain why the word *congruent* is essential for both theorems.

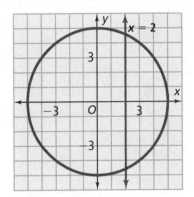

Find $m\overset{\frown}{AB}$. (*Hint:* You will need to use trigonometry in Exercise 30.)

28.

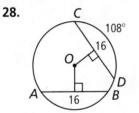

29.

30.

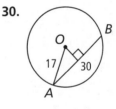

Proof 31. Prove Theorem 85.

Given: ℓ is the $\perp$ bisector of $\overline{WY}$.
Prove: ℓ contains the center of $\odot X$.

Proof 32. Given: $\odot A$ with $\overline{CE} \perp \overline{BD}$
Prove: $\overset{\frown}{BC} \cong \overset{\frown}{DC}$

 **Challenge**

Proof Prove each of the following.

33. Converse of Theorem 79: Within a circle or in congruent circles, congruent arcs have congruent central angles.

34. Converse of Theorem 80: Within a circle or in congruent circles, congruent chords have congruent central angles.

35. Converse of Theorem 81: Within a circle or in congruent circles, congruent arcs have congruent chords.

36. Converse of Theorem 82: Within a circle or congruent circles, congruent chords are equidistant from the center (or centers).

Proof 37. If two circles are concentric and a chord of the larger circle is tangent to the smaller circle, prove that the point of tangency is the midpoint of the chord.

8-5 Inscribed Angles

G.C.2 Identify and describe relationships among inscribed angles, radii, and chords . . . Also **G.C.3, G.C.4**

Objectives To find the measure of an inscribed angle
To find the measure of an angle formed by a tangent and a chord

Solve It! Write your solution to the Solve It in the space below.

An angle whose vertex is on the circle and whose sides are chords of the circle is an **inscribed angle**. An arc with endpoints on the sides of an inscribed angle, and its other points in the interior of the angle, is an **intercepted arc**. In the diagram, inscribed $\angle C$ intercepts $\widehat{AB}$.

Essential Understanding Angles formed by intersecting lines have a special relationship to the arcs the intersecting lines intercept. In this lesson, you will study arcs formed by inscribed angles.

take note

Theorem 86   Inscribed Angle Theorem

The measure of an inscribed angle is half the measure of its intercepted arc.

$$m\angle B = \tfrac{1}{2}\, m\widehat{AC}$$

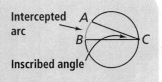

To prove Theorem 86, there are three cases to consider.

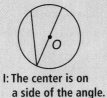

I: The center is on a side of the angle.

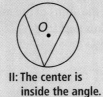

II: The center is inside the angle.

III: The center is outside the angle.

The following is a proof of Case I. You will prove Case II and Case III in Exercises 19 and 20.

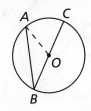

Given: $\odot O$ with inscribed $\angle B$ and diameter $\overline{BC}$

Prove: $m\angle B = \frac{1}{2}m\overset{\frown}{AC}$

Draw radius $\overline{OA}$ to form isosceles $\triangle AOB$ with $OA = OB$ and, hence, $m\angle A = m\angle B$ (Isosceles Triangle Theorem).

$m\angle AOC = m\angle A + m\angle B$	Triangle Exterior Angle Theorem
$m\overset{\frown}{AC} = m\angle AOC$	Definition of measure of an arc
$m\overset{\frown}{AC} = m\angle A + m\angle B$	Substitute.
$m\overset{\frown}{AC} = 2m\angle B$	Substitute and simplify.
$\frac{1}{2}m\overset{\frown}{AC} = m\angle B$	Divide each side by 2.

Problem 1 **Using the Inscribed Angle Theorem**

Got It?   **a.** In $\odot O$, what is $m\angle A$?

b. What are $m\angle A$, $m\angle B$, $m\angle C$, and $m\angle D$?

> **Plan**
> What is the intercepted arc of each angle?

c. What do you notice about the sums of the measures of the opposite angles in the quadrilateral in part (b)?

ⒶPractice Find the value of each variable. For each circle, the dot represents the center.

1.

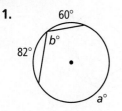

2.

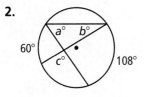

You will use three corollaries to the Inscribed Angle Theorem to find measures of angles in circles. The first corollary may confirm an observation you made in the Solve It.

---

take note

Corollaries to Theorem 86   The Inscribed Angle Theorem

Corollary 1

Two inscribed angles that intercept the same arc are congruent.

Corollary 2

An angle inscribed in a semicircle is a right angle.

Corollary 3

The opposite angles of a quadrilateral inscribed in a circle are supplementary.

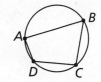

You will prove these corollaries in Exercises 24–26.

Got It?   In the diagram at the right, what is the measure of each numbered angle?

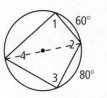

Think

What does the auxiliary line represent in the diagram?

Practice   Find the value of each variable. For each circle, the dot represents the center.

3.

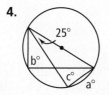

4.

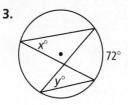

The following diagram shows point *A* moving along the circle until a tangent is formed. From the Inscribed Angle Theorem, you know that in the first three diagrams $m\angle A$ is $\frac{1}{2} m\,\overset{\frown}{BC}$. As the last diagram suggests, this is also true when *A* and *C* coincide.

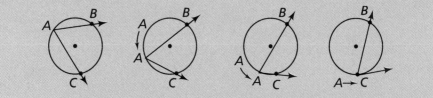

Theorem 87

The measure of an angle formed by a tangent and a chord is half the measure of the intercepted arc.

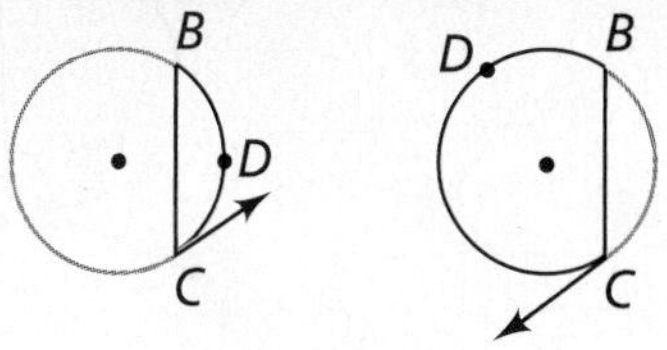

$$m\angle C = \tfrac{1}{2} m\,\widehat{BDC}$$

You will prove Theorem 87 in Exercise 27.

Problem 3 **Using Arc Measure**

Got It? **a.** In the diagram at the right, $\overline{KJ}$ is tangent to $\odot O$. What are the values of x and y?

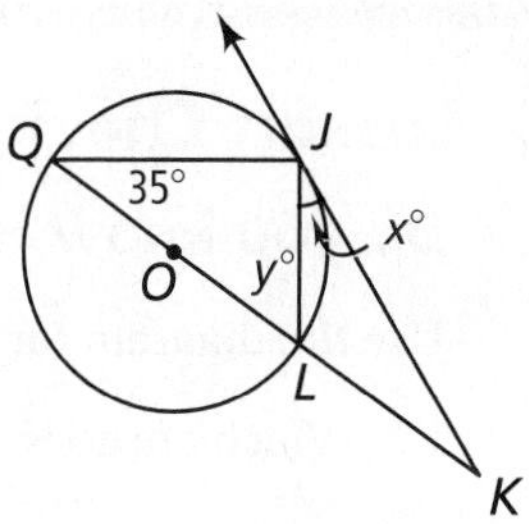

b. Reasoning In part (a), an inscribed angle ($\angle Q$) and an angle formed by a tangent and chord ($\angle KJL$) intercept the same arc. What is always true of these angles? Explain.

Ⓐ Practice In Exercises 5 and 6, find the value of each variable. Lines that appear to be tangent are tangent.

5.

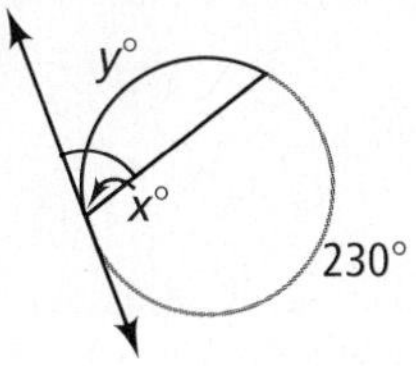

6.

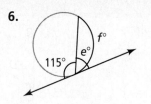

Lesson Check

Do you know HOW?

Use the diagram for Exercises 7–9.

7. Which arc does ∠A intercept?

8. Which angle intercepts $\overset{\frown}{ABC}$?

9. Which angles of quadrilateral *ABCD* are supplementary?

Do you UNDERSTAND?

⊚ **10. Vocabulary** What is the relationship between an inscribed angle and its intercepted arc?

⊚ **11. Error Analysis** A classmate says that $m\angle A = 90$. What is your classmate's error?

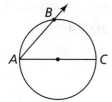

More Practice and Problem-Solving Exercises

Ⓑ **Apply**

⊚ **12. Writing** A parallelogram inscribed in a circle must be what kind of parallelogram? Explain.

Find each indicated measure for ⊙O.

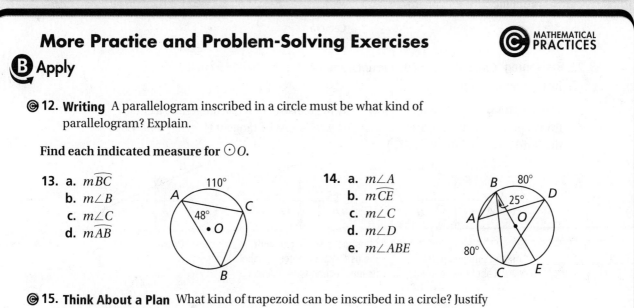

13. a. $m\widehat{BC}$
 b. $m\angle B$
 c. $m\angle C$
 d. $m\widehat{AB}$

14. a. $m\angle A$
 b. $m\widehat{CE}$
 c. $m\angle C$
 d. $m\angle D$
 e. $m\angle ABE$

⊚ **15. Think About a Plan** What kind of trapezoid can be inscribed in a circle? Justify your response.
 • Draw several diagrams to make a conjecture.
 • How can parallel lines help?

Find the value of each variable. For each circle, the dot represents the center.

16.

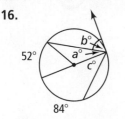

52°

b°
a°
c°

84°

17.

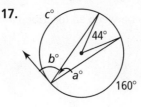

c°
44°
b°
a°

160°

18.

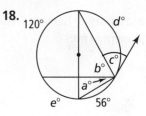

120°
d°
b° c°
a°
e°
56°

Write a proof for Exercises 19 and 20.

Proof 19. Inscribed Angle Theorem, Case II

Given: ⊙O with inscribed ∠ABC

Prove: $m\angle ABC = \frac{1}{2} m\widehat{AC}$

(*Hint:* Use the Inscribed Angle Theorem, Case I.)

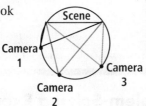

P
C
A
O
B

Proof 20. Inscribed Angle Theorem, Case III

Given: ⊙S with inscribed ∠PQR

Prove: $m\angle PQR = \frac{1}{2} m\widehat{PR}$

(*Hint:* Use the Inscribed Angle Theorem, Case I.)

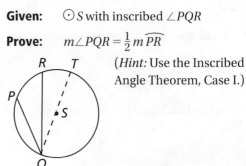

R   T
P
S
Q

21. Television The director of a telecast wants the option of showing the same scene from three different views.

  a. Explain why cameras in the positions shown in the diagram will transmit the same scene.

  b. Reasoning Will the scenes look the same when the director views them on the control room monitors? Explain.

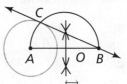

Scene
Camera 1
Camera 3
Camera 2

22. Reasoning Can a rhombus that is not a square be inscribed in a circle? Justify your answer.

23. Constructions The diagrams below show the construction of a tangent to a circle from a point outside the circle. Explain why $\overleftrightarrow{BC}$ must be tangent to ⊙A. (*Hint:* Copy the third diagram and draw $\overline{AC}$.)

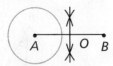

A   O   B

C
A   O   B

C
A   O   B

Given: ⊙A and point B
Construct the midpoint of $\overline{AB}$. Label the point O.

Construct a semicircle with radius OA and center O. Label its intersection with ⊙A as C.

Draw $\overleftrightarrow{BC}$.

Write a proof for Exercises 24–27.

Proof 24. Inscribed Angle Theorem, Corollary 1

Given: $\odot O$, $\angle A$ intercepts $\overarc{BC}$, $\angle D$ intercepts $\overarc{BC}$.

Prove: $\angle A \cong \angle D$

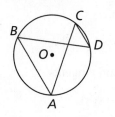

Proof 25. Inscribed Angle Theorem, Corollary 2

Given: $\odot O$ with $\angle CAB$ inscribed in a semicircle

Prove: $\angle CAB$ is a right angle.

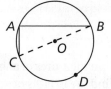

Proof 26. Inscribed Angle Theorem, Corollary 3

Given: Quadrilateral $ABCD$ inscribed in $\odot O$

Prove: $\angle A$ and $\angle C$ are supplementary. $\angle B$ and $\angle D$ are supplementary.

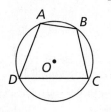

Proof 27. Theorem 87

Given: $\overline{GH}$ and tangent ℓ intersecting $\odot E$ at H

Prove: $m\angle GHI = \frac{1}{2} m\overarc{GFH}$

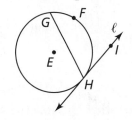

Challenge

⊚ Reasoning Is the statement *true* or *false*? If it is true, give a convincing argument. If it is false, give a counterexample.

28. If two angles inscribed in a circle are congruent, then they intercept the same arc.

29. If an inscribed angle is a right angle, then it is inscribed in a semicircle.

Proof 30. Prove that if two arcs of a circle are included between parallel chords, then the arcs are congruent.

31. Constructions Draw two segments. Label their lengths x and y. Construct the geometric mean of x and y. (*Hint:* Recall a theorem about a geometric mean.)

Angle Measures and Segment Lengths

G.C.2 Identify and describe relationships among inscribed angles, radii, and chords . . .

Objectives To find measures of angles formed by chords, secants, and tangents
To find the lengths of segments associated with circles

Solve It! Write your solution to the Solve It in the space below.

Essential Understanding Angles formed by intersecting lines have a special relationship to the related arcs formed when the lines intersect a circle. In this lesson, you will study angles and arcs formed by lines intersecting either within a circle or outside a circle.

take note

Theorem 88

The measure of an angle formed by two lines that intersect inside a circle is half the sum of the measures of the intercepted arcs.

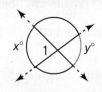

$$m\angle 1 = \tfrac{1}{2}(x + y)$$

Theorem 89

The measure of an angle formed by two lines that intersect outside a circle is half the difference of the measures of the intercepted arcs.

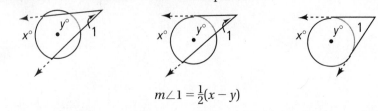

$$m\angle 1 = \tfrac{1}{2}(x - y)$$

You will prove Theorem 89 In Exercises 28 and 29.

In Theorem 88, the lines from a point outside the circle going through the circle are called secants. A **secant** is a line that intersects a circle at two points. $\overleftrightarrow{AB}$ is a secant, $\overrightarrow{AB}$ is a secant ray, and $\overline{AB}$ is a secant segment. A chord is part of a secant.

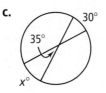 **Proof of Theorem 88**

Given: $\odot O$ with intersecting chords $\overline{AC}$ and $\overline{BD}$
Prove: $m\angle 1 = \frac{1}{2}(m\widehat{AB} + m\widehat{CD})$

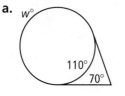

Begin by drawing auxiliary $\overline{AD}$ as shown in the diagram.

$m\angle BDA = \frac{1}{2}m\widehat{AB}$, and $m\angle CAD = \frac{1}{2}m\widehat{CD}$

Inscribed Angle Theorem

$m\angle 1 = m\angle BDA + m\angle CAD$

△ Exterior Angle Theorem

$m\angle 1 = \frac{1}{2}m\widehat{AB} + \frac{1}{2}m\widehat{CD}$

Substitute.

$m\angle 1 = \frac{1}{2}(m\widehat{AB} + m\widehat{CD})$

Distributive Property

Problem 1 Finding Angle Measures

Got It?   What is the value of each variable?

a.

$w°$

$110°$

$70°$

b.

$110°$

$30°$

$y°$

c.

$30°$

$35°$

$x°$

Ⓐ Practice **Algebra** Find the value of each variable.

1.

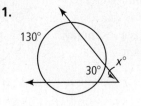

130°

30° x°

2.

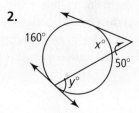

160°

x°

50°

y°

Problem 2 **Finding an Arc Measure**

Got It? **a.** A departing space probe sends back a picture of Earth as it crosses Earth's equator. The angle formed by the two tangents to the equator is 20°. What is the measure of the arc of the equator that is visible to the space probe?

Think

How can you represent the measures of the arcs?

Ⓒ **b. Reasoning** Is the probe or the geostationary satellite in Problem 2 closer to Earth? Explain.

Ⓐ Practice **3. Algebra** Find the value of each variable.

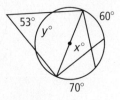

53°

y°

60°

x°

70°

4. Photography You focus your camera on a circular fountain. Your camera is at the vertex of the angle formed by tangents to the fountain. You estimate that this angle is 40°. What is the measure of the arc of the circular basin of the fountain that will be in the photograph?

Essential Understanding There is a special relationship between two intersecting chords, two intersecting secants, or a secant that intersects a tangent. This relationship allows you to find the lengths of unknown segments.

From a given point P, you can draw two segments to a circle along infinitely many lines. For example, $\overline{PA_1}$ and $\overline{PB_1}$ lie along one such line. Theorem 90 states the surprising result that no matter which line you use, the product of the lengths $PA \cdot PB$ remains constant.

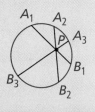

take note

Theorem 90

For a given point and circle, the product of the lengths of the two segments from the point to the circle is constant along any line through the point and circle.

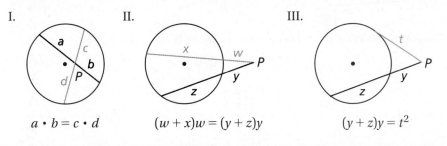

I.

$a \cdot b = c \cdot d$

II.

$(w + x)w = (y + z)y$

III.

$(y + z)y = t^2$

As you use Theorem 90, remember the following.

- **Case I:** The products of the chord segments are equal.
- **Case II:** The products of the secants and their outer segments are equal.
- **Case III:** The product of a secant and its outer segment equals the square of the tangent.

Here is a proof for Case I. You will prove Case II and Case III in Exercises 30 and 31.

Here is a proof for Case I. You will prove Case II and Case III in Exercises 30 and 31.

Proof **Proof of Theorem 90, Case I**

Given: A circle with chords $\overline{AB}$ and $\overline{CD}$ intersecting at P

Prove: $a \cdot b = c \cdot d$

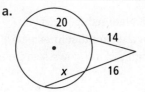

Draw $\overline{AC}$ and $\overline{BD}$. $\angle A \cong \angle D$ and $\angle C \cong \angle B$ because each pair intercepts the same arc, and angles that intercept the same arc are congruent. $\triangle APC \sim \triangle DPB$ by the Angle-Angle Similarity Postulate. The lengths of corresponding sides of similar triangles are proportional, so $\frac{a}{d} = \frac{c}{b}$. Therefore, $a \cdot b = c \cdot d$.

ONLINE PROBLEMS

Problem 3 **Finding Segment Lengths**

Plan

How can you identify the segments needed to use Theorem 90?

Got It? What is the value of the variable to the nearest tenth?

a.

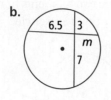

b.

Practice **Algebra** Find the value of each variable using the given chord, secant, and tangent lengths. If the answer is not a whole number, round to the nearest tenth.

5.

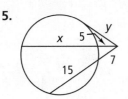

6.

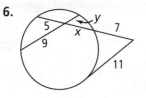

Lesson Check

Do you know HOW?

7. What is the value of x?

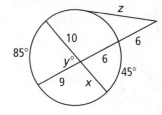

8. What is the value of y?

9. What is the value of z, to the nearest tenth?

10. The measure of the angle formed by two tangents to a circle is 80. What are the measures of the intercepted arcs?

Do you UNDERSTAND?

© **11. Vocabulary** Describe the difference between a *secant* and a *tangent*.

12. In the diagram for Exercises 7–9, is it possible to find the measures of the unmarked arcs? Explain.

© **13. Error Analysis** To find the value of x, a student wrote the equation $(7.5)6 = x^2$. What error did the student make?

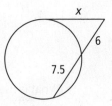

More Practice and Problem-Solving Exercises

B Apply

Algebra $\overline{CA}$ and $\overline{CB}$ are tangents to $\odot O$. Write an expression for each arc or angle in terms of the given variable.

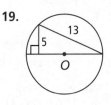

14. $m\,\widehat{ADB}$ using x **15.** $m\angle C$ using x **16.** $m\,\widehat{AB}$ using y

Find the diameter of $\odot O$. A line that appears to be tangent is tangent. If your answer is not a whole number, round it to the nearest tenth.

17.
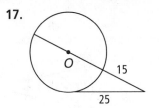

18.
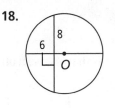

19.

20. A circle is inscribed in a quadrilateral whose four angles have measures 85, 76, 94, and 105. Find the measures of the four arcs between consecutive points of tangency.

Wankel engine

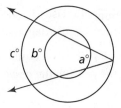

STEM 21. Engineering The basis for the design of the Wankel rotary engine is an equilateral triangle. Each side of the triangle is a chord to an arc of a circle. The opposite vertex of the triangle is the center of the circle that forms the arc. In the diagram below, each side of the equilateral triangle is 8 in. long.

  a. Use what you know about equilateral triangles and find the value of x.

  b. Reasoning Copy the diagram and complete the circle with the given center. Then use Theorem 90 to find the value of x. Show that your answers to parts (a) and (b) are equal.

22. Think About a Plan In the diagram, the circles are concentric. What is a formula you could use to find the value of c in terms of a and b?

  • How can you use the inscribed angle to find the value of c?

  • What is the relationship of the inscribed angle to a and b?

23. $\triangle PQR$ is inscribed in a circle with $m\angle P = 70$, $m\angle Q = 50$, and $m\angle R = 60$. What are the measures of $\widehat{PQ}$, $\widehat{QR}$, and $\widehat{PR}$?

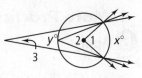

24. Reasoning Use the diagram at the right. If you know the values of *x* and *y*, how can you find the measure of each numbered angle?

Algebra Find the values of *x* and *y* using the given chord, secant, and tangent lengths. If your answer is not a whole number, round it to the nearest tenth.

25.   **26.**   **27.**

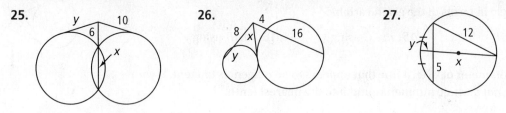

Proof 28. Prove Theorem 89 as it applies to two secants that intersect outside a circle.

Given: $\odot O$ with secants $\overline{CA}$ and $\overline{CE}$
Prove: $m\angle ACE = \frac{1}{2}(m\widehat{AE} - m\widehat{BD})$

Proof 29. Prove the other two cases of Theorem 89. (See Exercise 28.)

For Exercises 30 and 31, write proofs that use similar triangles.

Proof 30. Prove Theorem 90, Case II.   **Proof 31.** Prove Theorem 90, Case III.

32. The diagram at the right shows a *unit circle*, a circle with radius 1.
   a. What triangle is similar to $\triangle ABE$?
   b. Describe the connection between the ratio for the tangent of $\angle A$ and the segment that is tangent to $\odot A$.
   c. The secant ratio is $\frac{\text{hypotenuse}}{\text{length of leg adjacent to an angle}}$. Describe the connection between the ratio for the secant of $\angle A$ and the segment that is the secant in the unit circle.

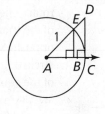

Ⓒ Challenge

For Exercises 33 and 34, use the diagram at the right. Prove each statement.

Proof 33. $m\angle 1 + m\widehat{PQ} = 180$ **Proof 34.** $m\angle 1 + m\angle 2 = m\widehat{QR}$

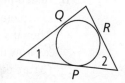

Proof 35. Use the diagram at the right and the theorems of this lesson to prove the Pythagorean Theorem.

Proof 36. If an equilateral triangle is inscribed in a circle, prove that the tangents to the circle at the vertices form an equilateral triangle.

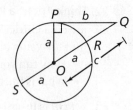

8-1 Circles and Arcs

Quick Review

A **circle** is the set of all points in a plane equidistant from a point called the **center**. The **circumference** of a circle is $C = \pi d$ or $C = 2\pi r$. **Arc length** is a fraction of a circle's circumference. The length of $\widehat{AB} = \frac{m\widehat{AB}}{360} \cdot 2\pi r$.

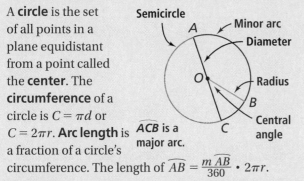

Semicircle

Minor arc
Diameter

Radius

$\widehat{ACB}$ is a major arc.

Central angle

Example

A circle has a radius of 5 cm. What is the length of an arc measuring 80°?

length of $\widehat{AB} = \frac{m\widehat{AB}}{360} \cdot 2\pi r$ Use the arc length formula.

$= \frac{80}{360} \cdot 2\pi(5)$ Substitute.

$= \frac{20}{9}\pi$ Simplify.

The length of the arc is $\frac{20}{9}\pi$ cm.

Exercises

Find each measure.

1. $m\angle APD$

2. $m\widehat{AC}$

3. $m\widehat{ABD}$

4. $m\angle CPA$

Find the length of each arc shown in red. Leave your answer in terms of π.

5.

6.

7.

8.

8-2 Areas of Circles and Sectors

Quick Review

The area of a circle is $A = \pi r^2$. A **sector of a circle** is a region bounded by two radii and their intercepted arc. The area of sector $APB = \frac{m\widehat{AB}}{360} \cdot \pi r^2$.

A **segment of a circle** is the part bounded by an arc and the segment joining its endpoints.

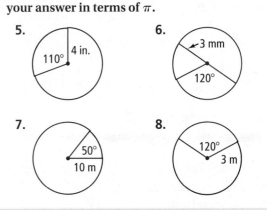

Sector of a circle

Segment of a circle

Example

What is the area of the shaded region?

Area $= \frac{m\widehat{AB}}{360} \cdot \pi r^2$ Use the area formula.

$= \frac{120}{360} \cdot \pi(4)^2$ Substitute.

$= \frac{16\pi}{3}$ Simplify.

The area of the shaded region is $\frac{16\pi}{3}$ ft².

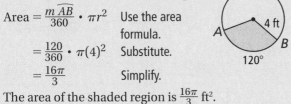

Exercises

What is the area of each circle? Leave your answer in terms of π.

9.

10.

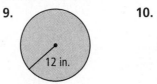

Find the area of each shaded region. Round your answer to the nearest tenth.

11.

12.

13. A circle has a radius of 20 cm. What is the area of the smaller segment of the circle formed by a 60° arc? Round to the nearest tenth.

8-3 Tangent Lines

Quick Review

A **tangent** to a circle is a line that intersects the circle at exactly one point. The radius to that point is perpendicular to the tangent. From any point outside a circle, you can draw two segments tangent to a circle. Those segments are congruent.

Example

$\overrightarrow{PA}$ and $\overrightarrow{PB}$ are tangents. Find x.

The radii are perpendicular to the tangents. Add the angle measures of the quadrilateral:

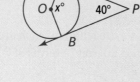

$x + 90 + 90 + 40 = 360$
$x + 220 = 360$
$x = 140$

Exercises

Use $\odot O$ for Exercises 14–16.

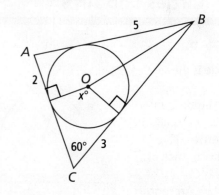

14. What is the perimeter of $\triangle ABC$?

15. $OB = \sqrt{28}$. What is the radius?

16. What is the value of x?

8-4 Chords and Arcs

Quick Review

A **chord** is a segment whose endpoints are on a circle. Congruent chords are equidistant from the center. A diameter that bisects a chord that is not a diameter is perpendicular to the chord.

The perpendicular bisector of a chord contains the center of the circle.

Example

Since the chord is bisected, $m\angle ACB = 90$. The radius is 13 units. So an auxiliary segment from A to B is 13 units. Use the Pythagorean Theorem.

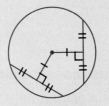

$$d^2 + 12^2 = 13^2$$
$$d^2 = 25$$
$$d = 5$$

Exercises

Use the figure below for Exercises 17–19.

17. If $\overline{AB}$ is a diameter and $CE = ED$, then $m\angle AEC = \underline{\ ?\ }$.

18. If $\overline{AB}$ is a diameter and is at right angles to $\overline{CD}$, what is the ratio of CD to DE?

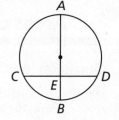

19. If $CE = \frac{1}{2}CD$ and $m\angle DEB = 90$, what is true of $\overline{AB}$?

Use the circle below for Exercises 20 and 21.

20. What is the value of x?

21. What is the value of y?

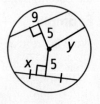

8-5 Inscribed Angles

Quick Review

An **inscribed angle** has its vertex on a circle and its sides are chords. An **intercepted arc** has its endpoints on the sides of an inscribed angle, and its other points in the interior of the angle. The measure of an inscribed angle is half the measure of its intercepted arc.

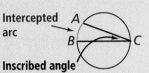

Example

What is $m\widehat{PS}$? What is $m\angle R$?

The $m\angle Q = 60$ is half of m, so $m\widehat{PS} = 120$. $\angle R$ intercepts the same arc as $\angle Q$, so $m\angle R = 60$.

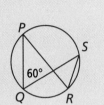

Exercises

Find the value of each variable. Line ℓ is a tangent.

22.   23.

25.

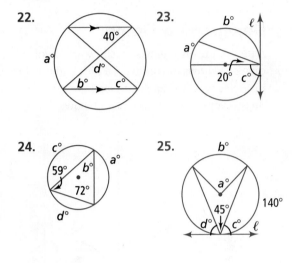

8-6 Angle Measures and Segment Lengths

Quick Review

A **secant** is a line that intersects a circle at two points. The following relationships are true:

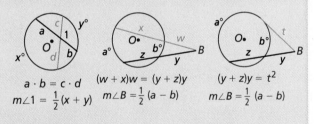

$$a \cdot b = c \cdot d$$
$$m\angle 1 = \tfrac{1}{2}(x + y)$$

$$(w + x)w = (y + z)y$$
$$m\angle B = \tfrac{1}{2}(a - b)$$

$$(y + z)y = t^2$$
$$m\angle B = \tfrac{1}{2}(a - b)$$

Example

What is the value of x?

$$(x + 10)10 = (19 + 9)9$$
$$10x + 100 = 252$$
$$x = 15.2$$

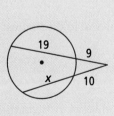

Exercises

Find the value of each variable.

26.   27. 145°

28.   29.

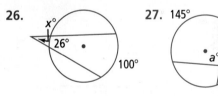

Pull It All Together

Designing a Game

A new game on a television show will involve flat circular disks falling into slots. The diagram shows the radius of a disk and the dimensions of a slot. The disks always fall in such a way that each one rests against a side of the slot, first on one side and then on the opposite side, as shown below.

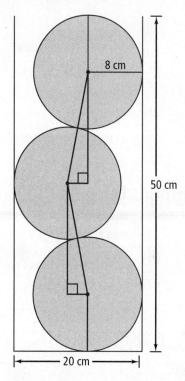

The game designer must verify that three disks will fit into a slot, without the top disk protruding from the top of the slot.

Task Description

Show that the vertical distance from the bottom of the slot to the highest point on the top disk is less than 50 cm.

- How would knowing the length of the longer leg of the right triangles in the diagram help you solve the problem?

- What are the lengths of the hypotenuse and shorter leg of the right triangles? How can you use these measurements to find the length of the longer leg?

Postulates and Theorems

Postulates

Postulate 1
Through any two points there is exactly one line.

Postulate 2
If two distinct lines intersect, then they intersect in exactly one point.

Postulate 3
If two distinct planes intersect, then they intersect in exactly one line.

Postulate 4
Through any three noncollinear points there is exactly on plane.

Postulate 5
Ruler Postulate
Every point on a line can be paired with a real number. This makes a one-to-one correspondence between the points on the line and the real numbers.

Postulate 6
Segment Addition Postulate
If three points A, B, and C are collinear and B is between A and C, then $AB + BC = AC$.

Postulate 7
Protractor Postulate
Consider $\overrightarrow{OB}$ and a point A on one side of $\overrightarrow{OB}$. Every ray of the form $\overrightarrow{OA}$ can be paired one to one with a real number from 0 to 180.

Postulate 8
Angle Addition Postulate
If point B is in the interior of $\angle AOC$, then $m\angle AOB + m\angle BOC = m\angle AOC$.

Postulate 9
Linear Pair Postulate
If two angles form a linear pair, then they are supplementary.

Postulate 10
Area Addition Postulate
The area of a region is the sum of the area of its nonoverlapping parts.

Postulate 11
Same-Side Interior Angles Postulate
If a transversal intersects two parallel lines, then same-side interior angles are supplementary.

Postulate 12
Parallel Postulate
Through a point not on a line, there is one and only one line parallel to the given line.

Postulate 13
Perpendicular Postulate
Through a point not on a line, there is one and only one line perpendicular to the given line.

Postulate 14
Side-Side-Side (SSS) Postulate
If three sides of one triangle are congruent to the three sides of another triangle, then the two triangles are congruent.

Postulate 15
Side-Angle-Side (SAS) Postulate
If two sides and the included angle of one triangle are congruent to two sides and the included angle of another triangle, then the two triangles are congruent.

Postulate 16
Angle-Side-Angle (ASA) Postulate
If two angles and the included side of one triangle are congruent to two angles and the included side of another triangle, then the two triangles are congruent.

Theorems

Theorem 1
Vertical Angles Theorem
Vertical angles are congruent.

Theorem 2
Congruent Supplements Theorem
If two angles are supplements of the same angle (or of two congruent angles), then the two angles are congruent.

Theorem 3
Congruent Complements Theorem
If two angles are complements of the same angle (or of two congruent angles), then the two angles are congruent.

Theorem 4
All right angles are congruent.

Theorem 5
If two angles are congruent and supplementary, then each is a right angle.

Theorem 6
Alternate Interior Angles Theorem
If a transversal intersects two parallel lines, the alternate interior angles are congruent.

Theorem 7
Corresponding Angles Theorem
If a transversal intersects two parallel lines, then corresponding angles are congruent.

Theorem 8
Alternate Exterior Angles Theorem
If a transversal intersects two parallel lines, then alternate exterior angles are congruent.

Theorem 9
Converse of the Corresponding Angles Theorem
If two lines and a transversal form corresponding angles that are congruent, then the two lines are parallel.

Theorem 10
Converse of the Alternate Interior Angles Theorem
If two lines and a transversal form alternate interior angles that are congruent, then the two lines are parallel.

Theorem 11
Converse of the Same-Side Interior Angles Postulate
If two lines and a transversal form same-side interior angles that are congruent, then the two lines are parallel.

Theorem 12
Converse of the Alternate Exterior Angles Theorem
If two lines and a transversal form alternate exterior angles that are congruent, then the two lines are parallel.

Theorem 13
If two lines are parallel to the same line, then they are parallel to each other.

Theorem 14
In a plane, if two lines are perpendicular to the same line, then they are parallel to each other.

Theorem 15
Perpendicular Transversal Theorem
In a plane, if a line is perpendicular to one of two parallel lines, then it is perpendicular to the other.

Theorem 16
Triangle Angle-Sum Theorem
The sum of the measures of the angles of a triangle is 180.

Theorem 17
Triangle Exterior Angle Theorem
The measure of each exterior angle of a triangle equals the sum of the measure of its two remote interior angles.

Corollary
The measure of an exterior angle of a triangle is greater than the measure of each of its remote interior angles.

Theorem 18
Third Angles Theorem
If two angles of one triangle are congruent to two angles of another triangle, than the third angles are congruent.

Theorem 19
Angle-Angle-Side (AAS) Theorem
If two angles and a nonincluded side of one triangle are congruent to two angles and a nonincluded side of another triangle, then the two triangles are congruent.

Theorem 20
Isosceles Triangle Theorem
If two sides of a triangle are congruent, then the angles opposite those sides are congruent.

Corollary
If a triangle is equilateral, then the triangle is equiangular.

Theorem 21
Converse of the Isosceles Triangle Theorem
If two angles of a triangle are congruent, then the sides opposite the angles are congruent.

Corollary
If a triangle is equiangular, then it is equilateral.

Theorem 22
If a line bisects the vertex angle of an isosceles triangle, then the line is also the perpendicular bisector of the base.

Theorem 23
Hypotenuse-Leg (HL) Theorem
If the hypotenuse and a leg of one right triangle are congruent to the hypotenuse and a leg of another right triangle, then the triangles are congruent.

Theorem 24
Triangle Midsegment Theorem
If a line segment joins the midpoints of two sides of a triangle, then the segment is parallel to the third side and is half as long.

Theorem 25
Perpendicular Bisector Theorem
If a point is on the perpendicular bisector of a line segment, then it is equidistant from the endpoints of the segment.

Theorem 26
Converse of the Perpendicular Bisector Theorem
If a point is equidistant from the endpoints of a line segment, then it is on the perpendicular bisector of the segment.

Theorem 27
Angle Bisector Theorem
If a point is on the bisector of an angle, then the point is equidistant from the sides of the angle.

Theorem 28
Converse of the Angle Bisector Theorem
If a point in the interior of an angle is equidistant from the sides of the angle, then the point is on the angle bisector

Theorem 29
Concurrency of Perpendicular Bisectors Theorem
The perpendicular bisectors of the sides of a triangle are concurrent at a point equidistant from the vertices.

Theorem 30
Concurrency of Angle Bisectors Theorem
The bisectors of the angles of a triangle are concurrent at a point equidistant from the sides of the triangle.

Theorem 31
Concurrency of Medians Theorem
The medians of a triangle are concurrent at a point that is two-thirds the distance from each vertex to the midpoint of the opposite side.

Theorem 32
Concurrency of Altitudes Theorem
The lines that contain the altitudes of a triangle are concurrent.

Theorem 33
If two sides of a triangle are not congruent, then the larger angle lies opposite the longer side.

Theorem 34
If two angles of a triangle are not congruent, then the longer side lies opposite the larger angle.

Theorem 35
Triangle Inequality Theorem
The sum of the lengths of any two sides of a triangle is greater than the length of the third side.

Theorem 36
The Hinge Theorem (SAS Inequality Theorem)
If two sides of one triangle are congruent to two sides of another triangle and the included angles are not congruent, then the longer third side is opposite the larger included angle.

Theorem 37
Converse of the Hinge Theorem (SSS Inequality)
If two sides of one triangle are congruent to two sides of another triangle and the third sides are not congruent, then the larger included angle is opposite the longer third side.

Theorem 38
Polygon Angle-Sum Theorem
The sum of the measures of the angles of an n-gon is $(n - 2)180$.

> **Corollary**
> The measure of each angle of a regular n-gon is $\frac{(n - 2)180}{n}$.

Theorem 39
The sum of the measures of the exterior angles of a polygon, one at each vertex, is 360.

Theorem 40
If a quadrilateral is a parallelogram, then its opposite sides are congruent.

Theorem 41
If a quadrilateral is a parallelogram, then its consecutive angles are supplementary.

Theorem 42
If a quadrilateral is a parallelogram, then its opposite angles are congruent.

Theorem 43
If a quadrilateral is a parallelogram, then its diagonals bisect each other.

Theorem 44
If three (or more) parallel lines cut off congruent segments on one transversal, then they cut off congruent segments on every transversal.

Theorem 45
If both pairs of opposite sides of a quadrilateral are congruent, then the quadrilateral is a parallelogram.

Theorem 46
If an angle of a quadrilateral is supplementary to both of its consecutive angles, then the quadrilateral is a parallelogram.

Theorem 47
If both pairs of opposite angles of a quadrilateral are congruent, then the quadrilateral is a parallelogram.

Theorem 48
If the diagonals of a quadrilateral bisect each other, then the quadrilateral is a parallelogram.

Theorem 49
If one pair of opposite sides of a quadrilateral is both congruent and parallel, then the quadrilateral is a parallelogram.

Theorem 50
If a parallelogram is a rhombus, then its diagonals are perpendicular.

Theorem 51
If a parallelogram is a rhombus, then each diagonal bisects a pair of opposite angles.

Theorem 52
If a parallelogram is a rectangle, then its diagonals are congruent.

Theorem 53
If the diagonals of a parallelogram are perpendicular, then the parallelogram is a rhombus.

Theorem 54
If one diagonal of a parallelogram bisects a pair of opposite angles, then the parallelogram is a rhombus.

Theorem 55
If the diagonals of a parallelogram are congruent, then the parallelogram is a rectangle.

Theorem 56
If a quadrilateral is an isosceles trapezoid, then each pair of base angles is congruent.

Theorem 57
If a quadrilateral is an isosceles trapezoid, then its diagonals are congruent.

Theorem 58
Trapezoid Midsegment Theorem
If a quadrilateral is a trapezoid, then

(1) the midsegment is parallel to the bases, and

(2) the length of the midsegment is half the sum of the lengths of the bases.

Theorem 59
If a quadrilateral is a kite, then its diagonals are perpendicular.

Theorem 60
Side-Angle-Side Similarity (SAS ~) Theorem
If an angle of one triangle is congruent to an angle of a second triangle, and the sides that include the two angles are proportional, then the triangles are similar.

Theorem 61
Side-Side-Side Similarity (SSS ~) Theorem
If the corresponding sides of two triangles are proportional, then the triangles are similar.

Theorem 62
The altitude to the hypotenuse of a right triangle divides the triangle into two triangles that are similar to the original triangle and to each other.

Corollary 1
The length of the altitude to the hypotenuse of a right triangle is the geometric mean of the lengths of the segments of the hypotenuse.

Corollary 2
The altitude to the hypotenuse of a right triangle separates the hypotenuse so that the length of each leg of the triangle is the geometric mean of the length of the hypotenuse and the length of the segment of the hypotenuse adjacent to the leg.

Theorem 63
Side-Splitter Theorem
If a line is parallel to one side of a triangle and intersects the other two sides, then it divides those sides proportionally.

Converse
If a line divides two sides of a triangle proportionally, then it is parallel to the third side.

Corollary
If three parallel lines intersect two transversals, then the segments intercepted on the transversals are proportional.

Theorem 64
Triangle-Angle-Bisector Theorem
If a ray bisects an angle of a triangle, then it divides the opposite side into two segments that are proportional to the other two sides of the triangle.

Theorem 65
Pythagorean Theorem
If a triangle is a right triangle, then the sum of the squares of the lengths of the legs is equal to the square of the length of the hypotenuse.

Theorem 66
Converse of the Pythagorean Theorem
If the sum of the squares of the lengths of two sides of a triangle is equal to the square of the length of the third side, then the triangle is a right triangle.

Theorem 67
If the square of the length of the longest side of a triangle is greater than the sum of the squares of the lengths of the other two sides, then the triangle is obtuse.

Theorem 68
If the square of the length of the longest side of a triangle is less than the sum of the squares of the lengths of the other two sides, then the triangle is acute.

Theorem 69
45°-45°-90° Triangle Theorem
In a 45°-45°-90° triangle, both legs are congruent and the length of the hypotenuse is $\sqrt{2}$ times the length of a leg.

Theorem 70
30°-60°-90° Triangle Theorem
In a 30°-60°-90° triangle, the length of the hypotenuse is twice the length of the shorter leg. The length of the longer leg is $\sqrt{3}$ times the length of the shorter leg.

hypotenuse = 2 • shorter leg longer leg 5 $\sqrt{3}$ • shorter leg.

Theorem 71
Area of a Regular Polygon
The area of a regular polygon is half the product of the apothem and the perimeter.

Theorem 72
Circumference of a Circle
The circumference of a circle is π times the diameter.

$C = \pi d$ or $C = 2\pi r$

Theorem 73
Arc Length
The length of an arc of a circle is the product of the ratio $\frac{\text{measure of the arc}}{360}$ and the circumference of the circle.

length of $\widehat{AB} = \frac{m\widehat{AB}}{360} \cdot 2\pi r$ or

length of $\widehat{AB} = \frac{m\widehat{AB}}{360} \cdot \pi d$

Theorem 74
Area of a Circle
The area of a circle is the product of π and the square of the radius.

$A = \pi r^2$

Theorem 75
Area of a Sector of a Circle
The area of a sector of a circle is the product of the ratio $\frac{\text{measure of the arc}}{360}$ and the area of the circle.
Area of sector $AOB = \frac{m\widehat{AB}}{360} \cdot \pi r^2$

Theorem 76
If a line is tangent to a circle, then the line is perpendicular to the radius at the point of tangency.

Theorem 77
If a line in the plane of a circle is perpendicular to a radius at its endpoint on the circle, then the line is tangent to the circle.

Theorem 78
If two segments are tangent to a circle from a point outside the circle, then the two segments are congruent.

Theorem 79
Within a circle or in congruent circles, congruent central angles have congruent arcs.

> **Converse**
> Within a circle or in congruent circles, congruent arcs have congruent central angles.

Theorem 80
Within a circle or in congruent circles, congruent central angles have congruent chords.

> **Converse**
> Within a circle or in congruent circles, congruent chords have congruent central angles.

Theorem 81
Within a circle or in congruent circles, congruent chords have congruent arcs.

> **Converse**
> Within a circle or in congruent circles, congruent arcs have congruent chords.

Theorem 82
Within a circle or in congruent circles, chords equidistant from the center (or centers) are congruent.

> **Converse**
> Within a circle or in congruent circles, congruent chords are equidistant from the center (or centers).

Theorem 83
In a circle, if a diameter is perpendicular to a chord, it bisects the chord and its arc.

Theorem 84

In a circle, if a diameter bisects a chord (that is not a diameter), it is perpendicular to the chord.

Theorem 85

In a circle, the perpendicular bisector of a chord contains the center of the circle.

Theorem 86

Inscribed Angle Theorem

The measure of an inscribed angle is half the measure of its intercepted arc.

Corollary 1

Two inscribed angles that intercept the same arc are congruent.

Corollary 2

An angle inscribed in a semicircle is a right angle.

Corollary 3

The opposite angles of a quadrilateral inscribed in a circle are supplementary.

Theorem 87

The measure of an angle formed by a tangent and a chord is half the measure of the intercepted arc.

Theorem 88

The measure of an angle formed by two lines that intersect inside a circle is half the sum of the measures of the intercepted arcs.

Theorem 89

The measure of an angle formed by two lines that intersect outside a circle is half the difference of the measures of the intercepted arcs.

Theorem 90

For a given point and circle, the product of the lengths of the two segments from the point to the circle is constant along any line through the point and circle.

Theorem 91

Lateral and Surface Areas of a Prism

The lateral area of a right prism is the product of the perimeter of the base and the height of the prism.

$$L.A. = ph$$

The surface area of a right prism is the sum of the lateral area and the areas of the two bases.

$$S.A. = L.A. + 2B$$

Theorem 92

Lateral and Surface Areas of a Cylinder

The lateral area of a right cylinder is the product of the circumference of the base and the height of the cylinder.

$$L.A. = 2\pi rh, \text{ or } L.A. = \pi dh$$

The surface area of a right cylinder is the sum of the lateral area and areas of the two bases.

$$S.A. = L.A. + 2B, \text{ or } S.A. = \pi rh + 2\pi r^2$$

Theorem 93

Lateral and Surface Areas of a Pyramid

The lateral area of a regular pyramid is half the product of the perimeter p of the base and the slant height ℓ of the pyramid.

$$L.A. = \tfrac{1}{2}p\ell$$

The surface area of a regular pyramid is the sum of the lateral area and the area B of the base.

$$S.A. = L.A. + B$$

Theorem 94

Lateral and Surface Areas of a Cone

The lateral area of a right cone is half the product of the circumference of the base and the slant height of the cone.

$$L.A. = \tfrac{1}{2} \cdot 2\pi r\ell \text{ or } L.A. = \pi r\ell$$

The surface area of a right cone is the sum of the lateral area and the area of the base.

$$S.A. = L.A. + B$$

Theorem 95

Cavalieri's Principle

If two space figures have the same height and the same cross-sectional area at every level, then they have the same volume.

Theorem 96

Volume of a Prism

The volume of a prism is the product of the area of the base and the height of the prism.

$$V = Bh$$

Theorem 97

Volume of a Cylinder

The volume of a cylinder is the product of the area of the base and the height of the cylinder.

$$V = Bh, \text{ or } V = \pi r^2h$$

Theorem 98

Volume of a Pyramid

The volume of a pyramid is one third the product of the area of the base and the height of the pyramid.

$$V = \tfrac{1}{3}Bh$$

Theorem 99
Volume of a Cone
The volume of a cone is one third the product of the area of the base and the height of the cone.

$V = \frac{1}{3}Bh$ or $V = \frac{1}{3}\pi r^2 h$

Theorem 100
Surface Area of a Sphere
The surface area of a sphere is four times the product of π and the square of the radius of the sphere.

$V = 4\pi r^2$

Theorem 101
Volume of a Sphere
The volume of a sphere is four thirds the product of π and the cube of the radius of the sphere.

$V = \frac{4}{3}\pi r^3$

Visual **Glossary**

A

Absolute value of a complex number (p. 780)   The absolute value of a complex number is its distance from the origin on the complex number plane. In general, $|a + bi| = \sqrt{a^2 + b^2}$.

Valor absoluto de un número complejo (p. 780)   El valor absoluto de un número complejo es la distancia a la que está del origen en el plano de números complejo. Generalmente, $|a + bi| = \sqrt{a^2 + b^2}$.

Example $|3 - 4i| = \sqrt{3^2 + (-4)^2} = 5$

Adjacent arcs (p. 468)   Adjacent arcs are on the same circle and have exactly one point in common.

Arcos adyacentes (p. 468)   Los arcos adyacentes están en el mismo círculo y tienen exactamente un punto en común.

Example

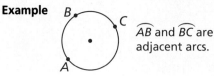

$\overset{\frown}{AB}$ and $\overset{\frown}{BC}$ are adjacent arcs.

Alternate interior (exterior) angles (p. 67) Alternate interior (exterior) angles are nonadjacent interior (exterior) angles that lie on opposite sides of the transversal.

Ángulos alternos internos (externos) (p. 67)   Los ángulos alternos internos (externos) son ángulos internos (externos) no adyacentes situados en lados opuestos de la transversal.

Example

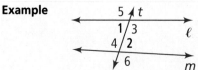

∠1 and ∠2 are alternate interior angles, as are ∠3 and ∠4. ∠5 and ∠6 are alternate exterior angles.

Altitude   *See* **cone; cylinder; parallelogram; prism; pyramid; trapezoid.**

Altura   *Ver* **cone; cylinder; parallelogram; prism; pyramid; trapezoid.**

Altitude of a triangle (p. 225)   An altitude of a triangle is the perpendicular segment from a vertex to the line containing the side opposite that vertex.

Altura de un triángulo (p. 225)   Una altura de un triángulo es el segmento perpendicular que va desde un vértice hasta la recta que contiene el lado opuesto a ese vértice.

Example

Altitude

Angle of elevation or depression (p. 447)   An angle of elevation (depression) is the angle formed by a horizontal line and the line of sight to an object above (below) the horizontal line.

Ángulo de elevación o depresión (p. 447)   Un ángulo de elevación (depresión) es el ángulo formado por una línea horizontal y la recta que va de esa línea a un objeto situado arriba (debajo) de ella.

Example

Horizontal line

B

Angle of depression

Angle of elevation

A

Horizontal line

Visual **Glossary**

English

Spanish

Apothem (p. 454)   The apothem of a regular polygon is the distance from the center to a side.

Apotema (p. 454)   La apotema de un polígono regular es la distancia desde el centro hasta un lado.

Example

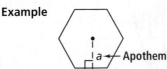

Arc length (p. 471)   The length of an arc of a circle is the product of the ratio $\frac{\text{measure of the arc}}{360}$ and the circumference of the circle.

Longitud de un arco (p. 471)   La longitud del arco de un círculo es el producto del cociente $\frac{\text{medida del arco}}{360}$ por la circunferencia del círculo.

Example

$$\text{Length of } \overset{\frown}{DE} = \frac{60}{360} \cdot 2\pi(5) = \frac{5\pi}{3}$$

Arithmetic mean (p. 966)   The arithmetic mean, or average, of two numbers is their sum divided by two.

Media aritmética (p. 966)   La media aritmética, o promedio, de dos números es su suma dividida por dos.

Example   The arithmetic mean of 12 and 15 is $\frac{12 + 15}{2} = 13.5$.

Arithmetic sequence (p. 964)   An arithmetic sequence is a sequence with a constant difference between consecutive terms.

Secuencia aritmética (p. 964)   Una secuencia aritmética es una secuencia de números en la que la diferencia entre dos números consecutivos es constante.

Example   The arithmetic sequence 1, 5, 9, 13, . . . has a common difference of 4.

Arithmetic series (p. 979)   An arithmetic series is a series whose terms form an arithmetic sequence.

Serie aritmética (p. 979)   Una serie aritmética es una serie cuyos términos forman una progresión aritmética.

Example $1 + 5 + 9 + 13 + 17 + 21$ is an arithmetic series with six terms.

Auxiliary line (p. 99)   An auxiliary line is a line that is added to a diagram to help explain relationships in proofs.

Línea auxiliar (p. 99)   Una línea auxiliar es aquella que se le agrega a un diagrama para explicar la relación entre pruebas.

Example

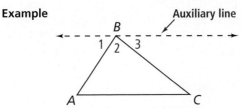

Axis of symmetry (p. 707) The line that divides a parabola into two matching halves.

Eje de simetría (p. 707) El eje de simetría es la línea que divide una parábola en dos mitades exactamente iguales.

Example

axis of symmetry

B

Base(s) *See* cone; cylinder; isosceles triangle; parallelogram; prism; pyramid; trapezoid.

Base(s) *Ver* cone; cylinder; parallelogram; prism; pyramid; trapezoid; triangle.

Base angles *See* trapezoid; isosceles triangle.

Ángulos de base *Ver* trapezoid; isosceles triangle.

Biconditional (p. 26) A biconditional statement is the combination of a conditional statement and its converse. A biconditional contains the words "if and only if."

Bicondicional (p. 26) Un enunciado bicondicional es la combinación de un enunciado condicional y su recíproco. El enunciado bicondicional incluye las palabras "si y solo si".

Example This biconditional statement is true: Two angles are congruent *if and only if* they have the same measure.

Binomial (p. 641) A polynomial of two terms.

Binomio (p. 641) Polinomio compuesto de dos términos.

Example $3x + 7$ is a binomial.

C

Center *See* circle; dilation; regular polygon; rotation; sphere.

Centro *Ver* circle; dilation; regular polygon; rotation; sphere.

Central angle of a circle (p. 467) A central angle of a circle is an angle whose vertex is the center of the circle.

Ángulo central de un círculo (p. 467) Un ángulo central de un círculo es un ángulo cuyo vértice es el centro del círculo.

Example

$\angle ROK$ is a central angle of $\odot O$.

English

Spanish

Centroid of a triangle (p. 223) The centroid of a triangle is the point of concurrency of the medians of the triangle.

Centroide de un triángulo (p. 223) El centroide de un triángulo es el punto de intersección de sus medianas.

Example P is the centroid of $\triangle ABC$.

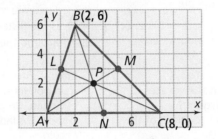

Chord (p. 498) A chord of a circle is a segment whose endpoints are on the circle.

Cuerda (p. 498) Una cuerda de un círculo es un segmento cuyos extremos son dos puntos del círculo.

Example

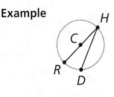

$\overline{HD}$ and $\overline{HR}$ are chords of $\odot C$.

Circle (p. 467) A circle is the set of all points in a plane that are a given distance, the *radius*, from a given point, the *center*. The standard form for an equation of a circle with center (h, k) and radius r is $(x - h)^2 + (y - k)^2 = r^2$.

Círculo (p. 467) Un círculo es el conjunto de todos los puntos de un plano situados a una distancia dada, el *radio*, de un punto dado, el *centro*. La fórmula normal de la ecuación de un círculo con centro (h, k) y radio r es $(x - h)^2 + (y - k)^2 = r^2$.

Example

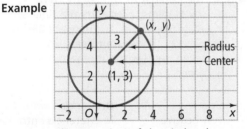

The equation of the circle whose center is (1, 3) and whose radius is 3 is $(x - 1)^2 + (y - 3)^2 = 9$.

Circumcenter of a triangle (p. 215) The circumcenter of a triangle is the point of concurrency of the perpendicular bisectors of the sides of the triangle.

Circuncentro de un triángulo (p. 215) El circuncentro de un triángulo es el punto de intersección de las bisectrices perpendiculares de los lados del triángulo.

Example

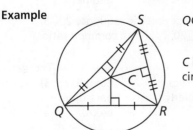

$QC = SC = RC$

C is the circumcenter.

Visual Glossary

Circumference (p. 470) The circumference of a circle is the distance around the circle. Given the radius r of a circle, you can find its circumference C by using the formula $C = 2\pi r$.

Example
$$C = 2\pi r$$
$$= 2\pi(4)$$
$$= 8\pi$$

Circumference is the distance around the circle.

Circunferencia (p. 470) La circunferencia de un círculo es la distancia alrededor del círculo. Dado el radio r de un círculo, se puede hallar la circunferencia C usando la fórmula $C = 2\pi r$.

Circumscribed about (p. 215) A circle is circumscribed about a polygon if the vertices of the polygon are on the circle. A polygon is circumscribed about a circle if all the sides of the polygon are tangent to the circle.

Example

$\odot G$ is circumscribed about $ABCD$.

$\triangle XYZ$ is circumscribed about $\odot P$.

Circunscritoa (p. 215) Un círculo está circunscrito a un polígono si los vértices del polígono están en el círculo. Un polígono está circunscrito a un círculo si todos los lados del polígono son tangentes al círculo.

Combination (p. 858) Any unordered selection of r objects from a set of n objects is a combination. The number of combinations of n objects taken r at a time is $_nC_r = \frac{n!}{r!(n-r)!}$ for $0 \le r \le n$.

Example The number of combinations of seven items taken four at a time is $_7C_4 = \frac{7!}{4!(7-4)!} = 35$. There are 35 ways to choose four items from seven items without regard to order.

Combinación (p. 858) Cualquier selección no ordenada de r objetos tomados de un conjunto de n objetos es una combinación. El número de combinaciones de n objetos, cuando se toman r objetos cada vez, es $_nC_r = \frac{n!}{r!(n-r)!}$ para $0 \le r \le n$.

Common difference (p. 964) A common difference is the difference between consecutive terms of an arithmetic sequence.

Example The arithmetic sequence 1, 5, 9, 13, . . . has a common difference of 4.

Diferencia común (p. 964) La diferencia común es la diferencia entre los términos consecutivos de una progresión aritmética.

Common ratio (p. 971) A common ratio is the ratio of consecutive terms of a geometric sequence.

Example The geometric sequence 2.5, 5, 10, 20, . . . has a common ratio of 2.

Razón común (p. 971) Una razón común es la razón de términos consecutivos en una secuencia geométrica.

Compass (p. 3) A compass is a geometric tool used to draw circles and parts of circles, called arcs.

Compás (p. 3) El compás es un instrumento usado para dibujar círculos y partes de círculos, llamados arcos.

English

Spanish

Complement of an event (p. 844) All possible outcomes that are not in the event. P(complement of event) = $1 - P$(event)

Complemento de un suceso (p. 844) Todos los resultados posibles que no se dan en el suceso. P(complemento de un suceso) = $1 - P$(suceso)

Example The complement of rolling a 1 or a 2 on a standard number cube is rolling a 3, 4, 5, or 6.

Completing the square (p. 760) A method of solving quadratic equations. Completing the square turns every quadratic equation into the form $x^2 = c$.

Completar el cuadrado (p. 760) Método para solucionar ecuaciones cuadráticas. Cuando se completa el cuadrado, se transforma la ecuación cuadática a la formula $x^2 = c$.

Example $x^2 + 6x - 7 = 9$ is rewritten as $(x + 3)^2 = 25$ by completing the square.

Complex conjugates (p. 784) Number pairs of the form $a + bi$ and $a - bi$ are complex conjugates.

Conjugados complejos (p. 784) Los pares de números de la forma $a + bi$ y $a - bi$ son conjugados complejos.

Example The complex number $2 - 3i$ and $2 + 3i$ are complex conjugates.

Complex number (p. 780) Complex numbers are the real numbers and the imaginary numbers.

Número complejo (p. 780) Los números complejos son los números reales y los números imaginarios.

Example $6 + i$, 7, $2i$

Complex number plane (p. 780) The complex number plane is identical to the coordinate plane except each ordered pair (a, b) represents the complex number $a + bi$. The horizontal axis is the Real axis. The vertical axis is the Imaginary axis.

Plano de números complejos (p. 780) El plano de los números complejos es idéntico al plano de coordenadas, a excepción de que cada par ordenado (a, b) representa el número complejo $a + bi$. El eje horizontal es el eje real. El eje vertical es el eje imaginario.

Example

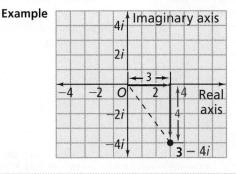

Composite function (p. 945) A composite function is a combination of two functions such that the output from the first function becomes the input for the second function.

Función compuesta (p. 945) Una función compuesta es la combinación de dos funciones. La cantidad de salida de la primera función es la cantidad de entrada de la segunda función.

Example $f(x) = 2x + 1$, $g(x) = x^2 - 1$
$(g \circ f)(x) = g(f(5)) = g(2(5) + 1)$
$= g(11) = 11^2 - 1$
$= 120$

English

Spanish

Composite space figures (p. 564)   A composite space figure is the combination of two or more figures into one object.

Figuras geométricas compuestas (p. 564)   Una figura geométrica compuesta es la combinación de dos o más figuras en un mismo objeto.

Example

Compound event (p. 865)   An event that consists of two or more events linked by the word *and* or the word *or*.

Suceso compuesto (p. 865)   Suceso que consiste en dos o más sucesos unidos por medio de la palabra *y* o la palabra *o*.

Example Rolling a 5 on a standard number cube and then rolling a 4 is a compound event.

Concentric circles (p. 470)   Concentric circles lie in the same plane and have the same center.

Círculos concéntricos (p. 470)   Los círculos concéntricos están en el mismo plano y tienen el mismo centro

Example

The two circles both have center *D* and are therefore concentric.

Conclusion (p. 19)   The conclusion is the part of an *if-then* statement (conditional) that follows *then*.

Conclusión (p. 19)   La conclusión es lo que sigue a la palabra *entonces* en un enunciado (condicional), *si . . . , entonces . . .*

Example In the statement, "If it rains, then I will go outside," the conclusion is "I will go outside."

Concurrent lines (p. 215)   Concurrent lines are three or more lines that meet in one point. The point at which they meet is the *point of concurrency*.

Rectas concurrentes (p. 215)   Las rectas concurrentes son tres o más rectas que se unen en un punto. El punto en que se unen es el *punto de concurrencia*.

Example

Point *E* is the point of concurrency of the bisectors of the angles of △*ABC*. The bisectors are concurrent.

Conditional (p. 19)   A conditional is an *if-then* statement.

Condicional (p. 19)   Un enunciado condicional es del tipo *si . . ., entonces . . .*

Example *If* you act politely, *then* you will earn respect.

English

Conditional probability (p. 874) A conditional probability contains a condition that may limit the sample space for an event. The notation $P(B \mid A)$ is read "the probability of event B, given event A." For any two events A and B in the sample space, $P(B \mid A) = \frac{P(A \text{ and } B)}{P(A)}$.

Example $= \frac{P(\text{departs and arrives on time})}{P(\text{departs on time})}$

$= \frac{0.75}{0.83}$

≈ 0.9

Cone (p. 552) A cone is a three-dimensional figure that has a circular *base*, a *vertex* not in the plane of the circle, and a curved lateral surface, as shown in the diagram. The *altitude* of a cone is the perpendicular segment from the vertex to the plane of the base. The *height* is the length of the altitude. In a *right cone*, the altitude contains the center of the base. The *slant height* of a right cone is the distance from the vertex to the edge of the base.

Example

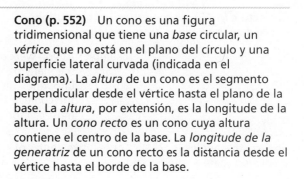

Right cone

Congruence transformation (p. 186) *See* isometry.

Congruent circles (p. 467) Congruent circles are circles whose radii are congruent.

Example

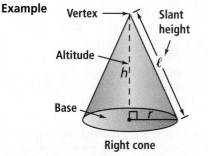

$\odot A$ and $\odot B$ have the same radius, so $\odot A \cong \odot B$.

Spanish

Probabilidad condicional (p. 874) Una probabilidad condicional contiene una condición que puede limitar el espacio muestral de un suceso. La notación $P(B \mid A)$ se lee "la probabilidad del suceso B, dado el suceso A". Para dos sucesos cualesquiera A y B en el espacio muestral, $P(B \mid A) = \frac{P(A \text{ y } B)}{P(A)}$.

Cono (p. 552) Un cono es una figura tridimensional que tiene una *base* circular, un *vértice* que no está en el plano del círculo y una superficie lateral curvada (indicada en el diagrama). La *altura* de un cono es el segmento perpendicular desde el vértice hasta el plano de la base. La *altura*, por extensión, es la longitud de la altura. Un *cono recto* es un cono cuya altura contiene el centro de la base. La *longitud de la generatriz* de un cono recto es la distancia desde el vértice hasta el borde de la base.

Transformación de congruencia (p. 186) *Ver* isometry.

Círculos congruentes (p. 467) Los círculos congruentes son círculos cuyos radios son congruentes.

English

Spanish

Congruent polygons (p. 121) Congruent polygons are polygons that have corresponding sides congruent and corresponding angles congruent.

Polígonos congruentes (p. 121) Los polígonos congruentes son polígonos cuyos lados correspondientes son congruentes y cuyos ángulos correspondientes son congruentes.

Example

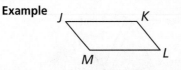

$\triangle DEF \cong \triangle GHI$

Conjecture (p. 12) A conjecture is a conclusion reached by using inductive reasoning.

Conjetura (p. 12) Una conjetura es una conclusión obtienda usando el razonamiento inductivo.

Example As you walk down the street, you see many people holding unopened umbrellas. You make the conjecture that the forecast must call for rain.

Consecutive angles (p. 271) Consecutive angles of a polygon share a common side.

Ángulos consecutivos (p. 271) Los ángulos consecutivos de un polígono tienen un lado común.

Example

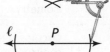

In $\square JKLM$, $\angle J$ and $\angle M$ are consecutive angles, as are $\angle J$ and $\angle K$. $\angle J$ and $\angle L$ are *not* consecutive.

Construction (p. 3) A construction is a geometric figure made with only a straightedge and compass.

Construcción (p. 3) Una construcción es una figura geométrica trazada solamente con una regla sin graduación y un compás.

Example

The diagram shows the construction (in progress) of a line perpendicular to a line ℓ through a point P on ℓ.

Contrapositive (p. 22) The contrapositive of the conditional "if p, then q" is the conditional "if not q, then not p." A conditional and its contrapositive always have the same truth value.

Contrapositivo (p. 22) El contrapositivo del condicional "si p, entonces q" es el condicional "si no q, entonces no p". Un condicional y su contrapositivo siempre tienen el mismo valor verdadero.

Example **Conditional:** If a figure is a triangle, then it is a polygon.
Contrapositive: If a figure is not a polygon, then it is not a triangle.

English

Spanish

Converge (p. 993) An infinite series $a_1 + a_2 + \ldots + a_n + \ldots$ converges if the sum $a_1 + a_2 + \ldots + a_n$ gets closer and closer to a real number as n increases.

Convergir (p. 993) Una serie infinita $a_1 + a_2 + \ldots + a_n + \ldots$ es convergente si la suma $a_1 + a_2 + \ldots + a_n$ se aproxima cada vez más a un número real a medida que el valor de n incrementa.

Example $1 + \frac{1}{2} + \frac{1}{4} + \frac{1}{8} + \ldots$ converges.

Converse (p. 22) The statement obtained by reversing the hypothesis and conclusion of a conditional.

Expresión recíproca (p. 22) Enunciado que se obtiene al intercambiar la hipótesis y la conclusión de una situación condicional.

Example The converse of "If I was born in Houston, then I am a Texan" would be "If I am a Texan, then I am born in Houston."

Coordinate proof (p. 319) *See* **proof.**

Prueba de coordenadas (p. 319) *Ver* **proof.**

Corollary (p. 159) A corollary is a theorem that can be proved easily using another theorem.

Corolario (p. 159) Un corolario es un teorema que se puede probar fácilmente usando otro teorema.

Example **Theorem:** If two sides of a triangle are congruent, then the angles opposite those sides are congruent.
Corollary: If a triangle is equilateral, then it is equiangular.

Corresponding angles (p. 67) Corresponding angles lie on the same side of the transversal t and in corresponding positions relative to ℓ and m.

Ángulos correspondientes (p. 67) Los ángulos correspondientes están en el mismo lado de la transversal t y en las correspondientes posiciones relativas a ℓ y m.

Example

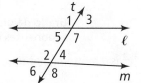

$\angle 1$ and $\angle 2$ are corresponding angles, as are $\angle 3$ and $\angle 4$, $\angle 5$ and $\angle 6$, and $\angle 7$ and $\angle 8$.

Counterexample (p. 14) An example showing that a statement is false.

Contraejemplo (p. 14) Ejemplo que demuestra que un enunciado es falso.

Example **Statement:** All apples are red.
Counterexample: A Granny Smith Apple is green.

Cross Products Property (p. 409) The product of the extremes of a proportion is equal to the product of the means.

Propiedad de los productos cruzados (p. 409) El producto de los extremos de una proporción es igual al producto de los medios.

Example If $\frac{x}{3} = \frac{12}{21}$, then $21x = 3 \cdot 12$

English

Spanish

Cylinder (p. 542) A cylinder is a three-dimensional figure with two congruent circular *bases* that lie in parallel planes. An *altitude* of a cylinder is a perpendicular segment that joins the planes of the bases. Its length is the *height* of the cylinder. In a *right cylinder*, the segment joining the centers of the bases is an altitude. In an *oblique cylinder*, the segment joining the centers of the bases is not perpendicular to the planes containing the bases.

Cilindro (p. 542) Un cilindro es una figura tridimensional con dos *bases* congruentes circulares en planos paralelos. Una *altura* de un cilindro es un segmento perpendicular que une los planos de las bases. Su longitud es, por extensión, la *altura* del cilindro. En un *cilindro recto*, el segmento que une los centros de las bases es una altura. En un *cilindro oblicuo*, el segmento que une los centros de las bases no es perpendicular a los planos que contienen las bases.

Example

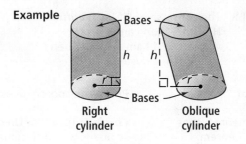

Right cylinder   Oblique cylinder

D

Deductive reasoning (p. 34) Deductive reasoning is a process of reasoning logically from given facts to a conclusion.

Razonamiento deductivo (p. 34) El razonamiento deductivo es un proceso de razonamiento lógico que parte de hechos dados hasta llegar a una conclusión.

Example Based on the fact that the sum of any two even numbers is even, you can deduce that the product of any whole number and any even number is even.

Degree of a monomial (p. 639) The sum of the exponents of the variables of a monomial.

Grado de un monomio (p. 639) La suma de los exponentes de las variables de un monomio.

Example $-4x^3y^2$ is a monomial of degree 5.

Degree of a polynomial (p. 640) The highest degree of any term of the polynomial.

Grado de un polinomio (p. 640) El grado de un polinomio es el grado mayor de cualquier término del polinomio.

Example The polynomial $P(x) = x^6 + 2x^3 - 3$ has degree 6.

Dependent events (p. 865) When the outcome of one event affects the probability of a second event, the events are dependent events.

Sucesos dependientes (p. 865) Dos sucesos son dependientes si el resultado de un suceso afecta la probabilidad del otro.

Example You have a bag with marbles of different colors. If you pick a marble from the bag and pick another without replacing the first, the events are dependent events.

English

Diameter of a circle (p. 467)   A diameter of a circle is a segment that contains the center of the circle and whose endpoints are on the circle. The term *diameter* can also mean the length of this segment.

Diameter of a sphere (p. 581)   The diameter of a sphere is a segment passing through the center, with endpoints on the sphere.

Example

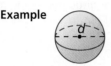

Difference of squares (p. 688)   A difference of two squares is an expression of the form $a^2 - b^2$. It can be factored as $(a + b)(a - b)$.

Example $25a^2 - 4 = (5a + 2)(5a - 2)$
$m^6 - 1 = (m^3 + 1)(m^3 - 1)$

Dilation (p. 393)   A dilation is a transformation that has *center* C and *scale factor* n, where $n > 0$, and maps a point R to R' in such a way that R' is on $\overrightarrow{CR}$ and $CR' = n \cdot CR$. The center of a dilation is its own image. If $n > 1$, the dilation is an *enlargement*, and if $0 < n < 1$, the dilation is a *reduction*.

Example

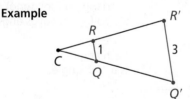

$\overline{R'Q'}$ is the image of $\overline{RQ}$ under a dilation with center C and scale factor 3.

Directrix (p. 814)   The directrix of a parabola is the fixed line used to define a parabola. Each point of the parabola is the same distance from the focus and the directrix.

Example

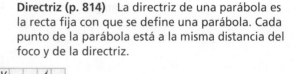

Spanish

Diámetro de un circulo (p. 467)   Un diámetro de un círculo es un segmento que contiene el centro del ciírculo y cuyos extremos estan en el círculo. El término *diámetro* tambien puedi referirse a la longitud de este segmento.

Diametro de una esfera (p. 581)   El diametro de unaesfera es un segmento que contiene el centro de la esfera y the sphere. cuyos extremos estan en la esfera.

Diferencia de dos cuadrados (p. 688)   La diferencia de dos cuadrados es una expresión de la forma $a^2 - b^2$. Se puede factorizar como $(a + b)(a - b)$.

Dilatacion (p. 393)   Una dilatacion, o *transformacion de semejanza*, tiene *centro* C y *factor de escala* n para $n > 0$, y asocia un punto R a R' de tal modo que R' esta en $\overrightarrow{CR}$ y $CR' = n \cdot CR$. El centro de una dilatacion es su propia imagen. Si $n > 1$, la dilatacion es un *aumento*, y si $0 < n < 1$, la a *reduction*. dilatacion es una *reduccion*.

Directriz (p. 814)   La directriz de una parábola es la recta fija con que se define una parábola. Cada punto de la parábola está a la misma distancia del foco y de la directriz.

English   # Spanish

Discriminant (p. 773) The discriminant of a quadratic equation of the form $ax^2 + bx + c = 0$ is $b^2 - 4ac$. The value of the discriminant determines the number of solutions of the equation.

Discriminante (p. 773) El discriminante de una ecuación cuadrática $ax^2 + bx + c = 0$ es $b^2 - 4ac$. El valor del discriminante determina el número de soluciones de la ecuación.

Example The discriminant of
$2x^2 + 9x - 2 = 0$ is 97.

Distance from a point to a line (p. 210) The distance from a point to a line is the length of the perpendicular segment from the point to the line.

Distancia desde un punto hasta una recta (p. 210) La distancia desde un punto hasta una recta es la longitud del segmento perpendicular que va desde el punto hasta la recta.

Example

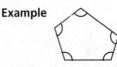

The distance from point P to a line ℓ
is PT.

Diverge (p. 993) An infinite series diverges if it does not converge.

Divergir (p. 993) Una serie infinita es divergente si no es convergente.

Example $1 + 2 + 4 + 8 + \ldots$ diverges.

E

Enlargement (p. 394) *See* **dilation.**

Aumento (p. 394) *Ver* **dilation.**

Equiangular triangle or polygon (p. 264) An equiangular triangle (polygon) is a triangle (polygon) whose angles are all congruent.

Triángulo o polígono equiángulo (p. 264) Un triángulo (polígono) equiángulo es un triángulo (polígono) cuyos ángulos son todos congruentes.

Example

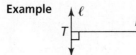

Each angle of the pentagon
is a 108° angle.

Equidistant (p. 207) A point is equidistant from two objects if it is the same distance from the objects.

Equidistante (p. 207) Un punto es equidistante de dos objetos si la distancia entre el punto y los objetos es igual.

Example

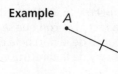

Point B is equidistant
from points A and C.

Equilateral triangle or polygon (p. 264) An equilateral triangle (polygon) is a triangle (polygon) whose sides are all congruent.

Triángulo o polígono equilátero (p. 264) Un triángulo (polígono) equilátero es un triángulo (polígono) cuyos lados son todos congruentes.

Example

Each side of the quadrilateral
is 1.2 cm long.

Visual **Glossary**

English

Spanish

Equivalent statements (p. 22) Equivalent statements are statements with the same truth value.

Enunciados equivalentes (p. 22) Los enunciados equivalentes son enunciados con el mismo valor verdadero.

Example The following statements are equivalent: If a figure is a square, then it is a rectangle. If a figure is not a rectangle, then it is not a square.

Event (p. 841) Any group of outcomes in a situation involving probability.

Suceso (p. 841) En la probabilidad, cualquier grupo de resultados.

Example When rolling a number cube, there are six possible outcomes. Rolling an even number is an event with three possible outcomes, 2, 4, and 6.

Expected value (p. 890) The average value you can expect for a large number of trials of an experiment; the sum of each outcome's value multiplied by its probability.

Valor esperado (p. 890) El valor promedio que se puede esperar para una cantidad grande de pruebas en un experimento; la suma de los valores de los resultados multiplicados cada uno por su probabilidad.

Example In a game, a player has a 25% probability of earning 10 points by spinning an even number and a 75% probability of earning 5 points by spinning an odd number.
expected value =
$0.25(10) + 0.75(5) = 6.25$

Experimental probability (p. 842) The ratio of the number of times an event actually happens to the number of times the experiment is done.

$P(\text{event}) = \dfrac{\text{number of times an event happens}}{\text{number of times the experiment is done}}$

Probabilidad experimental (p. 842) La razón entre el número de veces que un suceso sucede en la realidad y el número de veces que se hace el experimento.

$P(\text{suceso}) = \dfrac{\text{número de veces que sucede un suceso}}{\text{número de veces que se hace el experimento}}$

Example A baseball player's batting average shows how likely it is that a player will get a hit, based on previous times at bat.

Explicit formula (p. 955) An explicit formula expresses the nth term of a sequence in terms of n.

Fórmula explícita (p. 955) Una fórmula explícita expresa el n-ésimo término de una progresión en función de n.

Example Let $a_n = 2n + 5$ for positive integers n. If $n = 7$, then $a_7 = 2(7) + 5 = 19$.

Extended proportion (p. 348) *See* **proportion.**

Proporción extendida (p. 348) *Ver* **proportion.**

Extended ratio (p. 339) *See* **ratio.**

Razón extendida (p. 339) *Ver* **ratio.**

Glossary

English

Spanish

Exterior angle of a polygon (p. 101)   An exterior angle of a polygon is an angle formed by a side and an extension of an adjacent side.

Ángulo exterior de un polígono (p. 101)   El ángulo exterior de un polígono es un ángulo formado por un lado y una extensión de un lado adyacente.

Example

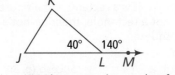

$\angle KLM$ is an exterior angle of $\triangle JKL$.

Extremes of a proportion (p. 340)   In the proportion $\frac{a}{b} = \frac{c}{d}$, a and d are the extremes.

Valores extremos de una proporción (p. 340)   En la proporción $\frac{a}{b} = \frac{c}{d}$, a y d son los valores extremos.

Example   The product of the extremes of $\frac{x}{4} = \frac{x+3}{2}$ is $2x$.

F

Factor by grouping (p. 694)   A method of factoring that uses the Distributive Property to remove a common binomial factor of two pairs of terms.

Factor común por agrupación de términos (p. 694)   Método de factorización que aplica la propiedad distributiva para sacar un factor común de dos pares de términos en un binomio.

Example   The expression $7x(x - 1) + 4(x - 1)$ can be factored as $(7x + 4)(x - 1)$.

Finite Series (p. 979)   A finite series is a series with a finite number of terms.

Serie finite (p. 979)   Una serie finita es una serie con un número finito de términos.

Flow proof (p. 84)   *See* **proof.**

Prueba de flujo (p. 84)   *Ver* **proof.**

Focal length (p. 814)   The focal length of a parabola is the distance between the vertex and the focus.

Distancia focal (p. 814)   La distancia focal de una parábola es la distancia entre el vértice y el foco.

Focus (plural: foci) of a parabola (p. 814)   A parabola is the set of all points in a plane that are the same distance from a fixed line and a fixed point not on the line. The fixed point is the focus of the parabola.

Foco de una parabola (p. 814)   Una parábola es el conjunto de todos los puntos en un plano con la misma distancia desde una línea fija y un punto fijo que no permanece en la línea. El punto fijo es el foco de la parábola.

Frequency table (p. 848)   A table that groups a set of data values into intervals and shows the frequency for each interval.

Tabla de frecuencias (p. 848)   Tabla que agrupa un conjunto de datos en intervalos y muestra la frecuencia de cada intervalo.

Example

Interval	Frequency
0–9	5
10–19	8
20–29	4

Visual Glossary

English

Fundamental Counting Principle (p. 855) If there are m ways to make the first selection and n ways to make the second selection, then there are $m \cdot n$ ways to make the two selections.

Example For 5 shirts and 8 pairs of shorts, the number of possible outfits is $5 \cdot 8 = 40$.

G

Geometric mean (p. 371, 975) The geometric mean is the number x such that $\frac{a}{x} = \frac{x}{b}$, where a, b, and x are positive numbers.

Example The geometric mean of 6 and 24 is 12.
$$\frac{6}{x} = \frac{x}{24}$$
$$x^2 = 144$$
$$x = 12$$

Geometric sequence (p. 971) A geometric sequence is a sequence with a constant ratio between consecutive terms.

Example The geometric sequence 2.5, 5, 10, 20, 40 ..., has a common ratio of 2.

Geometric series (p. 991) A geometric series is the sum of the terms in a geometric sequence.

Example One geometric series with five terms is $2.5 + 5 + 10 + 20 + 40$.

Great circle (p. 581) A great circle is the intersection of a sphere and a plane containing the center of the sphere. A great circle divides a sphere into two *hemispheres*.

Example Hemispheres   Great circle

Greatest integer function (p. 933) The greatest integer function corresponds each input x to the greatest integer less than or equal to x.

Spanish

Principio fundamental de Conteo (p. 855) Si hay m maneras de hacer la primera selección y n maneras de hacer la segunda selección, quiere decir que hay $m \cdot n$ maneras de hacer las dos selecciones.

Media geométrica (p. 371, 975) La media geométrica es el número x tanto que $\frac{a}{x} = \frac{x}{b}$, donde a, b y x son números positivos.

Secuencia geométrica (p. 971) Una secuencia geométrica es una secuencia con una razón constante entre términos consecutivos.

Serie geométrica (p. 991) Una serie geométrica es la suma de términos en una progresión geométrica.

Círculo máximo (p. 581) Un círculo máximo es la intersección de una esfera y un plano que contiene el centro de la esfera. Un círculo máximo divide una esfera en dos *hemisferios*.

Función del entero mayor (p. 933) La función del entero mayor relaciona cada entrada x con el entero mayor que es menor oigual a x.

Visual **Glossary**

Height *See* **cone; cylinder; parallelogram; prism; pyramid; trapezoid.**

Altura *Ver* **cone; cylinder; parallelogram; prism; pyramid; trapezoid.**

Hemisphere (p. 581) *See* **great circle.**

Hemisferio (p. 000) *Ver* **great circle.**

Hypotenuse (p. 165) *See* **right triangle.**

Hipotenusa (p. 165) *Ver* **right triangle.**

Hypothesis (p. 19) In an *if-then* statement (conditional) the hypothesis is the part that follows *if*.

Hipótesis (p. 19) En un enunciado *si . . . entonces . . .* (condicional), la hipótesis es la parte del enunciado que sigue el *si*.

Example In the conditional "If an animal has four legs, then it is a horse," the hypothesis is "an animal has four legs."

I

Imaginary number (p. 780) An imaginary number is any number of the form $a + bi$, where a and b are real numbers and $b \neq 0$.

Número imaginario (p. 780) Un número imaginario es cualquier número de la forma $a + bi$, donde a y b son números reales y $b \neq 0$.

Example $2 + 3i$, $7i$, i

Imaginary unit (p. 778) The imaginary unit i is the complex number whose square is -1.

Unidad imaginaria (p. 778) La unidad imaginaria i es el número complejo cuyo cuadrado es -1.

Incenter of a triangle (p. 218) The incenter of a triangle is the point of concurrency of the angle bisectors of the triangle.

Incentro de un triángulo (p. 218) El incentro de un triángulo es el punto donde concurren las tres bisectrices de los ángulos del triángulo.

Example

$XI = YI = ZI$

I is the incenter.

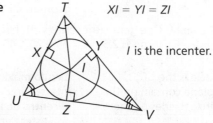

Independent events (p. 865) When the outcome of one event does not affect the probability of a second event, the two events are independent

Sucesos independientes (p. 865) Cuando el resultado de un suceso no altera la probabilidad de otro, los dos sucesos son independientes.

Example The results of two rolls of a number cube are independent. Getting a 5 on the first roll does not change the probability of getting a 5 on the second roll.

Index (p. 624) With a radical sign, the index indicates the degree of the root.

Índice (p. 624) Con un signo de radical, el índice indica el grado de la raíz.

Example index 2 index 3 index 4
$$\sqrt{16} \quad \sqrt[3]{16} \quad \sqrt[4]{16}$$

English

Spanish

Indirect measurement (p. 364) Indirect measurement is a way of measuring things that are difficult to measure directly.

Medición indirecta (p. 364) La medición indirecta es un modo de medir cosas difíciles de medir directamente.

Example By measuring the distances shown in the diagram and using proportions of similar figures, you can find the height of the taller tower. $\frac{196}{540} = \frac{x}{1300} \to x \approx 472$ ft

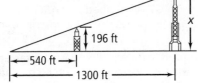

196 ft

540 ft

1300 ft

x

Indirect proof (p. 232) *See* **indirect reasoning; proof.**

Prueba indirecta (p. 232) *Ver* **indirect reasoning; proof.**

Indirect reasoning (p. 232) Indirect reasoning is a type of reasoning in which all possiblities are considered and then all but one are proved false. The remaining possibility must be true.

Razonamiento indirecto (p. 232) Razonamiento indirecto es un tipo de razonamiento en el que se consideran todas las posibilidades y se prueba que todas son falsas, a excepción de una. La posibilidad restante debe ser verdadera.

Example Eduardo spent more than $60 on two books at a store. Prove that at least one book costs more than $30. **Proof:** Suppose neither costs more than $30. Then he spent no more than $60 at the store. Since this contradicts the given information, at least one book costs more than $30.

Inductive reasoning (p. 11) Inductive reasoning is a type of reasoning that reaches conclusions based on a pattern of specific examples or past events.

Razonamiento inductivo (p. 11) El razonamiento inductivo es un tipo de razonamiento en el cual se llega a conclusiones con base en un patrón de ejemplos específicos o sucesos pasados.

Example You see four people walk into a building. Each person emerges with a small bag containing food. You use inductive reasoning to conclude that this building contains a restaurant.

Infinite series (p. 979) An infinite series is a series with infinitely many terms.

Serie infinita (p. 979) Una serie infinita es una serie con un número infinito de términos.

Inscribed angle (p. 509) An angle is inscribed in a circle if the vertex of the angle is on the circle and the sides of the angle are chords of the circle.

Ángulo inscrito (p. 509) Un ángulo está inscrito en un círculo si el vértice del ángulo está en el círculo y los lados del ángulo son cuerdas del círculo.

Example

$\angle C$ is inscribed in $\odot M$.

English

Spanish

Inscribed in (p. 218) A circle is inscribed in a polygon if the sides of the polygon are tangent to the circle. A polygon is inscribed in a circle if the vertices of the polygon are on the circle.

Inscrito en (p. 218) Un círculo está inscrito en un polígono si los lados del polígono son tangentes al círculo. Un polígono está inscrito en un círculo si los vértices del polígono están en el círculo.

Example

$\odot T$ is inscribed in $\triangle XYZ$.

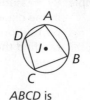

$ABCD$ is inscribed in $\odot J$.

Intercepted arc (p. 509) An intercepted arc is an arc of a circle having endpoints on the sides of an inscribed angle, and its other points in the interior of the angle.

Arco interceptor (p. 509) Un arco interceptor es un arco de un círculo cuyos extremos están en los lados de un ángulo inscrito y los punto restantes están en el interior del ángulo.

Example

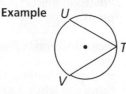

$\overset{\frown}{UV}$ is the intercepted arc of inscribed $\angle T$.

Inverse (p. 22) The inverse of the conditional "if p, then q" is the conditional "if not p, then not q."

Inverso (p. 22) El inverso del condicional "si p, entonces q" es el condicional "si no p, entonces no q".

Example **Conditional:** If a figure is a square, then it is a parallelogram.
Inverse: If a figure is not a square, then it is not a parallelogram.

Inverse function (p. 946) If function f pairs a value b with a then its inverse, denoted f^{-1}, pairs the value a with b. If f^{-1} is also a function, then f and f^{-1} are inverse functions.

Funcion inversa (p. 946) Si la función f empareja un valor b con a, entonces su inversa, cuya notación es f^{-1}, empareja el valor a con b. Si f^{-1} también es una función, entonces f y f^{-1} son funciones inversas.

Example If $f(x) = x + 3$, then $f^{-1}(x) = x - 3$.

Isometry (p. 181) An isometry, also known as a *congruence transformation,* is a transformation in which an original figure and its image are congruent.

Isometría (p. 181) Una isometría, conocida también como una *transformación de congruencia,* es una transformación en donde una figura original y su imagen son congruentes.

Isosceles trapezoid (p. 306) An isosceles trapezoid is a trapezoid whose nonparallel opposite sides are congruent.

Trapecio isósceles (p. 306) Un trapecio isosceles es un trapecio cuyos lados opuestos no paralelos son congruentes.

Example

English

Isosceles triangle An isosceles triangle is a triangle that has at least two congruent sides. If there are two congruent sides, they are called *legs*. The *vertex angle* is between them. The third side is called the *base* and the other two angles are called the *base angles*.

Example

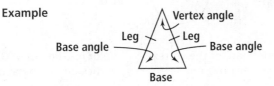

Vertex angle
Leg   Leg
Base angle   Base angle
Base

Spanish

Triángulo isósceles Un triángulo isósceles es un triángulo que tiene por lo menos dos lados congruentes. Si tiene dos lados congruentes, éstos se llaman *catetos*. Entre ellos se encuentra el *ángulo del vértice*. El tercer lado se llama *base* y los otros dos ángulos se llaman *ángulos de base*.

K

Kite (p. 310) A kite is a quadrilateral with two pairs of consecutive sides congruent and no opposite sides congruent.

Example

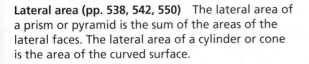

Cometa (p. 310) Una cometa es un cuadrilátero con dos pares de lados congruentes consecutivos y sin lados opuestos congruentes.

L

Lateral area (pp. 538, 542, 550) The lateral area of a prism or pyramid is the sum of the areas of the lateral faces. The lateral area of a cylinder or cone is the area of the curved surface.

Área lateral (pp. 538, 542, 550) El área lateral de un prisma o pirámide es la suma de las áreas de sus caras laterals. El área lateral de un cilindro o de un cono es el área de la superficie curvada.

Example

6 cm
5 cm
5 cm

$$\text{L.A. of pyramid} = \frac{1}{2}p\ell$$
$$= \frac{1}{2}(20)(6)$$
$$= 60 \text{ cm}^2$$

Lateral face *See* **prism; pyramid.**

Cara lateral *Ver* **prism; pyramid.**

Leg *See* **isosceles triangle; right triangle; trapezoid.**

Cateto *Ver* **isosceles triangle; right triangle; trapezoid.**

Limits (p. 982) Limits in summation notation are the least and greatest integer values of the index *n*.

Límites (p. 982) Los límites en notación de sumatoria son el menor y el mayor valor del índice *n* en números enteros.

Example

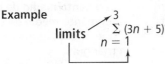

$$\text{limits} \nearrow \sum_{n=1}^{3} (3n + 5)$$

Major arc (p. 467) A major arc of a circle is an arc that is larger than a semicircle.

Arco mayor (p. 467) Un arco mayor de un círculo es cualquier arco más grande que un semicírculo.

Example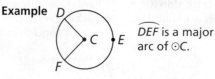

$\overset{\frown}{DEF}$ is a major arc of $\odot C$.

Maximum (p. 708) The y-coordinate of the vertex of a parabola that opens downward.

Valor máximo (p. 708) La coordenada y del vértice en una parábola que se abre hacia abajo.

Example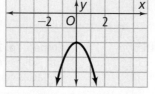

Since the parabola opens downward, the y-coordinate of the vertex is the function's maximum value.

Means of a proportion (p. 340) In the proportion $\frac{a}{b} = \frac{c}{d}$, b and c are the means.

Valores medios de una proporción (p. 340) En la proporción $\frac{a}{b} = \frac{c}{d}$, b y c son los valores medios.

Example The product of the means of $\frac{x}{4} = \frac{x+3}{2}$ is $4(x + 3)$ or $4x + 12$.

Median of a triangle (p. 223) A median of a triangle is a segment that has as its endpoints a vertex of the triangle and the midpoint of the opposite side.

Mediana de un triángulo (p. 223) Una mediana de un triángulo es un segmento que tiene en sus extremos el vértice del triángulo y el punto medio del lado opuesto.

Example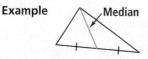

Midsegment of a trapezoid (p. 308) The midsegment of a trapezoid is the segment that joins the midpoints of the nonparallel opposite sides of a trapezoid.

Segmento medio de un triángulo (p. 308) Un segmento medio de un triángulo es un segmento que une los puntos medios de dos lados del triángulo.

Example ——Midsegment

Midsegment of a triangle (p. 199) A midsegment of a triangle is a segment that joins the midpoints of two sides of the triangle.

Segmento medio de un triángulo (p. 199) Un segmento medio de un triángulo es un segmento que une los puntos medios de dos lados del triángulo.

Example  Midsegment

English

Spanish

Minimum (p. 708) The y-coordinate of the vertex of a parabola that opens upward.

Valor mínimo (p. 708) La coordenada y del vértice en una parábola que se abre hacia arriba.

Example

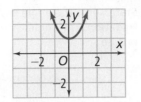

Since the parabola opens upward, the y-coordinate of the vertex is the function's minimum value.

Minor arc (p. 467) A minor arc is an arc that is smaller than a semicircle.

Arco menor (p. 467) Un arco menor de un círculo es un arco más corto que un semicírculo.

Example

$\widehat{KC}$ is a minor arc of $\odot S$.

Monomial (p. 639) A real number, a variable, or a product of a real number and one or more variables with whole-number exponents.

Monomio (p. 639) Número real, variable o el producto de un número real y una o más variables con números enteros como exponentes.

Example 9, n, and $-5xy^2$ are examples of monomials.

Mutually exclusive events (p. 868) When two events cannot happen at the same time, the events are mutually exclusive. If A and B are mutually exclusive events, then $P(A \text{ or } B) = P(A) + P(B)$.

Sucesos mutuamente excluyentes (p. 868) Cuando dos sucesos no pueden ocurrir al mismo tiempo, son mutuamente excluyentes. Si A y B son sucesos mutuamente excluyentes, entonces $P(A \text{ o } B) = P(A) + P(B)$.

Example Rolling an even number E and rolling a multiple of five M on a standard number cube are mutually exclusive events.
$$P(E \text{ or } M) = P(E) + P(M)$$
$$= \frac{3}{6} + \frac{1}{6}$$
$$= \frac{4}{6}$$
$$= \frac{2}{3}$$

N

Natural base exponential function (p. 909) A natural base exponential function is an exponential function with base e.

Función exponencial con base natural (p. 909) Ua función exponencial con base natural es una función exponencial con base e.

n factorial (p. 857) The product of the integers from n down to 1, for any positive integer n. You write n factorial as $n!$. The value of $0!$ is defined to be 1.

n factorial (p. 857) Producto de todos los enteros desde n hasta 1, de cualquier entero positivo n. El factorial de n se escribe $n!$. El valor de $0!$ se define como 1.

Example $4! = 4 \cdot 3 \cdot 2 \cdot 1 = 24$

Negation (p. 22) The negation of a statement has the opposite meaning of the original statement.

Negación (p. 22) La negación de un enunciado tiene el sentido opuesto del enunciado original.

Example Statement: The angle is obtuse.
Negation: The angle is not obtuse.

Oblique cylinder or prism *See* **cylinder; prism.**

Cilindro oblicuo o prisma *Ver* **cylinder; prism.**

Opposite angles (p. 270) Opposite angles of a quadrilateral are two angles that do not share a side.

Ángulos opuestos (p. 270) Los ángulos opuestos de un cuadrilátero son dos ángulos que no comparten lados.

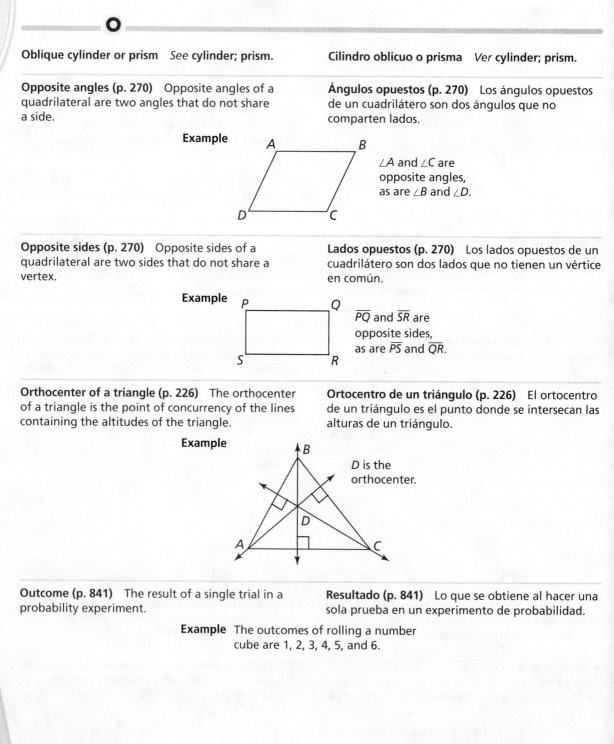

Example

∠A and ∠C are opposite angles, as are ∠B and ∠D.

Opposite sides (p. 270) Opposite sides of a quadrilateral are two sides that do not share a vertex.

Lados opuestos (p. 270) Los lados opuestos de un cuadrilátero son dos lados que no tienen un vértice en común.

Example

$\overline{PQ}$ and $\overline{SR}$ are opposite sides, as are $\overline{PS}$ and $\overline{QR}$.

Orthocenter of a triangle (p. 226) The orthocenter of a triangle is the point of concurrency of the lines containing the altitudes of the triangle.

Ortocentro de un triángulo (p. 226) El ortocentro de un triángulo es el punto donde se intersecan las alturas de un triángulo.

Example

D is the orthocenter.

Outcome (p. 841) The result of a single trial in a probability experiment.

Resultado (p. 841) Lo que se obtiene al hacer una sola prueba en un experimento de probabilidad.

Example The outcomes of rolling a number cube are 1, 2, 3, 4, 5, and 6.

Overlapping events (p. 869)   Events that have at least one common outcome. If A and B are overlapping events, then $P(A$ or $B) = P(A) + P(B) - P(A$ and $B)$.

Sucesos traslapados (p. 869)   Sucesos que tienen por lo menos un resultado en común. Si A y B son sucesos traslapados, entonces $P(A$ ó $B) = P(A) + P(B) - P(A$ y $B)$.

Example   Rolling a multiple of 3 and rolling an odd number on a number cube are overlapping events.

$P($multiple of 3 or odd$) = P($multiple of 3$) + P($odd$) - P($multiple of 3 and odd$)$

$$= \frac{1}{3} + \frac{1}{2} - \frac{1}{6}$$
$$= \frac{2}{3}$$

P

Parabola (p. 707)   The graph of a quadratic function.

Parábola (p. 707)   La gráfica de una función cuadrática.

Example

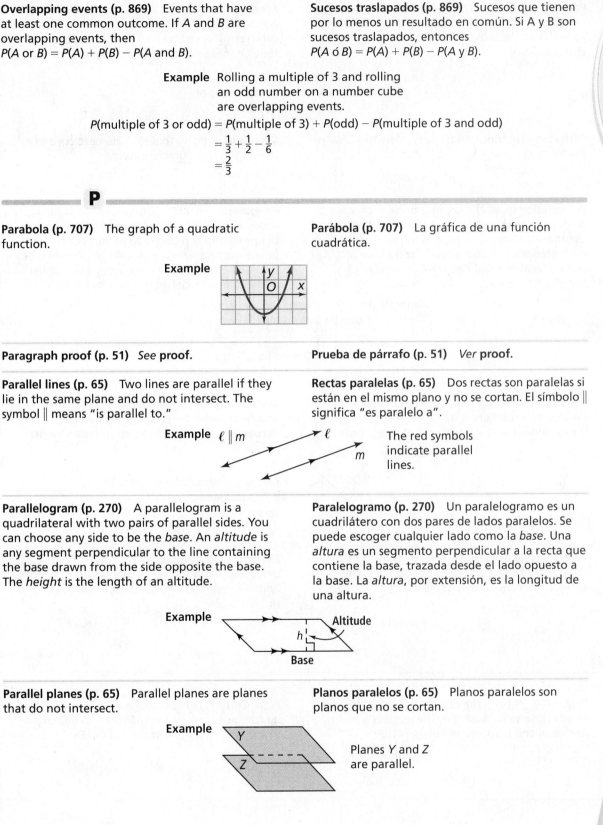

Paragraph proof (p. 51)   *See* **proof.**

Prueba de párrafo (p. 51)   *Ver* **proof.**

Parallel lines (p. 65)   Two lines are parallel if they lie in the same plane and do not intersect. The symbol ‖ means "is parallel to."

Rectas paralelas (p. 65)   Dos rectas son paralelas si están en el mismo plano y no se cortan. El símbolo ‖ significa "es paralelo a".

Example $\ell \parallel m$

ℓ
m

The red symbols indicate parallel lines.

Parallelogram (p. 270)   A parallelogram is a quadrilateral with two pairs of parallel sides. You can choose any side to be the *base*. An *altitude* is any segment perpendicular to the line containing the base drawn from the side opposite the base. The *height* is the length of an altitude.

Paralelogramo (p. 270)   Un paralelogramo es un cuadrilátero con dos pares de lados paralelos. Se puede escoger cualquier lado como la *base*. Una *altura* es un segmento perpendicular a la recta que contiene la base, trazada desde el lado opuesto a la base. La *altura*, por extensión, es la longitud de una altura.

Example

Altitude

h

Base

Parallel planes (p. 65)   Parallel planes are planes that do not intersect.

Planos paralelos (p. 65)   Planos paralelos son planos que no se cortan.

Example

Y

Z

Planes Y and Z are parallel.

English

Spanish

Parent function (p. 707) A family of functions is a group of functions with common characteristics. A parent function is the simplest function with these characteristics.

Función elemental (p. 707) Una familia de funciones es un grupo de funciones con características en común. La función elemental es la función más simple que reúne esas características.

Example $y = x$ is the parent function for the family of linear equations of the form $y = mx + b$.

Perfect square trinomial (p. 685) Any trinomial of the form $a^2 + 2ab + b^2$ or $a^2 - 2ab + b^2$.

Cuadrado perfecto (p. 685) Número cuya raíz cuadrada es un número entero.

Example $(x + 3)^2 = x^2 + 6x + 9$

Permutation (p. 857) An arrangement of some or all of a set of objects in a specific order. You can use the notation $_nP_r$ to express the number of permutations, where n equals the number of objects available and r equals the number of selections to make.

Permutación (p. 857) Disposición de algunos o de todos los objetos de un conjunto en un orden determinado. El número de permutaciones se puede expresar con la notación $_nP_r$, donde n es igual al número total de objetos y r es igual al número de selecciones que han de hacerse.

Example How many ways can you arrange 5 objects 3 at a time?

$$_3P_5 = \frac{5!}{(5-3)!} = \frac{5!}{2!} = \frac{5 \cdot 4 \cdot 3 \cdot 2 \cdot 1}{2 \cdot 1} = 60$$

There are 60 ways to arrange 5 objects 3 at a time.

Perpendicular bisector (p. 5) The perpendicular bisector of a segment is a line, segment, or ray that is perpendicular to the segment at its midpoint.

Mediatriz (p. 5) La mediatriz de un segmento es una recta, segmento o semirrecta que es perpendicular al segmento en su punto medio.

Example

$\overleftrightarrow{YZ}$ is the perpendicular bisector of $\overline{AB}$. It is perpendicular to $\overline{AB}$ and intersects $\overline{AB}$ at midpoint M.

Perpendicular lines (p. 5) Perpendicular lines are lines that intersect and form right angles. The symbol $\perp$ means "is perpendicular to."

Rectas perpendiculares (p. 5) Las rectas perpendiculares son rectas que se cortan y forman ángulos rectos. El símbolo $\perp$ significa "es perpendicular".

Example

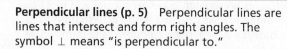

$m \perp n$

Pi (p. 470) Pi (π) is the ratio of the circumference of any circle to its diameter. The number π is irrational and is approximately 3.14159.

Pi (p. 470) Pi (π) es la razón de la circunferencia de cualquier círculo a su diámetro. El número π es irracional y se aproxima a $\pi \approx 3.14159$.

Example

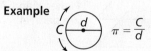

$\pi = \frac{C}{d}$

English

Spanish

Piecewise function (p. 930) A piecewise function has different rules for different parts of its domain.

Función de fragmentos (p. 930) Una función de fragmentos tiene reglas diferentes para diferentes partes de su dominio.

Point of concurrency (p. 215) *See* **concurrent lines.**

Punto de concurrencia (p. 215) *Ver* **concurrent lines.**

Point of tangency (p. 488) *See* **tangent to a circle.**

Punto de tangencia (p. 488) *Ver* **tangent to a circle.**

Polynomial (p. 640) A monomial or the sum or difference of two or more monomials. A quotient with a variable in the denominator is not a polynomial.

Polinomio (p. 640) Un monomio o la suma o diferencia de dos o más monomios. Un cociente con una variable en el denominador no es un polinomio.

Example $2x^2$, $3x + 7$, 28, and $-7x^3 - 2x^2 + 9$ are all polynomials.

Prism (p. 537) A prism is a polyhedron with two congruent and parallel faces, which are called the *bases*. The other faces, which are parallelograms, are called the *lateral faces*. An *altitude* of a prism is a perpendicular segment that joins the planes of the bases. Its length is the *height* of the prism. A *right prism* is one whose lateral faces are rectangular regions and a lateral edge is an altitude. In an *oblique prism*, some or all of the lateral faces are nonrectangular.

Prisma (p. 537) Un prisma es un poliedro con dos caras congruentes paralelas llamadas *bases*. Las otras caras son paralelogramos llamados *caras laterales*. La *altura* de un prisma es un segmento perpendicular que une los planos de las bases. Su longitud es también la *altura* del prisma. En un *prisma rectangular*, las caras laterales son rectangulares y una de las aristas laterales es la altura. En un *prisma oblicuo*, algunas o todas las caras laterales no son rectangulares.

Example

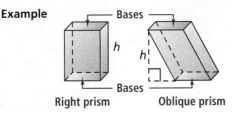

Right prism | Oblique prism

Probability (p. 841) How likely it is that an event will occur (written formally as P(event)).

Probabilidad (p. 841) La posibilidad de que un suceso ocurra, escrita formalmente P(suceso).

Example You have 4 red marbles and 3 white marbles. The probability that you select one red marble, and then, without replacing it, randomly select another red marble is $P(\text{red}) = \frac{4}{7} \cdot \frac{3}{6} = \frac{2}{7}$.

Visual Glossary

Probability distribution (p. 851) A probability distribution is a function that tells the probability of each outcome in a sample space.

Distribución de probabilidades (p. 851) Una distribución de probabilidades es una función que señala la probabilidad de que cada resultado ocurra en un espacio muestral.

Example

Roll	Fr.	Prob.
1	5	0.125
2	9	0.225
3	7	0.175
4	8	0.2
5	8	0.2
6	3	0.075

The table and graph both show the experimental probability distribution for the outcomes of 40 rolls of a standard number cube.

Proof (p. 44) A proof is a convincing argument that uses deductive reasoning. A proof can be written in many forms. In a *two-column proof*, the statements and reasons are aligned in columns. In a *paragraph proof*, the statements and reasons are connected in sentences. In a *flow proof*, arrows show the logical connections between the statements. In a *coordinate proof*, a figure is drawn on a coordinate plane and the formulas for slope, midpoint, and distance are used to prove properties of the figure. An *indirect proof* involves the use of indirect reasoning.

Prueba (p. 44) Una prueba es un argumento convincente en el cual se usa el razonamiento deductivo. Una prueba se puede escribir de varias maneras. En una *prueba de dos columnas*, los enunciados y las razones se alinean en columnas. En una *prueba de párrafo*, los enunciados y razones están unidos en oraciones. En una *prueba de flujo*, hay flechas que indican las conexiones lógicas entre enunciados. En una *prueba de coordenadas*, se dibuja una figura en un plano de coordenadas y se usan las fórmulas de la pendiente, punto medio y distancia para probar las propiedades de la figura. Una *prueba indirecta* incluye el uso de razonamiento indirecto.

Example

Given: $\triangle EFG$, with right angle $\angle F$
Prove: $\angle E$ and $\angle G$ are complementary.

Paragraph Proof: Because $\angle F$ is a right angle, $m\angle F = 90$. By the Triangle Angle-Sum Theorem, $m\angle E + m\angle F + m\angle G = 180$. By substitution, $m\angle E + 90 + m\angle G = 180$. Subtracting 90 from each side yields $m\angle E + m\angle G = 90$. $\angle E$ and $\angle G$ are complementary by definition.

Proportion (p. 340) A proportion is a statement that two ratios are equal. An *extended proportion* is a statement that three or more ratios are equal.

Proporción (p. 340) Una proporción es un enunciado en el cual dos razones son iguales. Una *proporción extendida* es un enunciado que dice que tres razones o más son iguales.

Example $\frac{x}{5} = \frac{3}{4}$ is a proportion.

$\frac{9}{27} = \frac{3}{9} = \frac{1}{3}$ is an extended proportion.

Pure imaginary number (p. 780) If $a = 0$ and $b \neq 0$, the number $a + bi$ is a pure imaginary number.

Número imaginario puro (p. 780) Si $a = 0$ y $b \neq 0$, el número $a + bi$ es un número imaginario puro.

Pyramid (p. 549) A pyramid is a polyhedron in which one face, the *base*, is a polygon and the other faces, the *lateral faces*, are triangles with a common vertex, called the *vertex* of the pyramid. An *altitude* of a pyramid is the perpendicular segment from the vertex to the plane of the base. Its length is the *height* of the pyramid. A *regular pyramid* is a pyramid whose base is a regular polygon and whose lateral faces are congruent isosceles triangles. The *slant height* of a regular pyramid is the length of an altitude of a lateral face.

Pirámide (p. 549) Una pirámide es un poliedro en donde una cara, la *base*, es un polígono y las otras caras, las *caras laterales*, son triángulos con un vértice común, llamado el *vértice* de la pirámide. Una *altura* de una pirámide es el segmento perpendicular que va del vértice hasta el plano de la base. Su longitud es, por extensión, la *altura* de la pirámide. Una *pirámide regular* es una pirámide cuya base es un polígono regular y cuyas caras laterales son triángulos isósceles congruentes. La *apotema* de una pirámide regular es la longitud de la altura de la cara lateral.

Example

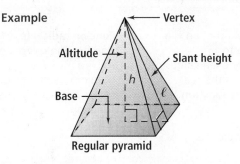

Vertex

Altitude

Slant height

Base

h ℓ

Regular pyramid

Pythagorean triple (p. 416) A Pythagorean triple is a set of three nonzero whole numbers a, b, and c, that satisfy the equation $a^2 + b^2 = c^2$.

Tripleta de Pitágoras (p. 416) Una tripleta de Pitágoras es un conjunto de tres números enteros positivos a, b, and c que satisfacen la ecuación $a^2 + b^2 = c^2$.

Example The numbers 5, 12, and 13 form a Pythagorean triple because $5^2 + 12^2 = 13^2 = 169$.

Q

Quadratic equation (p. 740) A quadratic equation is one that can be written in the standard form $ax^2 + bx + c = 0$, where $a \neq 0$.

Ecuación cuadrática (p. 740) Ecuación que puede expresarse de la forma normal como $ax^2 + bx + c = 0$, en la que $a \neq 0$.

Example $4x^2 + 9x - 5 = 0$

Quadratic formula (p. 768) If $ax^2 + bx + c = 0$ and $a \neq 0$, then $x = \frac{-b \pm \sqrt{b^2 - 4ac}}{2a}$.

Fórmula cuadrática (p. 768) Si $ax^2 + bx + c = 0$ y $a \neq 0$, entonces $x = \frac{-b \pm \sqrt{b^2 - 4ac}}{2a}$.

Example $2x^2 + 10x + 12 = 0$

$$x = \frac{-b \pm \sqrt{b^2 - 4ac}}{2a}$$

$$x = \frac{-10 \pm \sqrt{10^2 - 4(2)(12)}}{2(2)}$$

$$x = \frac{-10 \pm \sqrt{4}}{4}$$

$$x = \frac{-10 + 2}{4} \text{ or } \frac{-10 - 2}{4}$$

$$x = -2 \text{ or } -3$$

Quadratic function (p. 707)   A function of the form $y = ax^2 + bx + c$, where $a \neq 0$. The graph of a quadratic function is a parabola, a U-shaped curve that opens up or down.

Función cuadrática (p. 707)   La función $y = ax^2 + bx + c$, en la que $a \neq 0$. La gráfica de una función cuadrática es una parábola, o curva en forma de U que se abre hacia arriba o hacia abajo.

Example $y = 5x^2 - 2x + 1$ is a quadratic function.

Quadratic parent function (p. 707)   The simplest quadratic function $f(x) = x^2$ or $y = x^2$.

Función cuadrática madre (p. 707)   La función cuadrática más simple $f(x) = x^2$ ó $y = x^2$.

Example $y = x^2$ is the parent function for the family of quadratic equations of the form $y = ax^2 + bx + c$.

R

Radical function (p. 919)   A radical function is a function that can be written in the form $f(x) = a\sqrt[n]{x - h} + k$, where $a \neq 0$. For even values of n, the domain of a radical function is the real numbers $x \geq h$. *See also* **Square root function.**

Función radical (p. 919)   Una función radical es una función quepuede expresarse como $f(x) = a\sqrt[n]{x - h} + k$, donde $a \neq 0$. Para n par, el dominio de la función radical son los números reales tales que $x \geq h$. *Ver* también **Square root function.**

Example $f(x) = \sqrt{x - 2}$

Radicand (p. 624)   The expression under the radical sign is the radicand.

Radicando (p. 624)   La expresión que aparece debajo del signo radical es el radicando.

Example   The radicand of the radical expression $\sqrt{x + 2}$ is $x + 2$.

Radian Measure (p. 485)   The radian measure of a central angle of a circle is the ratio of the length of the intercepted arc to the radius of the circle. One radian is the measure of a central angle that intercepts an arc with length equal to the radius of the circle. On a unit circle, the radian measure of a central angle is the length of the arc it intercepts.

Medida en radianes (p. 485)   La medida en radianes de un ángulo central de un círculo es la razón de la longitud del arco interceptado al radio del círculo. Un radián es la medida de un ángulo central que intercepta un arco con una longitud igual al radio del círculo. En un círculo unitario, la medida en radianes de un ángulo central es la longitud del arco que este intercepta.

Radius of a circle (p. 467)   A radius of a circle is any segment with one endpoint on the circle and the other endpoint at the center of the circle. *Radius* can also mean the length of this segment.

Radio de un círculo (p. 467)   Un radio de un círculo es cualquier segmento con extremo en el círculo y el otro extremo en el centro del círculo. *Radio* también se refeiere a la longitud de este segmento.

Radius of a regular polygon (p. 454)   The radius of a regular polygon is the distance from the center to a vertex.

Radio de un polígono regular (p. 454)   El radio de un polígono regular es la distancia desde el centro hasta un vértice.

Example

English

Spanish

Radius of a sphere (p. 581) The radius of a sphere is a segment that has one endpoint at the center and the other endpoint on the sphere.

Radio de una esfera (p. 581) El radio de una esfera es un segmento con un extremo en el centro y otro en la esfera.

Example

Ratio (p. 337) A ratio is the comparison of two quantities by division.

Razón (p. 337) Una razón es la comparación de dos cantidades por medio de una división.

Example $\frac{5}{7}$ and $7 : 3$ are ratios.

Recursive formula (p. 956) A recursive formula defines the terms in a sequence by relating each term to the ones before it.

Fórmula recursiva (p. 956) Una fórmula recursiva define los términos de una secuencia al relacionar cada término con los términos que lo anteceden.

Example Let $a_n = 2.5a_{n-1} + 3a_{n-2}$. If $a_5 = 3$ and $a_4 = 7.5$, then $a_6 = 2.5(3) + 3(7.5) = 30$.

Rectangle (p. 289) A rectangle is a parallelogram with four right angles.

Rectángulo (p. 289) Un rectángulo es un paralelogramo con cuatro ángulos rectos.

Example

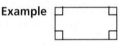

Reduction (p. 394) *See* **dilation.**

Reducción (p. 394) *Ver* **dilation.**

Regular polygon (p. 264) A regular polygon is a polygon that is both equilateral and equiangular. Its *center* is the point that is equidistant from its vertices.

Polígono regular (p. 264) Un polígono regular es un polígono que es equilateral y equiangular. Su *centro* es el punto equidistante de sus vértices.

Example

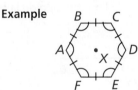

ABCDEF is a regular hexagon. Point *X* is its center.

Regular pyramid (p. 549) *See* **pyramid.**

Pirámide regular (p. 549) *Ver* **pyramid.**

Relative frequency (p. 848) The ratio of the number of times an event occurs to the total number of events in the sample space.

Frecuencia relativa (p. 848) La razón del número de veces que ocurre un evento al número de eventos en el espacio muestral.

Example

Archery Results				
Scoring Region	Yellow	Red	Blue	Black	White
Arrow Strikes	52	25	10	8	5

$$\text{Relative frequency of spinning 1} = \frac{\text{frequency of spinning 1}}{\text{total frequencies}}$$
$$= \frac{29}{100}$$

English

Spanish

Remote interior angles (p. 101) Remote interior angles are the two nonadjacent interior angles corresponding to each exterior angle of a triangle.

Ángulos interiores remotos (p. 101) Los ángulos interiores remotos son los dos ángulos interiores no adyacentes que corresponden a cada ángulo exterior de un triángulo.

Example

∠1 and ∠2 are remote interior angles of ∠3.

Rhombus (p. 289) A rhombus is a parallelogram with four congruent sides.

Rombo (p. 289) Un rombo es un paralelogramo de cuatro lados congruentes.

Example

Right cone (p. 552) *See* **cone.**

Cono recto (p. 552) *Ver* **cone.**

Right cylinder (p. 542) *See* **cylinder.**

Cilindro recto (p. 542) *Ver* **cylinder.**

Right prism (p. 538) *See* **prism.**

Prisma rectangular (p. 538) *Ver* **prism.**

Right triangle (p. 216) A right triangle contains one right angle. The side opposite the right angle is the *hypotenuse* and the other two sides are the *legs*.

Triángulo rectángulo (p. 216) Un triángulo rectángulo contiene un ángulo recto. El lado opuesto del ángulo recto es la *hipotenusa* y los otros dos lados son los *catetos*.

Root of the equation (p. 740) A solution of an equation.

Ráiz de la ecuación (p. 740) Solucion de una ecuación.

S

Same-side interior angles (p. 67) Same-side interior angles lie on the same side of the transversal *t* and between ℓ and *m*.

Ángulos internos del mismo lado (p. 67) Los ángulos internos del mismo lado están situados en el mismo lado de la transversal *t* y dentro de ℓ y *m*.

Example

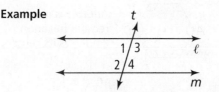

∠1 and ∠2 are same-side interior angles, as are ∠3 and ∠4.

Sample space (p. 841) The part of a population that is surveyed.

Muestra (p. 841) Porción que se estudia de una población.

Example Let the set of all males between the ages of 19 and 34 be the population. A random selection of 900 males between those ages would be a sample of the population.

English

Spanish

Scale (p. 352)   A scale is the ratio of any length in a scale drawing to the corresponding actual length. The lengths may be in different units.

Escala (p. 352)   Una escala es la razón de cualquier longitud en un dibujo a escala en relación a la longitud verdadera correspondiente. Las longitudes pueden expresarse en distintas unidades.

Scale drawing (p. 352)   A scale drawing is a drawing in which all lengths are proportional to corresponding actual lengths.

Dibujo a escala (p. 352)   Un dibujo a escala es un dibujo en el que todas las longitudes son proporcionales a las longitudes verdaderas correspondientes.

Example

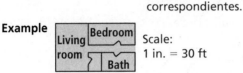

Scale:
1 in. = 30 ft

Scale factor (pp. 348, 393)   A scale factor is the ratio of corresponding linear measurements of two similar figures.

Factor de escala (pp. 348, 393)   El factor de escala es la razón de las medidas lineales correspondientes de dos figuras semejantes.

Example

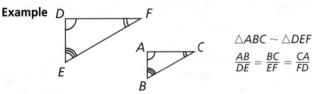

$\triangle ABC \sim \triangle DEF$

$\dfrac{AB}{DE} = \dfrac{BC}{EF} = \dfrac{CA}{FD}$

Scale factor of a dilation (p. 393)   The scale factor of a dilation is the ratio of the distances from the center of dilation to an image point and to its preimage point.

Factor de escala de dilatación (p. 393)   El factor de escala de dilatación es la razón de las distancias desde el centro de dilatación hasta un punto de la imagen y hasta un punto de la preimagen

Example

The scale factor of the dilation that maps $\triangle ABC$ to $\triangle A'B'C'$ is $\frac{1}{2}$.

Secant (p. 519)   A secant is a line, ray, or segment that intersects a circle at two points.

Secante (p. 519)   Una secante es una recta, semirrecta o segmento que corta un cículo en dos puntos.

Example

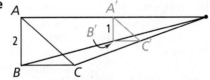

$\overleftrightarrow{AB}$ is a secant of $\odot C$.

Sector of a circle (p. 479)   A sector of a circle is the region bounded by two radii and their intercepted arc.

Sector de un círculo (p. 479)   Un sector de un círculo es la región limitada por dos radios y el arco abarcado por ellos.

Example

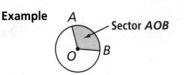

Sector *AOB*

Visual **Glossary**

Visual **Glossary**

Segment of a circle (p. 480)   A segment of a circle is the part of a circle bounded by an arc and the segment joining its endpoints.

Example

Segment of ⊙C

Segmento de un círculo (p. 480)   Un segmento de un círculo es la parte de un círculo bordeada por un arco y el segmento que une sus extremos.

Semicircle (p. 467)   A semicircle is half a circle.

Example

Semicircle

Semicírculo (p. 467)   Un semicírculo es la mitad de un círculo.

Sequence (p. 955)   A sequence is an ordered list of numbers.

Example   1, 4, 7, 10, …

Progresión (p. 955)   Una progresión es una sucesión de números.

Similar figures (pp. 348, 403)   Similar figures are two figures that have the same shape, but not necessarily the same size.

Example

Figuras semejantes (pp. 348, 403)   Los figuras semejantes son dos figuras que tienen la misma forma pero no necesariamente el mismo tamaño.

Similar polygons (p. 348)   Similar polygons are polygons having corresponding angles congruent and the lengths of corresponding sides proportional. You denote similarity by ~.

Example

$\triangle JKL \sim \triangle MNO$

Scale factor $= \frac{2}{5}$

Polígonos semejantes (p. 348)   Los polígonos semejantes son polígonos cuyos ángulos correspondientes son congruentes y las longitudes de los lados correspondientes son proporcionales. El símbolo ~ significa "es semejante a".

Similarity transformation (p. 403)   A composition of a rigid motion and a dilation.

Transformación de semejanza (p. 403)   Una transfomación que contiene un movimiento rígido y una dilatación.

Sine ratio (p. 438)   *See* **trigonometric ratios.**

Razón seno (p. 438)   *Ver* **trigonometric ratios.**

Skew lines (p. 65)   Skew lines are lines that do not lie in the same plane.

Example

$\overleftrightarrow{AB}$ and $\overleftrightarrow{EF}$ are skew.

Rectas cruzadas (p. 65)   Las rectas cruzadas son rectas que no están en el mismo plano.

English	Spanish
Slant height *See* **cone; pyramid.**	**Generatriz (cono) o apotema (pirámide)** *Ver* **cone; pyramid.**

Sphere (p. 581)   A sphere is the set of all points in space that are a given distance r, the *radius*, from a given point C, the *center*. A *great circle* is the intersection of a sphere with a plane containing the center of the sphere. The *circumference* of a sphere is the circumference of any great circle of the sphere.

Esfera (p. 581)   Una esfera es el conjunto de los puntos del espacio que están a una distancia dada r, el *radio*, de un punto dado C, el *centro*. Un *círculo máximo* es la intersección de una esfera y un plano que contiene el centro de la esfera. La *circunferencia* de una esfera es la circunferencia de cualquier círculo máximo de la esfera.

Example
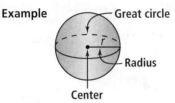
Great circle — Radius — Center

Square (p. 289)   A square is a parallelogram with four congruent sides and four right angles.

Cuadrado (p. 289)   Un cuadrado es un paralelogramo con cuatro lados congruentes y cuatro ángulos rectos.

Example
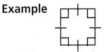

Square root function (p. 919)   A square root function is a function that can be written in the form $f(x) = a\sqrt{x - h} + k$, where $a \neq 0$. The domain of a square root function is all real numbers $x \geq h$.

Función de raíz cuadrada (p. 919)   Una función de raíz cuadrada es una función que puede ser expresada como $f(x) = a\sqrt{x - h} + k$, donde $a \neq 0$. El dominio de una función de raíz cuadrada son todos los números reales tales que $x \geq h$.

Example $f(x) = 2\sqrt{x - 3} + 4$

Standard form of a polynomial (p. 640)   The form of a polynomial that places the terms in descending order by degree.

Forma normal de un polinomio (p. 640)   Cuando el grado de los término de un de un polinomio disminuye de izquierda a derecha, está en forma normal, o en orden descendente.

Example $15x^3 + x^2 + 3x + 9$

Standard form of a quadratic equation (p. 740)   The standard form of a quadratic equation is $ax^2 + bx + c = 0$, where $a \neq 0$.

Forma normal de una ecuación cuadrática (p. 740)   Cuando una ecuación cuadrática se expresa de forma $ax^2 + bx + c = 0$, donde $a \neq 0$.

Example $-x^2 + 2x - 9 = 0$

Standard form of a quadratic function (p. 707)   The standard form of a quadratic function is $f(x) = ax^2 + bx + c$, where $a \neq 0$.

Forma normal de una función cuadrática (p. 707)   La forma normal de una función cuadrática es $f(x) = ax^2 + bx + c$, donde $a \neq 0$.

Example $f(x) = 2x^2 - 5x + 2$

Standard form of an equation of a circle (p. 824)   The standard form of an equation of a circle with center (h, k) and radius r is $(x - h)^2 + (y - k)^2 = r^2$.

Forma normal de la ecuación de un círculo (p. 824)   La forma normal de la ecuación de un círculo con un centro (h, k) y un radio r es $(x - h)^2 + (y - k)^2 = r^2$.

Example   In $(x + 5)^2 + (y + 2)^2 = 48$, $(-5, -2)$ is the center of the circle.

English

Spanish

Step function (p. 933) A step function pairs every number in an interval with a single value. The graph of a step function can look like the steps of a staircase.

Función escalón (p. 933) Una función escalón empareja cada número de un intervalo con un solo valor. La gráfica de una función escalón se puede parecer a los peldaños de una escalera.

Straightedge (p. 3) A straightedge is a ruler with no markings on it.

Regla sin graduación (p. 3) Una regla sin graduación no tiene marcas.

Surface area (pp. 538, 542, 550) The surface area of a prism, cylinder, pyramid, or cone is the sum of the lateral area and the areas of the bases. The surface area of a sphere is four times the area of a great circle.

Área (pp. 538, 542, 550) El área de un prisma, pirámide, cilindro o cono es la suma del área lateral y las áreas de las bases. El área de una esfera es igual a cuatro veces el área de un círculo máximo.

Example

$$\text{S.A. of prism} = \text{L.A.} + 2B$$
$$= 66 + 2(28)$$
$$= 122 \text{ cm}^2$$

T

Tangent to a circle (p. 488) A tangent to a circle is a line, segment, or ray in the plane of the circle that intersects the circle in exactly one point. That point is the *point of tangency*.

Tangente de un círculo (p. 488) Una tangente de un círculo es una recta, segmento o semirrecta en el plano del círculo que corta el círculo en exactamente un punto. Ese punto es el *punto de tangencia*.

Example

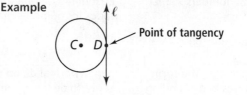

Point of tangency

Line ℓ is tangent to $\odot C$. Point D is the point of tangency.

Term of a sequence (p. 955) Each number in a sequence is a term.

Término de una progresión (p. 955) Cada número de una progresión es un término.

Example 1, 4, 7, 10, … The second term is 4.

Theorem (p. 48) A theorem is a conjecture that is proven.

Teorema (p. 48) Un teorema es una conjetura que se demuestra.

Example The theorem "Vertical angles are congruent" can be proven by using postulates, definitions, properties, and previously stated theorems.

Theoretical probability (p. 843) The ratio of the number of favorable outcomes to the number of possible outcomes if all outcomes have the same chance of happening.

$$P(\text{event}) = \frac{\text{number of favorable outcomes}}{\text{number of possible outcomes}}$$

Probabilidad teórica (p. 843) Si cada resultado tiene la misma probabilidad de darse, la probabilidad teórica de un suceso se calcula como la razón del número de resultados favorables al número de resultados posibles.

$$P(\text{suceso}) = \frac{\text{numero de resultados favorables}}{\text{numero de resultados posibles}}$$

Example   In tossing a coin, the events of getting heads or tails are equally likely. The likelihood of getting heads is $P(\text{heads}) = \frac{1}{2}$.

Transversal (p. 67)   A transversal is a line that intersects two or more lines at distinct points.

Transversal (p. 67)   Una transversal es una línea que interseca dos o más líneas en puntos precisos.

Example

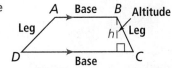

t is a transversal of ℓ and m.

Trapezoid (p. 306)   A trapezoid is a quadrilateral with exactly one pair of parallel sides, the *bases*. The nonparallel sides are called the *legs* of the trapezoid. Each pair of angles adjacent to a base are *base angles* of the trapezoid. An *altitude* of a trapezoid is a perpendicular segment from one base to the line containing the other base. Its length is called the *height* of the trapezoid.

Trapecio (p. 306)   Un trapecio es un cuadrilátero con exactamente un par de lados paralelos, las *bases*. Los lados no paralelos se llaman los *catetos* del trapecio. Cada par de ángulos adyacentes a la base son los *ángulos de base* del trapecio. Una *altura* del trapecio es un segmento perpendicular que va de una base a la recta que contiene la otra base. Su longitud se llama, por extensión, la *altura* del trapecio.

Example

In trapezoid $ABCD$, $\angle ADC$ and $\angle BCD$ are one pair of base angles, and $\angle DAB$ and $\angle ABC$ are the other.

Trigonometric ratios (p. 438)   In right $\triangle ABC$ with acute $\angle A$,

$$\text{sine } \angle A = \sin A = \frac{\text{leg opposite } \angle A}{\text{hypotenuse}}$$

$$\text{cosine } \angle A = \cos A = \frac{\text{leg adjacent to } \angle A}{\text{hypotenuse}}$$

$$\text{tangent } \angle A = \tan A = \frac{\text{leg opposite } \angle A}{\text{leg adjacent to } \angle A}$$

Razones trigonométricas (p. 438)   En un triángulo rectángulo $\triangle ABC$ con ángulo agudo $\angle A$,

$$\text{seno } \angle A = \text{sen } A = \frac{\text{cateto opuesto a } \angle A}{\text{hipotenusa}}$$

$$\text{coseno } \angle A = \cos A = \frac{\text{cateto adyecente a } \angle A}{\text{hipotenusa}}$$

$$\text{tangente } \angle A = \tan A = \frac{\text{cateto opuesto a } \angle A}{\text{cateto adyecente a } \angle A}$$

Example

Trinomial (p. 641)   A polynomial of three terms.

Trinomio (p. 641)   Polinomio compuesto de tres términos.

Example $3x^2 + 2x - 5$

Truth value (p. 21)   The truth value of a statement is "true" or "false" according to whether the statement is true or false, respectively.

Valor verdadero (p. 21)   El valor verdadero de un enunciado es "verdadero" o "falso" según el enunciado sea *verdadero* o falso, respectivamente.

Visual Glossary

Visual Glossary

Two-column proof (p. 44)   *See* **proof.**

Prueba de dos columnas (p. 44)   *Ver* **proof.**

Two-way frequency table (p. 873)   A table that displays frequencies in two different categories.

Tabla de frecuencias de doble entrada (p. 873) Una tabla de frecuencias que contiene dos categorías de datos.

Example

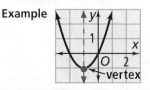

	Male	Female	Totals
Juniors	3	4	7
Seniors	3	2	5
Totals	6	6	12

V

Vertex of a parabola (p. 708)   The highest or lowest point on a parabola. The axis of symmetry intersects the parabola at the vertex.

Vértice de una parabola (p. 708)   El punto más alto o más bajo de una parábola. El punto de intersección del eje de simetría y la parábola.

Example

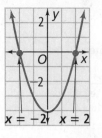

Vertex   *See* **angle; cone; polygon; polyhedron; pyramid.** The plural form of *vertex* is *vertices.*

Vértice   *Ver* **angle; cone; polygon; polyhedron; pyramid.**

Vertex angle (p. 156)   *See* **isosceles triangle.**

Ángulo del vértice (p. 156)   *Ver* **isosceles triangle.**

Volume (p. 559)   Volume is a measure of the space a figure occupies.

Volumen (p. 559)   El volumen es una medida del espacio que ocupa una figura.

Z

Zero of a function (p. 740)   An *x*-intercept of the graph of a function.

Cero de una función (p. 740)   Intercepto *x* de la gráfica de una función.

Example   The zeros of $y = x^2 - 4$ are ± 2.

$$x = -2 \quad x = 2$$

Zero-Product Property (p. 750)   For all real numbers a and b, if $ab = 0$, then $a = 0$ or $b = 0$.

Propiedad del producto cero (p. 750)   Para todos los números reales a y b, si $ab = 0$, entonces $a = 0$ ó $b = 0$.

Example $x(x + 3) = 0$
$x = 0$ or $x + 3 = 0$
$x = 0$ or $x - 3$

Index

M

Make a Conjecture exercises, 10, 114, 445, 546, 570, 571, 728, 929, 989

measurements
  of angles, 77, 78
  angles, 160
  Big Ideas, 64, 198, 262, 414, 466, 532
  indirect measurement, 196, 364
  multiplying powers with the same base, 604
  properties of parallelograms, 279
  Pull It All Together, 592
  using corresponding parts of congruent triangles, 149

medians and altitudes, 223–231, 258

Mental Math, 587, 693, 665, 667, 745, 746

midpoint formula, 197

midsegments
  of trapezoids, 309
  of triangles, 199–206, 257, 335

modeling
  falling objects model, 711
  linear, quadratic, and exponential models, 791–799
  modeling randomness, 888–894, 901
  multiplying binomials, 655
  probability models, 873–879, 900
  with quadratic functions, 732–739, 833
  vertical motion model, 722

monomials, 639–640, 646–647, 648

More Practice and Problem-Solving Exercises, 9–10, 16–18, 24–25, 31–33, 39–40, 46–47, 55–57, 70–71, 80–81, 89–90, 96–97, 104–106, 113–114, 127–128, 135–137, 146–147, 152–153, 162–164, 171–172, 179–180, 190–191, 205–206, 213–214, 221–222, 229–231, 237–238, 247–248, 255–256, 268–269, 278–279, 287–288, 295–297 304–305, 313–315, 322–323, 328–329, 346–347, 355–357, 367–368, 375–377, 387–389, 398–400, 407–408, 423–425, 433–434, 444–446, 452–453, 460–461, 474–476, 482–484, 496–497, 506–508, 515–517, 525–526, 546–548, 557–558, 566–568, 578–580, 587–589, 605, 613–614, 621–623, 630, 645, 651–652, 661, 669–670, 676–677, 683–684, 692–693, 700, 713–715, 724–726, 738–739, 745–747, 758–759, 766–767, 776–777, 789–790, 797–799, 808–809, 822–823, 831–832, 846–847, 853–854, 863–864, 871–872, 878–879, 886–887, 893–894, 912–914, 928–929, 936–937, 943–944, 961–963, 969–970, 977–978, 986–987, 997–998

Multiple Representations exercises, 25, 33, 329

multiplication
  binomials, 653–661, 702
  complex numbers, 783–784
  of expressions with exponents, 637
  factoring and, 646–652, 701
  of functions, 940
  of powers with the same base, 595–605, 634
  special cases, 662–670, 702

multiplication properties of exponents, 606–614, 634

mutually exclusive events, probability of, 868

N

negation, finding, 197

non-intersecting lines and planes, 66

number theory, 670

O

oblique cones, 576–577

oblique cylinders, 542

Open-Ended exercises, 17, 25, 31, 55, 71, 90, 126, 128, 180, 190, 206, 255, 268, 288, 297, 305, 313, 322, 328, 345, 346, 356, 389, 399, 407, 424, 434, 483, 546, 557, 566, 587, 605, 613, 621, 622, 630, 669, 683, 693, 700, 746, 747, 766, 789, 797, 807, 832, 833, 845, 871, 914, 928, 935, 944, 962, 968, 978, 987, 997

order of operations, 593

orthocenters, 226

outcomes, probability and, 841

overlapping events, probability of, 869

overlapping triangles, congruence in, 173–180, 194

P

paper folding and reflections, 230

paper-folding conjectures, 154–155

parabolas, 814–823, 837
  completing the square and, 762–763
  equations of, 732–733

  quadratic functions, 720
  quadratic graphs and, 710
  standard form of a quadratic function, 707–708

paragraph proofs, 51, 52, 94

parallel lines
  and perpendicular lines, 91–97, 107–114, 116, 117, 261
  properties of, 72–81, 115, 261, 335
  properties of parallelograms, 275
  proving lines parallel, 82–90, 116, 261
  Triangle Angle-Sum Theorem, 119
  and triangles, 98–106, 117

parallelograms
  proving theorems about quadrilaterals, 270–279, 280–288, 330, 331
  special parallelograms, 289–290

Parallel Postulate, 98

parallel segments, 200

patterns, 11–18, 57, 58, 62, 136, 953. *See also* sequences and series

percent change, finding, 593

percents, 839

perfect-square trinomials, factoring, 685–686

permutation notation, 857–858

permutations and combinations, probability and, 855–864, 899

perpendicular bisectors, 207–214, 257

Perpendicular Bisector Theorem, 208

perpendicular lines, 5
  constructing parallel and perpendicular lines, 107–114, 117
  parallel and perpendicular lines, 91–97, 116, 261

Perpendicular Postulate, 110

Perpendicular Transversal Theorem, 93

piecewise functions, 930–937, 951

planes, 66

point of concurrency, 215

points, lines, and planes, 109, 111

Polygon Angle-Sum Theorems, 263–269, 330

polygons
  areas of regular polygons, 454–461, 463
  similar polygons, 348–357, 409

polynomials
  addition of, 639–645, 701
  polynomial models, 649

Acknowledgments

Staff Credits

The people who made up the High School Mathematics team—representing composition services, core design digital and multimedia production services, digital product development, editorial, editorial services, manufacturing, marketing, and production management—are listed below.

Patty Fagan, Suzanne Finn, Matt Frueh, Cynthia Harvey, Linda Johnson, Roshni Kutty, Cheryl Mahan, Eve Melnechuk, Cynthia Metallides, Hope Morley, Michael Oster, Wynnette Outland, Brian Reardon, Matthew Rogers, Ann-Marie Sheehan, Kristen Siefers, Richard Sullivan, Susan Tauer, Mark Tricca, Oscar Vera, Paula Vergith

Additional Credits: Emily Bosak, Olivia Gerde, Alyse McGuire, Stephanie Mosely

Illustration

Jeff Grunewald: 25, 39, 55, 269, 284, 328, 346, 356, 357, 364, 376, 384, 385, 388; **Stephen Durke:** 86, 96, 102, 123, 132, 146, 153, 163, 180, 206, 209, 213, 217, 218, 222, 238, 247, 249, 251, 256, 376, 434, 444, 447, 448, 453, 474, 475, 476, 484; **Phil Guzy:** 423, 446, 470, 474, 475, 547, 548, 574, 581, 589, 992, 993; **Rob Schuster:** 914, 962, 963.

Technical Illustration

Aptara, Inc.; Datagrafix, Inc.; GGS Book Services

Photography

Every effort has been made to secure permission and provide appropriate credit for photographic material. The publisher deeply regrets any omission and pledges to correct errors called to its attention in subsequent editions.

Unless otherwise acknowledged, all photographs are the property of Pearson Education, Inc.

32, Material courtesy of Bill Vicars and Lifeprint; **55**, Jenny Thompson/Fotolia; **69**, Kevin Fleming/Corbis; **81**, photo courtesy of Frank Adelstein, Ithaca, NY; **89**, Robert Llewellyn/Corbis; **102**, Peter Cade/Iconica/Getty Images; **150**, Viktor Kitaykin/iStockphoto; **160**, John Wells/Photo Researchers, Inc; **171**, Image Source Black/Jupiter Images; **191 l**, M.C. Escher's "Symmetry E56" © 2009 The M.C. Escher Company-Holland. All rights reserved. www.mcescher.com; **191 r**, M.C. Escher's "Symmetry E18" © 2009 The M.C. Escher Company-Holland. All rights reserved. www.mcescher.com; **205**, Joseph Sohm/Visions of America, LLC/Alamy Images; **265 l**, Laurie Strachan/Alamy Images; **265 r,** BestShot/iStockphoto; **278**, Esa Hiltula/Alamy Images; **290 t**, Claro Cortes IV/Reuters/Landov LLC; **290 b**, Michael Jenner/Alamy Images; **304**, Rodney Raschke/Active Photo Service; **314**, Colin Underhill/Alamy Images; **376** ©James L. Amos/Corbis; **384** Victor R. Boswell Jr./Contributor National Geographic/Getty Images; **460** Dennis Marsico/Corbis; **496** Clive Streeter/©DK Images; **516** Vario Images GmbH & Co.KG/Alamy Images; **521** Melvyn Longhurst/Alamy; **525** dpa/Corbis; **546** Ron Chapple Stock/Alamy; **588** Stephen Sweet/Alamy; **700**, Kyla Brown.